More Joy of Art

KEYS TO APPRECIATING ART

Carolyn Schlam

ALLWORTH PRESS
NEW YORK

Allworth Press books may be purchased in bulk at special discounts for sales promotion, corporate gifts, fund-raising, or educational purposes. Special editions can also be created to specifications. For details, contact the Special Sales Department, Allworth Press, 307 West 36th Street, 11th Floor, New York, NY 10018 or info@skyhorsepublishing.com.

29 28 27 26 25   5 4 3 2 1

Published by Allworth Press, an imprint of Skyhorse Publishing, Inc. 307 West 36th Street, 11th Floor, New York, NY 10018. Allworth Press® is a registered trademark of Skyhorse Publishing, Inc.®, a Delaware corporation.

www.allworth.com

Library of Congress Cataloging-in-Publication Data
Names: Schlam, Carolyn Dobkin, 1947-
Title: More joy of art : keys to appreciating art / Carolyn Schlam.
Description: New York : Allworth Press, [2025] | Includes index. | Summary: "Find Even More Joy in Exploring and Appreciating Art, Guided by an Award-Winning Artist's Insights. Perhaps the best quality of art is that it challenges presumptions and forces a second look. Likewise, this sequel to popular art appreciation book The Joy of Art delves even deeper to decode and present the elements of visual art, leading the reader to a greater understanding and perception"-- Provided by publisher.
Identifiers: LCCN 2024030745 (print) | LCCN 2024030746 (ebook) | ISBN 9781621538455 (hardcover) | ISBN 9781621538462 (ebook)
Subjects: LCSH: Art appreciation.
Classification: LCC N7477 .S295 2025 (print) | LCC N7477 (ebook) | DDC 701/.18--dc23/eng/20240705
LC record available at https://lccn.loc.gov/2024030745
LC ebook record available at https://lccn.loc.gov/2024030746

Cover design by Mary Ann Smith
Cover image by Gustav Klimt

Print ISBN: 978-1-62153-845-5
Ebook ISBN: 978-1-62153-846-2

Printed in China

Thanks to art, instead of seeing
a single world, our own, we see it multiply
until we have before us as many worlds
as there are original artists.
—Marcel Proust

A joy shared is a joy doubled.
—Johann Wolfgang von Goethe

Contents

Part I

Keys to Understanding and Appreciating Visual Art

Introduction

Author's Intention and Approach

As we approach a task our ultimate destination is obscure. Our path ends at the horizon of our expectations. But then as we look back upon that point of embarkation, the internal logic may reveal itself. When I decided to write the book that would become *The Joy of Art: How to Look at, Appreciate, and Talk About Art* my goal was a simple one. From my perspective as a working artist, I wanted to provide a tool kit, or perhaps guidebook, for a visit to the museum. Something that the art lover could use to better understand, and hopefully appreciate, what they were looking at.

So I set out general and specific criteria for evaluating any artwork, and provided a working vocabulary of terms used to describe art techniques and principles. I then used these terms and criteria to look at the familiar genres and the artists who excelled at them. To compare and contrast. I hoped this might provide a roadway into the vast territory of this subject and its myriad forms and iterations.

I wanted it to be as simple as I could make it, but still give sufficient information to make a small dent in such a big subject. I wanted it to be accessible, not dense; friendly, not lofty; conversational, not dogmatic. I wanted it to be fun to read, but not so light that it failed at the task.

And I am so happy to report that judging from the many letters I have received from readers, I accomplished what I set out to do. People liked the book, said that it encouraged them to look at art in a new way, and looked forward to applying new insights and skills to future museum visits.

Thank you to everyone who read *The Joy of Art* and took the time to write and tell me.

That brings us to today. Readers, your encouragement led me to consider writing a sequel to *The Joy of Art* where I might endeavor to make art even more accessible, more understandable, and more interesting. So, I give you *More Joy of Art*, in which I will endeavor to dig a little deeper, a little broader, and offer more light into what makes art Art. What it is, and what it's for. How to read it and make sense of it. How we can use it, and how it enhances our lives.

I have had to make some hard choices in providing visual examples of artwork. Given the intransigent copyright restrictions that make photographs of most modern art unavailable to me, I've had to find other candidates that are in the public domain. That means that many of the most famous modern artists you are familiar with do not have a presence here. To make up for it, and to make sure there are examples of modern art forms, I have elected to include many works by living artists.

But this may inure to our benefit. There are many books in print that detail the premier artists of every period and extol their virtues and shortcomings. That is not my purpose here. The art for this book was not chosen to promote any particular artist, though you may discover someone here you choose to follow. Perhaps this will lead you to collect their work. That would be a wonderful side benefit.

The works of selected artists have been included because they illustrate or help to explain an idea, a principle, a mode or trend that we are studying, or they are fine examples of a technique or approach or intention. Taken as a totality, these artists will offer a glimpse into some of the possibilities and interpretations art encompasses.

I'm excited to bring these artists into the public eye. Some may be famous or familiar, but many are unknown or may just be new to you. How terrific that you will be using your newly informed eyes to view this new work. Because it is unfamiliar, you haven't already made assumptions about it. No one has told you that it's good or great or terrible. You don't have to like it. You'll be deciding that for yourself.

It has not been classified necessarily. Is it Impressionist, Expressionist, Dada, Baroque, Rococo, Classical, Romantic? Let's say it is "Other." We will need new language to describe and discuss it. Isn't this great? Let's challenge our eyes to form new conclusions, shall we?

In this book, though we will discuss art movements of the past, I will be expanding the definitions. I will endeavor to give you a bigger picture of the whole, and perhaps we will devolve new categories, or move past them entirely.

As I discussed in the first book, the world of art is complicated and complex, and we can't just read it historically. There were incredibly modern works executed centuries ago, and old fashioned and traditional ones are being conjured today. We will be looking at these exceptions and conundrums and discussing them, definitely "coloring outside of the lines." You might find yourself amazed. Truly.

What's important is that we lay out what to look for when looking at *any* work of art. Let's just say that though each artwork may contain similar ingredients and be made in a similar way, it is a world, an entity, unto itself, in the same way that no two snowflakes are exactly alike, or two human beings for that matter. We can break down the components but still appreciate each as a unique creation of a unique being at a never to be repeated point in time.

My approach to this topic does not fall neatly into one of the two main avenues of art analysis: formalism and contextualism. Had I taken a contextual approach, I would be discussing the artwork in the context of the environment in which it was created: the time, culture, place out of which it sprung. Choosing the formalist path, I would be looking at the work itself and focusing on its visual elements, regardless of other factors like the historical period, artist circumstances, or other factors that have influenced its creation.

Though I lean toward formalism and choose to see each work as a unitary creation, I find, as I believe you will too, that knowing the context amplifies and deepens our understanding of what we are looking at. As long as we don't get stuck in the classifications and can see each work for itself, not just a creature of an art movement, we can derive the greatest possible meaning from each and every work.

Our desire to know things definitively leads us to pigeonhole and overclassify. But just recognizing that a particular artwork has certain characteristics of say, "Cubism," is just the beginning of the story, not the end. We can, and should, both contextualize and study the work for its unique attributes and the myriad ways it both shares and violates the qualities of its own category.

Every work is both part of something bigger than itself and an anomaly, a unique creation. The degree to which we endeavor to understand both will be the measure of how close we can come to true appreciation.

For those of you who may not have read the first book, let me reiterate who I am and what I bring to this book. I am a working artist, a painter primarily, but I have worked in many other media including glass, ceramic, wood, collage, and mixed media. I am not a philosopher, although I am very interested in philosophy, have read a bunch of philosophy books, and enjoy thinking about these impossible questions that invite dialogue and debate.

I have a deep and abiding interest in art, respect and reverence for all who endeavor to make it, and an intimate, very personal understanding of what it takes to do so. It's hard to make something that others will admire. Hard to be judged for it. Hard to live up to one's own expectations and those of one's audience. Hard to work in the shadow of the greats. Hard to fail.

My love of art and respect for artists is in every sentence to come in this book. I will never be glib and make light of an artist's effort. You won't read any put-downs or snarky comments here. You will find a ferocious enthusiasm, but none of the promotional and sometimes pretentious babble that is attached to writings about art, making it drearily and downright incomprehensible to the average reader. You will not need a guidebook to obscure references or tangled art speak. I will try to speak as plainly and authentically as I can.

This is not art criticism per se. My goal is not to pass judgment on any particular artwork. Rather, I will be giving *you* the tools so *you* can recognize, identify, and name what the work offers in a positive way—its strengths, message, and particular vision. Knowing what to look for and where to find it will enable you to become a connoisseur of art and thereby, increase your enjoyment of it.

That's what we are here for.

I will also, as I did in *The Joy of Art*, pose lots of questions and ask that you take a crack at them and engage with this book. The more you do, the more you will take away with you when you turn the last page. We will start with vocabulary and move on to the questions. They provide the armature of this book that everything else depends on.

Just a bit of business before we get into our discussion. Please forgive mixed gender pronouns used in various ways in this book. It is inconvenient to use he/she/they in every context, but when I am referring to an artist and say he or she, the statement holds for all humans regardless of the pronouns utilized. My intention is not to exclude anyone.

When I wrote the first book, I never expected it would do well, be widely read, and enjoyed. I never expected I would find that I had even more to say on the subject and come to write *More Joy*.

But here we are. The journey continues, mine, and yours.

Joy to the world, to art, art makers, and art lovers. Let's turn the page to even more joy . . .

Chapter 1

The Vocabulary of Art and Art Criticism

When the first pictographs were drawn by humans on the walls of caves, this was an attempt by the maker to depict something visually, to express in pictorial form a physical object or idea, perhaps the hunt or some such activity. Let's say it was an animal. The maker was not necessarily trying to represent the animal with all its details, features, position, and characteristics illustrated. The pictograph is more like a symbolic representation, usually very simple, something we might today refer to as an icon.

I can tell you that as a working artist, even today in an age when full-blown images with scrupulous detail are readily available, if I endeavor to draw an animal, I might, without the benefit of these sources, draw something that resembles that cave pictograph. We all have mental images in our brains that are severely incomplete, and we know this when we set out to draw something.

Let's say we have the assignment to draw an elephant. Our brain tells us that the elephant is fat and has chubby and undifferentiated legs, big ears, and a trunk. But that's as far as we get without having an actual elephant in front of us to study or a picture of one to refer to. There's a lot more that goes into drawing the elephant than we have saved in our memory bank. We must know first our particular point of view, then we need to know the position of the elephant, how all his parts relate to one another, relative sizes, a relationship to the environment etc. There's a lot we need to know before we can even begin.

If we just try, what we will probably come up with is a drawing that looks like it was made by a five-year-old. That is because without lots of observation and drawing skill, our pictorial recall is extremely limited. We are all primitive humans drawing pictographs on cave walls.

So this is where we all start. It is entirely possible that the cave artists of yesterday had no concept whatsoever that they were making something called *Art*. They may have had no idea their cave drawings were superior to those of their fellow cave people. That they were important in any way. Certainly, that anyone would find them "collectible," want to possess them, and in some future day spend vast sums of money to do just that.

They may have had no concept that they were doing something anyone would care about at all, bother to comment on, or criticize. In all probability, the only purpose for making these drawings was to possibly make it more likely, in some weird connection between drawing and karma, that the "artist" might capture such animal being rendered and perhaps get to eat it.

When a baby begins eating food, and the idea of solid food is entirely new, they may really like the taste of the mashed bananas and yogurt, while the pureed veggies may just not appeal. But even so, at this point in time, before experience and discernment has taken hold, every morsel is miraculous. It will be that way for only a short while, until our preferences override the wonder and we, as children, clamor for pizza and hamburgers and ice cream. The good stuff, we think. But this is all subject to change as we become more educated.

When we start out looking at art, we may be like the baby, fascinated with every taste, but our adult brains soon take us to task, and we begin to compare and contrast. And then we may begin to form rigid eyes that assert we like this and we don't like that. We are convinced A is good, and B less so. So and so is the greatest. Impressionism is beautiful, but Surrealism's a drag. And so on.

What I am hoping I can help you accomplish with this book is to be the cave person or the baby again. To slough off the opinions you have formed about art (or at least put them to the side) while we look at art in a new fashion. Before judgment. To enjoy the full range of possibilities and the interesting and personal ways artists have explored them through the ages and continue to do so.

We are accustomed to looking at pictures and most of us have looked at zillions of them, mostly photographs. We basically look at them to gather information and can describe what we see. But just merely describing a work that has been created by an "artist" and is a work of "art" doesn't tell you much. Let's do this now and you will see what I mean.

This is a painting by the artist Edouard Manet. It is called *Berthe Morisot with a Bouquet of Violets*. (Ms. Morisot was a painter herself and you can see one of her works later in this book). It shows a woman in a black dress and hat. Perhaps she is in mourning.

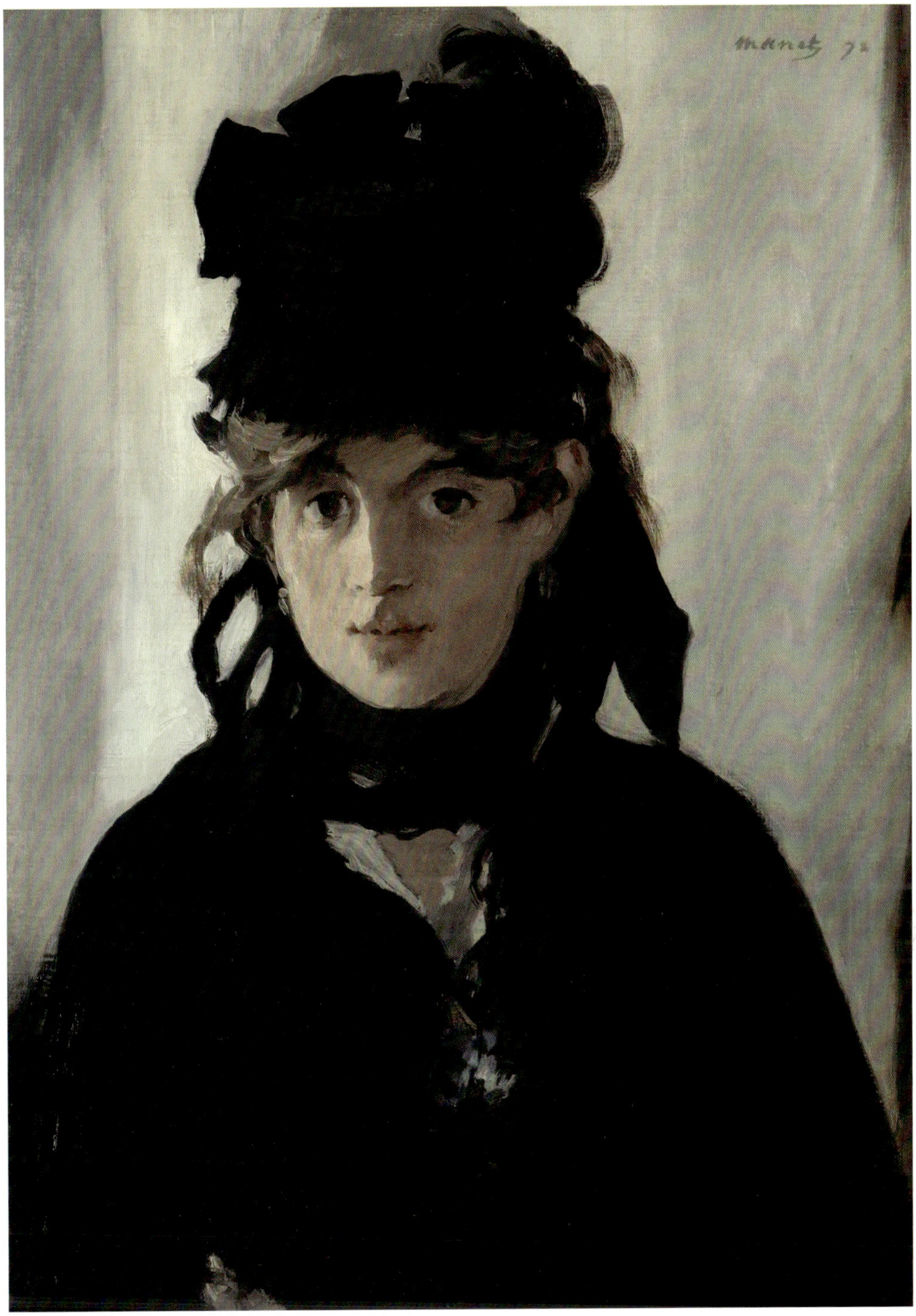

Fig. 1. Edouard Manet, BERTHE MORISOT WITH A BOUQUET OF VIOLETS.

Did you get much out of this matter-of-fact description? We need more information to form an opinion, don't we? What if I tell you that this painting is considered a masterpiece of Manet's work? The poet and critic Paul Valéry compared it in excellence to Vermeer's *Girl with a Pearl Earring*, a much-revered work. It has been much applauded and now is on the wall of the Musée d'Orsay in Paris. Are you liking the painting more now?

Well, you will have to look at Manet's other artworks to form an opinion for yourself. What makes it so good? You might have to look at other paintings of women to compare them to this one. Maybe you will need to look at Vermeer's portrait to discern how this one is different.

In fact, it is greatly simplified and quite elegant—Manet was renowned for his long **gamut** (the value range from light to dark) and his use of black. Even with the black, there is a tender touch in his rendering of the model's face and a perplexing expression. We wonder, since he mentioned the violets in his title for the painting, why he did not make them more visible.

One thing to keep in mind is that when we are looking at this painting by Manet, created in 1872, we are not only looking at a woman, but we are also looking at the style and ethos of the period in which she was painted. We are looking at France, where this year there was a meteor shower and a fellow named du Hauron made a very early color photograph and where, notably, Claude Monet began painting his famous work *Impression, Sunrise*, which would change painting forever. We are looking at this particular artist who, on this day, may have felt incredible happiness, or had a stomachache, or maybe ran out of red paint, the latter a total guess. So much went into this work that we will ever know.

The point here is that we need more data to truly appreciate this work, or any work of art for that matter. Describing what we see just scratches the surface. We need to read its emotional, psychological, spiritual, and aesthetic clues in order to form any kind of opinion at all.

The more open we are and the more we look at and look for, the more we will enjoy this work, respect it for its achievements, remember it for a quality of this or that, and understand it in relation to all of the other art we look at.

In *The Joy of Art*, I elaborated a vocabulary of art terms and principles, and I will not rehash them, except for the main categories and references we need to go forward here. We will be adding terms for qualities to consider as you look at art. Having the additional vocabulary will aid you in evaluating art in the deeper way we are advancing in this volume.

We spoke of the basic elements of visual art that elaborate in every work, regardless of the medium or style, though not necessarily to the same degree. To reiterate, they are light, color, line, shape, form, space, and texture. Before you even recognize what you are looking at, name the subject and style, or identify the medium, you can begin to think of these elements and how they are utilized and expressed in this particular work. To break it down, let's take each element one by one and note what to look for and what questions you might pose.

LIGHT

Light is the necessary condition for vision, as we know, and in visual art, it is key. In painting, light is created via the addition of white paint to our color mixtures, and it is the way the lights and shadows or darks are distributed that gives us the illusion of form. You have walked down the street in all probability with the sun at your back and noted the shadow your body casts before you. Have you noticed the odd shape your body forms? This is determined by the trajectory of the sun's rays as it strikes you. Imagine now, if you will, painting that shadow. It appears differently than it does in your mind's eye, doesn't it? This gives an inkling to something an artist might engage with—creating the shape of that shadow.

It is the way the light is described in the artwork that gives the work its feeling of authenticity, color, temperature, form, so it is all important. Remember that the artist Monet, and many, many others, spent countless hours studying the light and painting it at different times of day in the same place.

I first made an attempt as a young artist at working en plein air (from life outside) in the early morning to try and catch the light. The problem, I learned, was that the light changes more rapidly than you can dip your paint onto the colors and remix them. To gain that verisimilitude, one has to memorize a moment and keep it in mind so you may represent that light as something consistent. If you keep changing the mixtures as the light changes, you will never finish your painting.

Another work by the master Manet illustrates the impact of light in a work of art and the extent to which the shape and position of the light areas create the illusion of form and that sensation of authenticity I mentioned.

The light falling on the figure, especially upon the male boater, gives us a wealth of information: it tells us that the sun is behind the figures, illuminating the man's back and shooting over his head down to his legs. It tells us the time of day and the temperature—the light is soft and has already faded from the heat of midday. I read into it that perhaps the day is slightly overcast and not particularly hot.

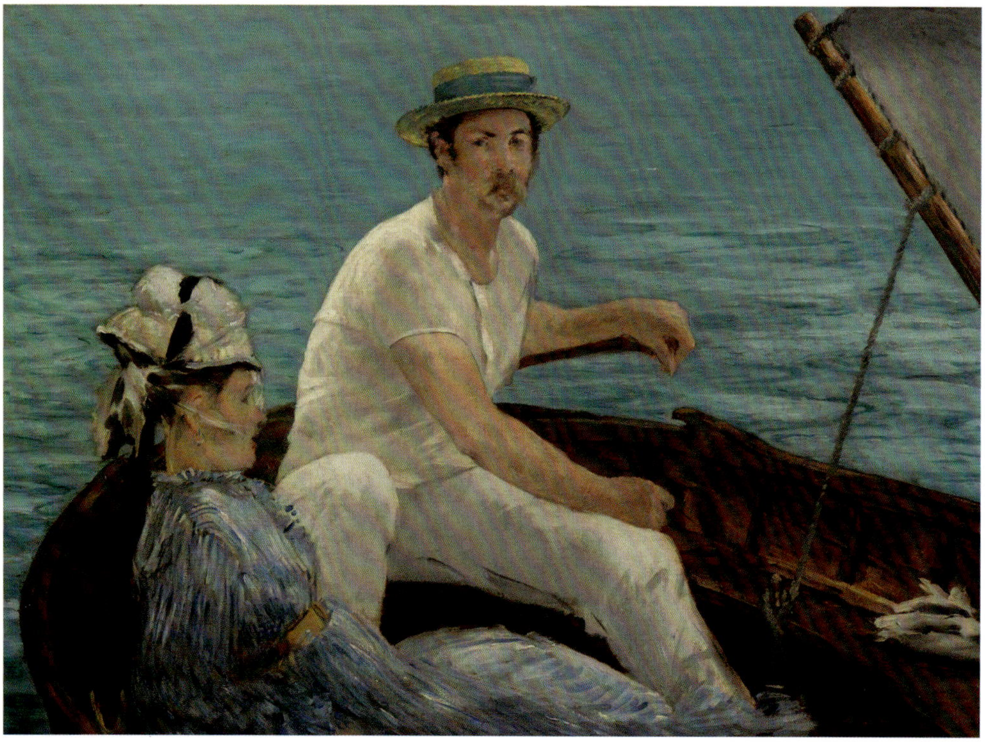

Fig. 2. Edouard Manet, BOATING.

"What a lovely time for a casual boat ride," Manet tells us, and we believe him because he has given us light conditions that are true, keenly observed, and thereby he has matched his vision with our experience.

Though light is an element in every work of visual art, to some artists it is the sine qua non, and that which they strive to create at every turn. The task for these artists is not only to create the believable, memorable light I referred to, but light so tender and beautiful that it makes us remember the most perfect light we have ever seen. The light of lights, so to speak. The one that inspires us, and makes us feel connected to the universe, to spirit, or even to God.

Do you believe that is a task an artist might ask of him/herself? If you answer in the affirmative, I will concur. Many of us are directed to such lofty goals and this one continues to challenge artists to spend a lifetime attempting to achieve it.

Here is an example of such a work.

In this painting by J. M. W. Turner painted in the latter part of his career, when he was seventy years old, you can see that the light itself has become the artist's obsession, obliterating anything that can be pointed to as an object. Since he painted in

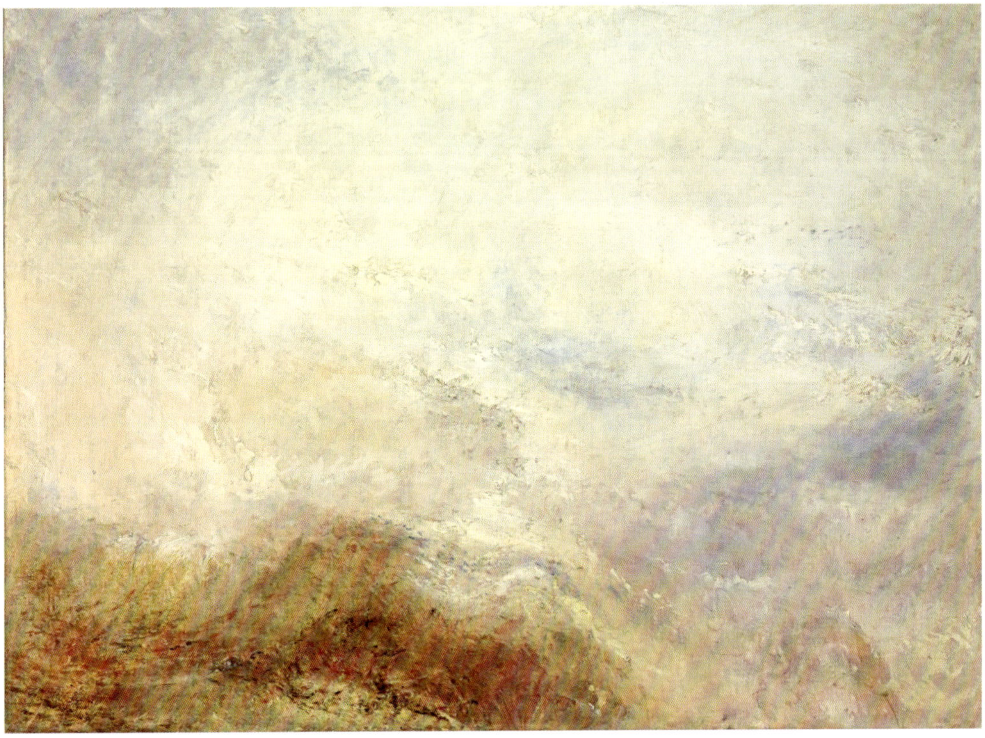

Fig. 3. J. M. W. Turner, A MOUNTAIN SCENE, VAL D'AOSTA.

the mid nineteenth century and the idea of abstraction was yet unformulated, he chose scenes, perhaps unconsciously, where extreme weather premised this sea of light and color. The work now appears as a quasi-abstract painting. In fact, he was attempting to realistically capture the light and swirling air.

Light is a factor in sculpture as well as wall art. As a solid form, sculpture stands in the light, and as such, will itself cast a shadow. Remember that the shadow is part of the sculpture. We see the light reflecting on the surface of the work itself and forming another shape on the ground. Remember too that sculptors choose materials for their sculptures partially because of reflective properties. You can notice and note reflective properties also when you look at glass art, both windows and sculpture.

Where the element of light is concerned, here are some "light" questions to ask when you look at art:

Is this a long or a short gamut (distance from lightest to darkest notes)? Long will make the work dramatic; short more subtle.

If I asked you to name the color of the light, what would be your answer? Light has an overall color that varies in different atmospheric conditions. In New

York, the light is gray; In Paris, more blue; in Greece, silvery. Now that you are looking at this in art, you can also observe it in nature. The same goes for water, which also has many colors, dependent on conditions. As you become attuned to noticing the colors specific light conditions engender in art, you will find your eyesight has become more sensitized in your daily life. Your eyes are becoming more educated.

Now look at the shadows. How has the artist represented them? With a solid mixture, a linear texture (marks comprised of lines), a transparency? Compare these to the way he or she has painted the light areas. Artists use different applications of paint to create volumes—thin washes to thick impasto paint. These are deliberate. Think about how the application of lights and darks differ and make the work more solid and more interesting. Your eyes are becoming more educated.

Because I love words, I will give you some examples of words that describe light, and then others in each category. To be discriminating, we need language, and without it, we cannot express to others exactly what we see and feel. Of course, I remind myself, that if the visual artist had been able to express his/her feeling/thought in words, that might have sufficed and the art never materialized. However, we are observers here, not creators, and we are communicating in words.

Words to describe light: soft, hard, sweet, bright, harsh, brilliant, blinding, flashing, sparkling, showy, dim, moody, dappled, patchy, gleaming, shining, radiant, glimmering, glistening, glittering, artificial, neon, glossy, incandescent, iridescent, transfiguring, luminescent, gloomy, stark, penumbral, phosphorescent, resplendent, spectral, translucent, saccharine, tawdry, fierce, nightmarish . . . there are more, I can assure you, but you get the idea.

As you look at art and consider the element of light, use these words and others to describe the quality of the light the artist has created. Recognizing that light is a major element in a work of art is a beginning but only that. What kind of light is it, and what does it tell you about the work and the artist's intention? Specificity is a sign of discernment.

COLOR

Color, as we know, is a leading actor in art making. All of us, whether we are working artists or not, have a lot to say about color. We all know what our favorite color is, though we may not know why. We know what colors look best on us, and those that do not, and what we prefer for our home environments, clothing, hair, and even our favorite shade of toaster.

I have written whole poems and treatises on color (one of my favorites is in my book *The Zen of Art*) and have commented on how we associate individual colors with things that are familiar to us, and this accounts, in large part, for the colors we prefer. Yellow for the sun, blue the sky, and the like. Paint manufacturers say that green is the most popular shade; its preponderance in nature's palette may account for this fact.

Color for an artist who paints goes a bit deeper than this bit about preferences, although we have our favorites like everyone else. Mine is a kind of blue green with white and black mixed in, a teal or aqua. Ironically, when I mix all my colors and wash them off my wooden paint palette, this is the color that remains. It is the distillation of my artistic effort.

Believe it or not, for the most part, painters do not always select colors based on preferences like these. The painter does not necessarily select and mix a color that he likes, but rather one that his painting likes, that it calls for. He may detest the color in and of itself, but the painting demands it, and so be it. Why, you ask, would the artist do that?

It could be for a number of reasons. One, that the artist is creating a specific mood that would be expressed by a group of tonal shades, or a limited palette of notes—think of something similar to the notes in a piece of music. Another, that he was expressing a certain quality of light that could best be featured in a certain color. Or perhaps he is depicting a detested figure and wants to show him in the most putrid of colors.

In other words, the color in art functions as a language in which the artist can deliver a specific message, whatever that might be. It is a tool, and a meaningful one at that. Modern artists and even some very astute traditionalists have clearly told us that the sky does not have to be blue or the sun yellow. It depends on the conditions of light at the time for a realist and can be just a matter of volition for the modernist, who just wants to give you a purple or an orange or a green sky, just because he or she feels like it and it makes the painting more effective.

When we are young, we tend to like colors that are pure and primary, bright and identifiable. As we mature, our tastes become more nuanced and our preferences turn to colors that are more tonal, subtler, and more complex, a combination of colors. And we may also become aware of what we call a color scheme, a selection of colors that complement or accent or set off one another.

These mixed tones may be more atmospheric—air- and light-filled—and act as minor notes that carry a mood. In painting, we achieve these shades mostly by adding white or black to our mixtures, which have the effect of softening and neutralizing the boldness of the pure pigment.

So, when you look at a piece of art, here are some questions about color you can pose (to yourself or others):

What is the color in this work trying to express?

Why did the artist probably choose this palette?

In a landscape work, what do the colors chosen tell me about the temperature? About the time of day?

In a figurative work, what do the colors chosen tell me about the character or expression of the figure?

In an abstract work, what do the colors chosen tell me about what the artist was thinking about?

Can I imagine this work in a different color scheme?

Colors can be warm: red, yellow, orange; or cold: blue, green, violet. Warm colors come forward and cool colors recede. This is the common way colors behave. In the distance, colors become more faint and conversely more vivid as they come close to your eye. This is all a function of what we call aerial perspective.

But you're not going to take my word for it, are you? So when you look at art, ask yourself:

How do the colors and values (the lightness of a hue) used serve to make the painting three-dimensional, in other words, have the illusion of depth?

Then ask yourself: **Would I change any of the colors?** If so, **Why?**

Let's look at two very different works and discuss them from the point of view of color:

The first, Fig. 4 is a 1909 painting by Wassily Kandinsky, who subsequently turned to abstraction. Here in his *Houses at Murnau* the artist delivers a raucous celebration of high-intensity color in a loose application where notes of color flicker and vibrate. One can see this work as a precursor to the artist's later abstractions where swirling color overrides any reference to land or sea.

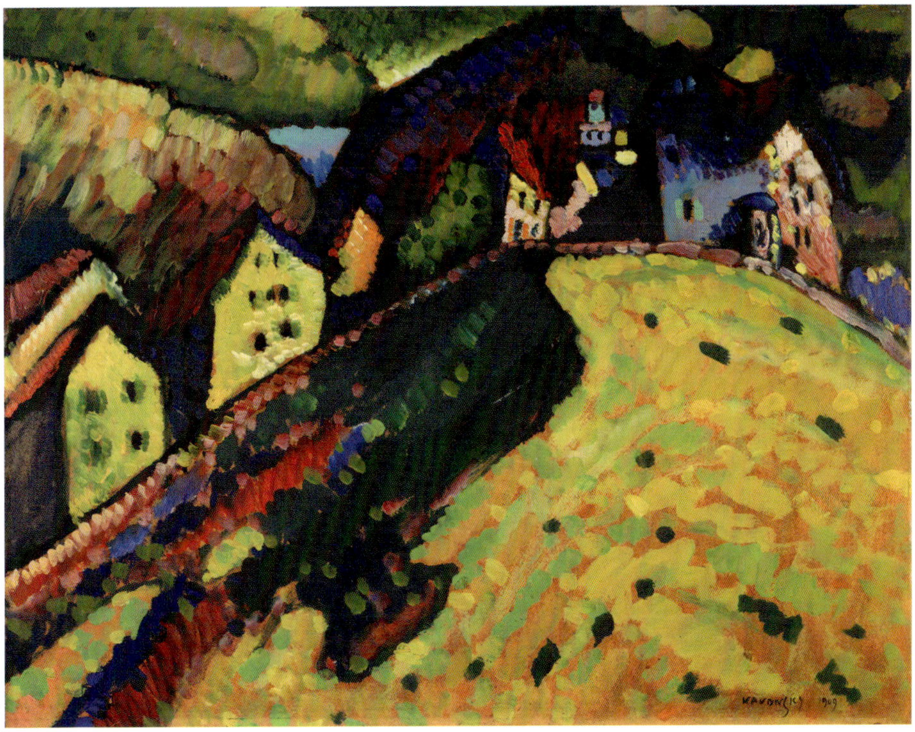

Fig. 4. Wassily Kandinsky, HOUSES AT MURNAU.

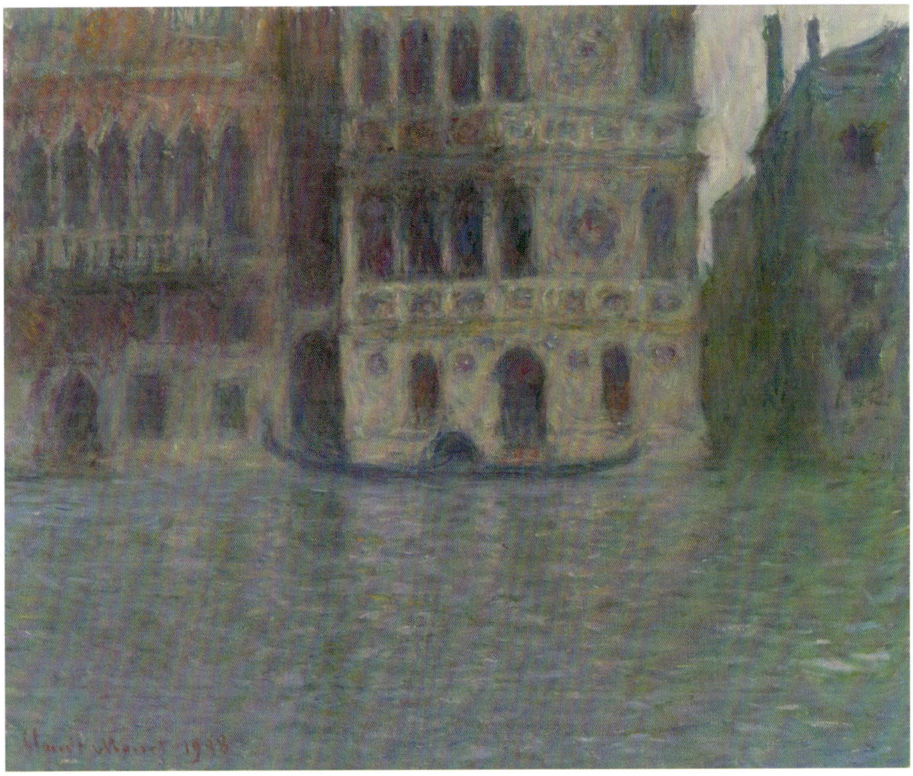

Fig. 5. Claude Monet, PALAZZO DARIO.

Contrast the color here to our second work, *Palazzo Dario* by Impressionist Claude Monet, painted concurrently in 1908. Here we see color that is soft, delicate, and muted, deliberately so, as the artist endeavors to deliver the atmospheric effects of light as it percolates into refraction of color. The main concern is to render the light, but in so choosing, Monet gives us the intimations of subtle pastel colors lurking in the greens of the water and the yellows of the buildings.

The two represent two entirely different interpretations where color is critically important in the message of the art. In each, the color serves a different master. In the Kandinsky, the color choices amplify the design and movement of the work; in the Monet, it is the light that commands.

Before we turn to our next element, once again let us make a list of some of the vocabulary associated with color: cold, warm, hot, fiery, ablaze, bold, bright, deep, delicate, muddy, somber, faint, festive, transparent, glowing, dull, vivid, tonal, local, electric, pale, bleak, sickly, pastel, chalky, blotchy, neutral, rustic, faded, saturated, healthy, primary, harsh, loud, childish . . . and so on.

Select a few to go with these two illustrations, or think about what these works make you think of or conjure. Do you enjoy both, for different reasons?

LINE

A line is an imaginary thing; there are no lines in nature. We use the line in art as a stand-in, a mechanism to define, isolate, separate. Close your eyes and imagine a black dot. Now imagine that black dot moving from the floor north to a set point, then east for a bit, south again and then west to the point of origination. You have made a square. When you follow a line back to its point of origination, you have created an enclosed flat shape, which can be geometric or organic, depending on the path of your line.

In our mind's eye we drew four connected lines, and they made a flat shape on our imaginary paper. If I add diagonal lines, I can create the appearance of a box, as here:

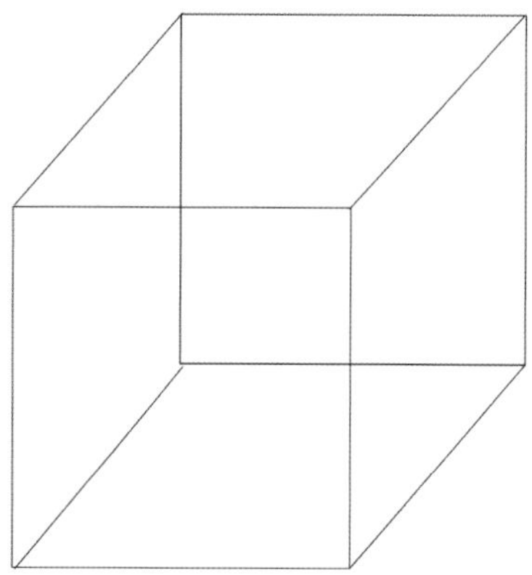

Remember that though the box appears three-dimensional, this is just an illusion of depth. Artists use principles of perspective—the diagonal lines are part of what we call "linear perspective"—to create that illusion of the third dimension. Using lines in this way while drawing is the artist's magic trick; the paper is still flat.

When an artist draws a line, he or she imagines the territory the line defines. If he is drawing something from life, as he traces what appears to be the outline—this too is imaginary—he also imagines that he is moving into depth, through the flat paper. When the line expresses well this imaginary journey, we say that he has drawn a "felt line," a line moving through space. I can tell you that when this is accomplished, it feels amazing.

Is there such a thing as a beautiful line? Yes, a line that is felt can be beautiful because it creates imaginary space. That is sublime.

But a line can also be made that has a sweep and a finesse that is lovely to look at, whether or not it defines deep space. It can be like calligraphy, just a well-made, decorative line. Chinese artists often excel at this latter form of line making as they are expert with the use of ink and have special quills and brushes for making these elegant lines.

An aside. I once participated in a workshop where the instructor asked us to make lines using a variety of found objects. I remember watching one of the students standing alongside his large sheet of paper on the ground and making sweeping lines with a long stick. Others used forks, ribbons dripped in ink, cotton balls, leaves. When we expand our vocabulary of tools, and retreat from tried-and-true habits, our creative possibilities can soar. That's why as advanced as we become as artists, we need to sometimes go back to school.

Lines can also be used as texture and we call this kind of line making **linear texture.** Now when you look at drawings especially, take note of how the artist has used small lines, crosshatching, stippling, scratching, graffito, or shading, to create a texture.

Here are other questions about lines:

Is this work primarily linear? In many works of art, even those that contain color, the linear aspect is primary. Instead of being a tapestry of color, the work looks like a drawing full of lines that are then colored in. This is perfectly acceptable, but just note that in these cases the lines are the main event. This can be equally true in abstract works—artists like Franz Kline and Robert Motherwell were linear artists and their black marks in many cases tell the entire story of their works.

Is the text in the work significant for the message or design, or both? Many artists like to incorporate text in their compositions. And text is linear. Even the signature of the artist can be seen as a linear element. When you look at a work with text,

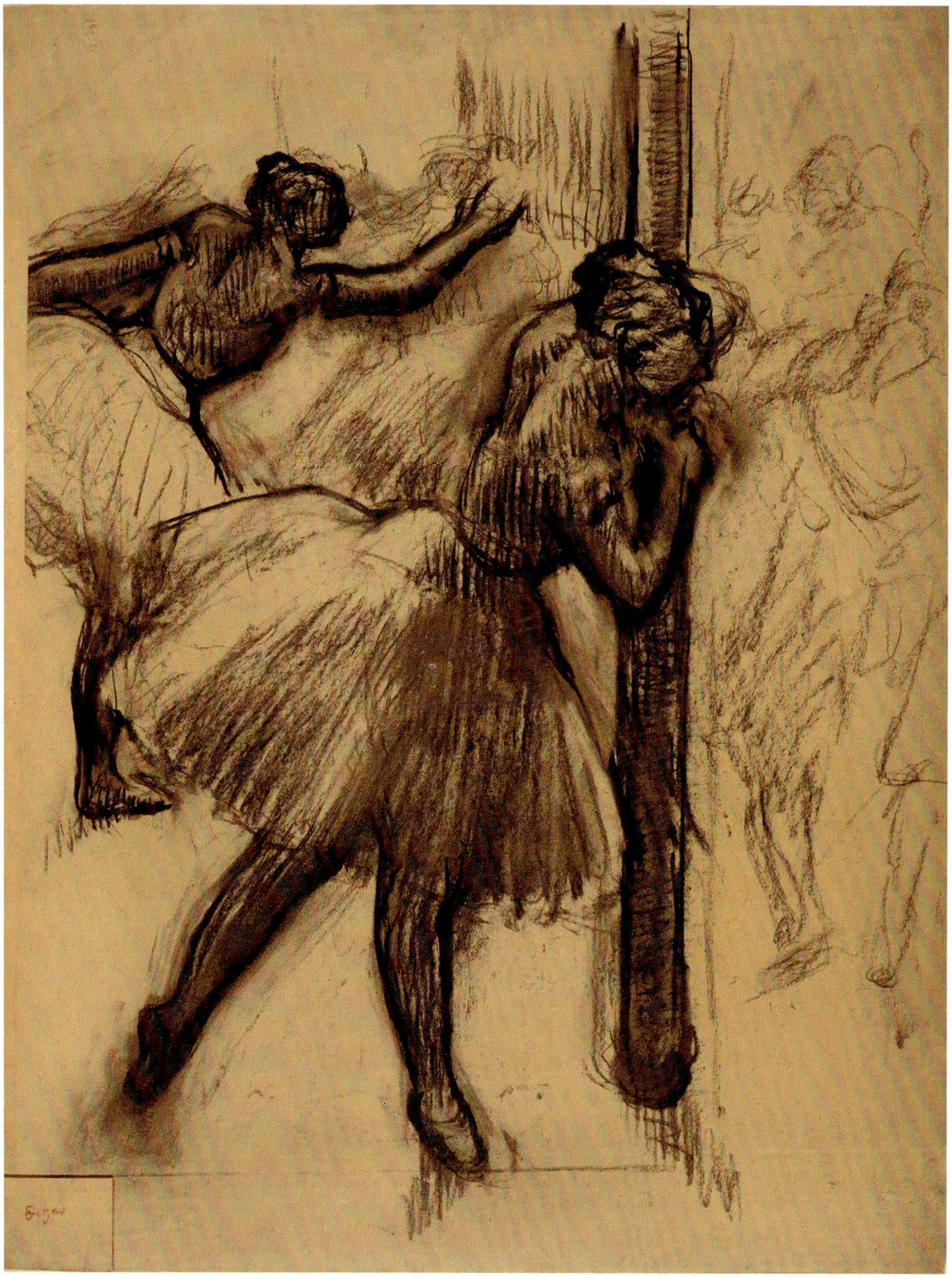

Fig. 6. Edgar Degas, DANSEUSE.

notice where the text was placed and ask whether this seems purposeful as a design element or to impart a specific message.

How does the line function in the composition? Think about this. A line can mean many things. It can be seen as an outline or perimeter of an object or shape. It can be a seam, or side, an end, or a road—pathway between two shapes. It can be just a crease within something—a crack, wrinkle, or furrow. It can form an important division between two opposing forces. Or it can be a vein, a lifeline that carries something from one place to another. It all depends on how you look at it. A close reader may be able to tell the difference.

We think of the line as being the major player in a drawing but not necessarily in a painting, where the line is disguised by the fill, the color. But the line is the foundation. We see it best revealed in a drawing, which may be made by the artist as a predicate or sketch for a more detailed painting, or as a finished work unto itself with no other purpose.

Degas was a wonderful draftsman and painter, and it is instructive to have a look at one of the drawings he made of dancers, a favorite subject, many of which were later elaborated in pastel or oil. In this charcoal drawing, he made a horizontal line to establish the floor and has drawn a pole to establish the vertical axis. This aids in establishing the position of the dancers. Notice also that he uses different intensities of the charcoal to indicate what is important, uses small lines as linear texture in the skirts, creates the entire scene just using a variety of lines.

Can you visualize how the lines create the armature for a painting? Can you close your eyes and visualize this drawing in full color?

Words that might describe lines include thin, fat, disjointed, wavy, s-curved, long, dotted, heavy, elegant, solid, broken, wispy, spiral. Can you think of others?

SHAPE, FORM, AND SPACE

Let's say I am an artist and I want to paint something that is realistic. I want it to look real, not like a cardboard cutout or a stick figure. Okay, so I draw a line and make a shape. But a shape is flat and even the oval I have made for the head doesn't work. I need to make something that looks thick and solid.

Well, thick and solid means not paper-thin but having depth. I'm working on a flat canvas so I can't get the depth there. The only thing I CAN do is to make something that LOOKS solid, isn't, but appears to be. I need to create the **illusion of form.**

There are a number of ways I can accomplish this. I can use color to show areas that come forward and go back. I can use light to show the form as it is illuminated in areas that greet the light, and shadow or darkness in receding areas and crevices that do not allow it to enter. The shape of the shadow further delineates the shape of the object I am trying to paint. I can break up the surface of objects to show

how the light falls on planes of the object, for instance, on the front of the apple, but not the underside of back. I can indicate reflective surfaces in the picture like windows and doors.

To show space in a landscape, for instance, I can use the principles of aerial and linear perspective to proportionately size the elements in my painting. Knowing that objects appear smaller and paler as they recede, and larger and more vivid as they come forward, assuming I size correctly, the image of space will be the result. I can also correctly shape and color what we call the negative space, the space between objects.

Now this is relatively simple to assess as you study realistic work. Note the sizes, the colors, the shadows, the areas of light, and as you do, try to imagine the vantage point of the artist. **Where was the light coming from?** You can follow the shadows to find out.

In an abstract painting, the feeling of space is also there, but you must hunt for it slightly differently. **Notice what shapes come forward and which go back? What is on top of what? Closest to your eye?**

Does the work of art illustrate deep space?

Estimate the imaginary depth? One foot, one mile, one hundred miles? Which is it?

Let's use this still life by Cézanne to examine form. He was an expert devotee of form making and is a father to many of the artists who followed him. Here in this simple painting of fruit on a plate Cézanne illustrates his methodology. Review the coloration, shadows of the fruit and under the plate, the surface and background, and how, through the distribution of shadow and light, the form is created.

You will note that generally speaking, when we track the light that illuminates a scene, where the light sources strikes most directly would be the lightest light, or **highlight**; where the light is evident but not does not shine directly would necessitate the **mid-tone**; where the light does not hit at all is the darkest spot (**core shadow**); the area on surrounding surfaces blocked by the object is the **cast shadow**; and lastly, the light reflected back onto to the object from the surrounding surfaces is called the **reflected light**. Taken together, these light and dark variations create the illusion of form.

As opposed to two-dimensional art like painting, sculpture makes form concrete. This can be accomplished in a myriad of formats include a solid form carved out

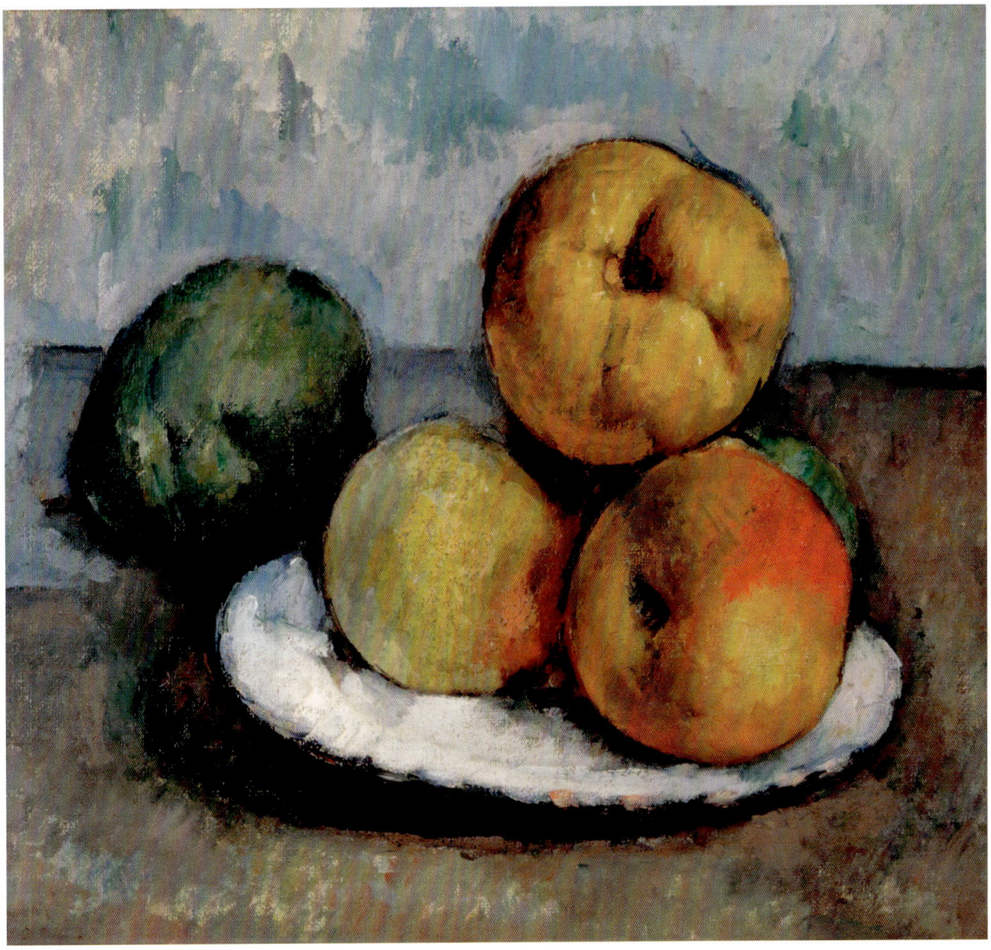

Fig. 7. Paul Cézanne, STILL LIFE WITH QUINCE, APPLES AND PEARS.

of a material like stone or molded like bronze; open, with a number of solid forms creating a work with air or negative space between them; constructed or assembled out of a variety of materials connected in a variety of ways; kinetic, or made of movable parts; and/or fashioned with a whole range of unusual materials like light, sound, earth, fabric, etc.

Sculpture can be composed of forms that are geometric, regular in shape, or organic, free-form in shape. It can be open or closed, a solid mass or composed of solid elements that encase a path of negative space which to the eye itself becomes a form. For the latter think of thin wire curved in shape to surround an area.

Most historical sculpture tends be solid form, with some exceptions. As I sought examples of sculpture that are what we call open form, I found many examples in African art, as the example I am providing in the next figure. How did the qualities in African art become more prevalent in the West?

The apocryphal story is that Matisse brought back a sculpture he acquired in Africa in 1905 and showed it to his fellow artists in France. Many of them became so enamored with it, that a kind of competition ensued to see who could bring this African influence into their modern painting and sculpture most dramatically. Matisse went on to create his *Bonheur de Vivre* painting in 1906, and the following year, Picasso created *Les Demoiselles d'Avignon*, the painting many deem to have opened the doorway to Modernism.

Suffice it to say, open-form sculpture characterizes much of modern sculpture, from the visually interlocking forms of the figurative modernist Henry Moore to the wire sculptures and mobiles of Calder.

Here are two examples of sculpture, one open and the other solid. Remember that in looking at any three-dimensional work, you want to view it in the round, from all angles. When it comes to an open form piece, consider the following:

1. We can look at the piece as a whole, including the negative space between the parts.
2. We can look at the solid parts and how they relate to one another.
3. We can also look at the negative spaces between the parts as a shape.

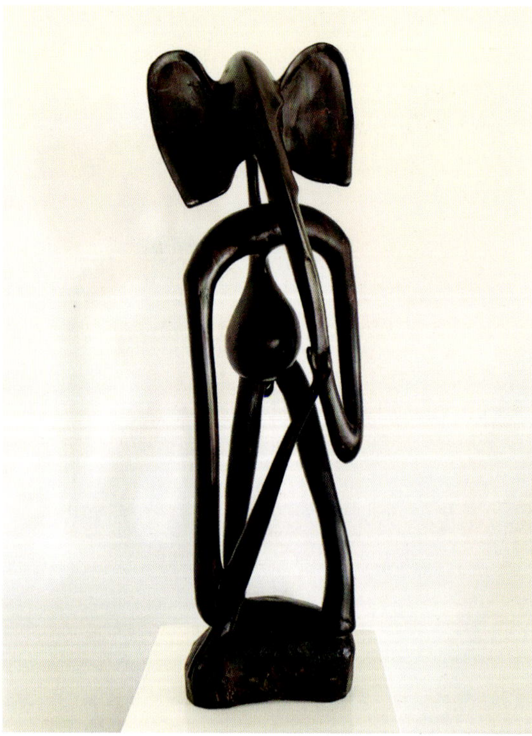

Fig. 8. Munfarid, ELEPHANT.

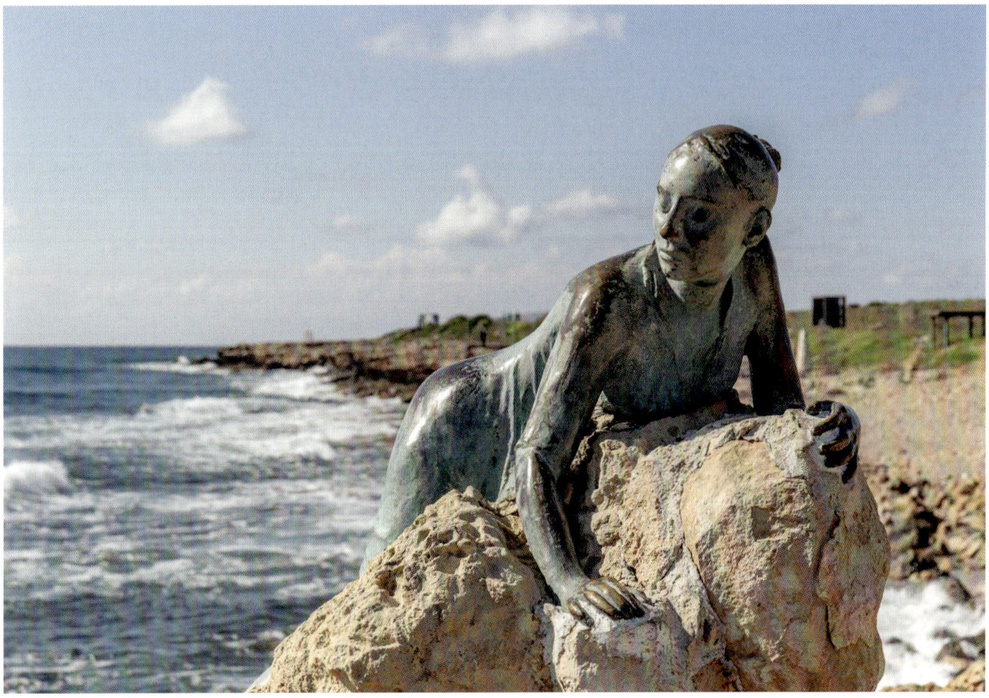

Fig. 9. Cypriot artist, MODERN APHRODITE.

This next work, a solid representative work, reminds us of another important way of viewing three-dimensional art. Sculpture is often placed outdoors. When it is, the artwork becomes part of the landscape and effectively the environs become part of the art and vice versa. Sculpture, regardless of whether it is sold or open, is often created in a monumental size, and as such, can provide a counterpoint to nature. We find it everywhere referred to as **public art**.

This Cypriot sculpture has turned a stretch of beachfront and a rock into a destination. But likewise, the destination has turned the sculpture into a bewitching sight. It would not be as effective climbing on a sculpted rock in a museum. When considering sculpture, always take into account how the art relates to its surroundings; how the elements of the work relate to the elements in nature, augmenting and providing counterpoint.

Consider the list of words to further define our terms: solid, empty, narrow, flat, round, curved, spherical, oval, geometric, organic, elongated, short, conical, elliptical, pyramidal, etc.

TEXTURE

Visual artists take their thoughts and feelings and put them into material form. Material is the matter from which a thing is or can be made. And what is matter but a physical substance? And physical substances, for the most part, at least, have texture, touch. We define texture as "the feel, appearance, or consistency of a surface or substance."

So, artists make texture and they use lots of substances to do so—paint—both oil- and water-based—oils, waxes, wax, metal, wood, clay, pencil, crayon, pastel, dirt, glass, stone, etc. They apply these on a variety of surfaces that are themselves textured and accept substances in a different way: canvas, paper, wood, metal, glass, etc. The substances and surfaces then combine to give off a very specific visual effect. This effect is in service to the very specific message the artist is attempting to convey in his or her work of art, and it becomes integral and essential to that message.

Unlike a literary work that would deliver the same message regardless of whether it was typed or handwritten, the work of visual art is dependent on its methodology and the materials used to create it. It might be similar in another medium, but not the same, and artists are very deliberate in the media they choose for particular works.

Like many artists, I have used a variety of different media, and can tell you firsthand that the medium has a decided effect on the message. When I worked melting and fashioning glass, I realized how very different that was from direct al primo painting on canvas. Even if the creator and his or her intention to create is the same, the mediums will deliver a different set of problems and effects and alter the ultimate result.

Painting directly on canvas is a direct process. I dip the brush in the paint mixture and voilà, right onto the canvas waiting to receive it. The painting is happening before my eyes, and I get into the flow of watching it develop. By its nature, it is a fast, al primo medium. This is not to say that there are not painters who work slowly and deliberately, fashioning layers of paint and then waiting until they dry to add additional notes. But the paint itself is plastic and pliable and the process is direct.

Working with warm glass (glass made in a kiln rather than blown utilizing a furnace), on the other hand, is a slower, more deliberate process. Even if my goal is to make what looks like a painting, I have to cut the pieces of glass, attach them to my surface, then wait a day or more until the glass melts in the kiln and I can view the resulting work. While I wait the vagaries of heat and cooling intervene in the process, affecting the outcome.

The different creative activities and the time it takes to perform them make for a different result. Whenever there are other factors and influences other than the direct work of the artist, unexpected consequences are possible. The artist can be quite dismayed and displeased when he views what the kiln has done to the work, even if it survives the process.

Do you assume that I prefer the direct painting process to the more time-intensive glass one? I will surprise you and say, no, not necessarily. Sometimes, the slower, more deliberate process makes for ultimately a better result, while I can get easily carried away on an unfortunate tangent during an overly quick painting session. I have found that success in the studio can be achieved in many different and unexpected ways.

This, by the way, is one of the reasons artists like to try out different media. They take us to different places.

Now, in regard to texture, the "feel," sense of touch of the artwork, here are some questions to ponder as you look at art:

Notice how the artist applied the paint or other medium. **Are some of the areas thin and transparent and others thick or is the texture consistent throughout?**

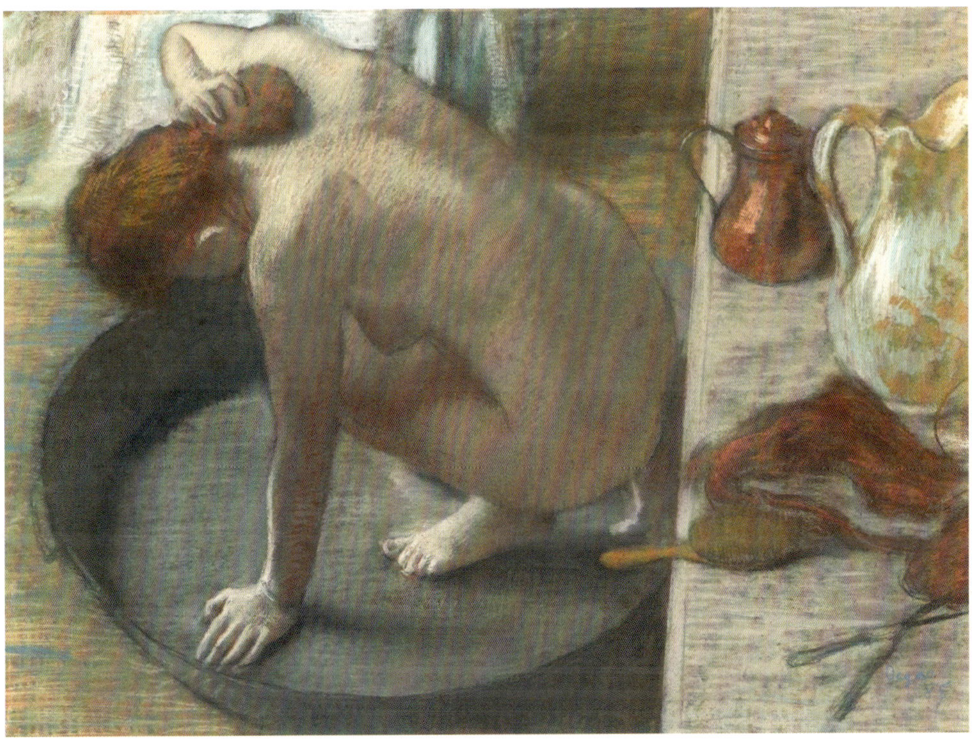

Fig. 10. Edgar Degas, LE TUB.

How does the texture contribute to the beauty of the work?

If the work is in a medium like glass or ceramic, can you imagine it in another medium?

If glass, notice how the transparency of this medium makes the work possible. Do the same for the opacity of the ceramic. Notice how a particular artist you are studying uses his medium in a particularly expert way.

Take an artist like Degas for instance. He is a painter, but I love his work in pastel; it is so special. **What is it about the chalkiness of pastel that suits Monsieur Degas's work so perfectly?**

Notice the little variations of color within each area, the dappled way the color mixtures are applied. Each area of color is vividly alive with strokes of slightly different values of the same color and notes of related colors. The dryness of the pastel is also stunningly lovely. Do you see what I mean? Do you concur?

Textures can be described as dry, wet, oily, gooey, thick, drippy, watery, slippery, airy, brittle, buttery, coarse, creamy, crisp, porous, silky, fine, sandy, fluffy, dense, crumbly, grainy, leathery, woodsy, hairy, furry, smooth, rough, meaty, feathery, spongy, gritty, waxy, and so on. Just think of a material or a substance and add the letter Y.

COMPOSITION

Now that we have elucidated the elements of art, we arrive at the concept of composition—how those elements work together to create a satisfying and effective work. We ask:

- How are the elements elaborated in a particular work?
- Are they utilized in such a way that the work is unified, balanced, and has a liveliness and feeling of movement?
- How has the artist specified his primary concern or is it ambiguous?
- Does the work exhibit focus and is the meaning clear?
- Is there interesting contrast or is the work more monotone?
- What about proportion—is the work symmetrical or seemingly out of kilter?
- Is the surface animated?
- Do we see a pattern in the design?

Let's look at a painting and ask these questions in context. This is a work by an American artist who worked in Europe and won many awards and accolades during his career. I selected this painting because I found the composition quite unusual and compelling.

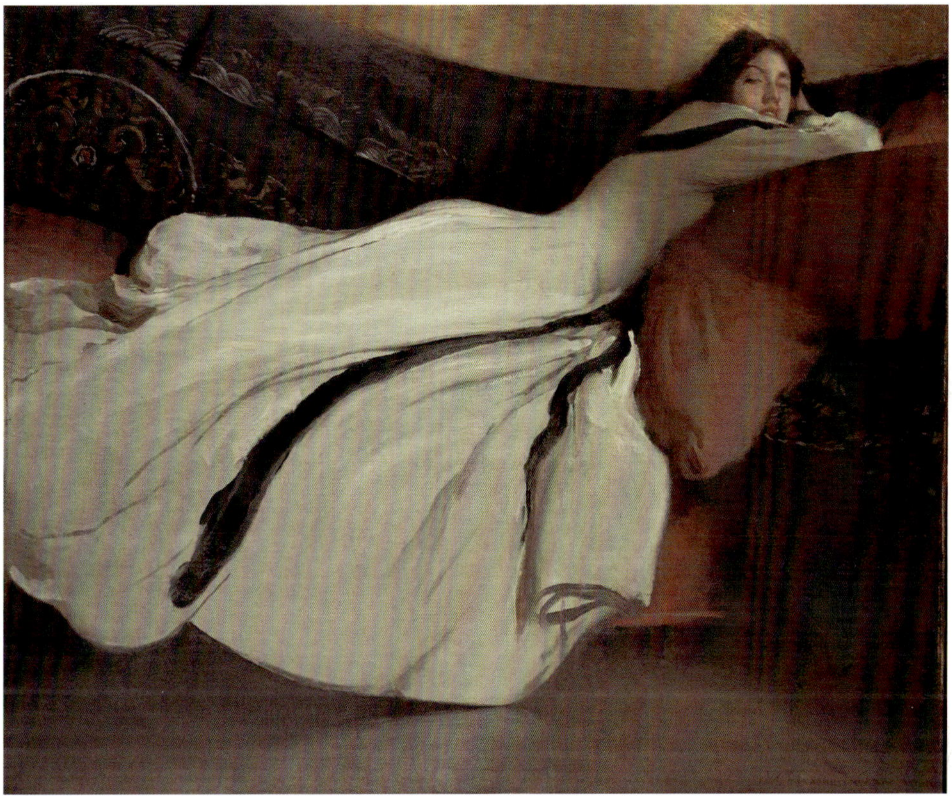

Fig. 11. John White Alexander, REPOSE.

This is a large oil arrayed on the horizontal. You may not be aware of it, but the composition of every work takes your eye on a little trip. There is an entry point and then a route by which the eye naturally travels.

In this painting, the shine on the floor sweeps us into the voluminous skirt and then into the very small head of the woman peering back at us. The fact that her face is so small does not distract from the fact of her engagement with us. This is what I find compelling. The sofa on which she lays is not straight and stiff, and this enlivens the work and gives it a feeling of movement.

So what does this composition present? Light and color are not extraordinary, rather prosaic. The space is shallow—we have an illusion of about 4 or 5 feet created by virtue of the relative size of dress and face. There is little patterning or decoration. But we do have movement, this is by virtue of the positioning of the figure, and some excellent drawing. We have unity—there are no discordant notes. And we do have focus and balance and harmony—the simple intention to render a figure in repose is realized in a creative way. I would deem this work to exhibit an excellent composition, and this makes up for a banality in the elements of color, light, and texture.

Taking note of the composition and asking these questions is another step in the process of reading a work of art.

SUMMARY: THE ART ELEMENTS

Our elaboration of the elements of art and how they relate to one another give us the beginning of a road map to search for aesthetic considerations in looking at visual art. As we search for these elements, and notice more and more what is available for us to see and feel in any work of art, it is as if we have now grasped the phonics and are able to read whole sentences and begin to make sense of art. We have taken a major step to deciphering and decoding the messages contained therein.

This also enables us to compare works as our vocabulary grows, and in turn, to understand more and more about the sweep of art in all its iterations, the logical way it has moved forward through the ages and all the stops taken along the way. Before long, we will be recognizing the major movements, their star practitioners, and the many artists who were enamored of this or that approach, style, medium.

This is not an art history book per se, rather one focusing on art appreciation and aesthetic theory. In the chapters on originality and modernity, we'll be looking more specifically at the ride of art through history. So, though this journey is not technically a historical one, or even a sequential one, we will touch on how art has progressed, what modern art is all about, and even where we go from here.

But first we will pose some pretty interesting questions about beauty, truth, and the puzzles that continue to fascinate all of us who enjoy art.

Chapter 2
Questions and Conundrums

What is Art? Art is expressive communication created by an artist to not only inform, but to evoke, elicit, distill, heighten, transform, personalize, stimulate, exalt, and glorify (I could go on) human emotion and thought in such a way that the viewer is moved, inspired, stirred, saddened, entertained, enthralled (I could go on) in a significant and meaningful way.

What is aesthetics? Aesthetics is a branch of philosophy that deals with art and all the questions and conundrums art engenders. The answers to these questions help us to understand visual art in all its incarnations and to appreciate it. That is the purpose of this book.

Here are some of the aesthetic questions we will tackle:

- What makes something a work of art?
- What are the characteristics of a work of art?
- What is the nature of beauty?
- How can we recognize it?
- How do you assess or judge what is beautiful?
- Is beauty even necessary in a work of art?
- Is beauty universal or totally subjective?
- In other words, is beauty attached to reality independent of human feeling?
- Is it, as the expression goes, "in the eye of the beholder"?
- Can everyone be a judge of beauty?
- Are more educated people more able to assess art?
- What is taste?
- Why does taste differ from person to person?
- Do some people have good taste and others bad?
- What is bad taste?

- Is there something that we can all agree is good?
- Can something deformed or ugly be beautiful?
- What is the definition of "ugly"?
- What does beauty have to do with truth?
- Does art have to be truthful to be good?
- What is the meaning of authenticity?
- Does art have to be skillfully made to be art?
- How can we compare one work to another and evaluate its value?
- How can you compare disparate works, a figurative work to an abstract one, for instance?
- What do great works of art have in common?
- Are there any universal values in art?
- How can I form my own judgments free of the opinion of others?

Let's start with an investigation into what art is and what it isn't. This is not an easy question at all, especially because many people write, draw, paint, dance, make music, act, participate in what we call the art forms. Are all of them making art? Not necessarily. I think we can probably agree that just performing the act of writing may make you literally a "writer" and the act of applying paint on a surface may make you "a painter," yet you are not definitely an "artist," one who is making art.

Just coming up with a definition of art has racked the minds of aesthetic philosophers for centuries and continues to do so as this is truly a perplexing question. How can we recognize what art is and what it isn't, what qualifies and makes the grade, and what falls short? Is what we call "bad" art simply not art at all? And what makes it bad?

We make a distinction between "fine art" and "commercial art" and that may provide some insight. The distinction has to do with the purpose of the work, or what we call its "intention." When we say a piece of visual art is commercial, what we mean is that its reason for being is to sell or promote something, a product perhaps, or an idea. This is opposed to the fine artwork whose only purpose is to communicate a feeling or thought and has no other ulterior reason for being.

So intention may be a factor in determining what is art. Now keep in mind that the work of commercial art may be, in fact, expertly made, and even beautiful, in fact even more so than the work of fine art. Does this confuse us in our assessment? What is the role of expertise in the creation of art?

Another complicating factor is that though a work of fine art may not have a commercial purpose, like an advertisement, artists' intention and hope is often to sell their work. This desire may throw a wrench into the creative process, as artists either wittingly or unconsciously alter their works in some way so they will please an audience.

This was certainly true for court painters or portraitists of the past, who had to please the individuals who commissioned them. Oil paintings of elite figures were status acquisitions, and this is one reason you will find the subjects adorned with all manner of finery, fur, and other glossy and expensive enhancements. Most assuredly, creating all these textures was good fun for the skilled painter, but they may not have represented what he or she really wanted to paint.

This is one of the reasons it is instructive to look at paintings these artists made just for their own amusement, like genre scenes and self-portraits, where pleasing the nobles was taken out of the equation. You likely will find a different quality of work when the need to please a patron is no longer a factor. A good example are the marvelous Rembrandt self-portraits, where the desire to prettify and flatter is replaced with the intention to portray a human soul.

This is an opportune moment to think about another distinction: that between what is referred to as "fine art," and another subset which is referred to as "folk art." The former is what we think of as a sophisticated product of an artist, and the latter a naive or unsophisticated product of an artisan or crafts person. But is there a difference and how can we identify it, or is this only a matter of what we might call a "class" distinction? This merits a deeper look.

Folk art is definitely thought of as the product of common or ordinary "folk," not the elite or well-educated upper classes. It is thought to arise out of tradition and to be a practice and form that may be passed down from generation to generation, defined within the parameters of an established cultural framework. Tradition and folk art go hand in hand, are inextricably linked.

Let's look at some other characteristics of folk art:

- It is usually mostly or entirely handmade and one of a kind, though multiple similar objects can be made repeatedly by the artist.
- Many of the items are functional or utilitarian, though they may be decorative and fanciful, like an urn shaped like a fish, or a wedding chest decorated with elaborate designs.
- For the most part, works of folk art are made to be used and displayed in the home, not in museums or public buildings.

- Folk art is a prevalent activity in remote or rural locations, away from population centers where commercialization and the standardization and availability of machine-made items may replace the handmade ones.
- When it comes to materials, folk artists often make use of inexpensive and readily available materials like straw or rope or shells or palm fronds. Where a fine artist might cast in bronze, the folk artist might use tin.
- A folk artist unschooled in perspective might use flat shapes and outlines and the work may lack verisimilitude.
- A folk sculptor might assemble parts in a crude or haphazard manner, lacking professional tools for finishing and polishing.
- Folk art often commemorates basic human events like births, weddings, holidays, while fine art may lean toward more esoteric subjects.
- Folk art is generally thought to be childlike and may predominantly utilize primary colors, as opposed to the tonal mixtures of fine art painters.
- Decoration is highly prized in folk art, and it can be stylized.

Here's the issue at hand: Do these characteristics of folk art make it a lesser art form than fine art? Is this just a distinction without a difference? Again, isn't art just art, regardless of its type?

What may give pause and confuse the issue are some of the derogative terms used in the context of folk art. "Naive" is one of these, suggesting inferiority. So is "primitive," suggesting ignorance or lack of education or sophistication. The modern term "outsider" used as a synonym also has a negative connotation—fine artists are "in" and folk artists are "out"? And what are they out of? The class? The club? The school? The aristocracy?

In fact, many "fine" modern artists have looked to folk art techniques, styles, and materials with envy and incorporated these into their own oeuvre. Think of "found art" sculpture. Collage and assemblage. Painting on odd-shaped surfaces. Using cheaper materials like chalk and house paint. Adding decorative elements with stencils and other tools. Mixed-media work is now widely available and prized. Yet these artists are not considered "folk" artists.

Whether "folk art" is a legitimate category of art anymore is questionable. Certainly subject matter is not determinative. One of my favorite artists comes to mind—the incredible Marc Chagall, whose whimsical works evoke in a very folksy manner the Russian villages he grew up in. I love his childlike flying goats, husbands, and brides and have no doubt that they are components of Art with a capital "A."

We have to be careful with language and aware of its connotations. Even the word "whimsy," which I have applied here is misleading. The dictionary definition of the word is "playfully quaint." Playfulness may not necessarily be derogative, though it connotes childhood, but quaintness does have a questionable taint. "Quaint" is defined as unusual or old fashioned. Taken in its totality, "whimsy" does connote a lack of sophistication and currency—it may be affiliated with "cuteness," a reference that is surely anathema in the world of art.

Let us not be confused by these terms and qualifications. What is colloquially referred to as "craft" is part of art making and may be significant. But what makes a work "art" supersedes the materials used in its construction and the techniques employed to craft it. The art is found in what the work says and evokes. Generally speaking, it's a good idea to avoid judging a work of art by its classification and to view it as if you have heard nothing at all about it. Let it speak to you with its own voice.

Let's get back, after this digression, to the idea of intention. Does art have to have a noble purpose? Does the subject have to be a worthy one? Modern art asks us whether art needs to have a subject at all, doesn't it? When Jackson Pollock laid his canvas on the floor and flicked and splattered and poured his bucket of paint on it, and created what we call "action painting," what was the subject he had in mind? Yet the art reviewers consider those splatter painting works of art, don't they?

Do you? We take a pause to consider this . . . don't decide just yet.

If art is a form of heightened communication, and I do not think anyone can disagree with this most basic definition, what did Pollock communicate? What did he say?

In truth, one of the things he told us was that it was okay to break the rules. One did not have to use a brush or an easel or any of the tools formerly associated with the art of painting. Through his act, breaking with convention, he did something new, original, and important, or at least he thought so in that moment. He undoubtedly had a breakthrough. And his accomplishment spurred other artists to experiment in their own way.

When we look at those resulting paintings, we, too, experience a breakthrough. We get rid of one assumption we have carried with us about how art HAS TO BE made. We experience a liberation of sorts, one that has influenced many, many people, artists and viewers alike. This is worthy but is it sufficient? We need more information to jump to a conclusion.

One of the theorists on art I have read on this topic was the great Russian writer Leo Tolstoy. In his attempt to define art and to differentiate it from nonart, he insisted that it meet certain discrete standards. The first of these is that the subject must be important. To Tolstoy, this was necessary, but again, not sufficient, and a poor or inadequate presentation could suffice to deny an important subject the status of art. Tolstoy further qualified the definition to say that the intention of the artist must be solely and exclusively the need to express with no tarnishing of an external inducement. If all three conditions were met: valuable content, excellent clarity in delivery (the latter also called beauty), and worthy intent, it would meet all criteria and Tolstoy would deem it ART.

Tolstoy's third requirement of worthy intent is specious in my view. What of those court painters who were hired and paid to make portraits of wealthy scions. Were all of these to be disqualified as art? (Some are quite marvelously painted.)

I think not, at least not necessarily. Even artworks made expressly for commercial purposes can and do sometimes rise to the status of art—think here of the posters of the marvelous Toulouse-Lautrec.

This may be an advertisement for a masked ball at the Moulin Rouge, but the art of Lautrec is what made the Moulin Rouge a symbol of fun and a memorable name, now totally associated with this very artful bit of promotion. It has surpassed its purpose as great art is wont to do.

Tolstoy further elaborates that these three requirements may be found in differing proportions and that works of art may stand out for one or more of these qualities. Some may excel in content, others in presentation, and a third group for the authenticity of their intent. This, I agree, is undeniable.

This gives us a clue and aid in evaluating art, and he elaborates the possible combinations:

1. Some will have content and beauty but lack sincerity.
2. Some may be beautiful to look at but lack content.
3. Some may have great authenticity but be crude.

And so on. This may give us a framework for analyzing artworks we will be applying as we go forward to look at individual works.

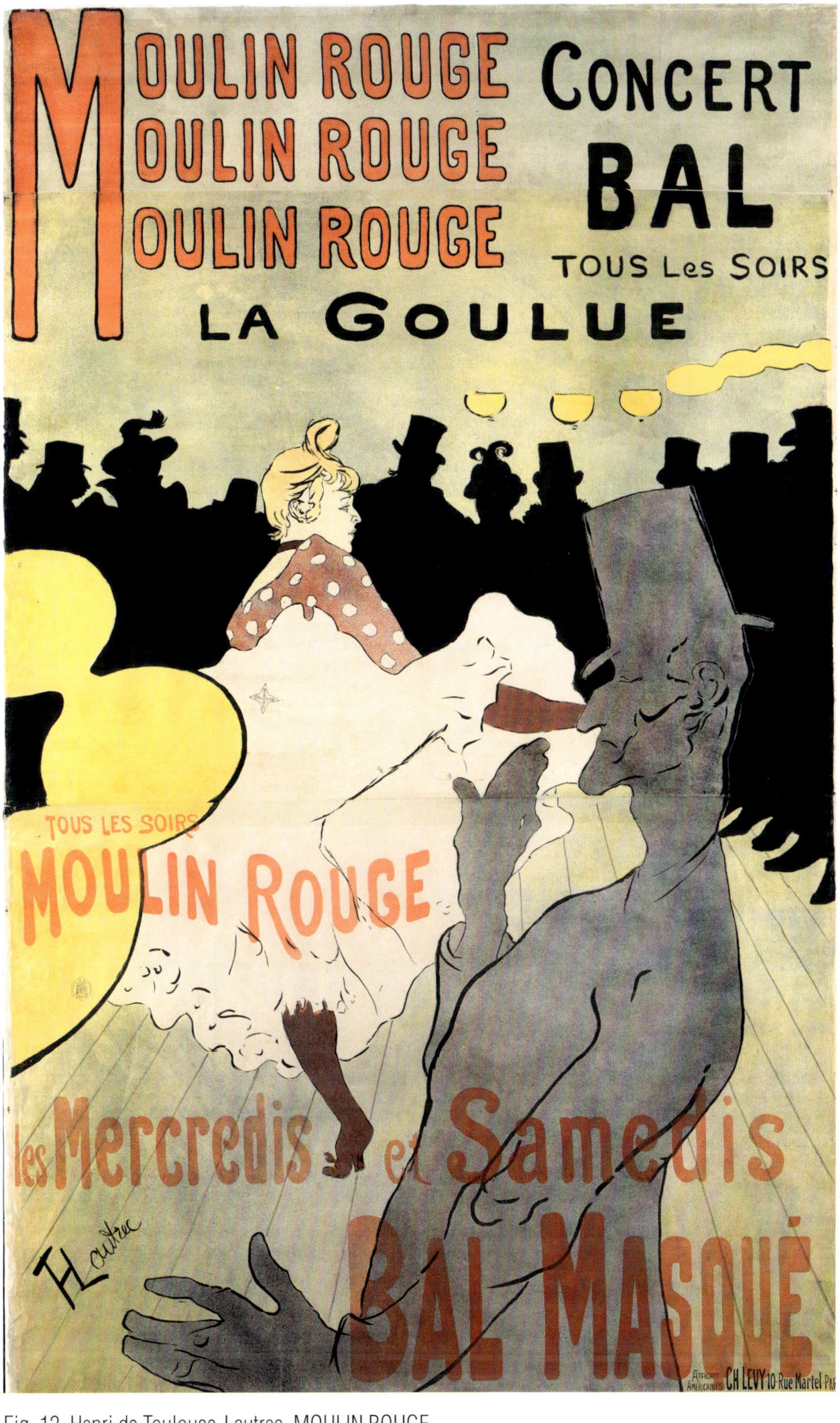

Fig. 12. Henri de Toulouse-Lautrec, MOULIN ROUGE.

Just to clarify, when Tolstoy speaks of delivery or presentation being clear and intelligible (he is probably mostly thinking of the art of writing), he extrapolates that it is therefore beautiful. Beauty to Tolstoy is synonymous with clarity. Let's keep this in mind as we will get into a more involved discussion of beauty in visual art in a later chapter in this book.

We will also be talking about the place of skill in art. Most people would assume that one of the qualities that differentiate art from nonart is skill, believing that artists are very skilled at their craft. Though in many instances this is the case, it does not therefore mean that extreme skill in an art form is a prerequisite for creating art. Tolstoy does provide for the idea that a less skilled artist can still create art, and also that skill alone will not automatically qualify a work as art. We will also be masticating on this in a later chapter with many examples.

As in many theories of art, these qualities or conditions are found in unequal measure, and when all are present to a high magnitude, we get into the realm of the masterpiece, a work of art that exemplifies all the requirements in elevated fashion. As every artwork is a unique combination of factors, recognizing them on a scale such as Tolstoy's helps us to understand and appreciate artworks for their strengths and weaknesses, and to compare and contrast them.

Another triad of qualities that come to mind were the conception of another theorist, St. Thomas Aquinas, as related by James Joyce in *A Portrait of the Artist as a Young Man*. The character Stephen Dedalus interprets the Aquinas theory to one of his classmates and enunciates his three features of beauty as "wholeness, harmony, and radiance." He defines wholeness as context, the perspective from which the purpose arises. Harmony is the relatedness of the elements, the details that relate to the whole, and radiance is the realization of the intention.

The terms are different, but compare these qualities to those outlined by Tolstoy. Aquinas asks: Is the intention clear, do the elements make sense and advance the idea, and do they in concert communicate something meaningful and moving? Very close indeed to the Tolstoy criteria!

These theorists of aesthetics, regardless of how they name their criteria, all allude to the idea that art is indeed "heightened" communication, as opposed to ordinary and common means of sharing feelings and ideas. Art is something special in that it not only tells us something; it expresses it in such a way that we not only learn of the feeling or thought the artist is communicating. We actually feel it; that is, the feeling is actually contained or embedded in the specific way the message is delivered.

Think of the saying, "The medium is the message." In art, the idea or feeling and the manner in which it is conveyed are inextricably combined.

I have discussed in previous books that a visual artist practices an advanced form of seeing that I refer to as "engaged." It is neither perfunctory nor merely attentive. It is a seeing that is enhanced by feeling and is deeply personal. In a way, an artist sees what he or she wants to see—wanting is attached to seeing.

As I define it, engaged vision is something an artist develops as they begin to inject their own self—preferences, passions, idiosyncrasies—into what they see. It is a kind of vision that is informed by the senses, certainly, but complicated by emotive, psychological choices.

Here's an interesting question to ponder: **Can a viewer of art, can you, also practice engaged seeing, and if so, how?**

As you study visual art, take note of the very personal and particular way the artist portrays his or her subject. In fact, no two artists will portray the same subject in an identical fashion, even if they are tasked to work from the same model or scene and are charged to copy it exactly. As you look at, for instance, the way an artist describes and depicts say, a tree, you will realize that your perfunctory idea of what a tree looks like, which sits in your mind's eye, will undergo a transformation.

After a passel of looking, you will realize that there is no such vision that is "tree" and that all the so-called trees you see in all the art you have looked at are not something Plato might call the form of a tree, or "treeness." Rather, each portrayal of a tree is much more specific and an entirely different art "species"—you can call it a Chagall-tree or a Monet-tree or a Hopper-tree. Now when you take a walk in the park, you, too will regard the trees in a way that is unique to you. We can affirm that now your vision and senses are "engaged."

Tolstoy opined that originality played a significant part in defining a work of art. He stated that a work of art must always contain something new, a revelation of sorts, but once again though this was necessary, it was not sufficient. Simply being new did not automatically qualify the work as achieving the mantle of art. It needed the content and excellent execution to make it so. One might argue that traditional paintings dedicated to the realistic depiction of objects, which are still made by many artists today, are not "new" or "original." Yet they may surely achieve the status of being beautiful or evocative. Would you disqualify them because they are traditional and the artist did not invent realism?

My more benevolent assessment is that artists may have the same goal, but the way they get there is totally their own. Originality is not the purview of any one style and realistic work can be as original as abstract. But a caveat: I say "can be," not "is." Let's take a case by case or "formalist" approach and analyze each work as the universe that it is, okay?

Before we close on this chapter—which provides the architecture of the house we are building that is this book—and move on to study the wonderful work of the many artists who have agreed to grace its pages, let's look at an iconic work of very original and electrifying visual art by the artist Gustav Klimt. (It was chosen for our cover.) Let's apply the Tolstoy theory to it, but more importantly, let's look at it with engaged vision.

We all know it and many of us love it. So let's investigate why, shall we?

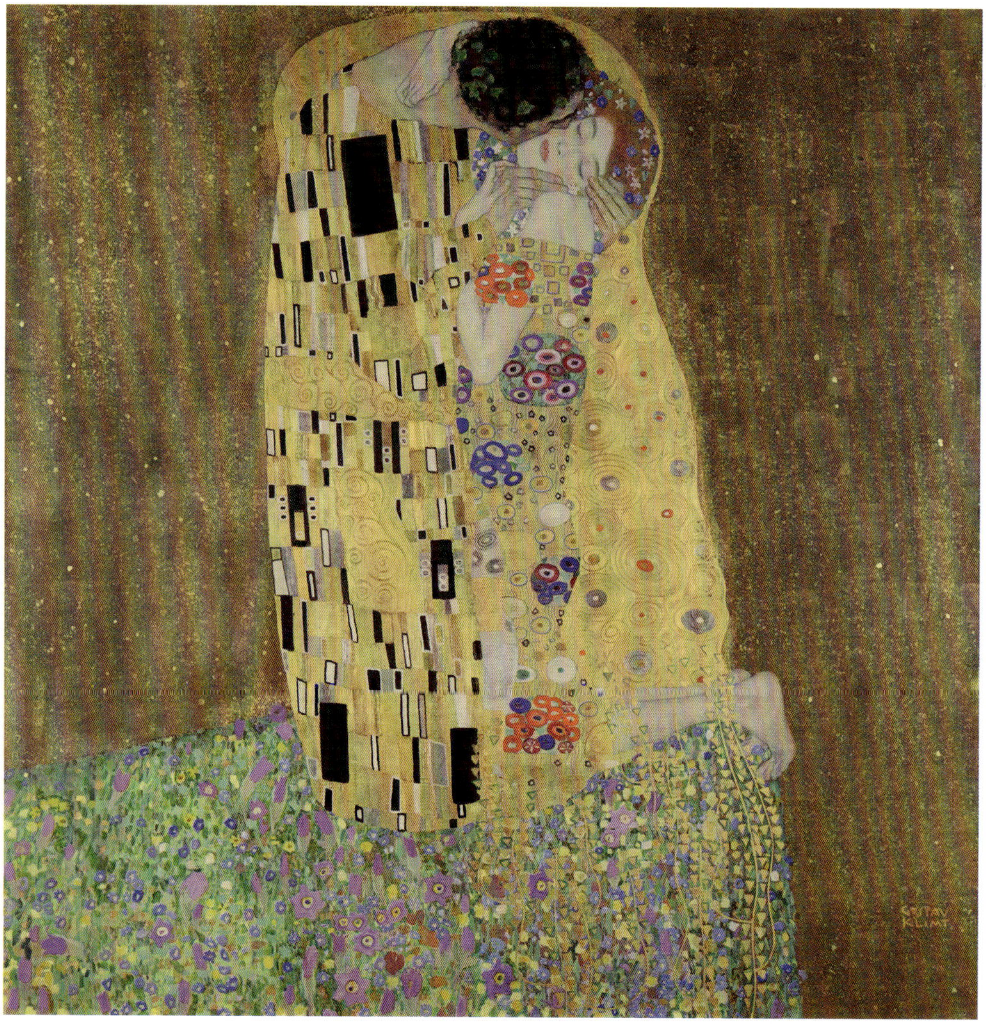

Fig. 13. Gustav Klimt, THE KISS.

Before we get into any details about the artist or this painting, let's just look at it. Toss aside any previous information you have about it, prior conclusions, and assumptions. Let's make believe we are seeing it for the first time.

We see a large square canvas. In fact, it is six feet by six feet. In the center we find two figures wrapped in a bright gold; the female figure is kneeling. These figures are surrounded by a field of golden rain, which frames them and makes them stand out. We can see the figures as a shape before we identify them and what they are doing. Only the faces, hands, and the lower legs of the female figure emanate from this golden shape, which is highly patterned. Part of the floor is patterned with a greenery motif though interestingly it does not span the entire area below the figures. Are they on a cliff?

There is nothing naturalistic about this work, no attempt at verisimilitude to conditions that reflect reality. This is a work of fantasy, though we see objects—figures—we can identify and name.

They are portrayed for us by the artist in flamboyant fashion—in an attempt to effect and evoke an emotion of passion. The elaborate ornamentation is the focus here, as well as highlighting the drawing of the figures in this dramatic pose where the man cradles the face of the woman in adoration and she responds with a blissful expression.

Klimt is a symbolist, and his elegant patterning is not just decoration. The man's robe is adorned with rectangles in white, black, and gray while the woman's garb is detailed with flowerlike swirls of color and wavy lines. These designs are not accidental or just plain old designs. His choices tell us something about his point of view. The colorless straight-lined shapes in the man's robe as opposed to the colorful curves of the woman's garb tell us that his is a traditionalist view of male and female personae.

This work is Klimt's most popular and is much admired. I will stun you perhaps and tell you that I find that its excess and extravagance of color and pattern, though expertly rendered and wrought, for me defeats the pure emotion of the passionate embrace. If I painted my own version of *The Kiss*, I think I would rather depict my lovers in rags so the connection between them is paramount. I find the decoration to be somewhat of a distraction.

But that's me. And this illustrates how an artist's choices reflect and express what is important to him or her, in individual philosophy and personality. Each choice of color, size, direction, and texture evokes and reveals what the artist is all about and what he or she is trying to communicate.

As you look at art, I recommend that you consider how *you* might portray the subject the artist has chosen. What would you like to change about the design, the color, the proportions, the texture? This is one way to become acquainted with your own personality regardless of whether or not you decide to make art on your own. Looking at art is one way to learn more about yourself.

Let's name what we discern from this work that defines the Klimt purpose: his imagery is sensual, yet crisp, in fact it can be hard edged, even flat. He is bold, a superb designer, and loves ornamentation. He is imaginative in his composition, decidedly not literal. His decorative abilities are truly outstanding.

How would he meet the Tolstoy standard of content, expertise, and sincerity? There is nothing questionable about the first two qualities, as Klimt stands as one of the most original, imaginative, and expert figurative painters in the pantheon of painting. If there is one quality that may be debated, it is surely the third—the factor of authenticity.

Exaggeration or aggrandizement in art is something many artists strive for. We find it in Greek marble statues that idealize the form of the human body. Aristotle commented on this in his *Poetics*—the representation in art of human bodies that are lifelike, yes, but more beautiful and perfect than they are in reality.

We will delve into this aspect of art in great depth in our chapter on Truth. Just note that artists fall all along the spectrum from the most naturalistic and *wabi sabi*[*] creations to the most unnatural and anti-natural fantastical iterations. Tolstoy had a decided preference, as did Aristotle, for art that leaned toward nature, but our purpose here is not to learn to recognize the distinctions, but not to denigrate any particular artistic choice.

In Klimt's work, we find an exemplar of the decorative aspect of art, a characteristic of many of his fellow Art Nouveau practitioners. In my estimation, we can love him for this while still admiring an artist like Cézanne or Soutine, artists who eschewed ornamentation. It's interesting to study them all and compare them, but we must extol them each for their virtues and personal vision. Our definitive value is vive la

* *Wabi sabi* is a Japanese term referring to the idea of naturalness and lack of adornment. Items that are wabi sabi may be weathered and old, remaining in their original state. Naturalness as beauty.

différence and to leave room in art for as many efforts as there are artists willing to make them. What they are, not what they are not. That is their gift to us.

The greatest artists and the ones we remember may be highly skilled, though there may be others that surpass them. Some may exhibit less technical or imitative skill, but more imagination, freshness, and heart. They may approach their work in myriad ways and for a variety of reasons.

What they have in common is their individuality. They are able and willing to express themselves in an innovative manner that startles us, interests us, and becomes consonant with an ineffable quality which we forever associate with them. In a sense, they create a "brand," an identifiable artistic signature.

It is something new that we may not have seen before, but now we know it. We may say, "That is a Matisse," or "That is so Matisse," about something other than an artwork, and our friend, providing he or she is into art, knows instantly what we mean. "Matisse" is not just a person, and "a Matisse" is not only an artwork; "Matisse" has now become an adjective.

We turn now to a discussion of Beauty, a key idea in aesthetics, and an interesting conundrum in the world of art.

Chapter 3
Beauty

If you stopped and asked the man on the street, What is art? it's a fair guess that he might include the word "beauty." The creation of something that is beautiful. So, let's get into this and talk about what this word means, how to apply it, and ultimately, whether it is, or is not, one of the criteria that makes art "art."

We start, as always, by defining our terms. The dictionary defines beauty as "a combination of qualities, such as shape, color, or form, that pleases the aesthetic senses, especially the sight." Simple enough. But, you rightly ask, exactly *what* quality of shape, color, or form makes something beautiful? Who is to decide that? And can we all agree?

To the last, whether we can agree, the easy answer is no. I daresay there is nothing all humans can agree upon. But wait . . . .

Can we reach consensus on anything? How about the blue sky? Flowers? A pristine beach on the Mediterranean Sea? The multifarious splendor of nature? Most would and do find these beautiful.

And on the other end of the spectrum? How about a bombed building? A corpse? Anything that is deformed or ruined or laid to waste? No beauty here surely.

But wait . . .

I give you now an example of a painting by a colleague of mine, the artist Jimmy Wright. He is a wonderful artist, much applauded, and is known for his paintings of flowers. Here is an example of one painted in 2001.

This is an exceptionally large work, and compelling. Though many may think of flowers as a noncontroversial subject, and one that epitomizes "beauty," there is a quality to these flowers that is unique. They are not "pretty" flowers; in my view they are "fierce." This tells us that even a subject we can all agree is pleasant and nonthreatening can be evoked in a manner that is expressive and personal.

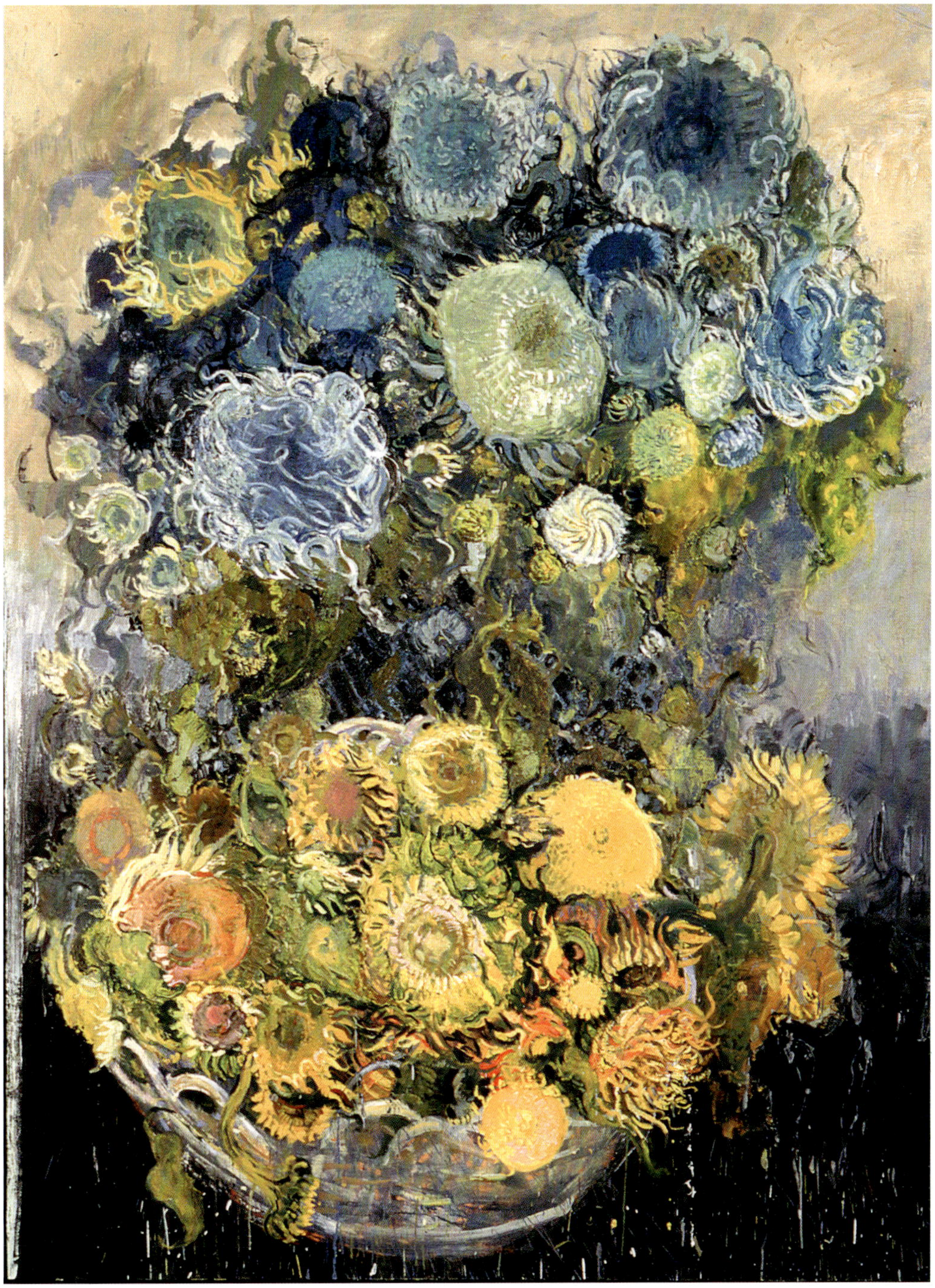

Fig. 14. Jimmy Wright, SUN AND SHADOW.

They can also be perceived and interpreted in a variety of ways. Mr. Wright has told me that his flower works have been recognized for their subtext of queer art, AIDS, and loss. He has also described his painting as "a record of time passed and emotions endured." No doubt, there is a lot more to art than meets the eye, at least in any superficial sense. The eye of the artist may and often does transcend clichés about objects and imbue them with a meaning that is idiosyncratic. This behooves us to not make assumptions or generalizations when interpreting art and always leave room for exceptions to commonly held beliefs.

Though judgment as to what is beautiful and what is not may skew in one direction or another, and there may even be general agreement, when we get into the nuances and specifics, we know that determinations of what is beautiful widely diverge, reflecting cultural, societal, and timely attitudes, norms, and biases.

Everyone knows and repeats the common phrase, "Beauty is in the eye of the beholder," which asserts that beauty is subjective, not actually attached to the object of adoration, belonging or part of it, but instead a sentiment that it provokes in the viewer. This sentiment can be generally classified as pleasure, or as many philosophers refer to it, an aesthetic emotion. It is experienced as enjoyment or appreciation. This sentiment may then engender the judgment on the object, that it is indeed beautiful.

It is this, the "judgment," that requires further analysis. No one minds the sentiment. If you enjoy looking at a sight and think what you see is beautiful, it's okay with me, even if I disagree. That is your prerogative, I say.

But if you make a judgment that Matisse is a lousy painter, and his painting is not beautiful, I have to take umbrage with that. Why, I think it is the cat's meow. It's beautiful to me and you must be wrong, uninformed, or just don't know anything about art.

But beautiful is such a general word. It covers a wide swath of aesthetic emotions and as we become more knowledgeable about art, we require a much larger aesthetic vocabulary to communicate the pleasure we take in art. Maybe if we widen our scope and get into the finer details, we can make sense of this.

I read the work of an interesting Ceylonese philosopher, A. K. Coomaraswamy (1877–1947), who identified the essential element in art with the word *rasa,* which translated means "flavor." *Rasa* is the equivalent of beauty; having *rasa* means imparting aesthetic emotion; the exact word for that is *rasavadana*.

He declared that to experience *rasa*—to recognize and enjoy beauty—one must be "competent," i.e. possess imagination. This suggests that though anyone and everyone can have feelings, sentiments, about what is beautiful, to make credible "judgments," one must be intelligent and imaginative. By the latter, I believe he was referring to one who might be considered a "connoisseur" of art.

I was taken by this word "*rasa*" as a substitute for the word "beauty" for a number of reasons. Firstly, it is clearly related to what we think of as "taste," our particular preferences. These preferences are certainly determined by what we experience—if we live in a culture where people are mostly short, we may think of height as a detriment; if we live in a desert, we may view denseness unfavorably, where the occupants of the jungle might find minimalism chilling. Or perhaps refreshing. But in any case, it would have a determinant effect on their aesthetic choices.

I also like the word because so many different qualifies can live under the banner of flavor that could never survive under the heading of beauty. Think about it. There are millions of flavors, and they appeal to some and not others and for different reasons. While most Russians like that pink soup called borscht, many wouldn't go near it. The Nordics are gobbling down herring, ick!, while in Mexico, the spice is so strong it burns my tongue, but tastes just right to millions. Right?

When it comes to art, I have in previous articles and books substituted the word "expressive" for the word "beautiful" because it, too, is a much larger umbrella for understanding and appreciating art. In chapter 13 of *The Joy of Art*, on "Decoding Works of Art, I provided some of the synonyms for the word "beautiful," and I have some 49 examples. I then moved on to providing some of the synonyms for the word "expressive," and I came up with 247.

This hews closer to the Tolstoy apprehension of beauty as what he referred as "effective communication." A work of art can be expressive when it is devised in such a way that it fulfills the artist's intention and makes that message clear and revelatory. To do so is to create beauty.

Beauty is customarily associated with certain distinguishing qualities of shape, color, and form. A certain proportion, regularity, and symmetry are features most people find beautiful. Bright primary colors as opposed to tonal or drab browns and grays. Smoothness as opposed to rough and scratchy textures. Certain subjects also flop into the beautiful slot—women, mountain tops, water.

Others are less likely to engender such exclamations—men, reptiles, swamps; we simply don't associate these with beauty.

These preferences depend in large measure on the prior experiences and milieu which the artist and his viewer occupy. These determine the artist's perspective and drive intention. We will be discussing cultural references in upcoming chapters but suffice it to remind us in this context, that in the determination of what is "beautiful," we must always refer to the context.

Our visual preferences are largely determined by the qualities of the environment we have grown up in and formed the basis of our visual vocabulary. If we grow up in a place of open spaces and dramatic topography and are accustomed to being able to look into the horizon at far distances, we may develop a preference for landscape paintings that depict vistas with deep space like this painting by the American artist Albert Bierstadt.

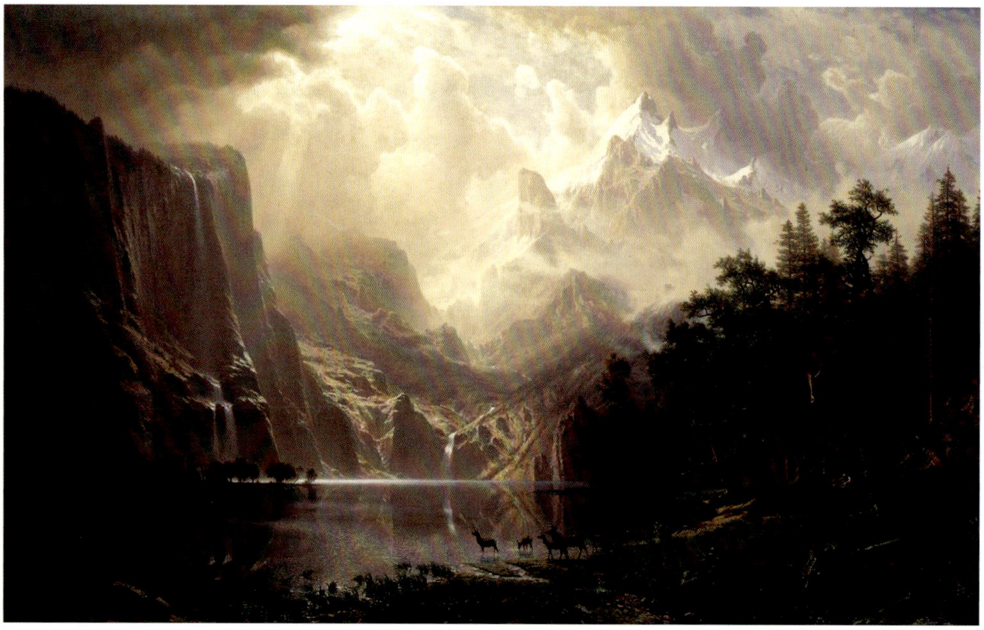

Fig. 15. Albert Bierstadt, AMONG THE SIERRA NEVADA.

Living in an open space, your eyes have become accustomed to looking deep so you are able to grasp the illusion created in this painting. If, on the other hand, you are grown up in a jungle or other dense environment, you might be quite confused looking at this work and even find it disconcerting.

In his essay on perspective, Richard L. Gregory pointed to the Zulus, who live in what he defines as a "circular culture." Their houses and even their doorways are rounded, and they eschew straight lines even in the plowing of their fields. They live in a dense environment with short views out of their rounded windows. If they had occasion to look at this Bierstadt painting, they would not perceive the depicted mountains as distant as they have not experienced distance in their normal visioning. The writer elaborated that people who lack this experience perceive distant objects not at far away, but simply small.

It is true that the painter who follows the principles of perspective deliberately draws distant objects as small to create that illusion they are far away. But a viewer accustomed to looking into the distance knows instinctively that the mountains are not small at all. Because of this, he is able to perceive the painting, the illusion of the scene, as acceptable, and even beautiful, while a Zulu person, from Gregory's example, may perceive it as a distortion and therefore displeasing or ugly.

Most reading this book and going to museums to look at Western art have accepted the spatial illusions as we have lived in an open culture, have traveled and perceived many environments and for this reason, we have a commonality of visual experience. So it makes sense that we have developed a similar set of visual preferences in the most general sense. Nonetheless, we all know some people who prefer open spaces like the beach, and others who prefer closed spaces with clear boundaries like caves, forests, interiors.

These preferences may coincide with our preferences in art and our decisions about what we judge to be beautiful. If you are an open space beach lover, you may be a fan of the fantastic artist J. M. W. Turner, and love this work that is so atmospheric that you judge it to be a work of abstract art. It is called *Venice with the Salute,* but Turner cared little for the storied bridges and villas we think of as Venetian. His fascination was with the air, the atmosphere, and for Turner, the stormier and soupier the better.

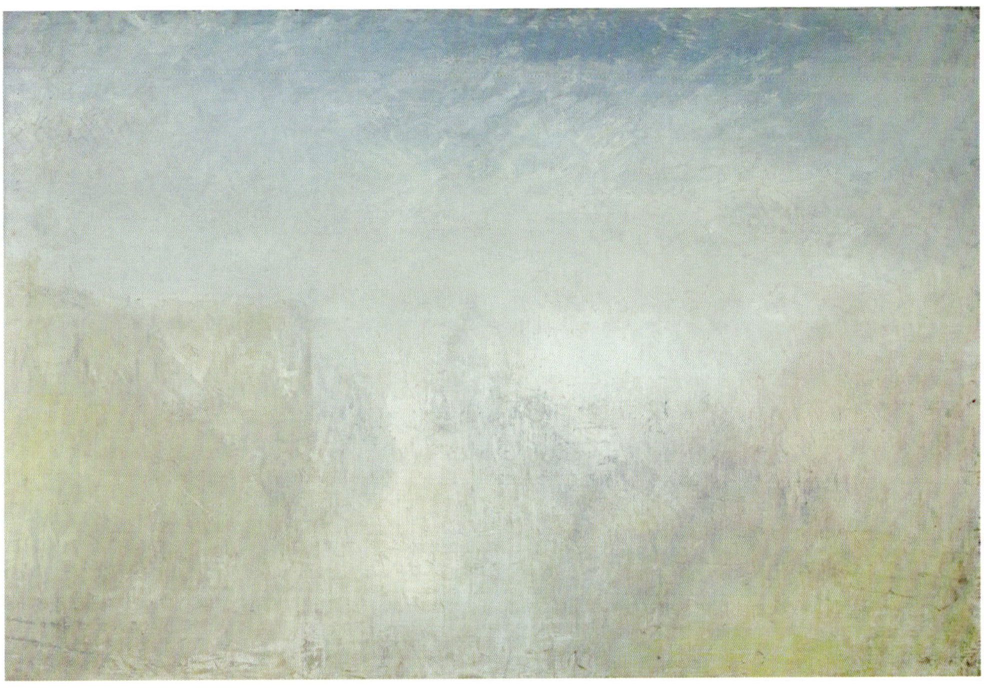

Fig. 16. J.M.W. Turner, VENICE WITH THE SALUTE.

And if you, beach lover, take a fancy to Turner, you will probably find modern abstract painters whose work you find beautiful as well, especially those we consider to be painterly, or use large swaths of color that also create an atmospheric effect, what we refer to as **color field**. Fig. 17 is a modern example of such a work.

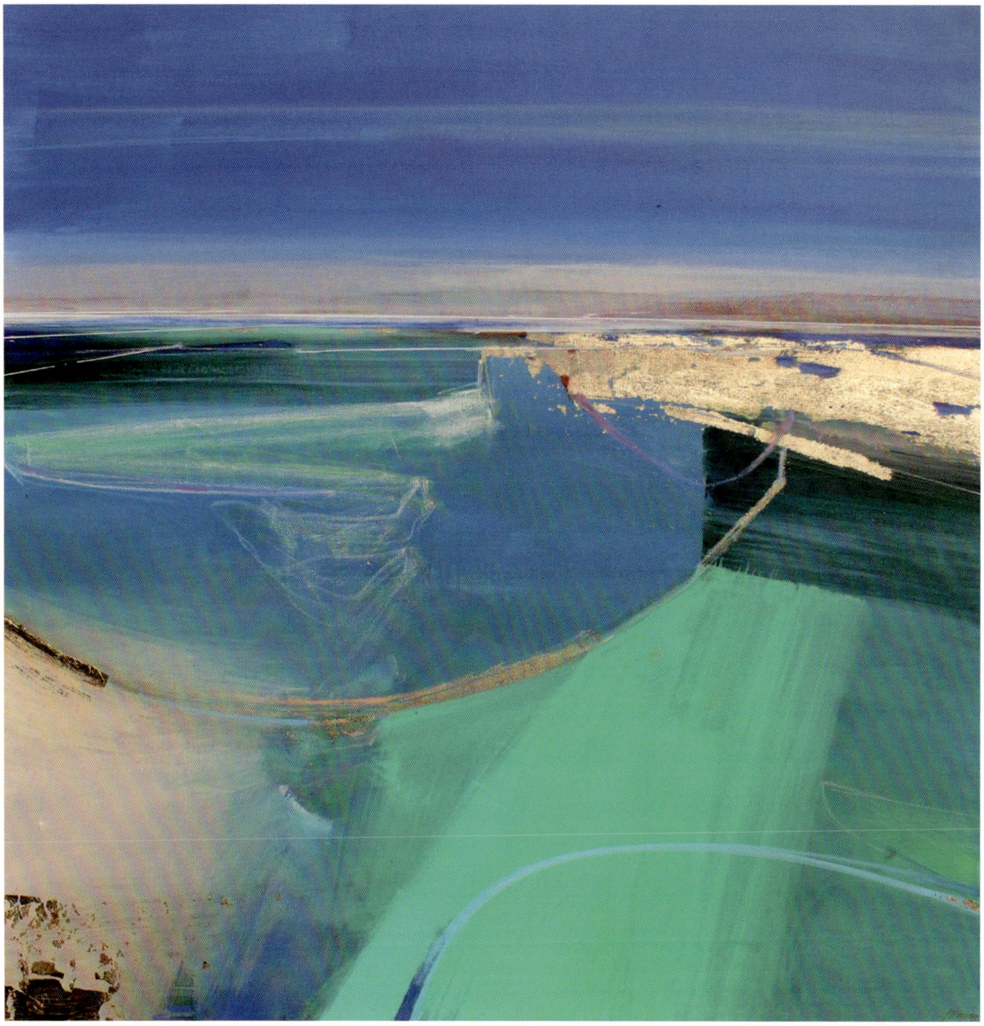

Fig. 17. Magdalena Morey, CATCHING THE WAVE.

In this work by the artist Magdalena Morey, the large areas of color and textured areas create the illusion of deep dimension. The piece is aptly titled *Catching the Wave*, which her adept composition enables you to do vicariously. Your vision takes a kind of thrill ride into imaginary space.

If, on the other hand, your propensities lean more toward closed spaces, you may fancy more descriptive works in general, perhaps interiors, and in abstract work,

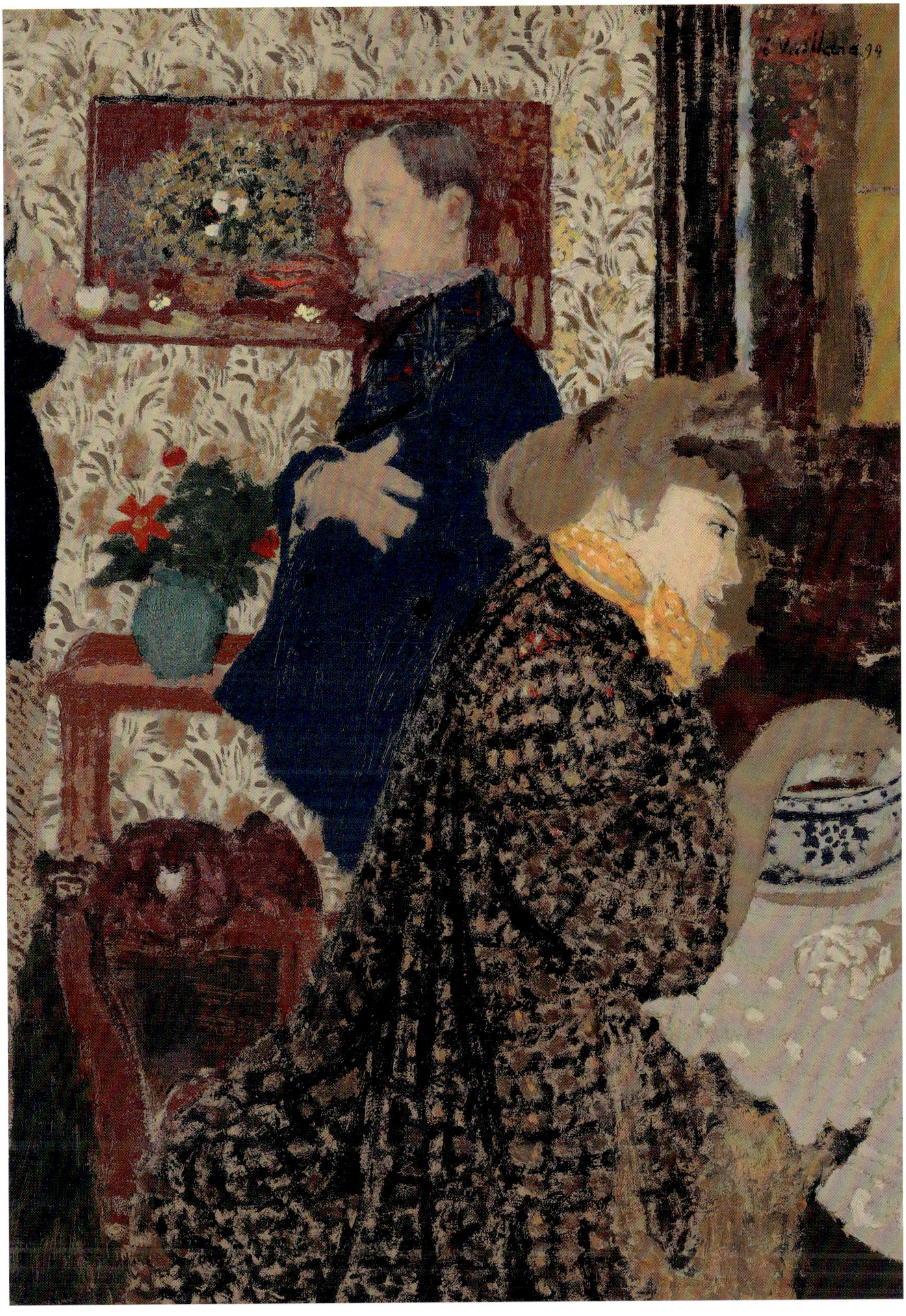

Fig. 18. Pierre Bonnard, MISIA ET VALLOTTON À VILLENEUVE.

pieces that are more geometric and/or decorative. Let's have a look at this example of a painting by the wonderful Pierre Bonnard, one of my very favorite painters of such typical scenes.

You may notice that in this work, not only is there an intimacy in the illusion of the space, the work appears sewed together like a tapestry, where each note of paint is connected to its neighbor, and there is little or no "negative space" or air between the surfaces and objects. The flowers in the vase are connected to the flowers in the wallpaper and to the flowers depicted in the painting on the wall. What we see is an enclosed world of texture and color that unifies the objects and figures depicted in the painting.

Nothing in the work stands alone or separate. Though the two figures shown in this painting look away from each other, all the color notes in the painting sweep them into the cozy homeyness of this lovely image. What we see reflected in this painting is the security and warmth, the privileged existence of this time and place.

At this moment in the book, we stop for a moment and realize what it is possible to read in a work on art. We recognize the elements, yes, but then think of what they reveal about the artist who created this particular work, and also what this recognition reveals about us, the viewers.

The artist and his viewer are partners. Both can interpret the artwork to better reveal through our choices and perceptions who we are and what matters to us. Art is the intermediary that communicates a very personal lesson for both artist and viewer.

Returning from this aside, let's just have a look at an abstract work that might have appeal to our viewer enjoying closed spaces. This is a work by Wassily Kandinsky, who experimented quite a bit with abstraction. Here is one of his more condensed works where the colored shapes are layered on top of one another, and literally cram the canvas.

I remind you here to look for areas of quiet when you look at art. This is a work that has little of it; instead it presents a cacophony of color and shape. On first blush, is this something that appeals or disturbs? Is the artist trying to say so much that his purpose is negated?

More is not necessarily more, as we know. Less can be more if it makes the imagery more potent, more recognizable, more interesting. More can be too much if it confuses or negates—what we might call an embarrassment of riches.

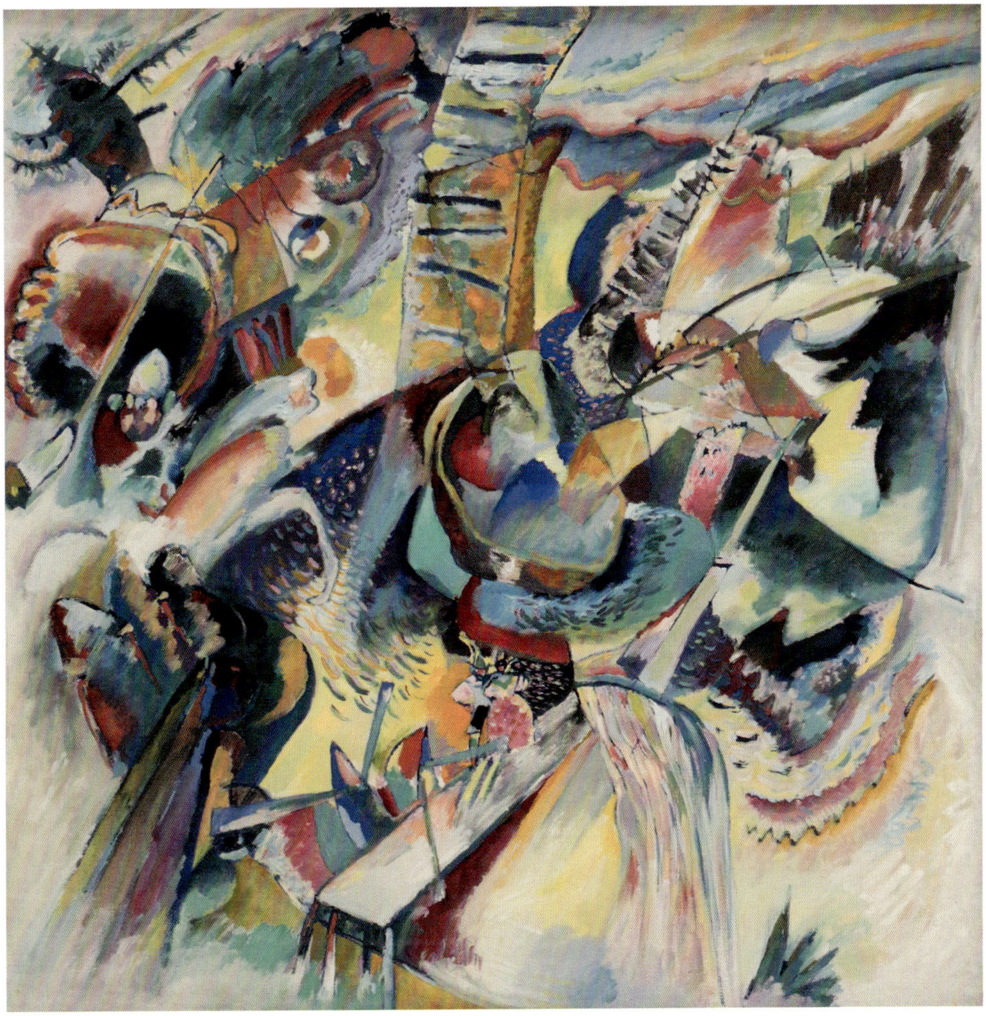

Fig. 19. Wassily Kandinsky, IMPROVISATION KLAMM.

This is an aesthetic criterion that you can employ when you look at any work of art. Does it say enough? Does it say too much? Or is the message so strikingly articulated that we can say it is loud and clear, just right? We are reminded here of the children's story "Goldilocks and the Three Bears." We can apply this standard—evaluating the three chairs—regardless of the subject or style.

We've provided some initial clues as to how our preferences are connected to what we find interesting and beautiful in art. But let's break that down a bit further.

When we speak of the qualities of art that encourage us to declare a particular work "beautiful" we know that this is not fixed, immutable, or even quantifiable and moreover, that what one viewer may think is beautiful will leave you cold. Our judgment depends on how moved we are by the work, and we know that varies tremendously and depends in large part on our former experiences, education, life circumstances, gender, culture, a host of factors, both intrinsic to us and learned, that make us who we are.

We may be much kinder in asserting that a work is "expressive," that though we don't like the message, the message is realized and well delivered. The standard of *rasa*—flavor—opens us up to so many possibilities. Let's delve into this and evolve a new vocabulary of flavors we can apply to our study and appreciation of art. Think of these as samples of expressive qualities that enable us to find value whether or not we determine that the work is indeed "beautiful."

VITALITY

Here's one to consider first: **vitality**. Can we not agree that this is a positive quality, indeed perhaps a standard for all others? Dictionary.com definition of the noun: "1. exuberant physical or mental vigor: 2. capacity for survival or for the continuation of a meaningful or purposeful existence 3. power to live or grow. 4. vital force or principle."

Artworks that exhibit vitality might be described using the following adjectives: muscular, vivacious, lively, powerful, energetic, enthusiastic, vibrant, fresh—all relating to the possession of a life force. You surely can name others.

And the antonyms: weak, flaccid, tired, desiccated, limp, exhausted.

Now let's look at two works that exhibit this quality of vitality. Again, we may not be able to agree that we find them "beautiful" but nonetheless concur that they can be described using one of the aforementioned adjectives. Be sure to pick one or give one of your own after you view the work.

This oil by Winslow Homer delivers us the ocean with all its ferocity and intensity. We feel the hardness and slipperiness of the rocks. His limited color palette is so effective as it gives us the temperature of the day, the coldness and turbulence of the air. He feels these conditions and provides them through his colors and animated application of paint. There are no discordant notes or confusion. We can imagine feeling fear if we were to find ourselves swirling in those waters. The painting has vitality, muscularity, vigor. It works.

In this case, the subject is one that is synonymous with vitality, but let's ask: Can a work on a tender scene still possess vitality, or do we attribute the vitality of the Homer to its subject?

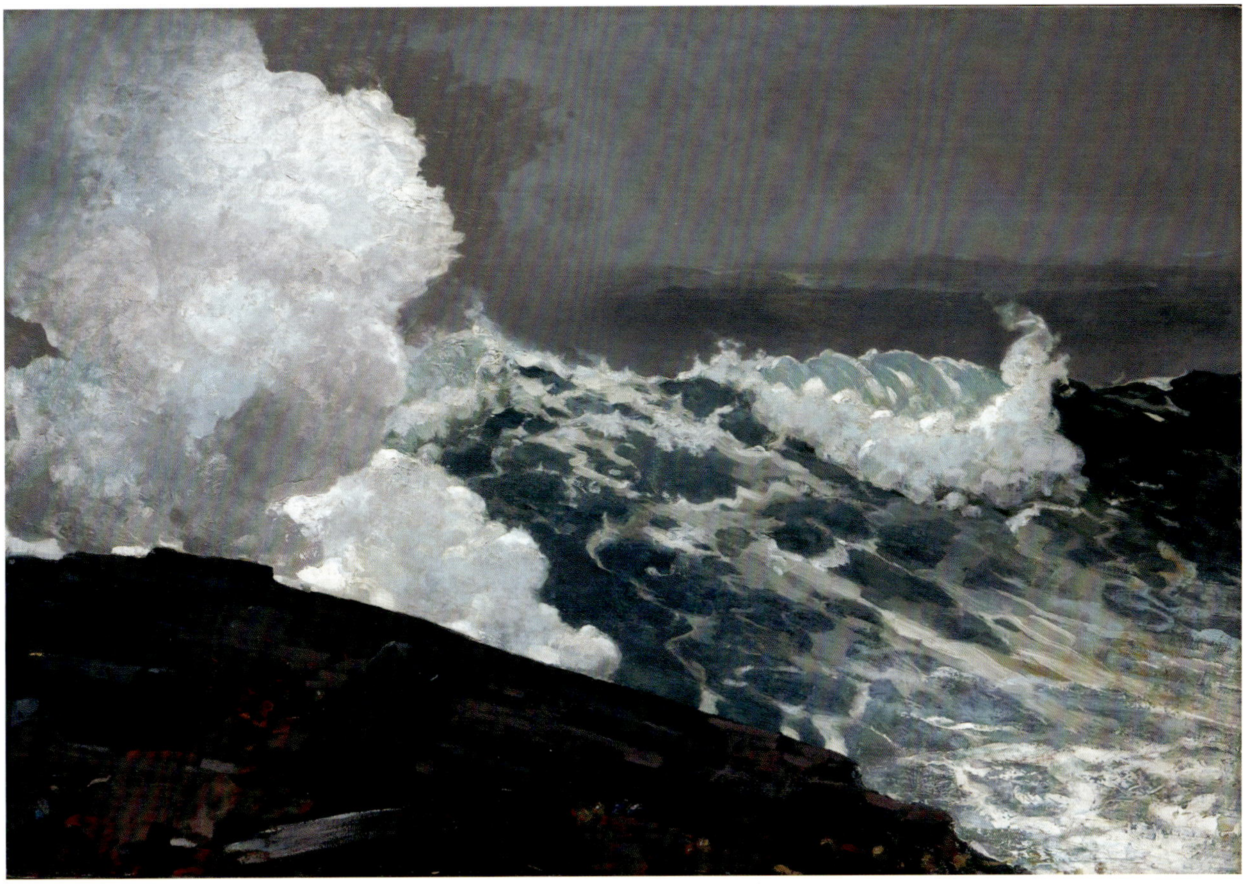

Fig. 20. Winslow Homer, NOREASTER.

Let's look at another painting and assess.

What more tranquil subject can you imagine than that of this painting by the American Impressionist Mary Cassatt of a woman sitting with a cup of tea in a garden? Yet it is the picture of vitality and verve with its loose brushstrokes and accents of color that allow you to move your eye from surface to surface in a delightful way. The whole surface sings with the dazzle of light punctuating every note.

Your eye comes to rest in the soft colorful shadow of the woman's contemplative face shielded from the sun by her bonnet. Then follow it to the glints of gold and silver on the cup and spoon. There is no labor evident in this lovely work of art which feels like it emerged full blown in an instant. It is the afternoon breeze incarnate in this masterly concoction that feels so very alive as it expresses the quiet and peace of the moment.

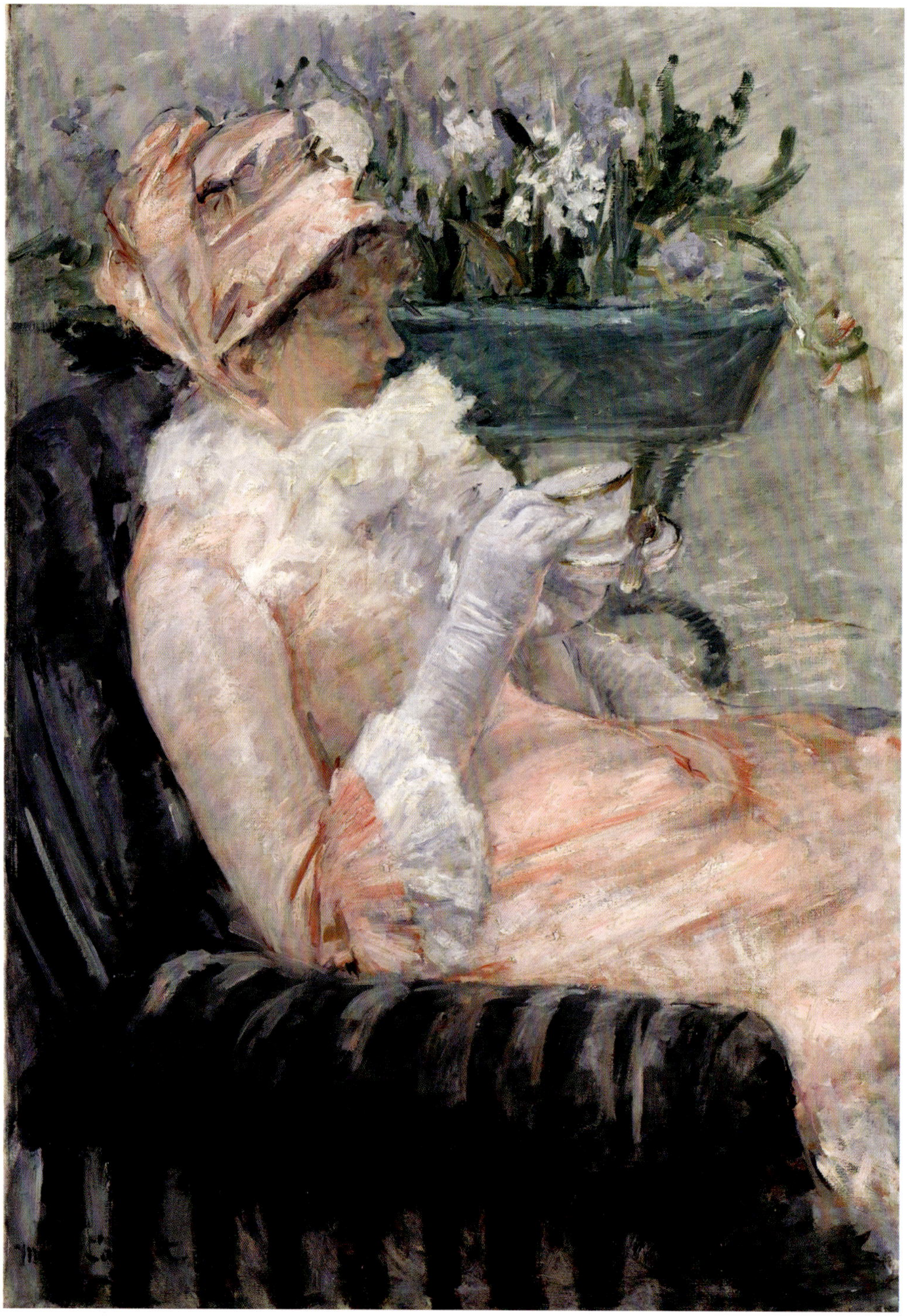

Fig. 21. Mary Cassatt, THE CUP OF TEA.

So, we see that the quality of vitality is not about the subject at all, but the artist's treatment of it. The vitality in the work of art may reside in the color, the application of paint, the movement captured in the design, or in a combination of factors. In the following example of a work by the American artist Marsden Hartley, painted in Germany at the beginning of World War I—a time when turbulence may have been the order of the day—Hartley delivers a vivid, color-charged work, quite modern for the time, an expressionistic work notable for its directness.

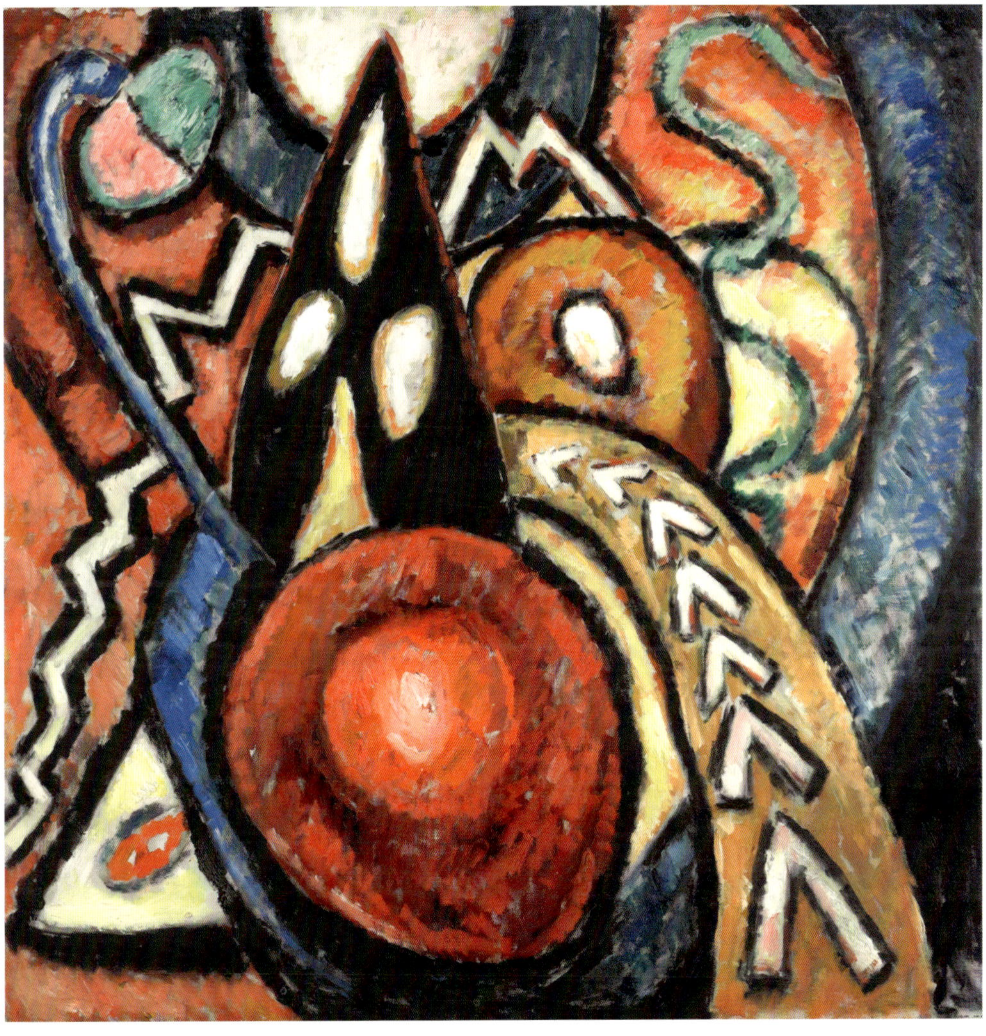

Fig. 22. Marsden Hartley, MOVEMENTS.

Take note of work that is particularly alive and vibrant, regardless of its period, or perhaps in spite of it, and possesses this quality of vitality. It is surely one of the characteristics of effective, expressive, and exemplary works of art.

POWER

How about the quality of "power"? Art that may not be deemed beautiful in the conventional sense—pleasing in shape, color, and form—may nonetheless register as "powerful." Again, let's begin with the definition: "1: having great power, prestige or influence, 2: leading to many or important deductions" (Merriam-Webster). Some synonyms: heavy-duty, important, influential, potent, significant, strong.

There are many visual artists whose work has been deemed powerful, some for its very execution that makes it more compelling than that of other practitioners of similar style or period. There are artists whose intention is to make a political statement with their art, and these messages delivered in visual form can be extremely powerful and compelling.

Other works are considered powerful for how they advanced the language and purview of visual art, created a movement that inspired other artists, or changed the way the public looks at art. We will look at the latter distinctions—artists who changed the way we look at art—in a subsequent chapter. Here let's just have a gander at some works that we consider powerful for their sheer force of execution or emotional intensity.

In utter force and monumentalism, there is no artist I can think of whose works are more powerful than those of the German artist Anselm Kiefer (b. 1945) who continues to create astounding works that push the barriers of boldness and psychological drama. He is best known for works that reflect and comment on German history and particularly on the horror of the Holocaust.

Taking off on the combines of Robert Rauschenberg, Kiefer incorporates all kinds of materials into often heavily impastoed, huge canvases that in and of themselves create a resonance—glass shards that speak pain, pieces of lead that add to the darkness and hard edge of the works and reference alchemy, dried flowers and strands of hair that speak of desiccation and death. All of these layered embellishments, as well as the generally dark or neutral palette, give his work a sober intensity. Truly, they can be hard to look at, but also, strangely, hard to look away from. That is their power to affect us.

These works are not descriptive but rather more like visual poetry that incorporates signs and symbols from myth, architectural structural shapes, disturbed and fierce textural landscapes, imagery that relates to German fairy tales, text from books and slogans, and even just scribbles.

It is powerful indeed, and though you probably would not use the word "beautiful" to describe it, would you say fascinating, resonant, inspired, even haunting? Look at this Kiefer work:

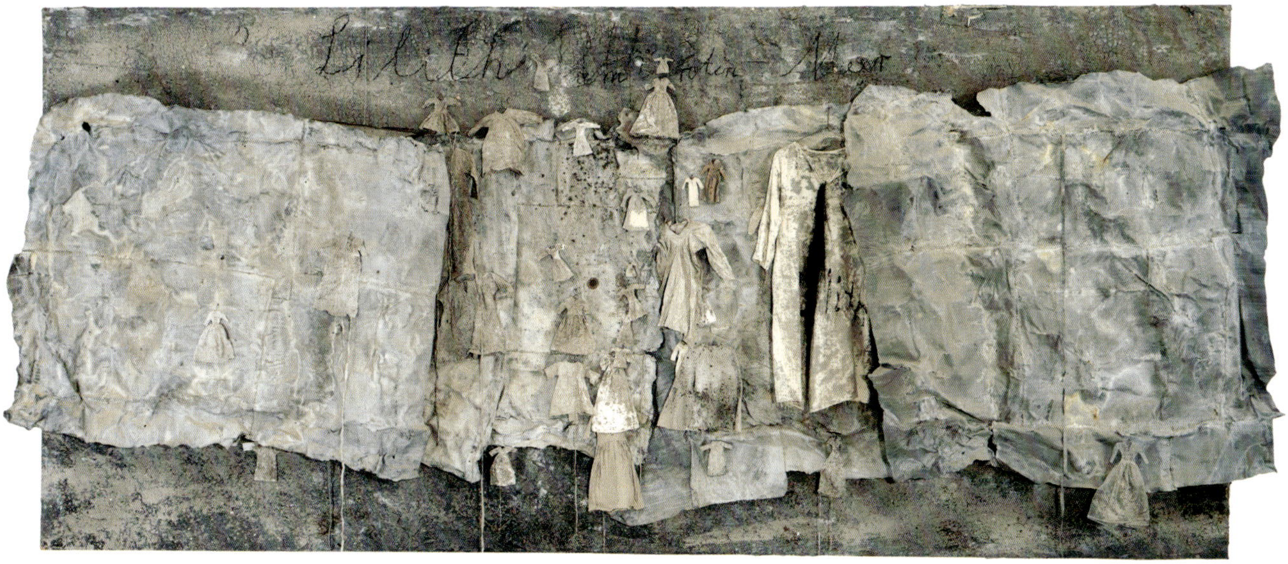

Fig. 23. Anselm Kiefer, LILITH AT THE RED SEA.

Ragged articles of clothing of all sizes, even doll-sized, hang on a surface the color and texture of dirt. There is an inscription at the top that is unintelligible, but it doesn't matter, does it? One can't exactly say why, but the work seems to talk to us about lives lost, squandered, left in the dirt, forgotten. Uncomfortable, surely, but unquestionably powerful!

The power of the Kiefer works is so extreme, it is difficult to find works that compare. Picasso's *Guernica* comes to mind; although that also touches on the horror of war, it is more descriptive and perhaps for that reason less evocative than the Kiefer. But artwork can be powerful regardless of whether the subject is one as weighty as death, or something more life affirming but rendered in an uncompromising manner.

All art is personal, as the personality of the artist comes through regardless of the subject. But in some cases, visual art can be so deliberately and intensely personal that it provides a view corridor into the psyche of the artist. This is powerful.

One artist we associate with psychological pain is the artist Edvard Munch, whose painting *The Scream* is one of the best known for its emotional draw. Here is another by Munch, titled *Melancholy*, in which he depicts a friend, Jappe Nilssen, who is suffering from despair due to a lost love.

What is interesting about this work is the placement of Nilssen on the canvas. Take note that placement and size of elements in art can be indicators of emotional relevance. I remember noting as a teacher of small children that one of the children in my class always drew her figures at the very bottom of the paper. When I questioned her mother to discern the possible meaning, she informed me that the child had taken a terrible fall and been injured. Now her placement of the figures made sense, surely not accidental at all, rather a depiction of her fear of falling.

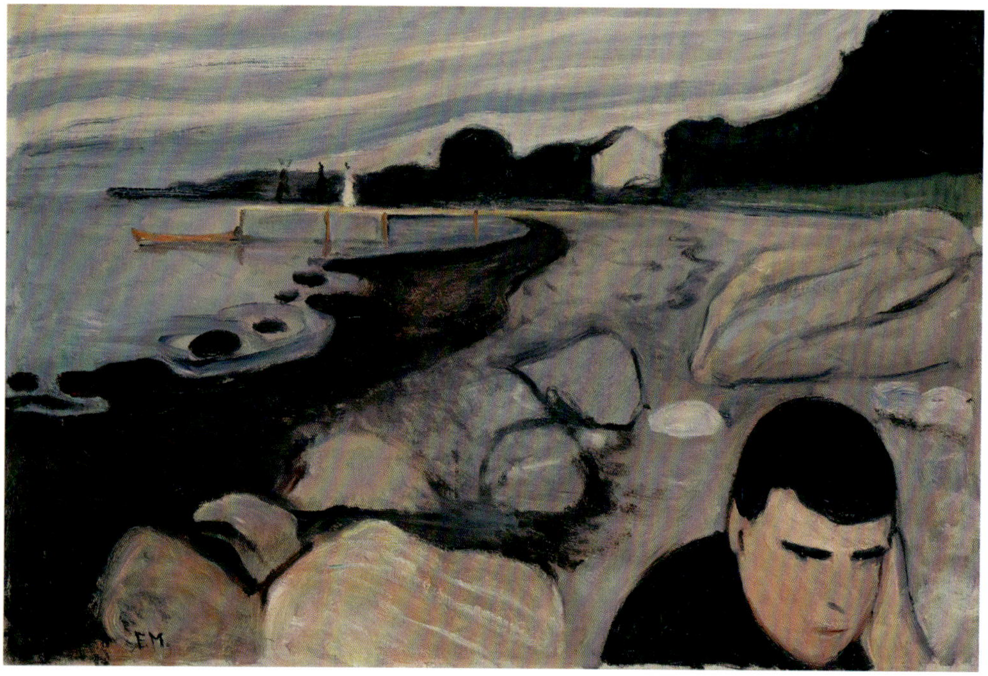

Fig. 24. Edvard Munch, MELANCHOLY.

What does the placement of the figure possibly represent? He is almost out of the picture, exactly what he has experienced in life, now in a state of melancholy as he is no longer relevant to the person he loved. Powerful, emotionally resonant works like this one transcend any concept of beauty, as it is not the artist's intention to deliver anything that is enhanced or embellished; quite the contrary. He is giving you the embodiment of psychological pain—here loneliness, isolation, rejection—and the only beauty is the authenticity and power of the naked truth.

These are works that go beyond providing the viewer with a pleasing image. The Munch work tugs at our hearts as we perceive this artist's camaraderie with his friend. And for Kiefer, his emotional canvas is even wider as his work delves not only into personal issues, but societal and historical ones as well, as he grapples with the horror of his German forebears.

Take note that it takes an inordinate amount of courage for an artist to both reveal his or her emotions in art, and also to present a work that does not have the familiar markers of conventional beauty. The artist's desire to express must transcend the desire to be liked or admired by the prevailing culture.

IMAGINATION

As we look at aesthetic criteria outside of the questionable concept of "beauty," let's look at another quality that describes myriad works of art and that is the factor of inventiveness or imagination, the ability to conjure visual imagery. Though all artists exhibit a perspective that is their own, some artists' works are distinguished by an exceptional novelty, freshness, or cleverness. Does an active imagination in itself give credibility to an artwork?

We looked last at a Munch work that is a powerful psychological portrait. But let us be clear that artworks possess more than one aesthetic quality. In fact, this work is also a striking example of original conception, as Munch found a personal pathway to make his emotion visual.

One of the most innovative, playful, and original artists was the Swiss artist Paul Klee (1879–1940). Though he was influenced by many visual artists of his time—Wassily Kandinsky, Cubists Braque and Picasso, and the colorists Delaunay and Macke—he developed a unique way of expressing himself, making whimsical marks and blocks and field of color that characterized his very expressive drawings, watercolors, and oils. Creative people like Klee often find many avenues to express themselves—Klee also wrote poetry and made music. You may be amazed to realize the potential output of such a creative individual—Klee produced nearly ten thousand artworks on paper alone!

Here is a fun fact that gives a window into how ingenuity might manifest. Klee was known to take scissors, cut off part of a work, and then reconnect it at a different juncture. Someone else might have preferred the symmetry and connectivity of the original but Klee was creative enough to find a more interesting arrangement. When I referred to him as "playful," you can see how apt that adjective is.

Playfulness and inventiveness are found in all periods of art making, on both ends of the spectrum from the positive and expansive versions like Klee, Warhol, and the kitsch of pop art to the wild and often dark nightmarish "*le fantastique*" of mannerist, Surrealist, visionary, and even grotesque art forms.

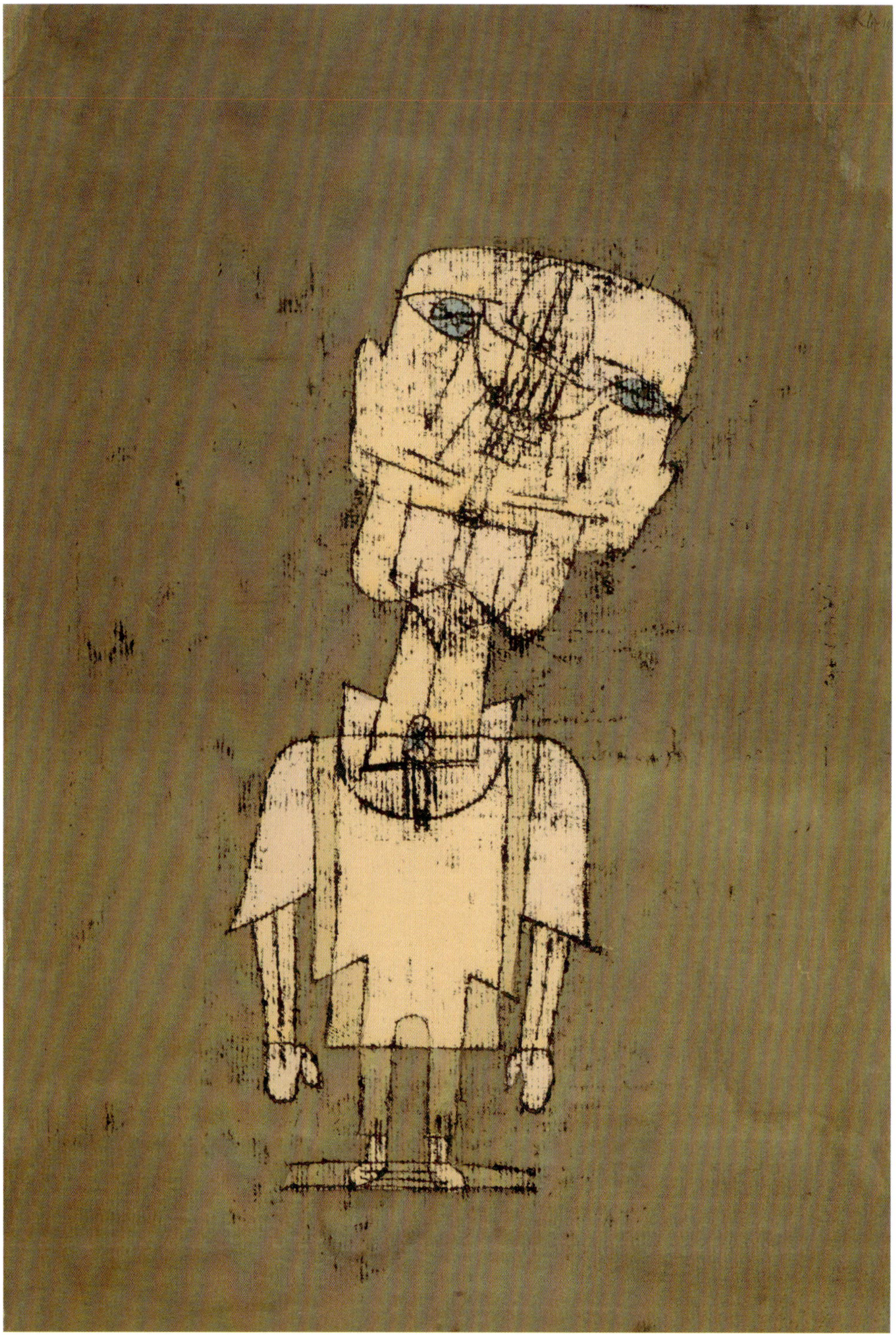

Fig. 25. Paul Klee, GHOST OF A GENIUS.

The latter comes to mind in the art of the infamous Hieronymus Bosch, working in the fifteenth and early sixteenth centuries, thought to be the first practitioner of fantastic art. You are probably somewhat familiar with his famous *The Garden of Earthly Delights*, which depicts in amazing detail and with aplomb his vision of heaven and hell.

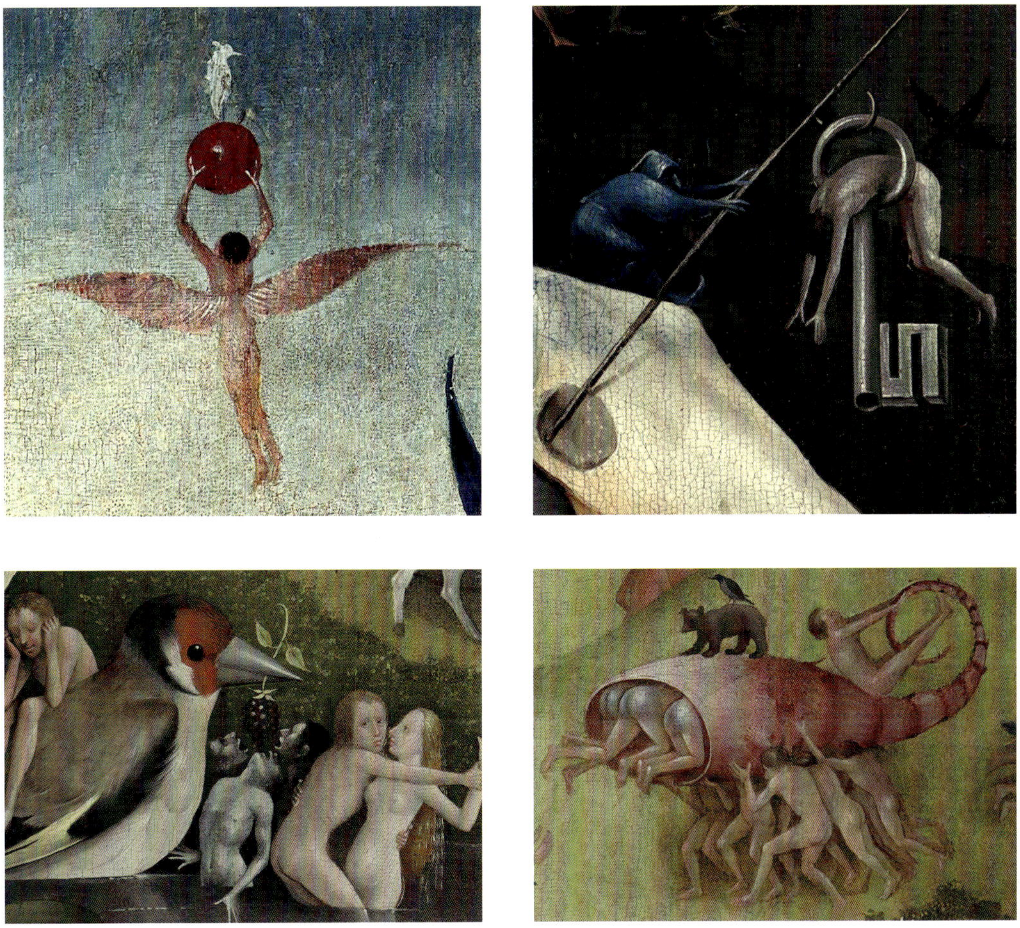

Fig. 26. Hieronymus Bosch, THE GARDEN OF EARTHLY DELIGHTS (details).

I show four images from this amazing work here so you can view the mind-blowing oddity and revolutionary nature of this early work—the distortion of proportions one would not associate with this era. They resemble images I might have taken from a modern film featuring creatures from outer space.

Looking at this Bosch imagery and knowing how long ago it was conceived, you might have expected the religious ferocity and ideas about heaven and hell you see displayed here, but the image of a figure on a huge bird, figures crammed in a giant lobster shell, or even a flying man—probably not. It may be wise to toss some of those assumptions out the nearest window and just continue to do lots of looking.

The Bosch imagery is the stuff of dreams, in which incongruity reigns supreme. In a dream, a person can be a cat, proportions can defy reality, clocks may drip (as in the famous Salvador Dalí painting *The Persistence of Memory*). Anything, indeed, is possible, and the more literally these impossibilities are realistically portrayed, the more believable they seem.

The word for the art form that champions these dream images, **Surrealism**, was coined in 1924. E. H. Gombrich in *The Story of Art* (1950) described the motivation of artists to create images "more real than reality itself." But here we see that we cannot hold fast to these definitions and conclusions, as we see Bosch creating these visions in the sixteenth century, more than three centuries before this description was even coined.

We may think of fantasy as a modern iteration, but it is obviously not, and, as you can see here, from an age of darkness where scientific knowledge is limited and conspiracy rages, the fantastic can proliferate. Dreams, especially nightmares, may seem more real than quotidian life.

Suffice it to say, oddities are everywhere to be found in the history of art and the question of whether there are only just so many visual ideas with an unlimited number of variations is not out of the question. Dream images like Bosch's have been wrought in visionary art of many periods, and this fascination culminates in the full-blown period of Surrealist works in the modern era. I encourage you to look at the work of Salvador Dalí and René Magritte and savor their imagery.

Here we have a modern Surrealist work by a Japanese artist, Harue Koga, one of the first Surrealist works executed in Japan in 1929.

Surrealist art often is heavily steeped in symbolism. It may not make sense on first glance. Though this image contains a series of water-related images—a swimmer, fish, a boat, a lighthouse, a blimp, and various mechanical parts, etc.—they are shown without regard to size or proportion or related in any sensible way. They appear the way they might in a dream from which you may awaken and, for the life of you, may not be able to reconstruct what seemed so potently real just moments ago.

Note that though the images are incongruous, they are very well organized. This is so consonant with the idea of a dream's believability at the moment you are having it and your sense of incomprehension and dismemberment from that moment when

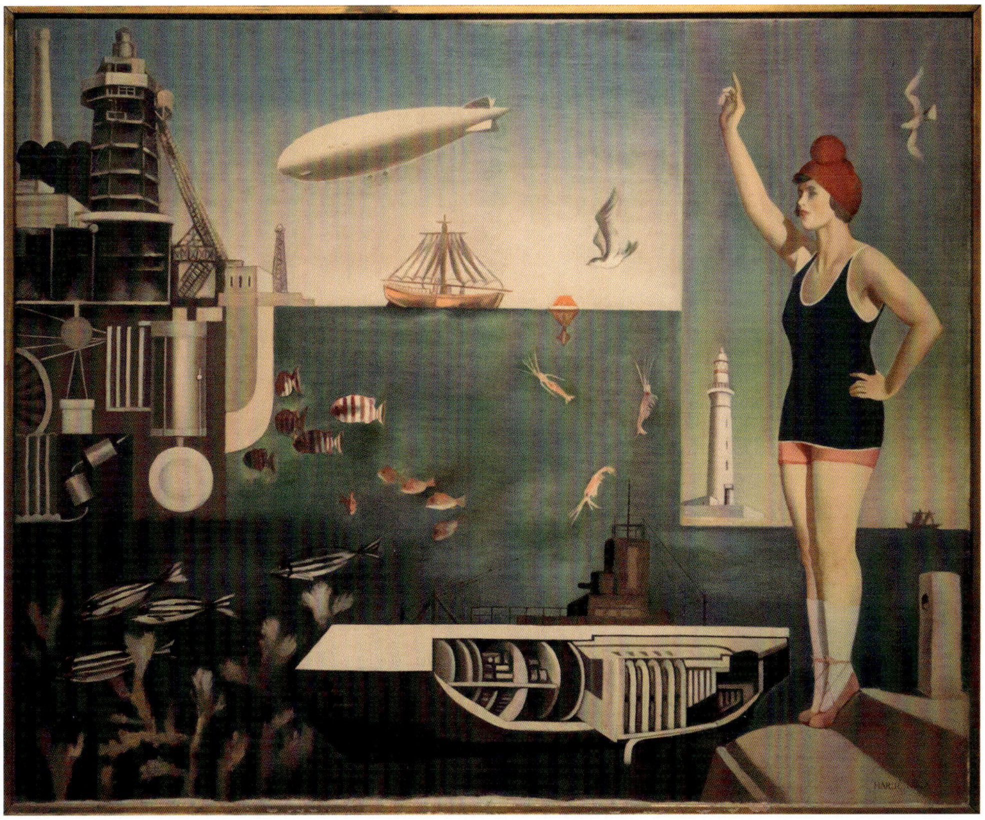

Fig. 27. Harue Koga, THE SEA.

you awaken and try to use your conscious mine to remember it. It made such sense, and now it is incomprehensible.

The artists whose work is imbued with this imaginative overlay are offering us a different state of consciousness in a visual format. In a sense, they are conjuring for us that dream state, where our minds are able to reshuffle elements we borrow from our conscious and reconstitute them into a new reality. This goes beyond any concept of beauty into creation itself.

THE UNEXPECTED

In language, we have the figure of speech referred to as an *oxymoron*. This strange word comes from the Greek: oxy means sharp, and moronos means dull. An oxymoron is a contradictory statement like "icy hot," "bittersweet," or "sad smile," where two opposites are paired. Now I ask: Is there something we might call a visual oxymoron, an image which is, in itself, a contradiction?

The answer is yes: a work of art may seem to contradict itself—children playing seemingly carefree but in a desolate environment that seems menacing; a depiction of death that is beautifully painted (think of Jacques-Louis David's *The Death of Marat*), or a jolly design in morbid colors. This kind of treatment is unusual and unexpected. It makes sense, doesn't it, to use bright, happy colors to suggest a positive scene, and dark, tonal colors to state the negative.

Look for visual oxymorons as you look at art. They are not common, but consider it a "find" when you spot one.

SENSUALITY

We have just taken a glance at art from the standpoint of vitality, power and imagination, all qualities that argue for expressive corollaries for beauty, but what of sensuality, the quality of the augmentation or delight of the senses. Surely that is another worthy candidate.

Sensuality in visual art is determined by the subject matter certainly, with some leading more toward feelingful treatment—figurative art, still lives, floral motifs, landscape—than others—war scenes, narrative, religious art, though the latter may be questionable—think of that Bosch work. But it is more likely that the sensuality is more directly related to the aesthetic elements—the color scheme, application of paint, feeling for light, form, quality of line, in other words, the painting and drawing finesse of the sensual artist.

Forgive me for such a comparison, but I offer two disparate works of art.

First, the painting of a young John the Baptist by the master Caravaggio, a religious painting which I include in this context because it is a true masterpiece and so stunning that I must share it with you here. The rendering of the form is so exceptional that you can feel each muscle and bone, the skin so magnificently delivered that you can sense its youthful spring, the folds of the cloth so perfectly painted you can stick your fingers in them, then grip the horns of the sheep, stroke the fur on the seat, all with your eyes.

Now if I explained to you that Caravaggio's great contribution was not only his expert rendering of the human form, and a startling sense of composition, but that he fashioned a kind of chiaroscuro called tenebrism, a kind of dramatic and stark lighting that illuminated a figure as if the light of God were shining directly on it, would that make you respect this work more?

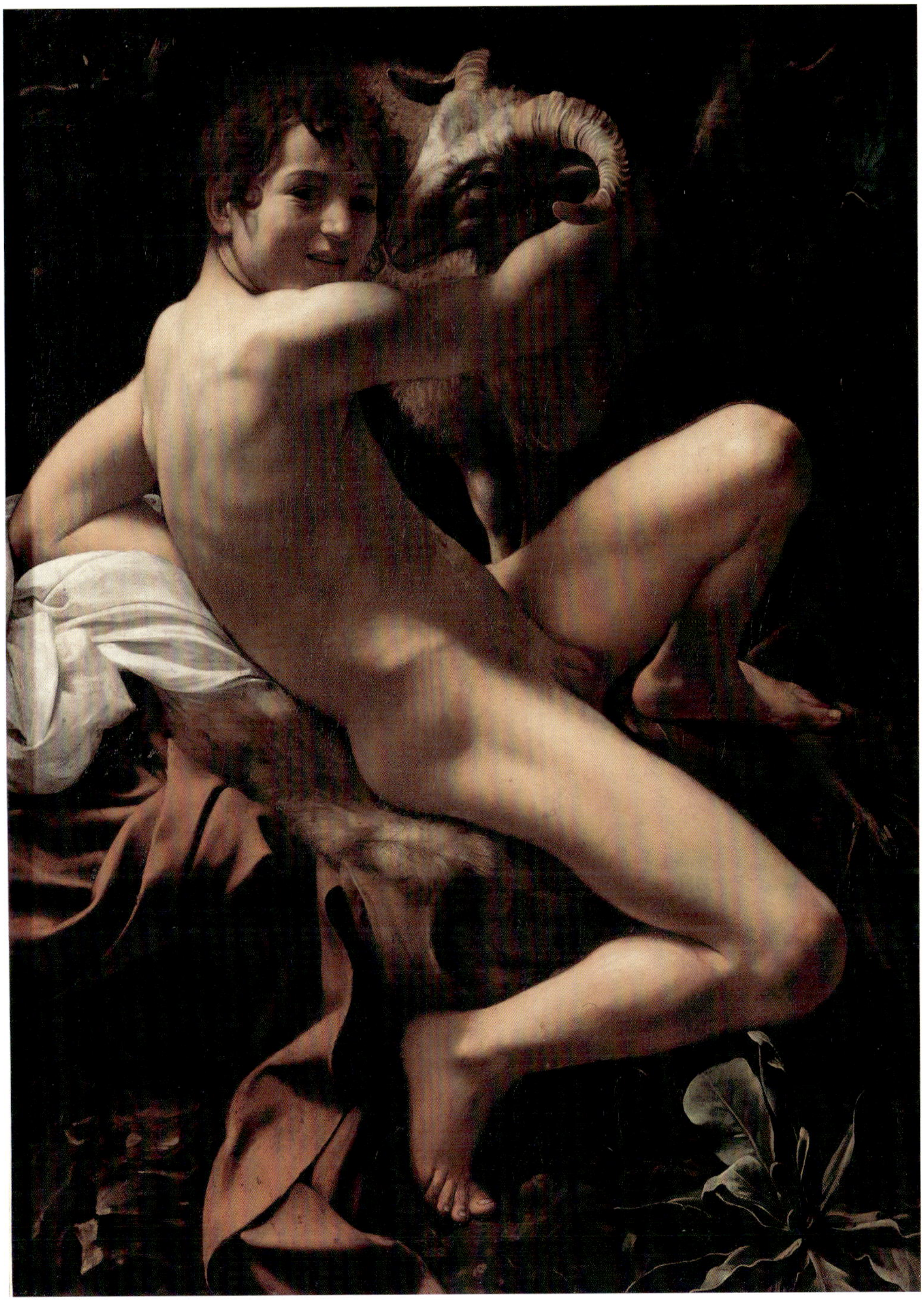

Fig. 28. Caravaggio, SAINT JOHN THE BAPTIST.

Yes, the form is idealized (I hear Tolstoy commenting). Yes, there is no daylight that is this transformative, nor artificial light available, certainly not in the early seventeenth century when this work was created (Tolstoy again wagging his finger). But, really, Tolstoy, look at it. Doesn't it just rock your world? I ask you. I, for one, stand in awe.

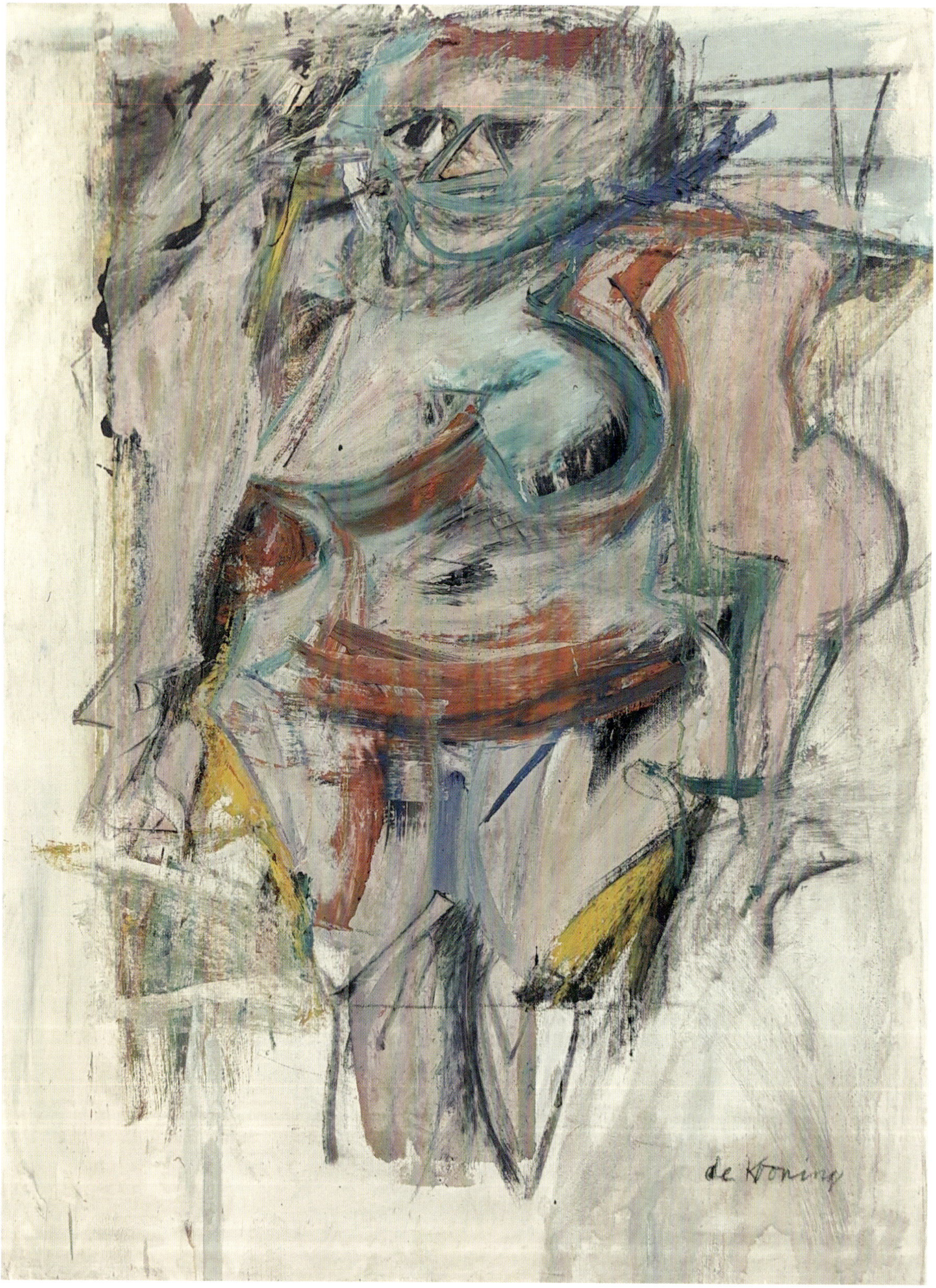

Fig. 29. Willem de Kooning, WOMAN STANDING: PINK.

Or would simply realizing the incredible empathy and feeling he possessed that enabled him to paint like this, just suffice?

Zooming now to the twentieth century, we encounter a sensualist of a different stripe, the fascinating Willem de Kooning (1907–1997), a Dutch American Abstract Expressionist whose most famous works are probably those that venture into figuration, his "Women," painted in the mid 1950s. At that time, Abstract Expressionism was in its heyday, and figurative work had fallen on the popularity totem pole. I encourage you to look at *Woman I* and show you here another similar work in this series.

It is within this context that de Kooning made this comment on beauty, giving us a clue to his mindset as iconoclast. In the Museum of Modern Art's catalog entry on *Woman I*, he is quoted saying, "Beauty becomes petulant to me. I like the grotesque. It's more joyous." That will frame our discussion about the Women series.

In fact, the Museum of Modern Art's collection committee found the painting "frightening" but vital nonetheless, which must have pleased the artist. They elected to acquire it but did not find it "beautiful," rather saying they "liked the quality of the color." Other fellow artists and viewers were not exactly on board, finding the piece sexist, anti-feminist, and even violent.

But to the maker (and I know this to be true because I have had similar feelings and thoughts as an artist about my own work) this was simply not true, could not be, because the artist sees his image not as a real woman, but literally a pile of paint. In these portrayals of women, he is subverting the pristine characterizations of women as sacrosanct objects of male fascination and beauty. He is getting into the sensuality of the paint itself, this evident in his statement, "Flesh is the reason oil paint was invented." A clue, perhaps, to why he chose this particular subject even though it was out of fashion.

De Kooning really went to town with the paint on *Woman I*—layering it on, thick and thin, on this giant canvas six feet by five feet, streaks and patches of color with thick ugly black outlines describing a distorted face with overlarge eyes and jagged mouth and teeth. No attempt is made to prettify her, quite the contrary, she is as unattractive as can be. You might conclude that he hated women, but that is not a necessary conclusion. Maybe he just loved the paint.

Did you guess that de Kooning made *Woman I* in an afternoon? It looks so carelessly made, does it not? But again, do not make assumptions. In fact, he worked on it for almost two years, making studies, painting again and again after scraping down whole sections and beginning anew. The seeming carelessness is a ruse. In fact, it often takes much work to make something that looks as fresh and spontaneous as *Woman I*.

De Kooning is quoted as saying, “I refrain from finishing,” in 1958. In 1960, he added, “I was never interested . . . [in] how to make a good painting. . . . I didn’t want to pin it down at all.”

This statement is belied by the fact that he worked on *Woman I* for so long. What was he trying to accomplish in all the time he spent on this piece if not beauty or perfection?

I can testify here as a painter, that getting the paint to feel a certain way is absolutely crucial for most painters and can drive them to scrape down or wash out areas of a painting, or indeed the whole painting, because the feeling of the paint is just not good enough, not right, they will tell you. Painting is a sensualist’s obsession, and not for those in a hurry. Time is our partner in just getting it to “feel” just right.

IN CONCLUSION

After our discussion of the expressive qualities of vitality, power, inventiveness, and sensuality, we close this chapter to address our subject “beauty” and the questions we posed about it.

Is beauty universal or totally subjective?

Since we may all appreciate and love the astounding variance and splendor of the earth we inhabit together, there are many images that all or most humans might agree to call “beautiful.” We can agree, but this does not make it so; it is simply a shared belief. The perception and resulting judgment that something is indeed “beautiful” is subjective, and as such, not necessarily true in any universal sense.

Do we know what we mean when we use the word? What we mean is that what we see pleases us, and therefore, we recognize it as something worthy of our pleasure.

In other words, is beauty attached to reality independent of human feeling?

No. We cannot say that it is, only that we think it is.

Is beauty even necessary in a work of art?

We will never stop appreciating what we find pleasing to our eyes, senses, and minds. But it is not necessary for something to be "beautiful" to be a work of art. What makes something a work of art is that IT is a communication from an artist that we can see, feel, and recognize as possessing any number of myriad qualities—we have just looked at four—that are important in some way or another.

It can evoke ANY feeling, express ANY emotion, communicate ANY thought, and still be art.

It must give us more than information, more than describe. It must make us feel something.

That leaves lots of room for creativity, which is just what we want, isn't it?

A suggestion: I have selected four qualities to elucidate expressiveness and I have provided examples of artworks that exhibit these qualities to an extreme degree. I could have chosen others. I invite you to think of some additional criteria you find in works of art and to select your own candidates to highlight them. Here are a few to get you started on this assignment: peculiarity, joyousness, elegance, complexity, spiciness, warmth . . . I could go on, but you can take it from here . . .

And the last: What does beauty have to do with truth?

Ah, this is a biggie. In fact, it merits its very own chapter, which we turn to next.

Chapter 4
Authenticity

WHAT DOES ART HAVE TO DO WITH TRUTH?

Here we tackle the question of whether art is about truth, or not, and whether this matters and why. Is it the artist's job to tell the truth? If so, does this mean the truth as he or she sees it, or prefers to see it? Or some agreed-upon or recognized standard? How in the world do we authenticate what the truth is? How can we know truth and recognize it? Is there one truth that exists for everyone and overrides subjective truths?

I am thinking of other art forms—writing, music, drama, film—and their analogies in the world of visual art. In writing, we have the major forms of prose and poetry and the genres of fiction and nonfiction. In film, likewise, the documentary and the feature, corollaries of nonfiction and fiction in writing. When I think about music, of course we have many forms and formats, but since music is abstract, there are no two categories that divide "truth" and material that is "made up."

Let's take the art of writing. When we say a writing is a work of nonfiction, we assume there is an attempt to say something that is true or attempts to speak truthfully. Of course, the author will have a point of view that is his or hers alone, and this will surely be prejudicial in one way or another, but nonetheless, we guess the writing will have some basis in reality.

On the other hand, were we handed a work of fiction, we should have such expectation of truthfulness. It might arise from something that happened, but the writer is admitting that they are not remaining faithful to a set of facts. That at the very least it will be embellished, altered, or transformed into something "made up."

A similar pattern would be echoed in the world of film, where a documentary, we believe, is a retelling of facts or happenings, and a feature film tells a story that did not necessarily happen, or at least, not as an actual retelling might—that it is invented. As opposed to writing, which may have only one author, film is a collaborative process, so that does make a bit of difference. Even a documentary film may have elements that belong in the fictionalized sphere, with people and events illustrated by stand-ins or look-alikes to imitate the actual participants and places. But likewise, the work of fiction may have elements that are taken from reality.

How does this pertain to our topic, you ask? Well, I am setting out to explore whether there is such a thing as truth in visual art, and if so, how it might be defined and recognized. I am asking whether the distinctions of poetry and prose, fiction and nonfiction, documentary and feature, have any relevancy here.

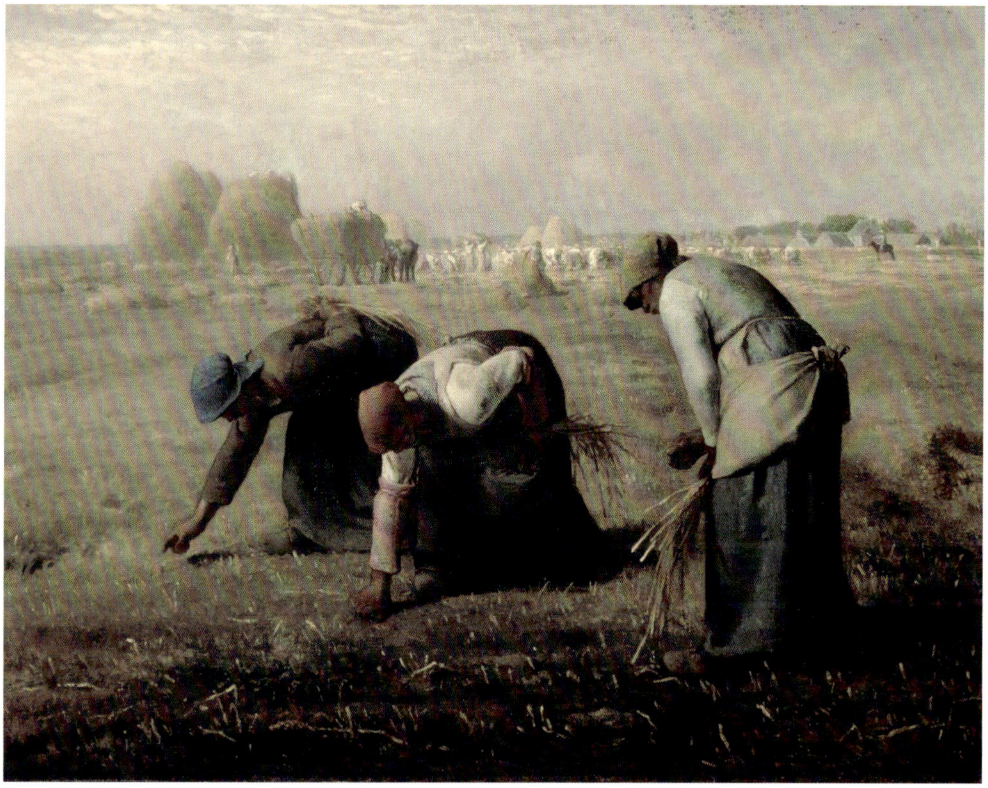

Fig. 30 Jean-François Millet, THE GLEANERS.

You might counterpose that in visual art we now have works that we might call "realistic" and others "abstract," and argue that the former would equate with nonfiction and the latter with fiction.

But this is quite a bit more complex.

"Realism" in art is actually the name of a movement, both aesthetic and political, that originated in France in the mid-nineteenth century in reaction to romantic painting. Artists in the "romantic" style focused on the grandiose representations of exceptional individuals and events, and the "realists" turned to ordinary individuals and scenes of quotidian life. *The Gleaners* is an example of a realist work by the artist Jean-François Millet.

Millet's devotion to the ordinary, you may be interested to learn, was much admired by none other than the painter Vincent van Gogh. If you are familiar with Van Gogh's work, you may be surprised, as Van Gogh's work takes realism to a different place entirely. Later in this chapter we will discuss how Van Gogh's approach to "realism" became emblematic for a philosopher who used it as an example of how art can lead us to a higher truth.

Van Gogh was inspired by Millet's faithfulness to his subject, but his larger personality and emotional nature led Van Gogh to speak perhaps more flamboyantly about his subjects. Millet was more sober but a wonderful painter, as you can clearly see in *The Gleaners*. His drawing is so excellent you can almost feel the pain in the backs of these agricultural workers, and his attention to the soft atmospheric light is palpable.

The history of art is the story of movements that build on but also reject prior movements. Just as Realism was a reaction to Romanticism, Impressionism, Postimpressionism, and ultimately Abstraction were reactions to Realism. Back and forth, back and forth, the trends go.

Artists went on to react to abstraction, too, and to create an even more concentrated and deliberate realism. You will find artworks that fall into the category of photorealism—painted works that are so detailed you would swear they are photographs—and others that we might call hyperrealistic—fantastical images rendered in such a detailed manner that we are astounded. In fact, you might say that these super realistic works are so unnaturally perfected that, in fact, they appear artificial, not realistic at all.

So is realistic work more truthful than abstract work? Though it may appear that a realistic work accurately represents an object or scene, it is not necessarily so, and an abstract work may possess a different, yet believable reality, even though it is not descriptive. The answer is there is no simple answer.

Let's look to the philosophers to have a look at the way they see it. How do they address questions like: Does it matter that a work of art contains elements of truth, or is true? What does it mean to be true? What is the place of truth in art? I am guided here by the book *Aesthetics: The Classic Readings* (edited by David E. Cooper, published by Wiley Blackwell, 2019).

The two poles are represented by the philosopher Plato (427?–347 BCE) on one side and Oscar Wilde (1854–1900) on the other. Plato was a very conservative thinker and he valued truth and moral values above all. He posited his theory of universal truths—ideas that he considered immutable and perfect—which he placed above all else. The rest fell into a subcategory deemed lesser in value. As for art, he considered it a deception, a weak representation or imitation, not the real thing.

Plato was a materialist and kind of a truth junkie. To him, material objects were a step down, representing only some of the characteristics of the form to which they belonged—a chair, not "chairness," the overriding form. As to the artist who rendered the chair in a work of art, he was an illusionist, a fraud, a trickster. Art was just too fanciful, too distant from reality, to make Plato a fan.

Plato's student Aristotle, less a left-brain rationalist and more even tempered, was more forgiving and more appreciative of art. He lived from 384 to 322 BC and repudiated Plato's denigration of the artist as a prevaricating maker of illusions. Aristotle did not cotton to Plato's concept of art as deceptive; he believed that artistic work made an important contribution to society. In his writings (*Poetics*), he extols the pleasure art may bring, and finds value in the "truth" of emotions that are revealed in art.

Aristotle spoke of mimesis, his word for imitation, which he believed was a propelling force for artists and which, when executed well, was able to convey "truths" about our lives, situations, and the like. This he found worthy. Through imitation, art could impart information that would be educational for the audience and bring knowledge as well as pleasure.

Now Oscar Wilde, the writer, and his fellow thinker Walter Pater (1839–1894), were on the other end of the spectrum when it came to the subject of art and truth. They considered these questions: Was truthfulness essential to art? Could good art trump truth?

Their conclusion: Art was just swell and should be applauded for its aesthetic value ONLY. It mattered not a whit whether what was communicated was the truth, the whole truth, and nothing but the truth. No sir. The only thing that was pertinent was whether it did a good job, communicated well, was entertaining and smart and maybe beautiful—apply here any number of aesthetic judgments you can come up with.

This idea came to be called "Art for art's sake," and it is still a phrase quoted and utilized by many in the arts. The theory put truth to bed when it came to art criticism. It is as if these critics were saying, "Truth, —when it comes to art, just take a walk."

Other artists and theorists landed somewhere in the middle of these two extreme points of view. Consider Pablo Picasso, who famously said, "Art is a lie that makes us realize truth."

What in the world did he mean by this? There is a lot to unpack in this phrase indeed.

Let's take the first half "Art is a lie . . . " I think that Picasso was expressing what he believed to be the totally subjective nature of art, both from the point of view of the artist and also of the viewer. You might argue that the artist provides "*their* truth" as they exhibit in the work what interests them, and what they want to say about it. But he recognizes this is just true for him, only in that moment. He might change his mind tomorrow and do something utterly contrary.

In other words, the artist may intend to tell the truth at the time, but it is certainly not any kind of universal truth, and in fact, it is possible that not another person on the planet would agree with them. In fact, only Pablo Picasso on Thursday afternoon of June 26, 1946, would ever create such a work. Ever again.

So art cannot be Truth with a capital T. In this sense, it is a lie.

But let us now finish Picasso's sentence, " . . . that makes us realize truth." Though the work of art is not itself truth, it may speak to me, the viewer. I may see in it something that has meaning for me, for one reason or another. Seeing this image may give me an insight into something that pertains to me alone or perhaps to many people—this is entirely possible. You may be moved by it as well: it may give you pleasure, it might sadden you, it might remind you of something forgotten. It may arouse in you any number of feelings and thoughts, which you believe to be a personal truth and which you accept as such.

It was the artist's truth, and it can be the viewer's truth. But this truth may not be one and the same. Ergo: "Art is a lie that makes us realize truth."

Aristotle did note that artists might tend to idealization, representing their subjects, "though lifelike, more beautiful than they are." This tendency to exaggeration or aggrandizement might jibe with Picasso's statement that art is a lie. Indeed, the artist's desire to improve upon nature is fairly prevalent in art through the centuries, and we will note this as we look at examples.

Another thinker, the philosopher Martin Heidegger (1889–1976), also opined on this idea. In his book *Being and Time* (1927), he discusses it, using, interestingly enough, a painting by the artist Van Gogh as illustration.

This painting is one that appeared in *The Joy of Art* as well, and I show it again here so you can see it in this context. Heidegger devotes many pages to the description of the "peasant shoes" depicted in this painting, and he sees in them much more than a pair of shoes. He sees the entirety of the peasant's experience and visualizes "her slow trudge through the far-spreading and ever uniform furrows of the field swept by a raw wind." He also imagines the loneliness of her path, the silent call of the earth, her anxiety about lack of bread, and the struggle of her daily life unto death.

All this in the painting of the shoes. He remarks that the painting has "spoken" or at least speaks to him, as we described in relation to Picasso's comment.

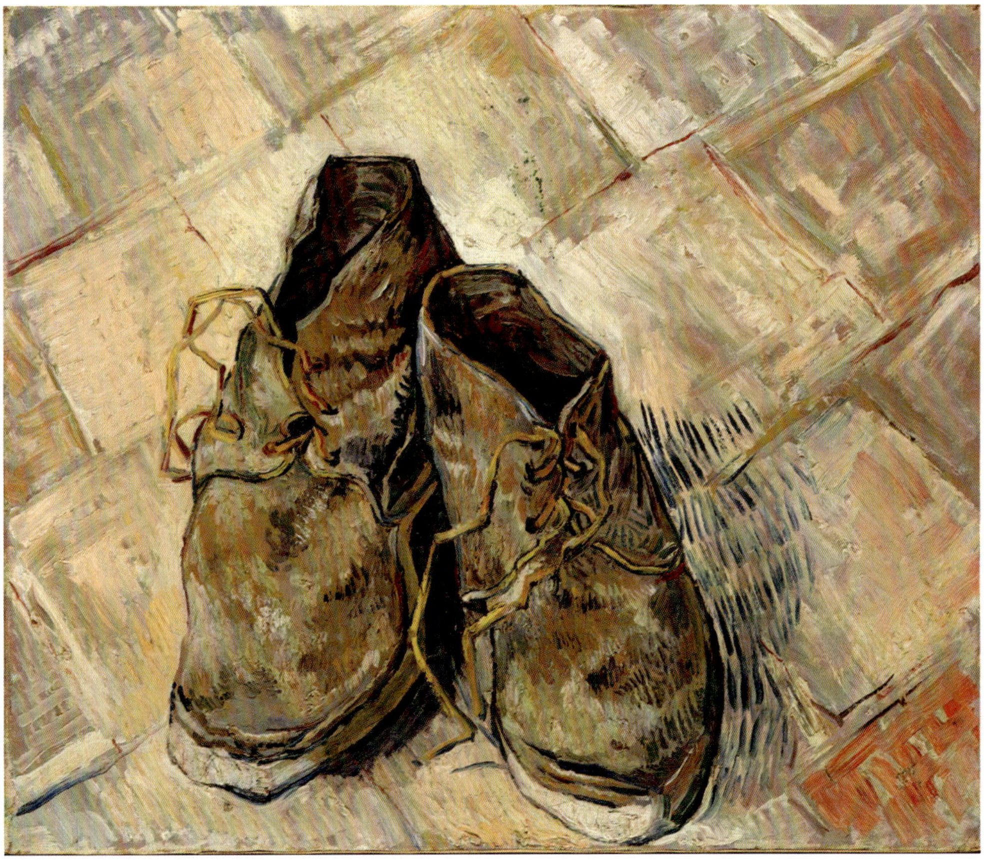

Fig. 31. Vincent van Gogh, SHOES.

Heidegger goes on to assert that what the artist has accomplished here is not the faithful reproduction of the object, but rather its general essence. Its value is that by virtue of the authenticity of its representation, it points to a higher truth and becomes revelatory—it reveals that greater truth. For Heidegger, this is what makes it art.

How is that accomplished? In this case, Van Gogh's peasant shoes, the artist has paid very close attention to the very specific way the shoes have been deformed by the feet of the wearer and the necessity of his daily travail, so much so that when you see them, you can unconsciously connect with the peasant. His life is embodied in the shape those shoes have taken, their scuffed and worn surface, their tangled shoelaces. They are placed in the painting in such a way so that they are set off for our close perusal against the texture of the floor where they have been laid to sit, after presumably that hard day's work.

Van Gogh's artistry has enabled this. His dedication to expressive painting and the care he applies in delivering an honest "take" on the shoes communicates this message to us. To Heidegger, this *aletheia* (the Greek word for truth) means "correspondence." The art is the deliverer of the message, and this is the mission of the artist, to be truthful.

The distinction between beauty and authenticity, or truth, is clearly understood in this Van Gogh example. These peasant shoes are not particularly attractive or pleasing to the eye in any sense of the word "beautiful." We admire them for the sensitivity of their portrayal, which gives context and meaning. For this reason, we celebrate them as excellent, and this painting as expressive and worthy of approbation.

We recognize, however, that this "truth" is forever changing. As we look at art through the ages, we can view it as a record of the beliefs of an ever-evolving culture—a statement of what is viewed as important and valuable at that time. Art also performs the function not only of reflecting culture but often of shaping it, as artists are often cultural vanguards and introduce ideas and fashion which become adopted as a new standard.

The "truth" of one era may be outdated or rejected in the next, as a new way of thinking takes hold. What seems revolutionary and new may before long become forgotten or no longer relevant, as a new truth sweeps into town. But we recognize that the truth of that work still makes it outstanding "for its time."

We have discussed how the criteria of "beauty" is not a universal value, but a subjective determination. So, what about truth? Is there a universal truth that finds its way into art, or is it, too, a matter of opinion? Does the truth morph and change through the passage of time or is it resolute?

There has been a lot written on this topic by philosophers and a lot of it is arcane, difficult to understand, and even harder to apply. So I am going to answer this question not as a philosopher, but as an artist.

Every artist when they begin a work has an intention—something they are setting out to accomplish. This can be very detailed and specific, or just a brief glimmer of a direction, a road they think they would like to follow. There must be something, so he or she can initiate a work—that enables her to choose a medium, the surface, and then take an action. To choose a color, choose a thickness of paint, and then apply it; choose a lump of clay and shape it; find a chunk of wood and take the first bite out of it. An action. And then another. And another. Maybe the work begins to reveal itself after the artist has smeared around the paint a bit. Or it suddenly occurs when a chunk of wood falls to the floor.

There will always be an intention, sooner or later. Now some artists are motivated primarily by an intention to make something that is appealing, decorative, or "beautiful" in some way. And others don't give a hoot about making something attractive. They have something to say with their work and they want to say it as effectively as they can. I refer to this latter artist as a "truth seeker."

I can identify a truth seeker by certain very clear markers. The truth seeker is one who will be happy with his work if gets that intention realized, regardless of "how it looks." The pretty surface will only bring a happy conclusion if it simultaneously gets the point across, and in all probability, will not. That's because the truth, the real truth, is usually not pretty. It is not symmetrical. It is not unblemished. It is certainly not perfect. It is more likely deformed and worn like those shoes of Mr. Van Gogh.

I can vouch for this because I have often experienced this and seen it in the work of students and fellow artists. The attempt to perfect a work is often the kiss of death. Instead of making it better, this action to "beautify" winds up destroying what is there and replacing it with something much less effective. This is because though the initial intention was to express something, this action runs counter to it. It arises from a different mindset—to fix, not to create.

Think of it this way: Though something in nature can be deemed to be "beautiful" in appearance, the attempt to "beautify" in art may lead to falseness. It is the intention, not the object, that creates the lie. The imperfect is a reflection of nature, reality, and most importantly, ourselves, because all humans are imperfect and in the imperfection of their work, we find them, and we can relate unconsciously and empathize.

When I was an art student, my painting teacher, Norman Raeben, pierced my ego when he named me the "plastic surgeon" of the class, accusing me of attempting not to render my still life as diligently as possible, but instead to "make it beautiful." I can still feel the sting of that appellation.

I encourage you to look at art with this idea in mind. Note that your eyes and mind accept the little flaws—the smearing of a color, the drips, the imperfect shapes, the unfinished portions of a work. Somehow, these make the work more real, more personal, more human, and yes, more beloved.

In every period, every movement, you will find certain artists whose intention is to create beautiful surfaces and tapestries of radiant paint and elegant drawing, and others who plumb the depths of reality and show us something not so pretty that perhaps makes us appreciate it for another reason, that it rings true and we recognize that. This idea arises out of my own experience as a working artist, and I can tell you that the same artist can have both intentions at different times, though in all probability will lean toward one or the other in their body of work.

In *The Joy of Art*, I discussed this dichotomy in other terms and described it as the contrast of the classical and romantic points of view. These two ways of identifying artists has some commonality, though one does not fit neatly alongside the other.

Characteristics of the classicists include a reverence for tradition, order, symmetry, clean lines, while romantics embrace individuality, quirkiness, imagination, and self-expression. The desire for order and symmetry is more consonant with the inclination to create idealized, beautiful forms, while a quest for originality may lead the more romantic to, ironically, resemble truth tellers, as they value authenticity over effect.

Both tendencies may lead the artist away from the literal definition of truth: accuracy and a lack of embellishment. Regardless of style or approach, the desire to express is, by its very nature, a pathway from fact to the glories of fiction, as the artist strives to make the visual personal and charged with emotion.

Before we embark upon a speed date with some of the prominent artists in each of a series of art movements, I think it is important to say something about categorization and how it relates to this discussion we are having about so-called truth in art.

The big chapter headings just give a slight clue to the intention of the artist. Two artists may employ the intention of producing a representational, let's say, a figurative work, and yet have an entirely different aesthetic and direction. Let's have a look at two assuredly realistic figurative works of art and peer into the artists intention and emphasis.

These are both late nineteenth-century works. The Seurat is a modest drawing of his mother executed circa 1882, rather small, in Conté crayon on paper. The second is a work by the French painter Jean-Léon Gérôme completed in 1868, a medium-sized oil on canvas. They are both portraits.

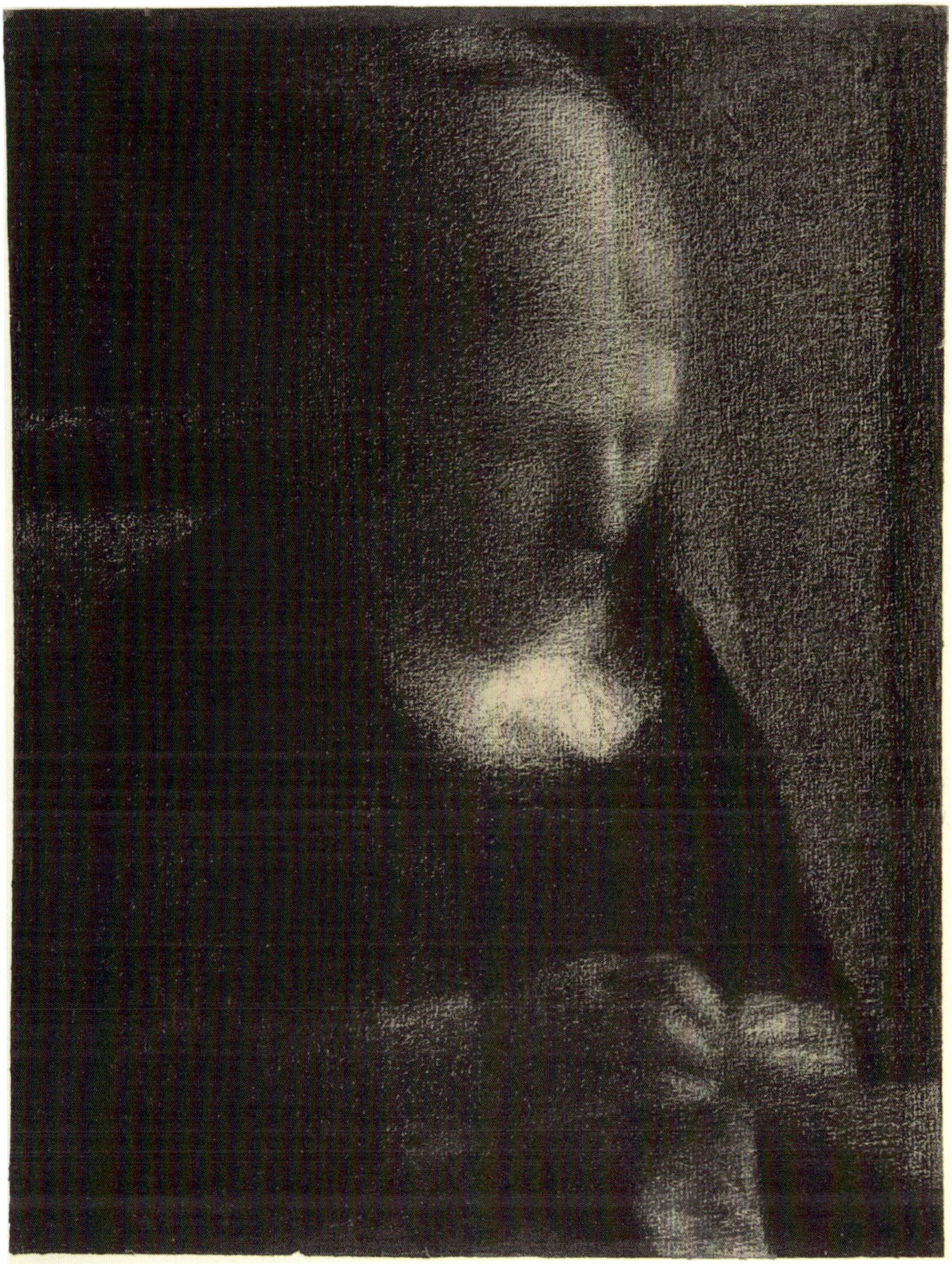

Fig. 32. Georges Seurat, THE ARTIST'S MOTHER.

The Seurat is a tender rendering in monotone—Seurat favored the Conté crayon as a preferred drawing implement. The woman is shown sewing and the tonal notes of black and white appear almost as if they have been sewn together—the work is a subtle tapestry where the figure of the woman emerges and comes into resolution.

The Metropolitan Museum description of Seurat's drawings, of which this is an example, quotes Seurat's fellow artist Paul Signac, who called them "the most beautiful painter's drawings that ever existed."

They are lovely, subtle, and subdued; there is nothing overdone or glorified. The work is, as we say, "of a piece."

What was the artist's intention here? I think it was to make this beloved figure just be born on the paper in utter tranquility and peace, as if she were always there.

Now the Gérôme painting is something else entirely. It is, what we call a tour de force, a work that shouts its command of the art form. The Seurat speaks almost in a whisper, but the Gerome makes itself heard, does it not? Even the title speaks emphatically.

This painting was made following Gérôme's journey to the Near East and is of a model he dressed in clothing he acquired on his trip. He is depicting a soldier but has dressed him not for battle, but rather for pomp and circumstance in a silk tunic. What is the purpose of this dress-up?

To show off, of course. Gérôme is a virtuoso painter, capable of creating magnificent, implied textures—metal and silk and the creamy skin of the young model in his elaborate headdress. It is an absolutely gorgeous, awe-inspiring painting.

Is there a message here? Not really. Do we learn anything by looking at it? No. Does it represent something important or even interesting? Again no. It is a feast for the eyes and a case study for the artist's amazing talent for verisimilitude. It is just stunning, and it amazes us with what this human was able to achieve. Just that.

What would you answer if I asked you which of these two works was more truthful? You might answer quickly and choose the Seurat because it is more modest, and the Gérôme is aggrandized and a show piece. But each artist did what was important to them—they revealed what motivated them and inspired them about art. Seurat was called a pointillist because he created his works out of dots or marks that coalesced to reveal an image. His intention was for his images to be revealed, not made. Gérôme was more direct—he was so capable he just made the brush imitate the surfaces he saw and felt before him.

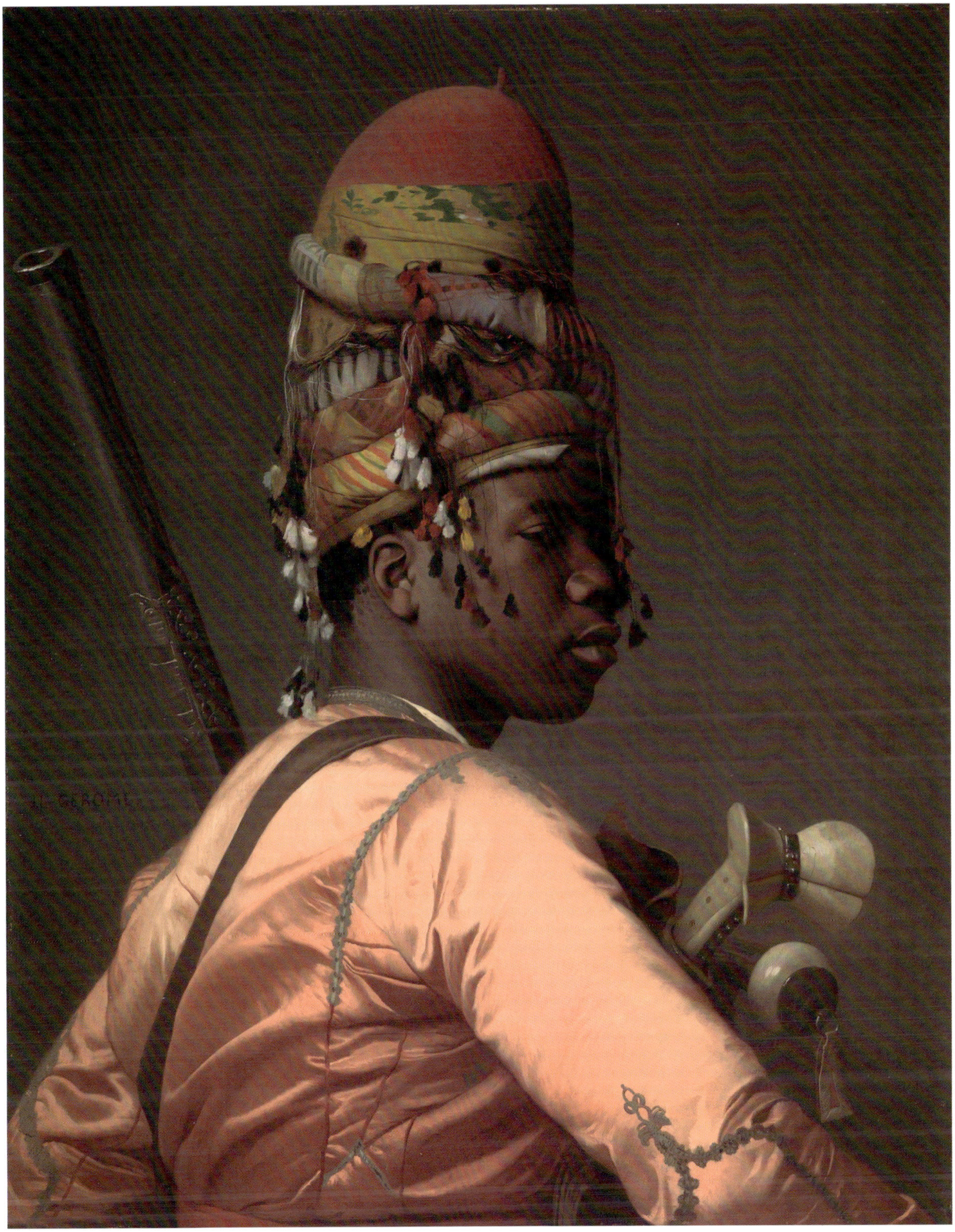

Fig. 33. Jean-Léon Gérôme, BASHI-BAZOUK.

Which method and intention interests and enchants you more? Let's not jump to conclusions without mulling this over. I say, truthfully, they are both wonderful—I just prefer the Seurat a teeny bit more. It just hews closer to my aesthetic preferences, not the right answer by any means. You?

Before we depart from these ideas regarding truth and authenticity in art, I want to introduce another issue, that of whether a work can be deemed genuine, and have, as we might call it, "good intentions."

Here is a magnificent work of sculpture, a bust, made by the French sculptor Jean-Baptiste Carpeaux in 1868. The artist studied in Rome and was enamored with the sculptures of the great Italians—Michelangelo, Donatello, and Verrocchio. During the Baroque period when movement was a calling card, he worked from actual models and ventured beyond classicism.

The work we are looking at is called *Why Born Enslaved* and depicts a Black woman, apparently a slave, as she is featured tied with rope. Slavery was abolished in the French colonies in 1848, twenty years before this bust was carved. I was riveted to this image at first glance as it is incredibly vivid and visceral, revealing a whole host of emotions in its marble incarnation—defiance, resistance, pain. It has the anatomical accuracy Carpeaux was known for, but more than that—not only a physical reality, but a psychic one as well.

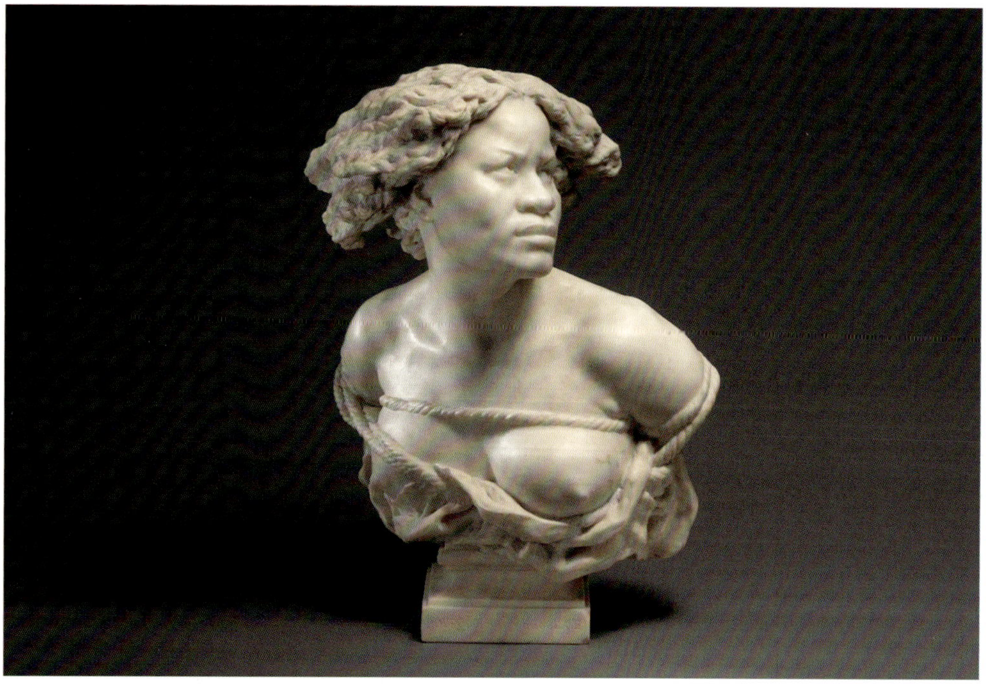

Fig. 34. Jean-Baptiste Carpeaux, WHY BORN ENSLAVED.

But here is the question. This bust was debuted in Paris in 1868 under another title, that of "Negresse." Why that title? The artist is clearly depicting this Black woman as a slave. But why? Was he doing it to make an antislavery message or to use her condition—show her bound and struggling, with her breast exposed—only to create a passionate rendering of a subject rarely depicted at the time? Could he even have conceived of carving an image of a free Black woman?

Critics have applauded the beauty of this sculpture while simultaneously decrying it as a manipulation—portraying a Black individual as connected to slavery, as if the conditions of Blackness and subjugation were inseparable. This does not alter the tremendous skill exhibited in the work, but it gives us pause, perhaps diminishing our approval, if not our appreciation.

So we must ask whether a bad intention can possibly degrade a work of art. We know that a good one can elevate our admiration, but is the reverse also true? Of course, we cannot vouch for the artist's point of view and know whether he saw pathos in the vision of a slave and just wanted to communicate it. It begs the question of whether seeing a Black person portrayed such runs counter to a message of opposing the mistreatment of a whole group of innocent people.

The artist did not give this woman a name. She remains nameless, called only a slave. Is she represented to serve an idea or recognized as a person? Where do you come down on the issue? How do you see this work of art?

Reading a work of art for sure takes more than a quick view. This is a good example of how the context—when, where, why, and how a work was created—is relevant in understanding and appreciating it. In reading written material, we may have more clarity about what the author is saying and why. In visual art, this may not be immediately apparent. Can you think of a similar circumstance in writing when something you knew about the author influenced your evaluation of their work?

Again, though we would prefer easy answers and chapter headings and definitive movements and patterns, art is just more complicated. We can categorize, but we have so many exceptions, we must qualify everything we promulgate as fitting into this or that generalization.

That being said, there are details to look at, and commonalities, and so now I shall put aside this aside (though not minimizing it in the least) and review with you some of the classified art movements and their characteristics. The scope of art is long and wide, and though what I offer here is a mere glimpse, it is useful to have some sense of the progression of attitudes and practices throughout the history of western art.

A CASUAL STROLL THROUGH THE HISTORY OF ART

For the purpose of this walkthrough, we start with the Renaissance (1400–1600) and will end with Realism (1848–1900). In the next chapter on Modernity, we shall continue our stroll starting with art movements of the twentieth and twenty-first centuries.

Of course, art, as we know it, was a part of human life from millennia before, from prehistoric (40,000–4,000 BC) through ancient (4,000 BC–AD 400) and medieval (500–1,400) times.

Each period featured artworks that were in keeping with the culture and resources of the time with prehistoric art focused on rock carvings and paintings depicting animals and other natural features; ancient art, featuring the design and decoration of utilitarian objects; and medieval art, concentrating on religious themes and grotesques that suited this dark and fearful time.

The Renaissance (1400–1600)

A time of enlightenment literally and figuratively. Emerging from the darkness of ignorance and religious persecution, artists arose whose life-affirming imagery changed the face of art. I love this self-portrait by the painter known by his first name only—Raphael (1483–1520)—painted circa 1506 when he was only twenty-three years old. Take away the hat and frills on the shirt and you can imagine him in a twenty-first-century advertisement. The quizzical expression. So sincere and straightforward in presentation, so simple and unadorned. It is wonderful to look at, isn't it? In an imaginary range of works from the most truthful and unadorned to the most embellished and grandiose, I would place it in the more naturalist (unadorned) camp. As we have mentioned, this is often the case with a self-portrait where ego takes a back seat to humility.

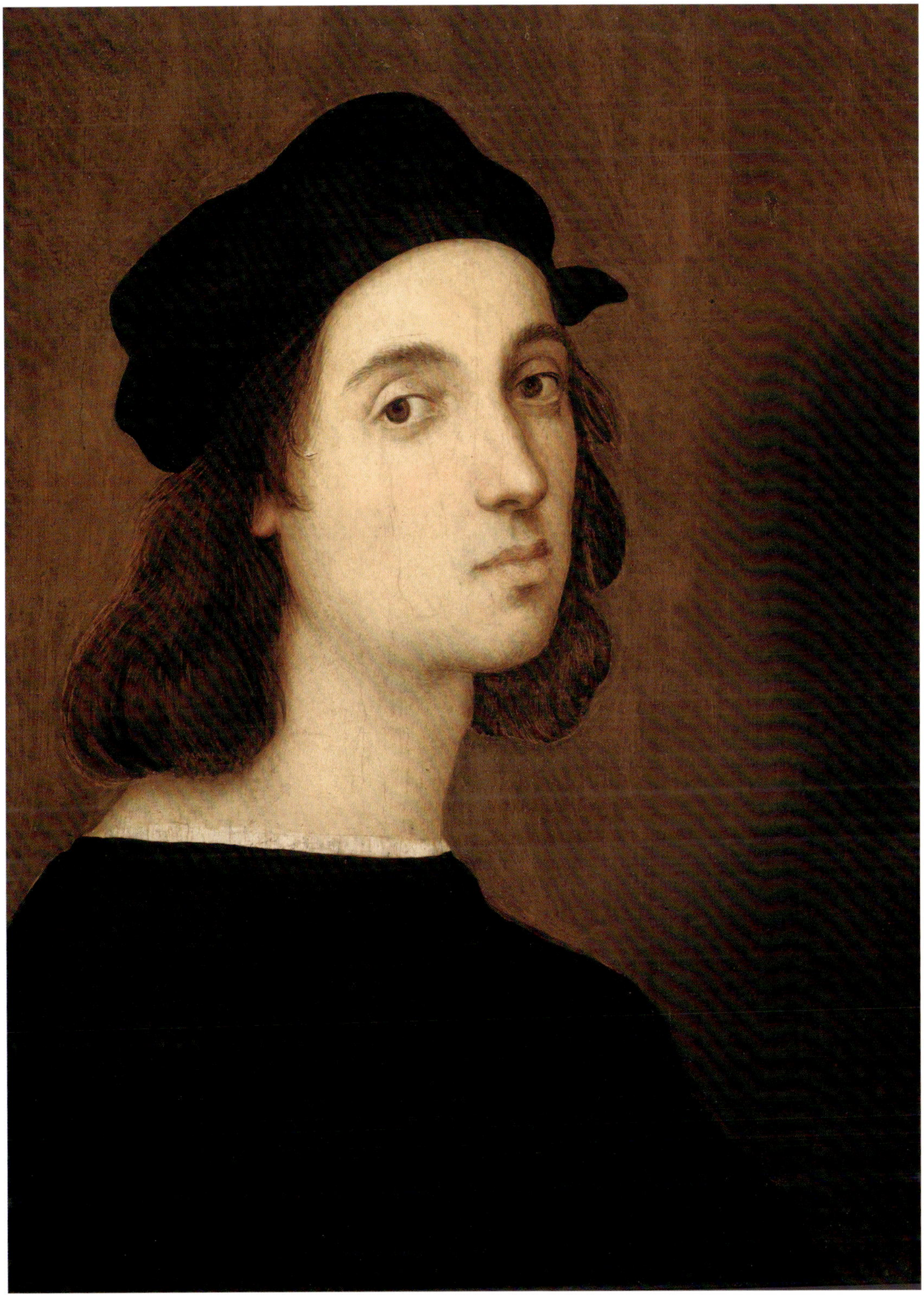

Fig. 35. Raphael, SELF PORTRAIT.

Mannerism (1527–1580)

Following the Renaissance, we find the art movement of Mannerism, which persisted for a short time, with exemplars Giorgio Vasari and Bronzino. Here we have a look at a work by a student of Bronzino called Alessandro Allori, who typifies one of the notable qualities of this period, an over-polishing of the surface that gives a kind of lifelessness to the image. We've referred to this tendency toward aggrandizement before, and here is a good example of it in another self-portrait.

It just seems a bit overcooked and stiff as compared to the more relaxed Raphael. Well done, certainly, but—curiously—not as pleasant to look at, just unnatural. These are small differences that, in the end, make one artist revered, like Raphael, or largely forgotten, like Allori.

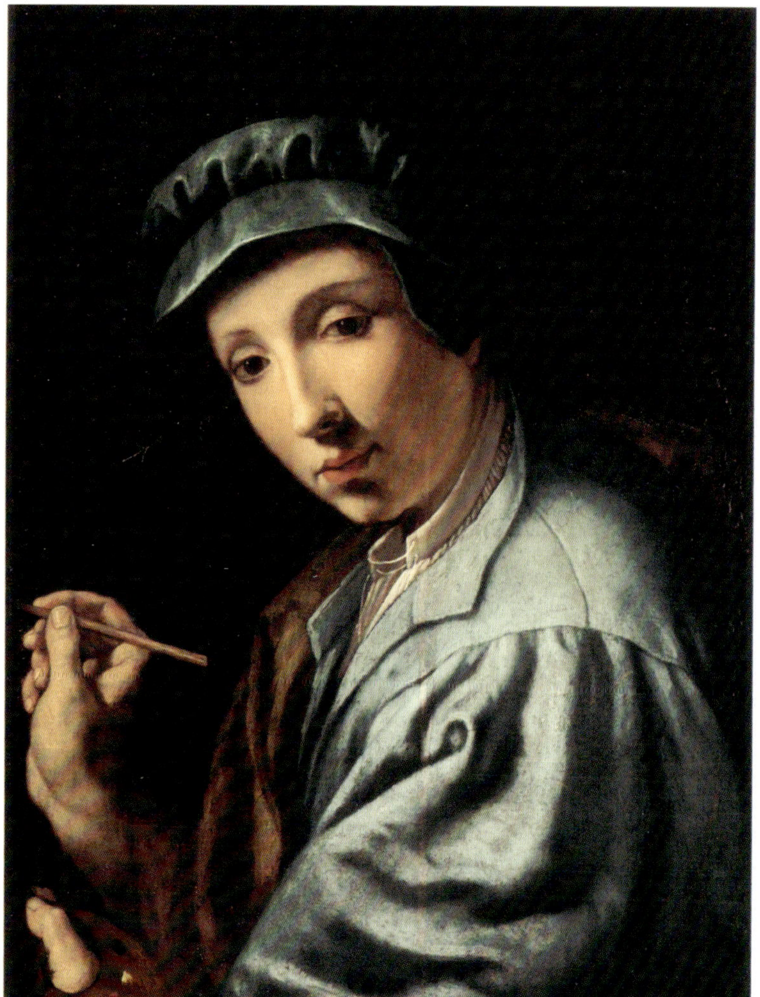

Fig. 36. Alessandro Allori, SELF PORTRAIT.

The Baroque (1600–1750)

This propensity for elaboration went into overdrive in the period following the Mannerist era, a very significant period in visual art we refer to as the Baroque. More than a century long, this era produced some of the most exceptional and revered artists who are beloved to this day, most principally two known by one name only, the artist Caravaggio (1571–1610) of Italy and the incomparable Rembrandt (1606–1669) of the Netherlands.

We looked at Caravaggio in our discussion last chapter of sensuality in art, which is attributable to several distinguishing features of his painting. He employed a stark chiaroscuro in his works that created a dramatic effect. The long gamut, punctuated shafts of light and dark shadows, make the figures stand out as if they are carved by the light and dark. He accentuates this dramatic lighting by depicting violent scenes with his figures struggling and taking intense poses where every muscle is attenuated, and dark shadows fall between the figures.

Study this figure of Cupid as an example. Utilizing a paucity of color but intense light and shadow, the figure is literally a sculpture of light. The drama of the work is heightened by the composition: everything is askew, falling; the figure is contorted, the face animated. I suggest you zoom into this work and examine every facet and crevice. The attention to detail is truly phenomenal.

Rembrandt was born several generations after Caravaggio and the influence of the master of chiaroscuro had great influence on the Dutch artist. Though greatly enhanced and dramatized, Caravaggio's incredible skill and accuracy at figurative painting was an inspiration to countless followers and certainly to Rembrandt, but Rembrandt possessed a quality that perhaps Caravaggio did not have, or at least not to the same extent.

Caravaggio's figures are magnificent, yes, but Rembrandt's figures have a grit and reality that takes them beyond "beautiful." In addition to vast skill, the artist possessed an empathy and connection to his subjects that made him pierce the veil of the superficial and take us into the very soul of the individual. He did this in many of his works, but none so emotionally resonant as in his self-portraits.

I love to look at and analyze self-portraits because this is a subject that reveals the true intention of the artist. Commissioned portraits must please their sitters, but self-portraits are a true reflection of what the artist finds important, how he expresses himself when no one is looking—or paying, for that matter.

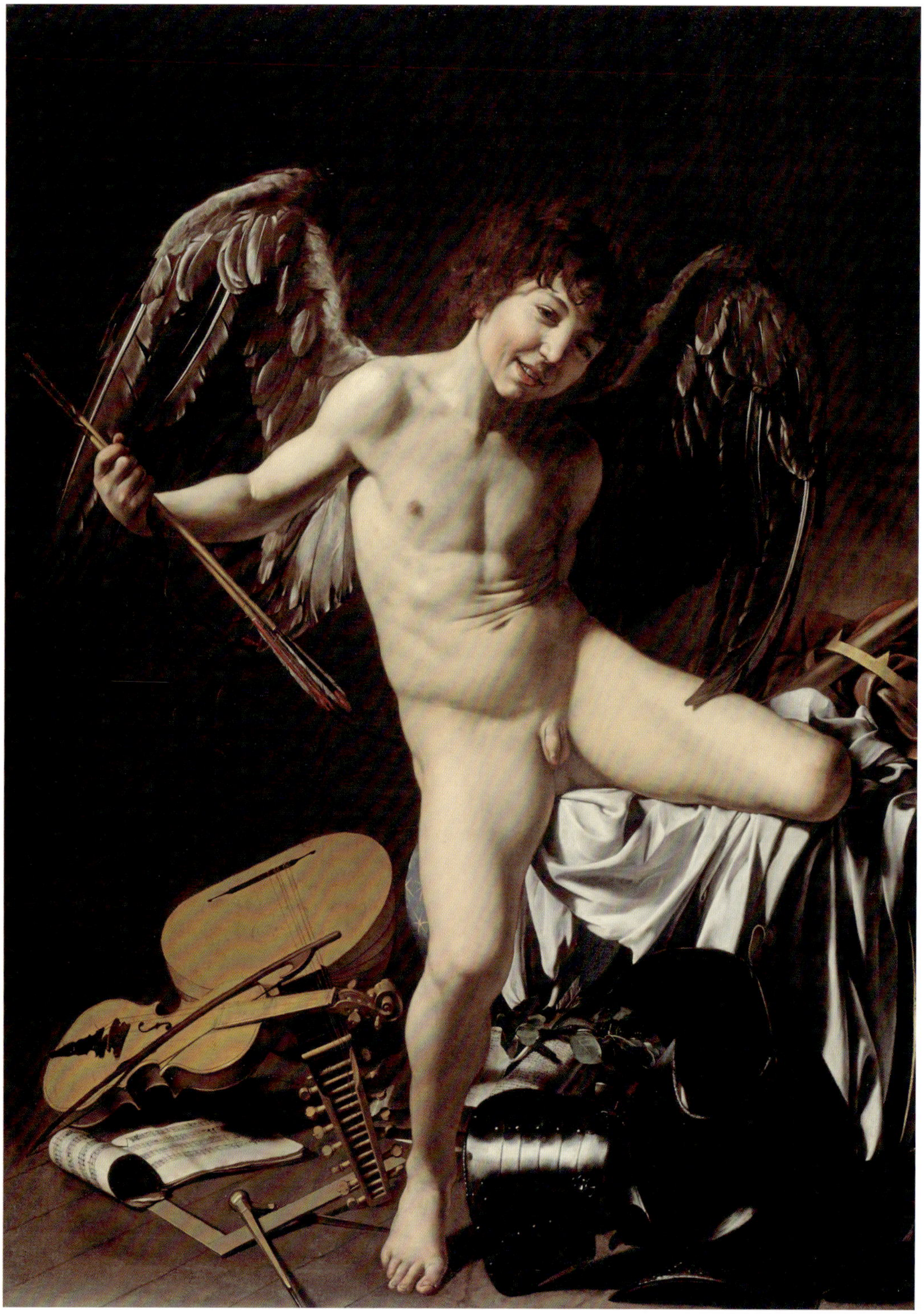

Fig. 37. Caravaggio, CUPID.

Let's look at this otherworldly self-portrait and discuss it. We clearly see here the influence of Caravaggio: the light arising out of deep shadow, here a bit more colorful than in the senior artist. The lightest lights are on the hand, the gold of the cloth and the nose and mouth, with part of the face in semi-shadow and the hat in deep shadow. Though the light and dark are dramatic, this work has a much softer general appearance than the Caravaggio Cupid we just looked at. The softness makes the figure more sympathetic and makes us want to gaze longer at it, especially at the face which seems permeated with emotion. He is showing us his character, his strength, but also his kindness. He is someone we admire and have the privilege of gazing upon. All this is evident in the masterful, yet very truthful and caring way Rembrandt presents himself to us.

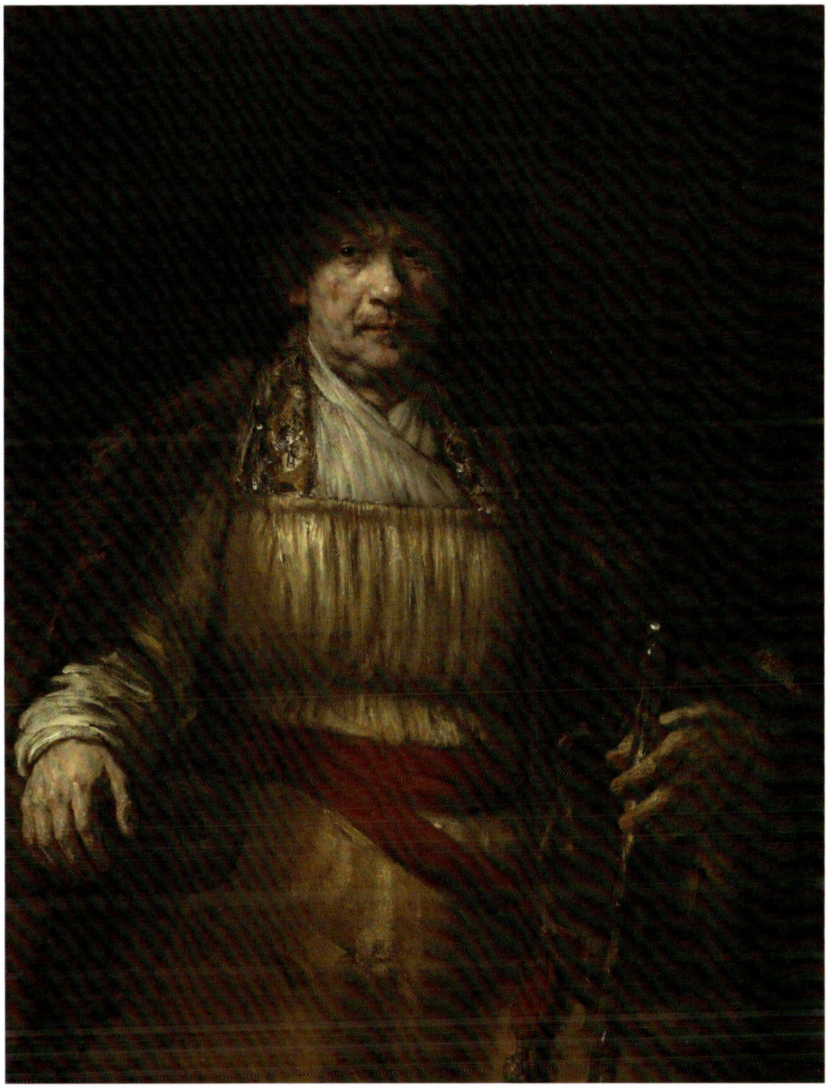

Fig. 38, Rembrandt, SELF PORTRAIT.

In Rembrandt we see the consummate artist steeped in truthfulness. Though he wishes to impress us with his understanding of light and shadow, his ability to create solidity of form, the textural complexities (you can feel the oiliness of the skin) and atmospheric tone, there is nothing prettified here. It has a reality that is potent and unmistakable.

Rococo (1699–1780)

As we've seen, art tends to seesaw from one preoccupation to the next. The eighteenth century was a time for a bit more frivolity in art as seen in the art movement called Rococo. See this painting by the French artist François Boucher—a portrait of Madame de Pompadour, who herself was a champion of this style.

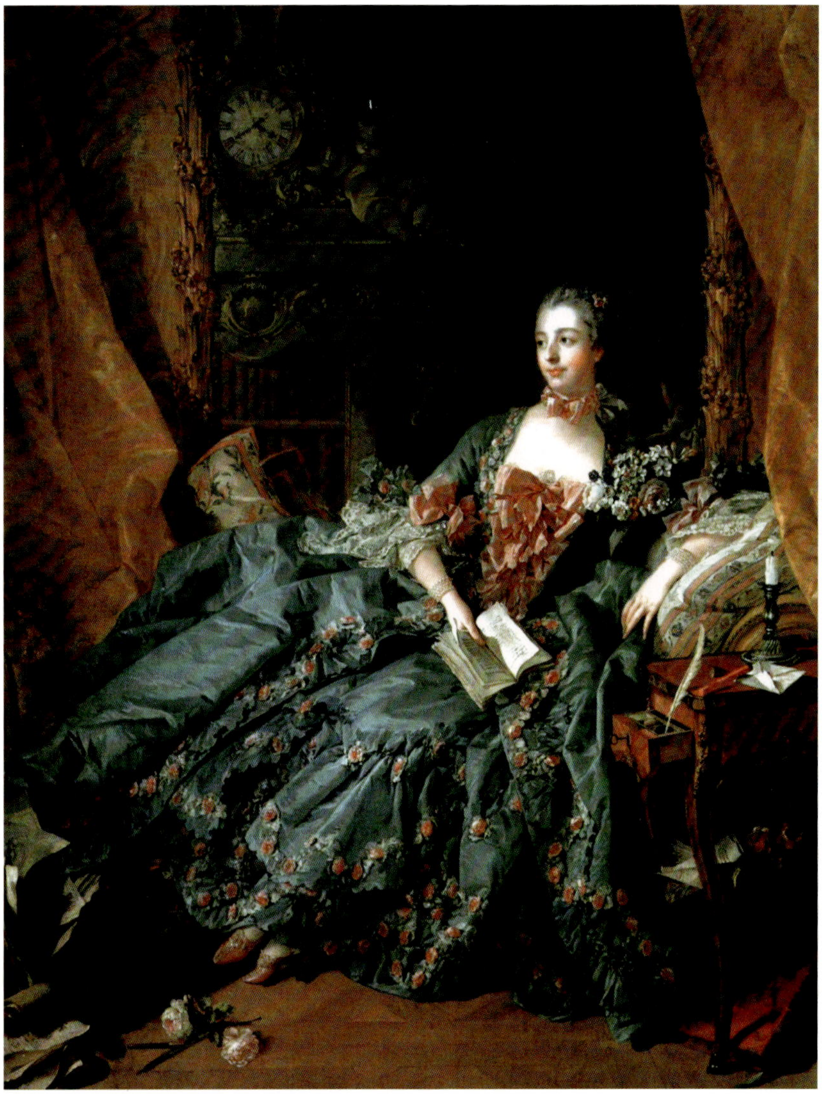

Fig. 39. François Boucher, PORTRAIT OF MADAME DE POMPADOUR.

As appropriate to this time of pomp and circumstance, artists like Boucher and Jean-Antoine Watteau introduced decoration into their works in the way of curves, curlicues, flowers, pastel colors, and all manner of ornamental touches. This was a time where fashion and ruffles and bows became the rage.

By the way, the name "rococo" was taken from a practice of decorating fountains and other architectural features in a kind of mosaic of shells and other glittery things. Likewise in the fine arts. Rigor and truth were replaced by theater and adornment.

It stands to reason that from the grandiosity of the Baroque and "froufrou" of Rococo, a return to order was called for. And that's exactly what happened. The art world said, "enough of that" and re-embarked on some new iterations: Neoclassicism and Romanticism. Moving from the late eighteenth century into the mid-nineteenth century, and coinciding with the Age of Reason, these two simultaneous movements had a different focus.

You might see these two diversions as two sides of the coin—Neoclassicism as a return to a familiar, tried-and-true art form championing virtue and morality, and Romanticism as a foray into a more daring form of personal expression—one looking back and the other forward.

Neoclassicism (1780–1850)

A revival of a beloved and trusted art form: the Classics. The art of ancient Greece was known for its simplicity, symmetry, and regularity. These values reappeared during this period, in a newer version—the curves and excesses of Rococo giving way to lovely, elegant straight lines and order, with idealization, a feature of classicism, still in force. More focus on beauty, just a less frivolous kind. Practitioners included Jean Auguste Dominique Ingres, Jacques-Louis David, and William-Adolphe Bouguereau.

Romanticism (1780–1830)

In counterpoint to Neoclassicism, we had Romanticism, a movement that stressed individuality and imagination. Influences such as the French Revolution and the rise of industrialization purportedly gave rise to a kind of libertarian spirit that manifested in art in very deliberate fashion. This was a time of glorification of the self, typified by Caspar David Friedrich's well-known painting *Wanderer above the Sea of Fog*. Here stands the heroic figure facing down the wildness and unpredictability of nature.

You might say the Romantics were in our parlance, "full of themselves," and here is a perfect example of this grandiosity in art, a painting by a lesser-known Romantic, the Swiss artist John Henry Fuseli. Here is his attempt to paint a bad dream with all the emotion he can muster; it rings false in its overdramatization, even seems a bit silly, and it clearly shows what may have motivated the realists who followed this art movement.

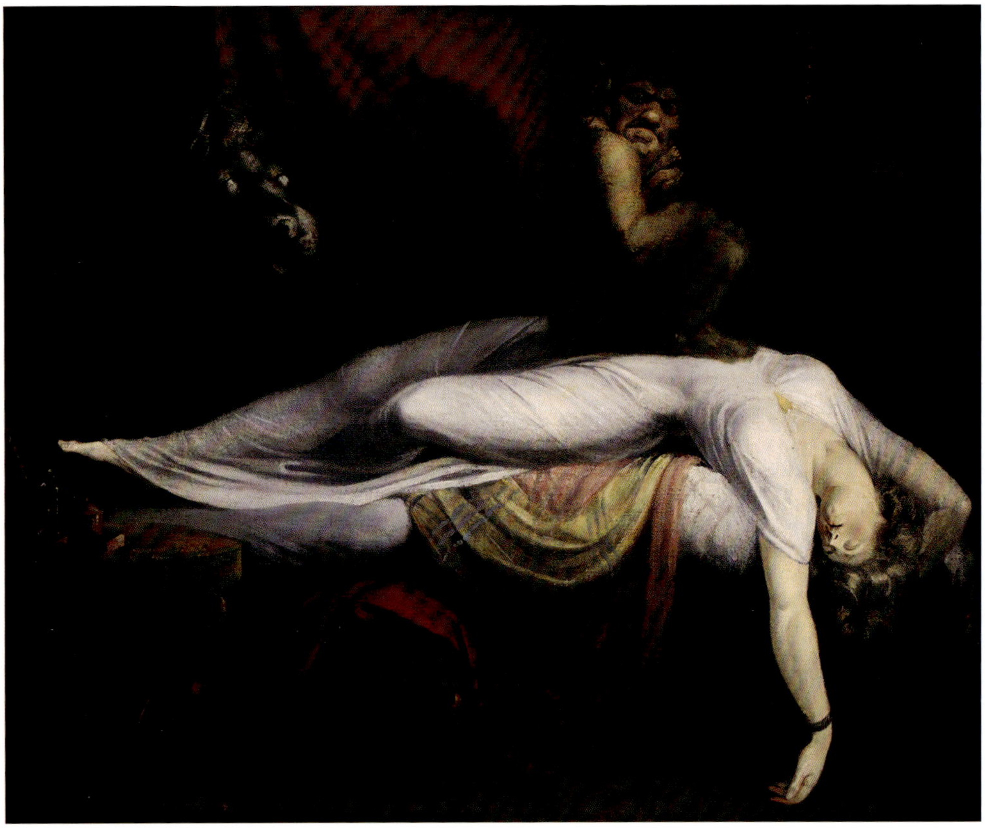

Fig. 40. John Henry Fuseli, THE NIGHTMARE.

The search for meaning and truth is an ongoing one in art. But, as we have seen here, truth is a moving ball, and it is interpreted and perceived in the light of so many factors, that it is difficult to recognize. There is the truth of what we see, and also the truth of what we feel, and these two truths do not necessarily walk the same path.

IN SUMMARY

We have seen how artists, who are both seekers of truth and individuals who want to express their feelings, find different ways to serve these two masters: truth and beauty. And the history of art is one where one or the other predominates and takes prominence.

Take a note here before we move on. If you look at all the works I have offered in this section, with the exception of the Van Gogh and the Millet (modern works), what do you notice as a point of commonality? Answer: the dark backgrounds. Remember that before Monet and his compatriots saw the light, painters worked "from the shadows up." They literally were in the dark.

From this point we are traveling into modern times, where the struggle becomes even more frenzied, and everything speeds up. From just a handful of art movements, we enter a dizzying period where dozens of movements rise and take the stage, all dealing with the same dilemmas and aesthetic questions, but finding new ways to express the argument. Truth or Beauty.

Remember Tolstoy believed originality to be an essential component of art. He would not be disappointed with the originality that governed the nineteenth, twentieth, and now twenty-first centuries.

Let's dive in now.

Chapter 5
Originality

Probably the most original artist who ever lived, Pablo Picasso, is purported to have said the following: "Good artists copy, but great artists steal." He likely even stole this comment, as variants of this quote have been attributed to others, including W. H. Davenport Adams, T. S. Eliot, William Faulkner, Lionel Trilling, and Igor Stravinsky. True to his word, that Picasso! This is a great way to begin our discussion of originality in any case.

The general public, I believe, sees artists as having a singular ability, not present in the average person. It is not that artists are necessarily more intelligent than nonartists though some surely do excel in that area. It is not that they are cleverer, or funnier, or better looking. No, none of these.

What they are is "creative," which means they seemingly have the ability to invent things. They have what we call "imagination" and the decided knack for coming up with and implementing ideas that we call "original."

Well, if they are so original, I hear you asking, why do they need to steal? Why does Picasso say it is not only okay to steal, but advisable? Whatever does he mean?

Have you ever heard anyone say, "There are only twelve great ideas"? Of course, there are more than twelve, certainly, but the idea is that knowledge, if not endless, is nestled around major conceptual structures, and each new bit added by some original thinker has built on what has gone before.

In the course of living, each person accumulates a vast number of thoughts and pictures that comprise his or her knowledge library, and since we all live in the same world under similar conditions, a great deal of these pictures and thoughts are shared.

The wheel has been invented and there is no need to reinvent it, right? You have heard that expression too. But wheels continue to be refined all the time, just like everything else.

The artist may have some thoughts and pictures in his mental library not commonly shared by the average person. Why? Well, if you're not inclined to make a picture yourself, the myriad techniques others have previously used to make pictures are just not relevant and worth holding top of mind.

To the visual artist, those images are exceedingly relevant, given utmost consideration, and frequently downloaded. When Pablo Picasso, the ultimate image maker, stumbled upon African art, his entire organism leapt in happiness. Here was something fabulous that he was not formerly familiar with, something he could relate to, admired tremendously, and yes, wanted to take for his very own. He saw immediately how he could adapt elements of African artistry to his own visual preferences, and, without hesitation, confiscated it immediately.

But he did not copy it. He did more; he appropriated it. To copy is to imitate or even to plagiarize; it is pretense. But to steal in this context means to want something so much that you dare to take it, and then to make it your own.

We all do this. All artists use sources. All of our work arises from multiple experiences—from life, photographs, and other visual materials, including the art of all who have come before us that we have had the privilege to experience.

If being original meant creating something entirely new with no connection to anything else, there would be no such thing as originality. Only Adam and Eve, perhaps, were able to be original. The rest of us borrow and steal and adapt information we gain through our senses, and recycle it, reconfigure it, personalize it, and reinvent it, so someone else can look at it and call it original.

And think about it. It *is* original. Did anyone else ever before or since visually describe love quite like Klimt did in *The Kiss*? Did anyone ever capture the horror of war like Picasso did in *Guernica*? Did anyone ever paint the pathos in a man's eyes like Rembrandt? No, never. These are exceptional masterpieces, yes, but even if you compare paintings by lesser landscape painters, you will recognize differences, smaller perhaps, but perceptible. Every hand has a unique signature.

I find it interesting that as time goes by and people gather more and more information, and artists presumably get to see more and more of the work of their fellows, that the desire to be "original" accelerates. In our chapter on truth, we looked at the period between the Renaissance and the birth of Realism, some five-hundred years. And there were changes, and one art movement led to the next, but all in all fewer than ten movements solidified.

But when we look at the period between 1900 and today, only 123 years, the number of revolving art movements grows exponentially, and the length of each movement shrinks radically. The ride we will take in our next chapter on Modernity from Realism to the present state of art will be fast and furious. The pace will make your head spin as the race to be original reaches a crescendo.

Before we go there, we're going to have some fun and look at the most original works ever created and some of the inventions and advancements that made those creative leaps possible. I am thinking it will be exhilarating to hit the heights as we look at some of the most remarkable feats of the imagination ever conjured in the world of visual art.

Just keep in mind that the pejorative term "derivative," which is commonly employed by critics to deride particular artworks as "unoriginal" could actually be applied to even the innovators mentioned here. ALL artists "derive" their imagery from somewhere, be it any of the art they have seen, or the myriad other bits of imagery they encounter—in nature, in books, or in the culture of their day or prior days. It is what we do with it—how we reinvent it, recycle, upgrade, alter it, revise it—in the light of our own experience that is relevant.

The way we do that moves the culture into the future and also invariably alters our view of the past. As T. S. Eliot said, "The past is altered by the present as much as the present is altered by the past."

So, let's take our developing perspective into the past and have a look at the best reinventors of their time.

1. CHAUVET CAVE HORSES

We must start our conversation about originality by looking and talking about works of art that appeared at the dawn of human life, when visual art was literally born. Discovered in 1994, the Chauvet Cave in southern France is the site of the oldest-known rock art paintings in the world. These works have been dated to the Aurignacian Era, some 30,000 to 36,500 years ago.

When we think of prehistoric rock art, we conjure images of simple pictographs or petroglyphs that depict animals like stick figures, like these found in Azerbaijan.

But the amazing artists who drew and painted on the walls of Chauvet with red ocher and charcoal accomplished a feat that is truly remarkable, if baffling. Who were these humans who painted with sensitive line and captured not only the appearance of the animal but its very power and movement?

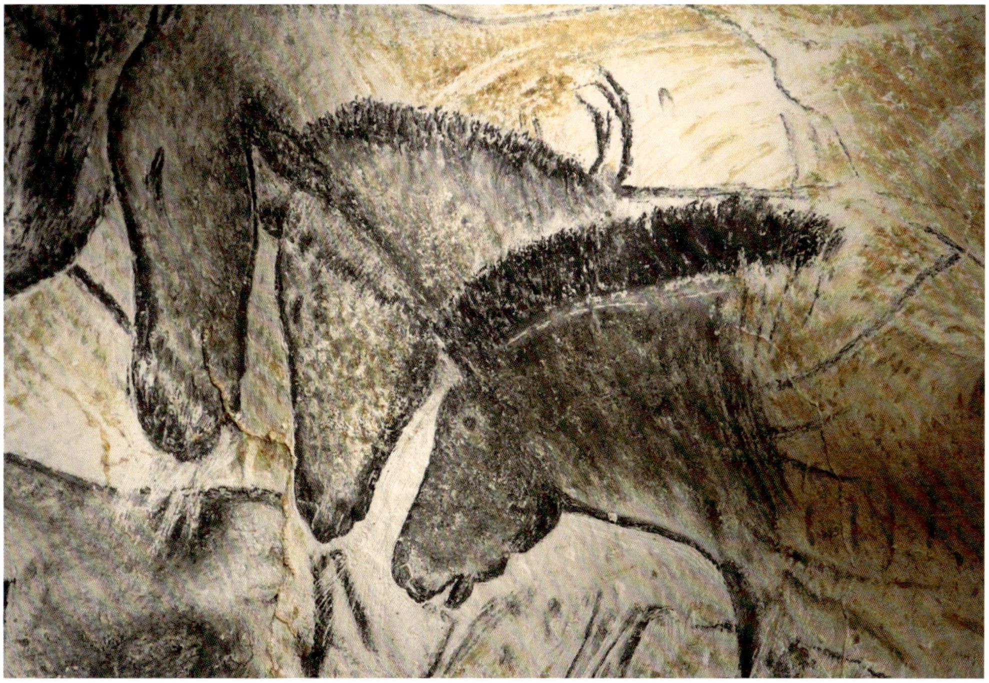

Fig. 41. Unknown Artist, CHAUVET CAVE PAINTING.

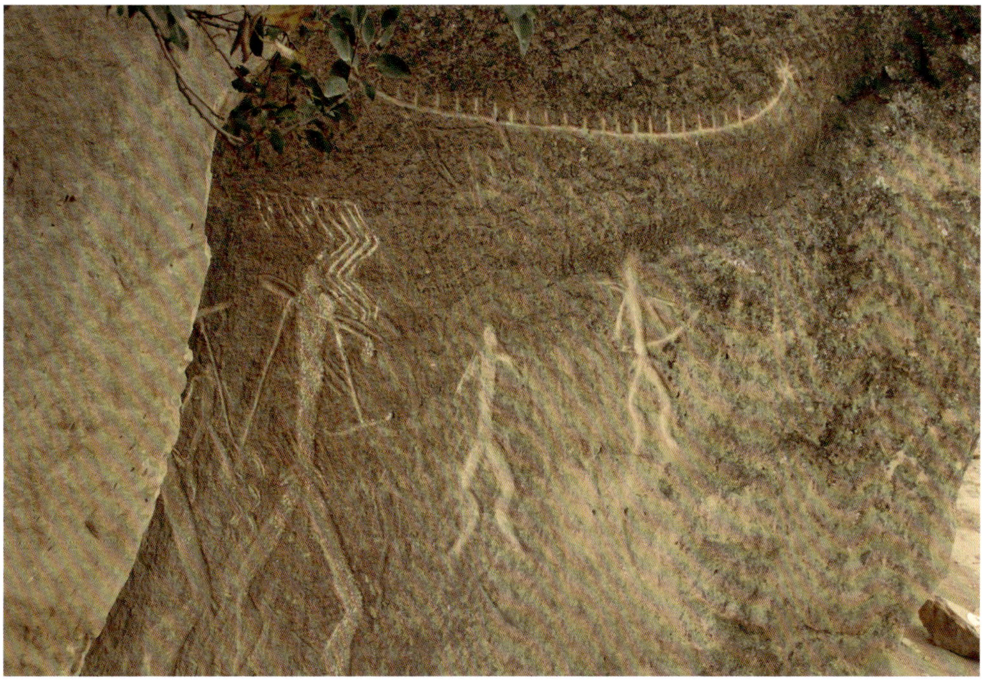

Fig. 42. Unknown Artists, PETROGLYPHS OF QOBUSTAN.

From where did they gain the intuition to scrape the surface upon which they worked free of debris, to create a smooth surface upon which to paint? What gave them the artistic vision to paint not singular icons of animals, but animals interacting with one another, in an active state?

The originality—and beauty—of these paintings is staggering. No one can debate the originality here. These artists had no one to follow—they literally originated art itself! A movie made about the cave in 2010 was called *Cave of the Forgotten Dreams*. I guess it is we—the people of today—who have forgotten these dreams. Let us now remember, and honor, their accomplishment.

2. FIRE

What made the first prehistoric human connect forming something with clay, a stiff layer of earth, and throwing it into a fire? No one knows, but it must have happened a very long time ago because ceramic figures have been found and carbon-dated back to 29,000 BC. These were made in what is called a pit kiln. The kind of enclosed kilns or ovens we are familiar with today were available to the Greeks, Romans, and Chinese, from around AD 200.

Human ingenuity, as typified by the use of fire to literally turn dirt into art, is an essential trait, making expressive communication possible. The urge to create is a driving force in this ingenuity, as is the human need to make objects that have permanence and will outlive us. It is the drive for immortality that has driven the human race to make art, which is our legacy and inspiration to those who follow us, to history itself.

3. MONA LISA

How can we exclude the most famous, most visited, most discussed, most valuable, and most copied and parodied painting ever created from this discussion of originality? I have not said it is the best, but it is universally lauded as Leonardo da Vinci's (1452–1519) masterpiece, and it is emblematic of one of the most cherished of all art periods and locations, the Italian Renaissance.

I'm including it here, not because of its originality, rather because of its amazing fame. Though it is a forward-looking work, and Leonardo an exceptional artist, I would be more likely to call it competent than to praise it to the skies. But the fact is that it is unquestionably a "star," and we have to ask what makes it so.

Let's look at it closely. It is a portrait of an Italian noblewoman, though it never belonged to her or her family. It was painted on a wood panel, and it is told that

Leonardo worked on it, on and off, for many years, as late as 1517. It arrived at the Louvre in Paris in 1797 and has been visited by millions since then. Per Wikipedia, it was valued at over $870 million in 2021, probably making it the most valuable painting ever created.

Why is it so lauded, so beloved?

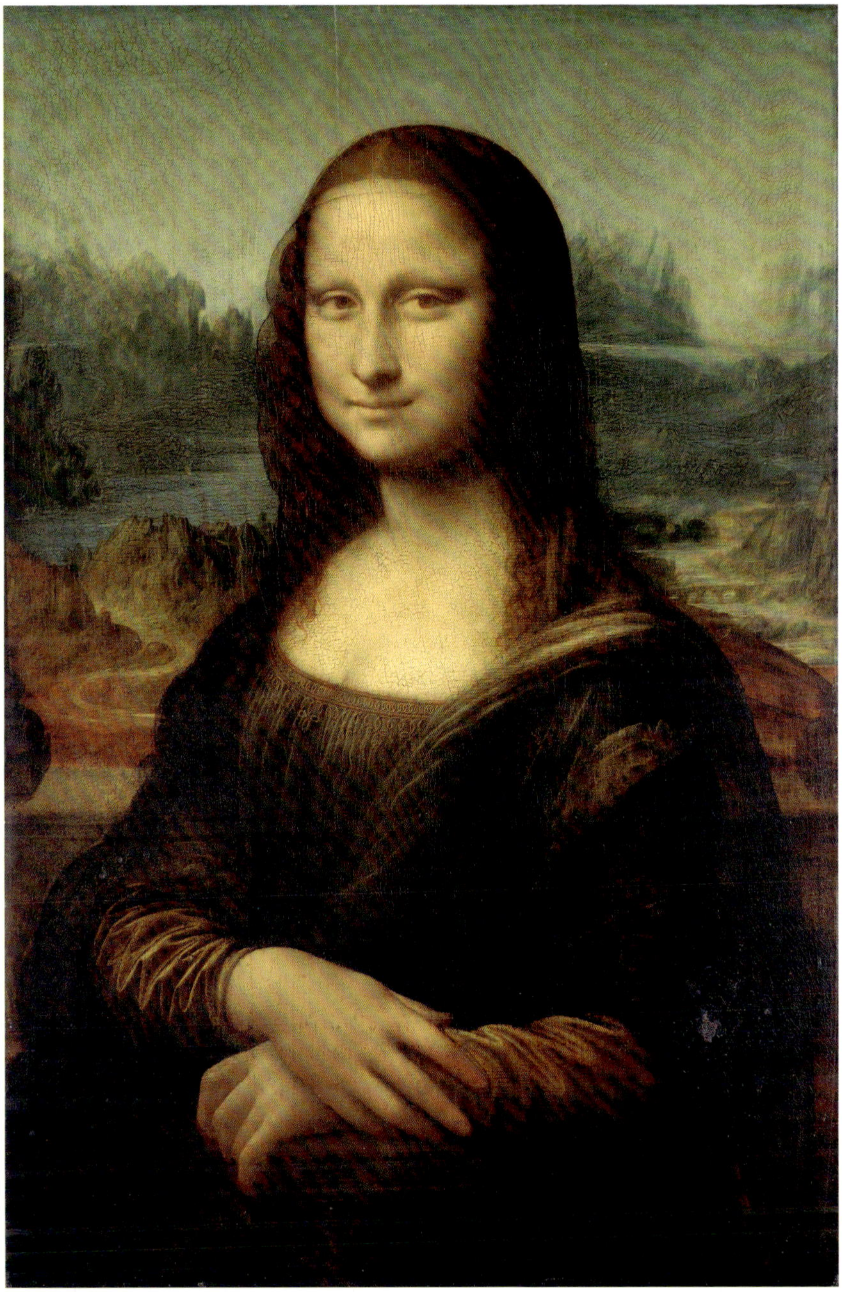

Fig. 43. Leonardo da Vinci, MONA LISA.

To my modern pair of eyes, the colors are drab and the background resembles a flat stage set, but I know this is typical of the period. On the other hand, the form of the figure is well felt, the hands in particular beautifully drawn. There is something about her gaze that compels you to look at it, and I get it that her half-smile is ambiguous and enigmatic.

The *Mona Lisa* is not a particularly beautiful work, nor is the woman depicted a beauty. Perhaps what is most remarkable about her is that so many people have found this painting so captivating. She has been sought after, prized, stolen, traveled the world, debased, and ridiculed, and now she sits encased in glass in the Louvre.

In truth, she has become a spectacle, an object people can project their feelings and thoughts on, and this, by no means, attests to her worthiness. It could have been another work by another artist that achieved this level of notoriety, as there is nothing intrinsic about this work that places it above all others.

Humans love to compare and figure out which is "best," and this goes for every category. When it comes to understanding and appreciating art, it is wise not to get carried away by fashion, trends, and favorites, as these all just make for entertaining dinner party conversation. Appreciate each work for its unique set of attributes, and your love of art will grow. Perhaps you will find many works, even by unknown or lesser-known artists, that move you far more than *Mona Lisa* and which you ultimately deem, if not to be the best ever, just works of art, for reasons you can now articulate, that speak to you.

4. MICHELANGELO: UNFINISHED

The great Renaissance artist known as Michelangelo (1475–1564) was retained to create statuary to adorn the tomb of Pope Julius II in 1505. He subsequently created four sculptures of figures he designated as slaves: *The Youthful Slave*, *The Awakening Slave*, *The Bound Slave*, and *The Bearded Slave*. All of these were unfinished to varying degrees, though it is not known whether this was intentional, or if they were left incomplete for other reasons.

I have included them here in this section on originality not only because Michelangelo was acclaimed as a painter and sculptor and created some of the most magnificent works in the history of sculpture, most notably *David* and the *Pietà*. I chose these because whether or not they were intentionally left unfinished, leaving them in this state has resulted in the creation of exceptionally moving works. Allowing them to remain such (and this would lend credence to the idea that leaving them unfinished was indeed intentional) is a perfect evocation of the humanity of the subjects. They are slaves, prisoners, and as such, they are bound, stuck in the marble and seemingly struggling to escape, as they are in actuality.

Leaving them unfinished gives the impression that the figures are trying to rise from the stone, and this has the effect of animating the sculptures. We feel their struggle; they seem alive. We also feel like we have joined in the act of creation as these figures are literally in a state of becoming. Michelangelo could not have found a more meaningful way to express this truth that perhaps all of us are prisoners of mortality and that, though we writhe and strain, we cannot become free of the reality of our lives.

There is no better example of "the medium is the message" than these works. Can you feel the poignancy in this sculpture? Can you see how finishing it would have defeated his artistic purpose? Can you now also apply this thinking when you look at other works that are left unfinished or at least, in a more rudimentary state?

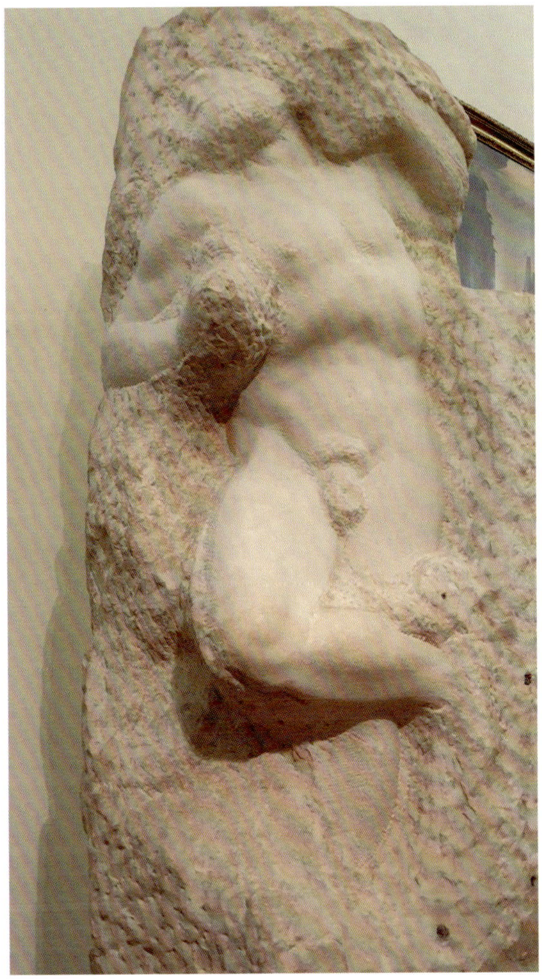

Fig. 44. Michelangelo, THE AWAKENING SLAVE.

Here is a quote, supposedly from Michelangelo, that may be apocryphal, but is nonetheless revelatory: "I saw the angel in the marble and carved until I set him free."

This is the process of visualization, or visioning, that many artists experience. I have felt it many times myself when I was creating—that the work already existed in another realm and that I was just making it manifest. It is in these moments when the artist feels like they are being led by an unseen force, or perhaps experiencing their destiny, living both in the moment and in the future.

All artists put forth a unique vision, but some, like Michelangelo, create signature works that leave their mark on the artists that follow them. They are truly "originals." Our next artist was also one of these.

5. THE CARAVAGGISTI: LEGACY OF CARAVAGGIO

The brilliant Baroque painter Caravaggio (1571–1610), whose work we have already looked at and noted here, was a rogue, a scoundrel, possibly even a murderer, and he lived less than forty years. He met a probably violent death, possibly from lead poisoning or an assassin. In his short time on earth, he created somewhere between forty and eighty astounding paintings, and as the star of Baroque painting, he influenced many artists who were to follow him and changed painting forever.

Here are some of the comments reported to have been made about him by critics:

Robert Longhi in the 1920s: "Ribera, Vermeer, La Tour and Rembrandt could never have existed without him. And the art of Delacroix, and Manet would have been utterly different."

Bernard Berenson: "With the exception of Courbet, no other Italian painter exercised so great an influence."

André Berne-Joffroy: "What begins in the work of Caravaggio is, quite simply, modern painting."

Caravaggio accomplished this without attempting to do so. He had no workshop, as did many prominent painters of this era. He was not a philosopher who set out his principles and techniques to a school of followers. Though he achieved fame during his short tenure in the limelight, his notoriety and influence waned after his death.

But the painters who followed were taking notice. They could not help but be taken with Caravaggio's dramatic imagery, the shafts of light that illuminated and animated the figures, the deep shadows that punctuated the scenes, creating a previously unseen dynamism and power. These admirers had a name. They were called the "Caravaggisti." These included Italian painters as well as Dutch, Belgian, and French; the most prominent being Rubens, de Ribera, Vermeer, La Tour, Bernini, Rembrandt, Delacroix, Courbet, and Manet.

Let's have a look at one of these admirers—the wonderful Dutch painter Johannes Vermeer (1632–1675) and his painting *The Milkmaid*, painted circa 1660 when he was only in his twenties. It is a painting of light, which the artist obviously studied and attempted to reproduce with much devotion. Just study the painting of the wall behind the figure and the way the shadows in the corner are so believable and the gradations of light from the window so perfectly elaborated.

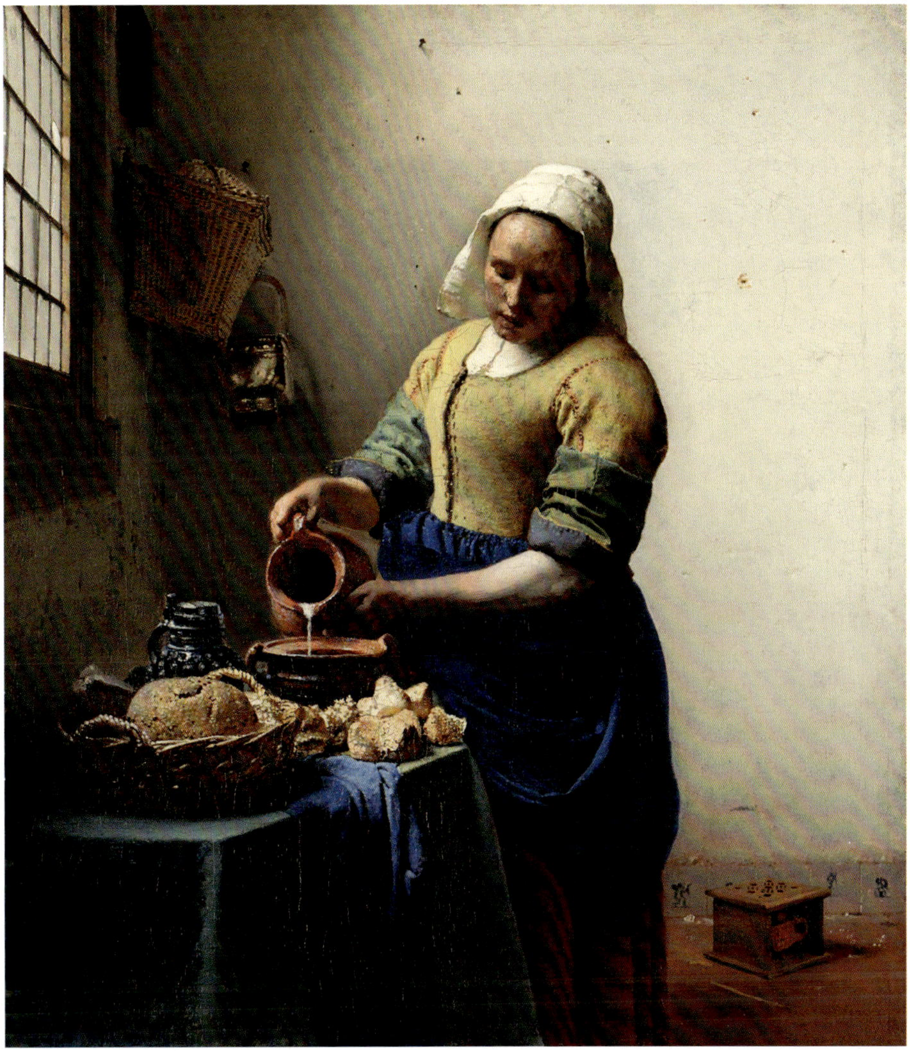

Fig. 45. Johannes Vermeer, THE MILKMAID.

The play of light is so effective and the desire to describe it has determined how the milkmaid is placed with the light spilling over and defining her ample form. One can easily see in this beautiful painting how the dynamic forces of chiaroscuro promoted by Caravaggio have impressed and influenced Vermeer.

Study how the light beats down on the table illuminating the highly detailed items. The artist has given an equal amount of loving care to the treatment of the breads and other inanimate objects, painting the breads with swirls and dots of different color mixtures. The naturalism of this style is apparent in the nail holes on the wall and crack in the window. No stone is left unturned, even the broken windowpane casts its reflection on the window frame. There is no attempt here to idealize this scene; this is realism at its most observant. When you realize this work is rather small, about eighteen inches by sixteen inches, the detail is even more remarkable.

As opposed to Caravaggio, Vermeer has here introduced a rather vivid color palette especially for his time, making use of a color not much used at the time because of its cost. Ultramarine blue was made from crushed lapis lazuli; Vermeer used it here to great effect as he combined it with a pungent yellow and offset it with the green of the table and dark red of the skirt.

There are so many things to like about this extraordinary work—the excellent composition positing the figure front and center with the busyness of the figure set off by the rather large expanse of floor and wall. That quiet makes it possible to draw our attention to the moment captured here: the pouring of the milk.

This is a captured moment portrayed in such an expert manner that it makes this piece of time immortal. Caravaggio's influence is undeniable, but we see how Vermeer in his deftness took his ingenuity to an entirely new and personal dimension.

Berenson compared Caravaggio to Michelangelo in the scope and range of his influence from the Baroque period all the way to the doorstop of Impressionism. He was bold, reckless, maybe even cruel, but he was a genius. He was a virtuoso of painting, had an incredible eye, and was able to work from his subjects directly in oil from life, painting them without drawing first or making studies. In other words, he worked *al primo*,** a very modern practice for a seventeenth-century artist. He eschewed idealism for direct, naturalistic imagery, using prostitutes and neighborhood figures as models for saints and bible figures.

** *al primo* or alla prima is a direct painting approach where paint is applied wet on wet without letting earlier layers dry. In Italian, the term alla prima means "at first attempt."

We can find other incredible talents in the world of painting, artists so facile that they make extraordinary works seem easy. This degree of enormous technical talent is often accompanied by a wildness and panache that others of lesser skill envy and endeavor to achieve but cannot.

Caravaggio was a leader in this arena, but he was not alone. Rembrandt possessed a talent on this level, as did Picasso, Monet, and others we discuss here. Ingres, less of an innovator, could draw like few could, and there are artists working today who are virtuoso performers as well. We will look at some of these in later chapters.

Let's not dismiss the many quieter voices as worthy of mention and applause. We will not forget these as we continue, for their original voices may not be as loud, but their influence and contribution equally as worthy.

6. DARKNESS: FRANCISCO GOYA

We enter a dark world when we visit the artworks of the Spanish Romantic painter, Francisco Goya (1746–1828). Beset by many troubles in his life—illness, deafness, mental illness—his gloomy pessimism and misery penetrated his canvases and determined a subject matter replete with death, murder, witches and supernatural demons, and political and religious corruption.

These paintings portray a dark vision and are also executed with a preponderance of dark notes punctuated by harshly lit subjects. Perhaps because he was driven by his own personal demons, he made no attempt to depict anything or anyone in a flattering manner, and instead was drawn to grotesques of all kinds.

Goya has been named the last old master and the first modern artist. This, too, was driven by his extreme unhappiness and rejection of normality. In his later years, he painted a series of Black Paintings on the walls of his house, which were later removed and placed on canvas to be exhibited. *Judith and Holofernes* is one of them.

It is not a particularly fetching image, but the Black Paintings suggest how Goya can be thought of as the first modern artist, and these paintings are known to have influenced another great Spanish modern artist, Pablo Picasso.

They display modernity in the subject matter, the composition, the rendering, and the intention. The intention is not, as has been articulated in the past, to render a beautiful image, a subject lit in a dramatic light, or anything one might consider appealing. It is rather to express a passionate, though troubled, emotion first and foremost, and might therefore lead one to say it is a precursor

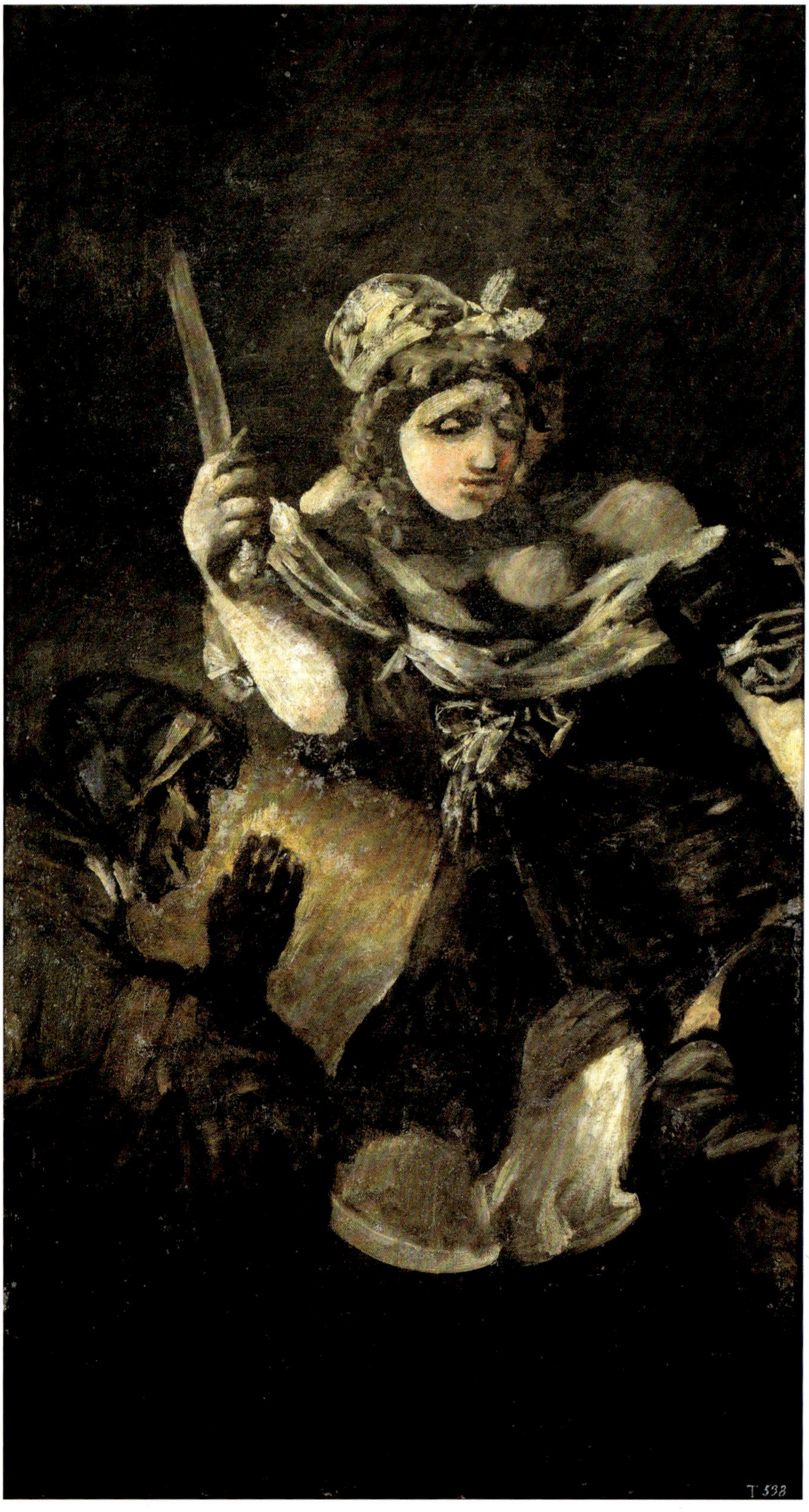

Fig. 46. Francisco Goya, JUDITH AND HOLOFERNES.

to expressionism. The compositions are odd, with figures placed off center, and only fragments of the figures visible: this too is a mark of modern compositional approaches.

This work may lead one to see Goya's work also as a harbinger of Surrealism, in which dream images became the subject of art. In Goya's case, they were nightmares. Whether one appreciates Goya's bleak art, his contribution to modern art is notable and important. He may have been driven by unfortunate circumstances, but nonetheless the work stands as a doorway to many other iterations that may not have occurred if not for him.

7. BACK TO NORMALITY: GUSTAVE COURBET

The French painter Gustave Courbet (1819–1877) was a man of the people, a socialist, and a pragmatist. As such, it makes sense that his intention was to paint only what he could see. His ideology commanded that he eschew subjects of privilege and concentrate on paintings of ordinary citizens in their ordinary lives. He was even more a devotee of this approach than his fellow realist Millet, whose work *The Gleaners* we viewed in a previous chapter. *The Gleaners* was too idealized for Courbet, who hewed to an even greater naturalism, with all its faults and irregularities.

You might say that he lived his philosophy in his work, and so is thought of as the father of Realism and an important practitioner. He inspired Delacroix, Manet, Whistler, and even the Impressionists, who took his eye to the next level.

Courbet wrote that he wanted to create "living art," putting down on canvas what he actually saw as closely and carefully as he was able. His dedication to this principle is evident in a painting he created called *The Origin of the World*, in which he depicted a woman's genitals in full frontal view. The boldness of this work is elucidated by the fact that though this work was painted in 1866, it was not exhibited until 1988, over a century later.

Can you imagine that a work this faithful to its subject would be deemed too radical for the eyes of the populace for so long? That a work of realism, not fantasy, was too bold to be offered for view? Courbet, the revolutionary? No, just a man who did not invent, a faithful interpreter of life as he saw it, a simple man, who painted these apples quite faithfully indeed.

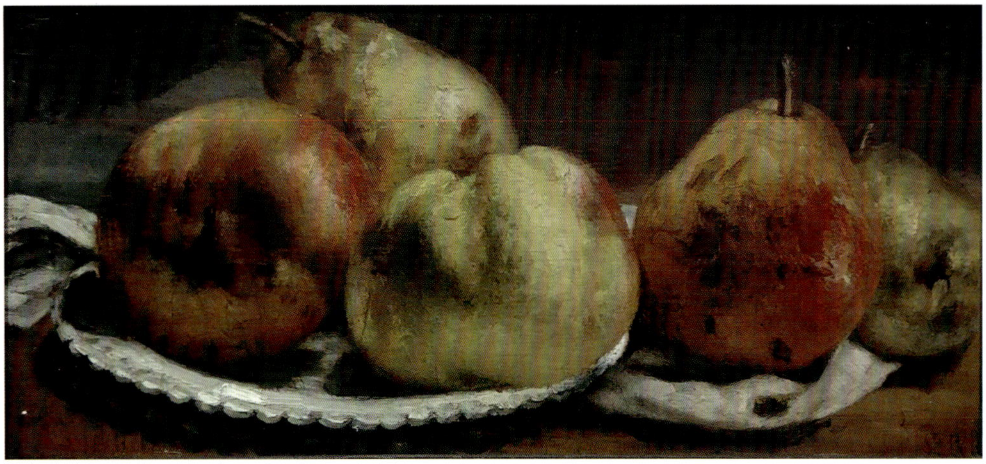

Fig. 47. Gustave Courbet, FRUIT.

8. FLIGHTS OF FANCY: ANTONI GAUDÍ

It is axiomatic that visual art creators love their materials and tools of the trade, and many enjoy experimenting with media. Of course, it takes time and hard work to learn the ways of a new medium, and some prefer to stick to one and master it. But for those innovators who venture out, there is the opportunity to speak in many languages, and some of the most prolific and innovative artists have done just that.

Let's mention a few:

- Picasso was a master of two-dimensional media (paint, drawing) but also worked in sculptural media (ceramics, wood, mixed media).
- Chagall, a painter, created magnificent windows in stained glass.
- Michelangelo wrote three hundred sonnets.
- Matisse made paintings, cutouts, and sculpture and designed a church.
- Modigliani, and many other painters, both painted and sculpted.
- Vincent van Gogh wrote over two thousand letters.
- Vuillard designed theater sets and programs, made prints, and did interior design.
- Klee was a multitalented artist who wrote poetry and played the violin.
- Many artists have written about art, including Philip Guston, David Hockney, Robert Motherwell, and Elaine de Kooning.

Following the determination of Realism, artists around the turn of the nineteenth century began to have a decided yen for its opposite. In place of strict adherence to the seen, the desire for decoration and embellishment was reborn in Europe and then spread to the United States. We call this period where flourish replaced forensics Art Nouveau, but it had other titles, and in Spain it was referred to as Modernismo.

This period of history is called the belle epoque, and it was a short, but delightful period of creative fervor that abruptly ended with the onset of World War I in 1914.

The most famous proponent of Spanish Art Nouveau was not a painter, or technically a visual artist at all. He was the architect Antoni Gaudí (1852–1926) of Barcelona who devoted a good portion of his artistic life to creating what is now the most visited attraction in all of Europe: the magnificent church La Sagrada Família in Barcelona.

The Art Nouveau movement reawakened and elevated the use of what incorrectly had been considered "craft" media—stained glass, ceramics, ironwork, and wood carvings—into the vocabulary and status of fine art. Art of this period is characterized by sinuous curves, floral motifs, and organic shapes rendered graphically, and works are instantly recognizable as Art Nouveau. Probably most recognizable are the delightful posters of this period created by Toulouse-Lautrec.

Not only did Gaudí design buildings, but he also incorporated artwork made of these media into his designs, making art an integral part of both his exteriors and interior spaces; he even designed furniture. Particularly noteworthy are the mosaic works, which, though formerly common in churches, function much more fancifully as part of Gaudí's oeuvre.

Gaudí's great passion, La Sagrada Familia, incorporates both Art Nouveau- and Modern Gothic-influenced themes. It was an incredible labor of love for the architect and artist, and he invested his life energy into its creation. The building was started in 1882 and it remains unfinished to this day; completion is projected for 2027, 145 years since its inauguration.

Gaudí's dogged determination to create this masterpiece made him an incredible innovator. He not only worked in a multiplicity of media, he found new ways to use these materials to shape his personal vision, for example: using ceramic fragments in new combinations, or creating a transfixing light in the church by a new approach to the stained glass, varying the thickness of the glass panels to graduate the light and stacking different colored-glass sheets to create new colors.

To create some of the sculptural forms, he studied anatomical forms and human skeletons, made photographs of models from different perspectives and then plaster casts, and was cognizant of appropriate sizes for these casts depending on where they would be placed and seen. Then and only then would he have the figure cast in stone.

It is important to note by Gaudí's example that meticulous attention to detail is not a feature of realistic portrayal as you might think. Here it was applied by an artist on the other end of the spectrum, one who was a true artist of the imagination.

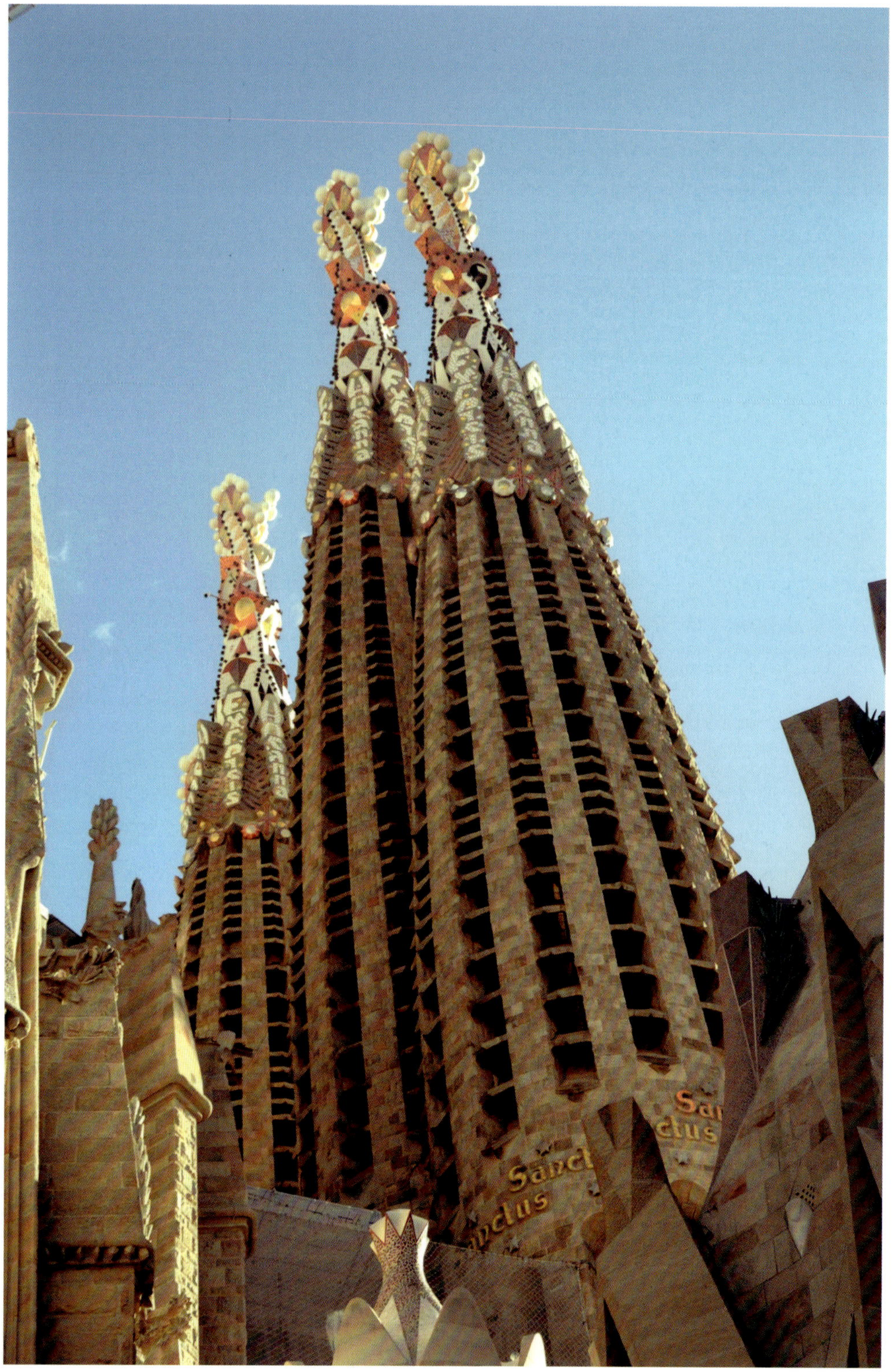

Fig. 48 Antoni Gaudí, LA SAGRADA FAMILIA.

Was he a Surrealist in training perhaps? Salvador Dalí, the bona fide Surrealist, reportedly worshipped Gaudí. Another Catalan artist, Picasso, was not as much of a fan. Interesting! A battle of geniuses is the only way to describe their disagreement.

I had the great pleasure of visiting La Sagrada Familia and stood in awe like all those privileged to have experienced it. That the work of a true visionary has been brought to realization is a testament to the human spirit and its manifestation in art. No photograph, though I offer one here, can do it justice.

Let me just pause in this way station to comment that I hope that the keys to understanding and appreciating art that I am providing in this book will encourage you to seek out the many treasures we are discussing and visit them. An artist like Gaudí devoted his life to creating this masterpiece and generations of other artists and artisans kept his dream alive and completed Gaudí's ambition. It is your privilege that you may be able in your lifetime to stand in this building and experience it.

9. THE BREAKTHROUGH TO MODERNITY: IMPRESSIONISM AND CLAUDE MONET

It hardly seems like a radical idea—to go outside and paint—but the so-called Impressionists who did just that changed painting forever. And it wasn't just a coincidence. In fact, a little invention may have played a giant role in making this all happen: the paint tube. An American portrait painter, John Goffe Rand, is credited with this innovation. Fed up with oil paints that dried up and were wasted being stored in pig bladders, which did not sufficiently close, or jars that were too cumbersome to carry, he devised the handy-dandy metal paint tube, and in the American can-do spirit, went on and patented them.

The inventor did not live to discover the impact his little invention would have on painting, but it made it possible for artists to go outside and paint, and voilà: Impressionism. Later on the invention was improved with the addition of a screw-able cap, which made oil paints less expensive, easier to use right out of the tube, and of more dependable consistency.

The term *Impressionism* arises from a painting from the premier Impressionist, Claude Monet, who exhibited a work called *Impression, Sunrise*, which was critically panned, with the critic (Louis Leroy) discrediting it as merely a sketch, not a real painting. Wow, did he get that wrong!

It turns out that Impressionism, characterized by loose brushstrokes of light-filled color mixtures painted mostly al primo en plein air (directly from life outdoors), was and continues to be immensely appealing to many art lovers to this day, with exhibitions of Impressionist works more popular than any other period or style. An accentuation of color was achieved by allowing bits of color to lay side by side unblended so that they seem to vibrate.

The father of Impressionism, and its most ardent practitioner, was none other than Claude Monet (1840–1926). Criticized early in his career (*Impression, Sunrise* did not sell when it was offered at the exhibition of the Anonymous Society of Painters, Sculptors and Engravers), Monet went on to achieve great recognition.

Monet was called "the eye" for his devotion to what he could see and his fascination with painting the light in exactitude. Since the light changes throughout the day, and is represented by entirely new color schemes, he took to painting the same scene at multiple times of day. As he matured as an artist, and was dedicated to painting the "seen," rather than inventing it, he had the gardens and ponds he wanted to paint created by landscapers. He would attempt to complete a painting in a single sitting, as if to hold onto the light with a short memory.

Take a long time and sit comfortably to study this Monet painting of a women with a parasol standing in the sunshine of a beautiful day. I confess that I have secretly yearned to live at this time in the second half of the nineteenth century so I could paint beautiful women in the park with long flowing dresses and parasols. What a time for a painter of the "seen" to live and work.

I love the perspective of this work, looking up from a lower vantage point into the parasol and the sky dotted with puffy clouds, the woman's face in shadow with the light behind her. How glorious! You can see the light and feel the air—looking at this painting is like taking a deep breath and echoing a sigh. Monet has painted the world the way he wanted to see it. We want to see it this way too, don't we? "The eye" as our eye.

Monet was one of the greatest innovators at the dawn of the modern era. And he took an even further step late in his life when he became obsessed with painting the ponds at his estate in Giverny. I visited this estate a few years ago with a group of painters. The Monet grounds, now a tourist attraction, were closed for the day so the painters could work at the ponds. I was thrilled, as you can imagine, with this opportunity and when I entered the estate with my colleagues, I found myself bursting into tears. I was overwhelmed that I was walking in the great Monet's footsteps and that I would soon be standing in his stead at the lily ponds. What a day that was!

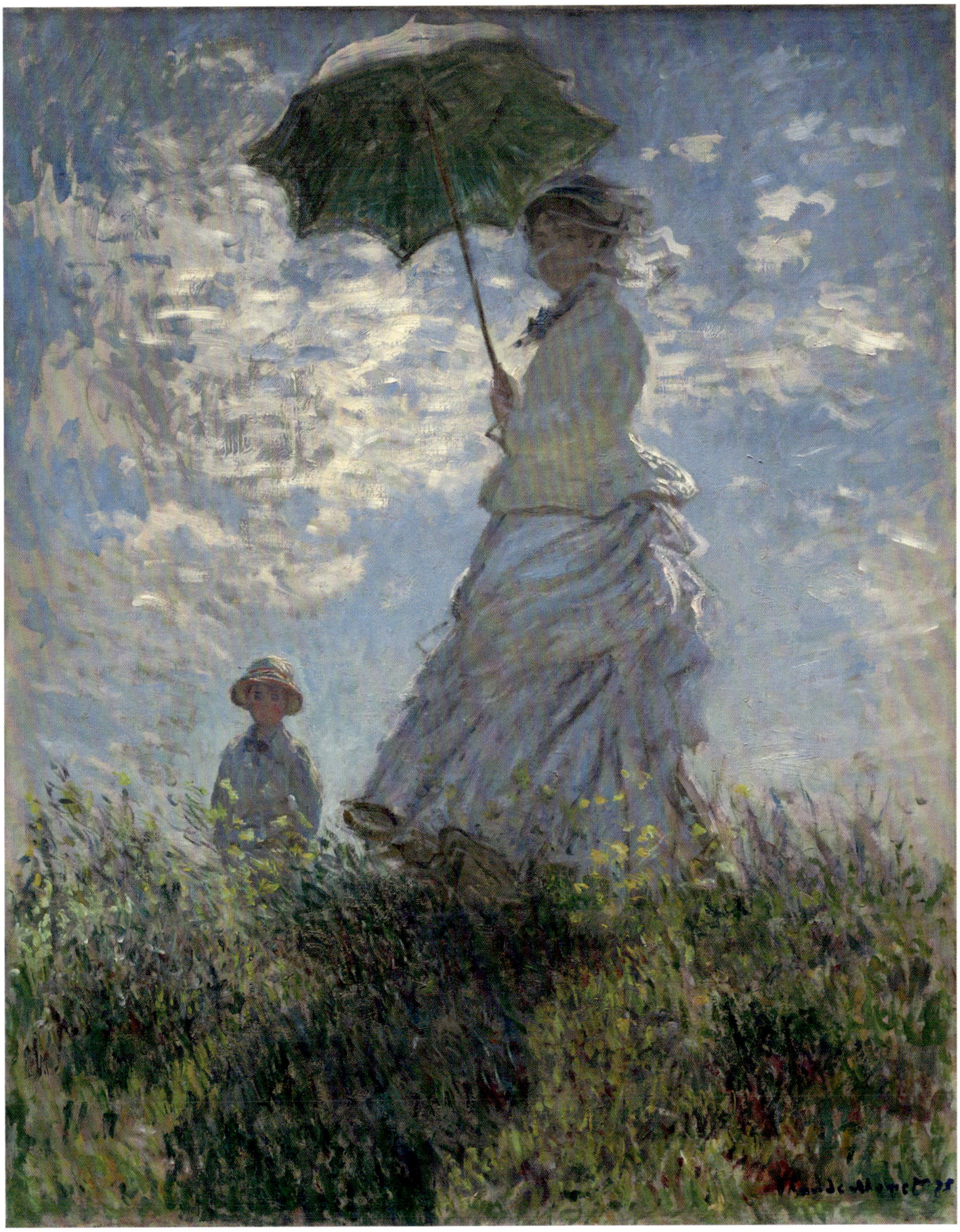

Fig. 49. Claude Monet, WOMAN WITH A PARASOL.

Monet painted these ponds starting in 1899 and this absorbed his interest for nigh on twenty years. It is interesting to note that during these years he developed cataracts and feared having them surgically removed, a practice more primitive at that point in time. He lived with them for many years and perhaps this had an impact on his treatment of the water lilies.

Regardless of the reason, Monet began to see the ponds more and more abstractly, as a moving swirl of colors, transparencies, intensities, blurred shapes, and textures, and the paintings became less and less descriptive, and more like a field of vibrating vision. I realized this when I, too, stood at the shore gazing into the pond, which shimmered in hypnotizing fashion. I was mesmerized by the shifting colors and saturations, with their periodic impasto elements. It is undeniable that this work is merely a stone's throw to pure abstraction—a slight shift in intention, and you have arrived.

Like many great painters who preceded him, notably Turner, Monet's raison d'être and the heart of his painting was the light and atmosphere. Like Turner, he loved to paint weather—mist, rain, and storms—and often worked on a bunch of canvases at the same time, switching as the light changed, and then returning when it came back again. With scientific precision—empirical evidence—he made art a record of time. Genius!

10. VINCENT VAN GOGH: EMOTION IN PAINT

I find it so terribly sad that the artist Vincent van Gogh (1853–1890), so distressed and overlooked in his lifetime, would be so aggrandized today. During his short lifetime, though he produced thousands of works of art, he suffered from extreme depression, failed to find commercial success or fame, and died by suicide.

Given his unfortunate life, it is certainly ironic and maybe even grotesque that today his artworks are sold for millions, and crowds flock to see blown-up photographs of his beloved work splashed on screens in these so called "immersive" displays. I can just imagine how Van Gogh would have hated these overblown, glorified treatments of his hard work.

Compare this to the absolute humility of his work, the fragility of his temperament, the fact that he required the support of his brother Theo, his relatively short career as a painter—he only painted for about ten years—and probably most poignantly, the authenticity of his work.

We all know the story of how he cut off a part of his ear with a razor after a confrontation with his friend Paul Gauguin, how he failed to take care of himself, did not eat well, drank, and spent time in mental hospitals. We know him as an emotional basket case, and yet . . . His work . . . so memorable, so personal, and recognized only after his death. He never knew what he had accomplished.

This is undeniably sad, with the tragedy now fused to every display of his work. He was a superb painter, and we appreciate how he took his turbulent state of mind and transferred it to the canvas, as here in his *Starry Night*, in which he transformed the sky in a way that is indelibly marked on the consciousness of all who have seen it.

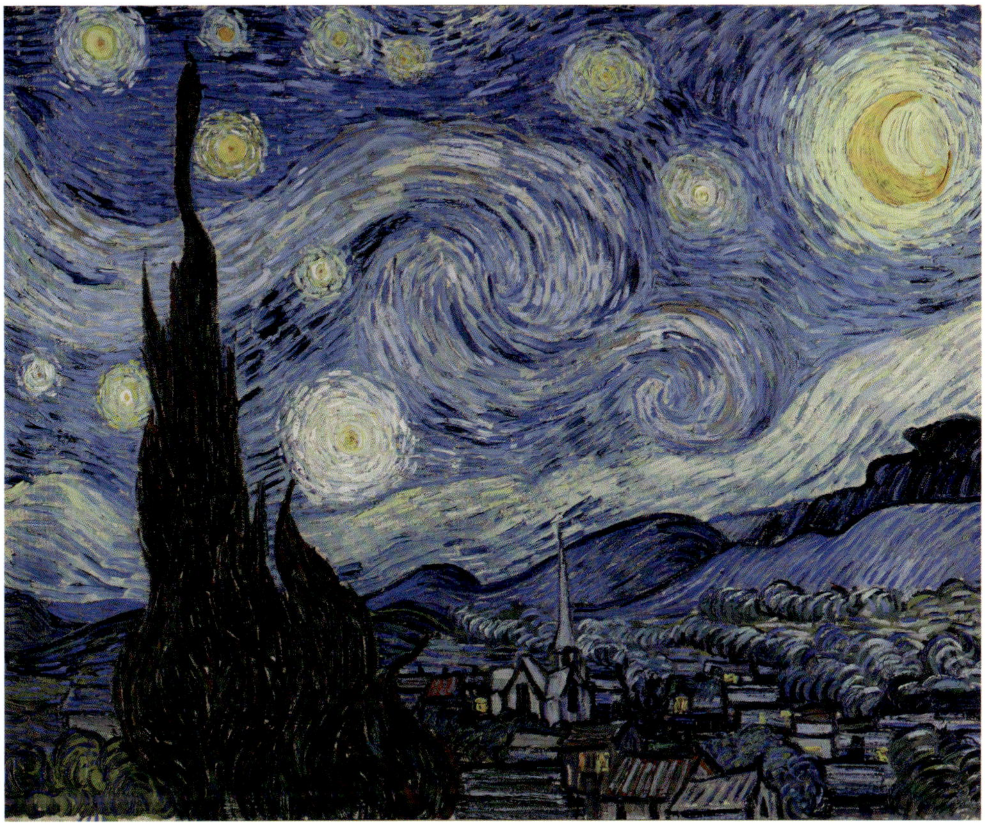

Fig. 50. Vincent van Gogh, STARRY NIGHT.

In fact, I was not surprised to read that Van Gogh was critical of this work and thought he had strayed too far from reality. This may be apocryphal, but I know that Van Gogh admired the work of realists like Millet and Courbet. It is entirely possible that he believed he had ventured out of his comfort zone here and that the work had become too stylized. Authenticity was his hallmark, and he was undoubtedly more self-critical than his audience. I know, as an artist, that we are our own worst critics.

So, which is it? Is he the greatest of the greats? Or just a very emotional man who put his extreme feeling into his paint?

It is important to appreciate art but at the same time not to over-romanticize or exalt it. The hyping and merchandising of Van Gogh does an injustice to his journey and to other terrific painters who, for one reason or other, may be out of favor at the moment. I treasure Van Gogh for his sincere attempt to work honestly, his vibrant use of color, and the vitality of his paint. And you should too. Just don't neglect all the others who may be unrecognized, or who have a different kind of song to sing. It takes all the voices in the chorus to reveal the magnificence of the music.

11. LARGER THAN LIFE: PAUL GAUGUIN

The meme or cliché about artists or artistes, if you will, is that of the starving outlier, conjuring wild images in a slovenly attic garret in frantic abandon. This may be the case for the movie version, but most artists are just like everyone else, certainly in appearance and lifestyle. They do mostly have what we refer to as a "calling," an intense desire to express themselves.

But the cliché has not risen out of thin air. One exemplar of what was undeniably an unusual life path was the French post-Impressionist Paul Gauguin, famous for his escape to Polynesia to paint intensely colorful renderings of the people and environment. You may be surprised to learn that this escape was prefaced by a rather conventional lifestyle. Gauguin was actually a stockbroker for eleven years and had a wife and five children. Following the stock market crash in France in 1891, penniless, he abandoned his family and fled to Tahiti to paint.

Gauguin has been criticized for his selfish behavior and accused of racial stereotyping based on a colonialist perception, but even given this, his achievements and originality in art, and his widespread influence on other painters, is undeniable. It is a truism that he gave his all for art, and his calling to express transcends any denunciation of his life choices. Though he may have hurt many, his contribution to art was outstanding and lives on.

Gauguin was a prodigious artist, wrote on art, and worked in many media including printmaking and ceramics. He was a lifelong friend to Edgar Degas and other prominent artists of the era. These are some of the movements he participated in originating:

Cloisonnism: a style characterized by flat forms outlined by dark lines. This painting style is imitative of the art of cloisonnè, where areas of powdered glass are surrounded by solder.

Symbolism: Gauguin was a proponent of and participant in this movement, a form of Romanticism that encompassed many art forms including prose, poetry, and visual art. Other symbolists in art included painters Klimt, Redon, Latour, Kahlo, Moreau, and the sculptor Rodin. As the title suggests, the imagery in Symbolist works is representative of an idea, which in many cases is personal to the artist and not immediately understandable. It is the transmission of a meaningful, even if obscure, image.

Symbolist work exalts individuality, subjectivity, mysticism, magic, the occult, allegory, eroticism, and sensation. The word synesthesia is utilized to express the

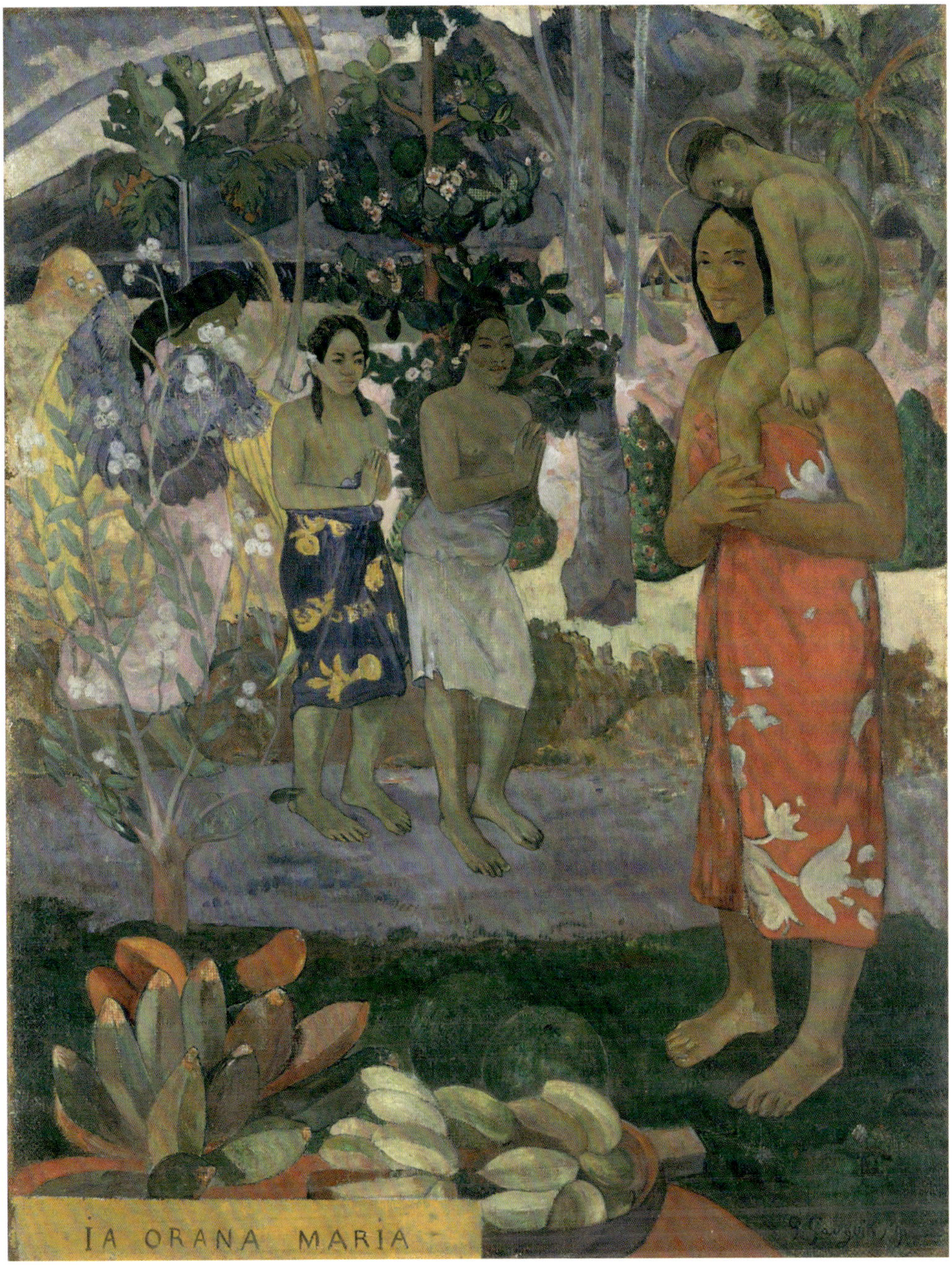

Fig. 51. Paul Gauguin, HAIL MARY

evocation of other senses—taste, touch, smell, sound—in the visual. Gauguin, for instance, thought of his work as not only visual, but musical.

Synthetism: As differentiated from Impressionism, this style championed large flat areas of color. A kind of clarity of color, shape and line was sought, as opposed to the feathered quality of Impressionism paint.

Primitivism: The art of Africa, Oceania, and other Indigenous people fascinated European artists of this period. The freshness, simplicity, and raw power of these works infiltrated the thinking of these artists and compelled them to create their own iterations in paint and sculpture. In our next section, we will discuss the latter. In the case of Gauguin, his reverence for painting Polynesian women was tarnished by his sexual exploits and, unfortunately, colors their appreciation for some.

In this early Symbolist work, Gauguin depicts Mary and Jesus as Polynesians. To their left you see an angel with yellow wings. Note the pleasing array of colors applied in that flat application we spoke of.

Folk Art or Pastoral Art: One of the reasons for the celebration of Primitivism is the belief that rural or country folk, or groups far removed from so-called civilized societies, were capable of a directness and purity in their artistic expressions. This engendered a longing on the part of many trained artists to capture that spontaneity in their work.

There is no overstating the influence of Paul Gauguin upon generations of artists, not to mention the absolute absorption with his life and practice. His journey has been regaled in novels like W. Somerset Maugham's *The Moon and Sixpence*; films like *Lust for Life*, in which Anthony Quinn played Gauguin, and *Paradise Found* starring Kiefer Sutherland; and as the subject for two operas. The man was larger than life and an inspiration—the artist who lived for art above all else.

12. MODERN SCULPTURE: BORROWING FROM THE ANCIENT

I need say little here that cannot more easily be expressed by these two images. Here is a Cycladic sculpture from 2500–2700 BCE, a very long time ago indeed. Notice the utter simplicity of this marble head.

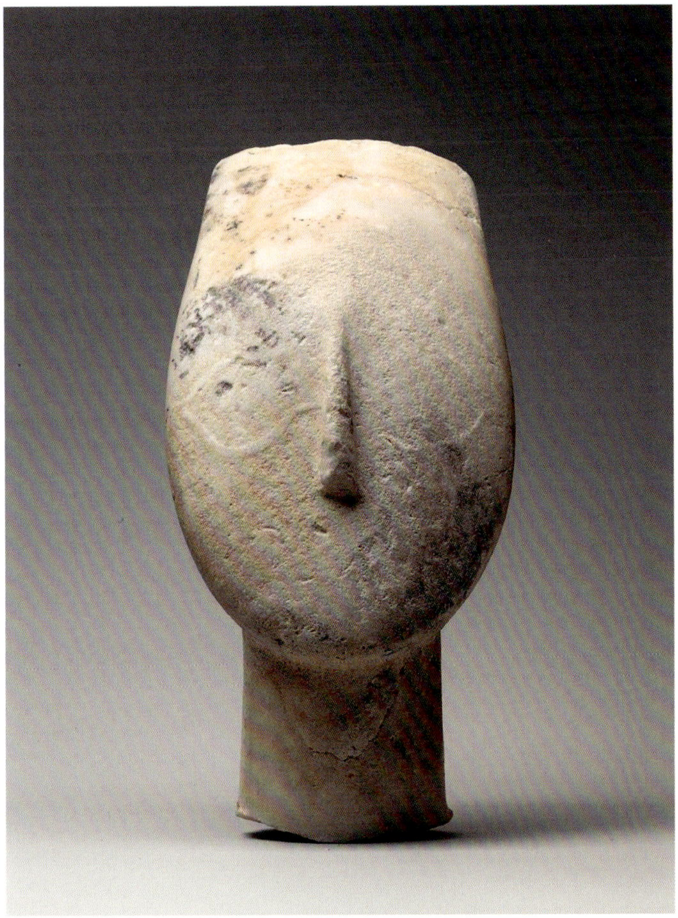

Fig. 52. Unknown Artist, CYCLADIC SCULPTURE.

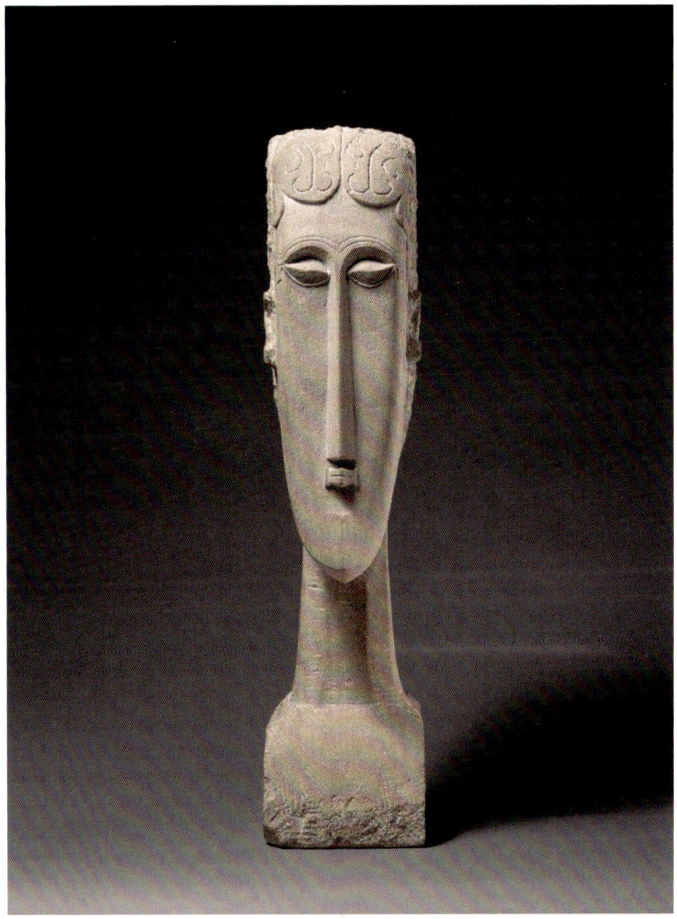

Fig. 53. Amadeo Modigliani, WOMAN'S HEAD.

Now have a look at this sculpture of a woman's head by the artist Modigliani, created in 1912.

It is said that the painter and sculptor Modigliani became acquainted with the art collection of Frank Burty Haviland, an American artist and collector of African art. This interest also spurred Modigliani to study ancient art, which included Cycladic works similar to the work here. You will surely agree that the resemblance is unmistakable.

If you study the paintings of Modigliani, you will clearly read his affinity for the elongated features, lack of detail, and simplified elements that are evident in these early sculptural works and later incarnations. The artist must have been totally exhilarated to discover these ancient works that so reflected his artistic preferences.

We do not have permissions to show you much of modern sculpture in these pages, but in your future museum going, look for the following:

Find sculpture in every art movement. Whether it be Cubism, Minimalism, Abstract Expressionism, Pop Art, or any other modernist art movement, you will find sculptural works as well as two-dimensional wall art. Have fun seeing if you can recognize the corollaries.

Look for other ways to make sculpture. Modern sculpture moved away from the solid form, or rather opened up the possibilities. Look for constructions—parts assembled like three-dimensional collages.

Sculpture became abstract. Paring down to essences was the trend in sculpture as well as painting. Look at Brancusi's famous *Bird in Space* as an example.

New materials came into the fore. No longer just marble, modern technology made a whole slew of new materials and tools available to create sculpture out of steel, polymers, resins, you name it.

Sculpture became kinetic. Modernist sculpture doesn't have to be static. It can move; it can have light and sound elements, screens for video elements—it has come alive!

Contextual integration an important factor. A lot of sculpture is designed and made to be placed in a specific environment as public art. Look at the environment as part of the art.

Ceramic art more prevalent and valued. No longer a lesser craft material associated with pottery, ceramic is a viable material for sculpture.

Installation art. Singularity in sculpture is no longer the norm.

Earth art: The canvas is now the earth. Is the solar system next?

13. THE MANY FACES OF PABLO PICASSO

When I think of Pablo Picasso (1881–1973), I think of the bulls he liked to draw. So different than the forlorn Van Gogh, Picasso had a vibrant, bellowing personality, which he manifested in an extraordinarily varied body of creative work. His confidence and bravado spilled out on the canvas, in the sculpture studio, in the ceramic workshop. There was no stopping him, and no competing with him. He was a force unto himself, a whirlwind of imaginative output.

I think his tremendous joie de vivre allowed Picasso to go in many directions, to borrow from the primitive work he so admired, to work without hesitation, and therefore to move any art form he worked into a new level. He was a marvelous draughtsman, and he knew this. Drawing well is a predicate for so much in art and those that do it well have a decided edge on others not so gifted. And Picasso was gifted—he could draw anything and that meant he could draw whatever he wanted.

There was nothing he had to prove. He was free to be . . . himself. The bull, the one who is not afraid of anything. (And he was only five feet, five inches tall.)

There was so much Picasso achieved that was worthy of great admiration, so much, and it is all very well documented. Here are some of the highlights:

- He worked with limited palettes in his Blue (1901–1904) and Rose (1904–1906) periods, creating emotionally resonant paintings.
- Along with Braque, he invented Cubism.
- He was the first artist to utilize collage in his Synthetic Cubism period.
- He brazenly incorporated African motifs in his painting to the chagrin of the art establishment. (*Les Demoiselles d'Avignon* was not exhibited for nine years).
- He incorporated symbolic imagery like the Minotaur in many works that become iconic.
- He created political art, most notably the celebrated mural *Guernica*.
- In addition to his artwork, Picasso was an avid writer, credited with over three hundred poems.
- He did not hesitate to make his own version of works by masters. He made over fifty versions of Velázquez's *Las Meninas* and also worked from Manet, Goya, Courbet, Poussin, and Delacroix.
- Picasso even appeared in films, always as himself.
- Picasso was one of the most prolific artists who ever lived. He made almost 16,000 paintings and drawings, and thousands of sculptures and ceramics.
- He was incredibly inventive in his use of materials in his sculpture, introducing wire, rope, sheet metal, and all manner of unlikely items.
- Picasso was able to paint and draw from his imagination and did not need models to create believable representations. He had, therefore, an astounding visual memory, quite uncommon, even to most visual artists who depend on source materials.
- In addition to painting and drawing, Picasso created an amazing body of work in ceramics, printmaking, and other techniques. Where in

> the world did he find the time to do all of this, we must wonder—especially in view of the fact that he had a robust personal life with multiple wives and children, not to mention paramours.

Even though Picasso's career was incredibly diverse, he hewed close to the representational. There is much that is treated in a semiabstract fashion, but he did not make the leap to full abstraction. He had too much to say about the real world and just found a unique way to express that world in every creative iteration.

One innovation I want to select out and write a bit more about is Picasso's artistic decision to adopt more than one point of view for the sake of simultaneously painting multiple views of the face and figure. This is a total departure from the idea of perspective adopted by every painter since the Masaccio perspective was proposed in the Renaissance. It never occurred to anyone that there was no reason to not put multiple views into one painting.

This is a radical idea, breathtaking in its influence and meaning in the world of visual art. It is a permission slip to see the world the way you want to see it, and to hell with the consequences. And we owe this freedom to Picasso, presumably the most amazing artist who ever lived. Look up *Portrait of Dora Maar* as an example of this multiple view. I was not able to show it to you here due to copyright restrictions.

If you wish, you can see the liberty Picasso allowed himself as the true initiation of modern art. Even though others are credited with this distinction, just realize that once an artist gives himself permission to see both sides of the face simultaneously, every other restriction just flies out the window. If this is possible, then anything is. Just imagine it and you can create it. If this is not the ticket to the show of what we call modern art, tell me what is?

Picasso was much rewarded in life. He lived a long time, and he lived large in every component of his life. He achieved fame and fortune and recognition at the highest level. There is no doubt that Picasso stands as the embodiment of la dolce vita and creative freedom. His accomplishments are legendary and will probably never be duplicated. His is surely one of the most amazing tales in the history of art.

14. THE OUTSIDER: HENRI ROUSSEAU

I remember seeing *The Dream* by Henri Rousseau at the Museum of Modern Art when I was a girl. I remember staring at it and loving it, but not knowing why. I have lived a lifetime since then, and now I can say I know why, and I am happy to tell you.

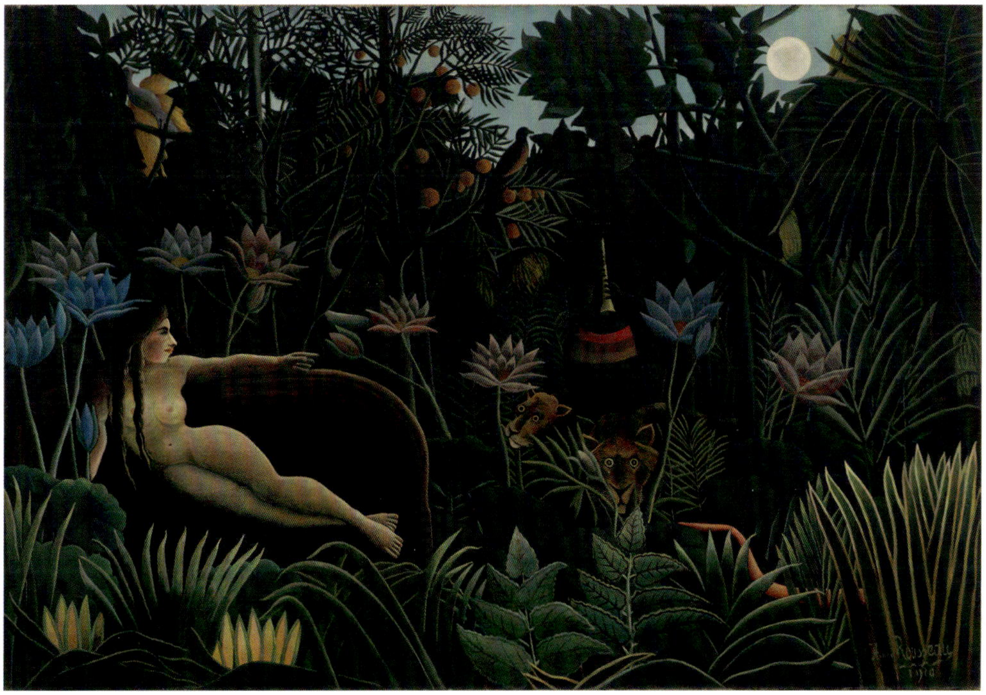

Fig. 54. Henri Rousseau, THE DREAM

First let me tell you about its creator, the French artist Henri Rousseau. He was not a trained artist, and though he painted these jungle scenes, he never saw a jungle. In fact, he never left France. He was called a naïf, or naive artist, or in today's lingo, an "outsider." He did not start painting until he was in his forties, and before that he was a customs inspector. He worked as a busker playing his violin in the street, and critics of the day said he painted like a child.

But Picasso made him a party and many artists came, and Sylvia Plath wrote a poem, a work of ekphrasis based on *The Dream* called "Yadwigha on a Red Couch Among Lilies." The last lines of that poem are these:

> Yadwigha, pose on, that he put you on the couch
> To feed his eye with red, such red! under the moon,
> In the midst of all that green and those great lilies!

The Dream was exhibited in March of 1910. Six months later Rousseau died of gangrene.

I still love *The Dream* and think it is an example of pure imagination. It doesn't matter that Rousseau did not paint from life and instead went to botanical gardens and natural history museums to do his research. He did not paint true-to-life jungles, but when I think of a jungle, I conjure up Rousseau's version. It is iconic.

People have tried to count how many shades of green are in this painting and have gotten up to fifty. This painting makes an argument for not studying, because here Rousseau has been able to create unburdened by ideas of what makes a good painting. He can make impossible connections, putting his childhood nurse, Yadwigha, on a couch in a fictional jungle, exactly like one might do in a dream.

Rousseau takes us into his dream and gives us one of our own. I read that instead of studying other artists, he looked at children's books for inspiration. Perhaps that is why I stood in front of this work as a child and can still remember that moment to this day.

This painting reminds us that in spite of the fact that there is so much to learn in the world of visual art, and so much to know as an artist, at its very heart is this urge to create—like a child, like an outsider, like a naïf—a vision that a little girl sixty years later will marvel at, and be inspired by. This is what art can do at its best and is more important to know than anything else you are learning in this book.

I have included an outsider artist in the section on living artists and hope you enjoy his work as much as I do.

15. COMMERCIAL ART: DOGS PLAYING POKER

You will probably be surprised that I am adding Cassius Marcellus Coolidge (1844–1934), known by his nickname, Kash Koolidge, to this list of art originals because you may not know his name. Even if you do, you might not recognize him as a bona fide fine artist. He is best known for creating eighteen paintings in his Dogs Playing Poker series.

Coolidge, an untrained artist, was commissioned by publishing company Brown & Bigelow to create these works in 1903. They were utilized in promotional items like calendars, ads, and posters. Each of the paintings shows incredible lifelike and expressive anthropomorphized dogs doing a variety of things, particularly playing cards.

Coolidge was pretty much laughed at and mocked for these works, which were considered "kitsch," a name for low art. It wasn't the theme that was the problem, as plenty of modern painters painted card players, notably Caravaggio, Manet, Paul Cézanne, and Georges Braque—but of course, those players weren't dogs. But Coolidge's dogs were expertly painted, and hilarious to boot. They became stars in TV, film, video games, album covers, and even books. They were beloved while their creator was vilified.

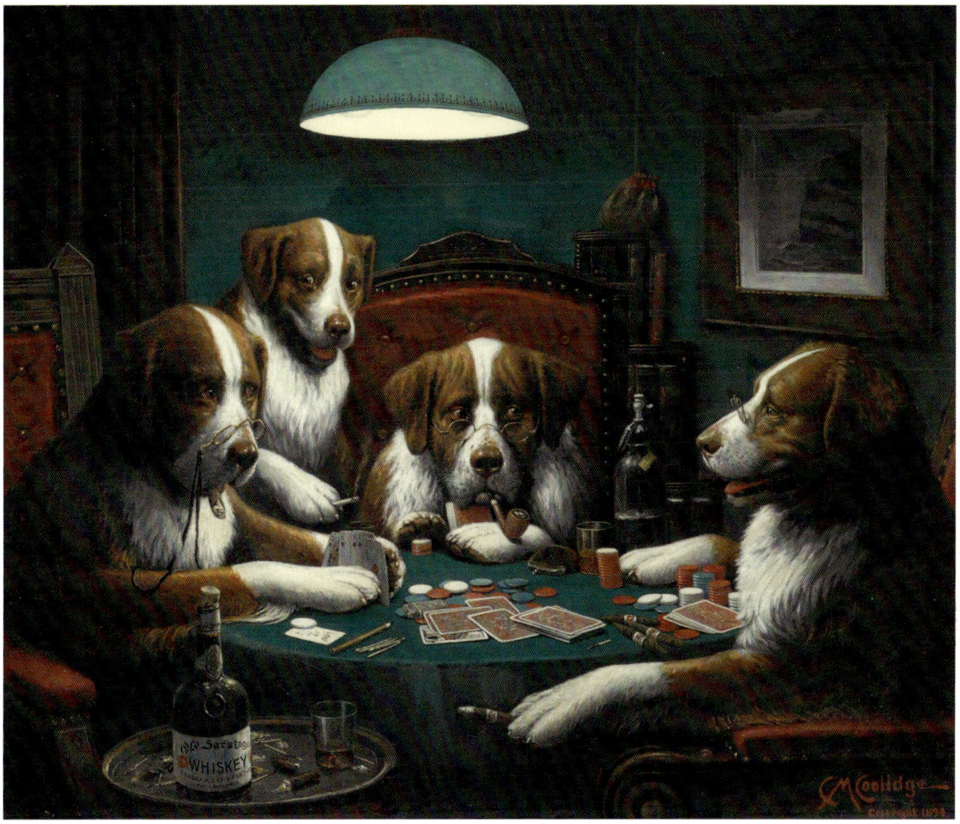

Fig. 55. Cassius Marcellus Coolidge, DOGS PLAYING POKER.

People, regular people, loved Coolidge's dogs, but critics shot them down. But we won't be doing that here. I, for one, think they are fabulous, incredibly well done, and super clever. Coolidge had some major talent, which he surely could have applied to all sorts of subjects but didn't.

Coolidge didn't achieve fame, but the dogs did, and his obituary was as understated as can be. It read, "He painted many pictures of dogs."

That he did, and kudos to him.

I include him because we can get so puffed up about art, snooty even, putting down commercial art while aggrandizing theoretical work that is conceptual or minimalist. We accept a bowl of fruit as a legitimate subject; why not a group of dogs? I'm sorry Coolidge didn't take up other subjects because I would have loved to see them. I bet he could have painted the best damn apples. He just didn't want to, and that's okay. We'll enjoy the dogs.

No judgment, just joy . . .

IN SUMMARY

Art is like any discipline: it is something an artist adopts and grows into. Bright ideas come to mind, and creative people try to materialize them. Through trial and mainly through error, eventually we learn what works and what doesn't, and *how* to make it work. Our intentions do not always lead us to successful outcomes; sometimes they are dead ends and we are forced to retrench and take a step back.

I have found that these errors of judgment and false alleys often lead to great leaps. When this happens, it feels like the universe has rewarded us for not settling for something that is not as excellent as we want it to be.

"Good for you," it seems to say. "Now you're onto something."

Originality is not a magical thing. It comes from learning what works, considering what might work, and trying it. "Why not?" is a great reason and often is what sends the ball rolling down a long, long hill. Sometimes, ideas and innovations turn out to be transformative, as were those discussed in this chapter. They are only some of the more influential examples of original thought and action that define the history of art.

The thing is that the more you do, the more you want to do and can do. In the next chapter we are turning our attention to modernity and the many innovations that took hold in the art world after Impressionism. It's a fast-moving train and it's pretty fascinating, but it took a long time to cover that territory. There are still artists working today who continue to explore the many techniques and movements from yesteryear. Of course, they are doing it with modern tools and consciousness. Welcome aboard for the ride . . .

Chapter 6
Modernity

My painting teacher believed that each art student lives the history of art in his or her own development as an artist. We all start as primitives and go through similar stages as those in art history until we can become modern artists. The point is that you need to experience the basics of image crafting before you can individuate and develop your own style. You can see this in the work of many modern artists as well. They start out copying their predecessors before they embark on their own unique direction.

Some students progress more quickly than others, but the journey is a similar one nonetheless. I say that the differentiation between people as to drawing ability is due to the fact that some people are capable of much closer observation, and they have therefore collected more visual information in their banks than others. But those others can catch up if they do the work. Of course, the work is demanding, and a deep commitment is in order.

When I was in art school, my teacher had a particular lesson that illustrates this point. He would set up a still life on a table in room A and mark a line on the floor where we were to stand and study it. Then after whatever period of time we wished, we would return to room B, where our easel and canvas were set up and we would put down on the canvas whatever we remembered from our viewing. We could keep going back and forth until we were satisfied.

This was an incredibly difficult assignment, and it illustrated clearly that our memories, even short-term memories, were severely lacking, as the information we collected seemed to completely vanish when we returned to the canvas. Only the most obvious and the simplest shapes and colors stuck. And what were those—well something very akin to the petroglyph.

So what did committed artists do with this understanding? How did artists who wanted to make detailed images accomplish this? They did what the students in my art class knew they had to do after their frustrating exercise. They studied! They used their eyes—and all of their senses—to closely, repeatedly, and more diligently *observe*.

They put the still life or the animal or the landscape or the person in front of them and they noticed and imitated every nook and cranny, every direction, color subtlety, with the utmost care, commitment, and intensity they could muster, and they copied and looked again and corrected and changed what was on the paper or canvas until it actually resembled the object in question.

And they created what we call representational art.

Now remember, centuries ago, there were no cameras, digital or otherwise, and every representation had to be drawn. Remember that before you had a calculator, you probably could add a column of figures much faster and better than you can now. That's because you've gotten lazy relying on the handy tool.

But artists of old had no such luxury. Their eyes got sharper, their powers of observation more acute, and their desire to reproduce what they saw felt even more compelling. Just like the calculator user, you would be hard pressed today to find an artist with the visual acuity of Caravaggio, or Michelangelo or Rembrandt, who seemed to see so deeply he revealed not only the outer resemblance, but the inner soul.

When it occurred to artists that it might be advantageous, interesting or meaningful to draw and paint complex images that had greater and greater **verisimilitude** to the object, they began to realize that what they were doing was creating an **illusion** of three-dimensional space on a two-dimensional surface. This illusion was arrived at by drawing and painting the image in **perspective**, that is, from a specific point of view.

In our brains, objects are visualized as basically flat shapes. But in order to depict the object in all three dimensions—length, width, and depth—on a flat paper or canvas, we must distort the shape. That is because from a visual point of view, objects appear smaller as they recede in distance from our eye. We call this **linear perspective**. They also appear less vivid in terms of saturation of hue. We call this **aerial perspective**.

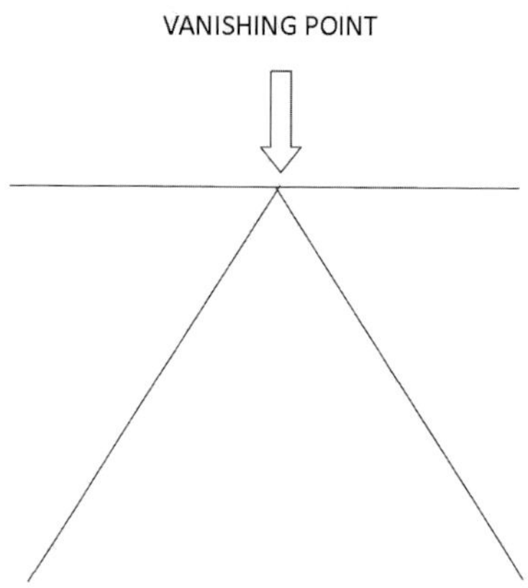

If the illusion of three-dimensional space is *not* created by virtue of aerial and linear perspective, the image will appear flat, like the pictograph or a stick figure drawn by a child.

Remember this: All representational painting is illusory, or an illusion. It fools you into believing that what you see is three-dimensional. This is foundational.

Painters of old applied these rules of perspective to objects, people, and animals, but it took a while before they treated the background—the setting—in the same fashion. Many of them actually cheated a bit. They drew their main subjects directly from life, assuring a greater accuracy and likeness, but they filled in the scenery, so to speak, without direct study.

It is as if the figures were actors in a play, living beings, surrounded by what resembled a stage set, a hastily painted backdrop to frame them. It is remarkable, but it took a while for artists to discover **plein air** painting and go outside to paint the landscape. To give it equal billing, so to speak, not backdrop status.

Incidentally, the whole idea of a **background** comes into question in modern art. It presupposes something that is important, say the figures, and something less important that frames them, like a landscape or interior. A modern work of art may have no background at all, as when the entire canvas is the subject.

This is something to look for when you study a work of art. Has the entire canvas been given the same attention by the artist? Or does it perhaps appear less authentic or more hastily made?

From our vantage point today, when information and goods are almost instantaneously available, it is difficult to imagine the context in which these representational painters of centuries ago lived and worked. But the work they did was inventive and even revolutionary, as artists made discoveries we now consider traditional.

They expressed their individuality within the confines of the knowledge and ethos of their day, and their particular version of painting what they observed became their signature. We can all instantly recognize those intimate and complex interiors of Vermeer, with his fascination with mirrors and other reflective surfaces. We can pick out a Frans Hals for his vivacity, a Rembrandt for its intensity, a Titian for its jubilant color.

But what they have in common is the desire to create the illusion—the illusion that what you see is an actual scene. It is intended to fool your eye that what you see is not just paint on a canvas. Through images fixed and still, it represents something that might be moved—that might get up and walk off the canvas. It has form, volume. It might even be alive!

So how do we get from this place to modern art?

The answer is rooted in science, evolutionary processes, culture, historical events, and human development. A very significant factor is the introduction of the camera, as photography made reproducing images by drawing and painting, if not unnecessary, then certainly nonexclusive. The first attempts to create a camera began centuries before the invention of photographic processes, which would make it possible to preserve images.

The very first actual preserved photograph was made in 1816 by Nicéphore Niépce when he exposed a paper coated with silver chloride to light. George Eastman pioneered the use of film in 1885 and the camera came into its own. In 1888–1889, Eastman switched from paper film to celluloid and offered the "Kodak," his first camera, for sale.

As soon as it became possible to make pictures with a camera, the making of pictures by artists in the studio utterly changed from a necessary occupation to a discretionary one. And the idea of modern art—art created for expressive purposes and not simply reproduction—was born.

Once the party began, so to speak, anything was possible, and the race to invent new ways to express was underway. The very purpose of art was challenged, and the possibilities seemed to glisten in the light of a new day.

In fact, the liberation led artists to leave their studios and go outdoors to paint, and this proved to be the factor that would shake up art making more than anything had to date. When artists made this radical step, they were pelted with a new obsession—the light itself. Not lighting, as observed indoors, but light, fabulous light, that felt now as palpable and fascinating as anything they had ever previously observed.

Everything looked different. Since color is refracted light, suddenly color blossomed and became something to study and adore in its own right. And the light blew everything else apart. Instead of tight molecules of paint creating a tight surface, with no hint of the brushstrokes used to create it, suddenly the pixels of paint started to float and stray, the strokes became visible, and the surface came alive.

Once artists became liberated from the necessity of rendering realistic objects and scenes, a new vocabulary of imagery was born which elaborated and commented on these objects and scenes, without copying them. Some of these were modifications of objects where the reference is obvious. We call these works **semiabstract**. Others obviate likeness altogether and do not give a clue as to what they might represent. These we refer to as **abstract.**

Liberation is self-perpetuating. Once representation was no longer a singular goal, there arose many different approaches, techniques, philosophies, and styles, and we will soon be looking at many of these as I endeavor to explain and illustrate the most prevalent and interesting practitioners.

The development and introduction of the camera caused a paradigm shift in visual art. But it is certainly not the only factor that engendered the experiments of the late nineteenth and twentieth centuries that we refer to as modern art. Artists are strongly influenced by the culture in which they live and work, and this period of modernity saw incredible changes in society; movements in other art forms, especially writing; the emergence of psychology as a science; the introduction of social theories; and new insights on human behavior; as well as cataclysmic events like two world wars.

Most of the early modern artists we will discuss were European, but America was becoming a cultural behemoth of its own as emigration from Europe to the United States accelerated in the early years of the twentieth century. In fact, many of the practitioners of Abstract Expressionism were Americans, and this movement came to be associated very much with the American experience.

Just as painting and visual art in general was undergoing this shift, much was simultaneously erupting in other areas of thought. The fracturing and deconstruction of the object was mirrored in the works of politics and social planning, in Karl Marx; in psychology with the work of Freud and Jung; in science, with Albert Einstein; and in the writings of Jean-Paul Sartre, Camus, and other philosophers of Existentialism.

These upheavals—historical events and cultural and political movements—worked their way into the psyches of visual artists and onto their canvases. The societal restraints were loosened, and artists responded in kind. Permission had been granted to express oneself, to be an individual, to be creative and bold and experimental. There is no coincidence that in music the same openness and spirit of innovation led to the creation of jazz. In fact, it is not impossible to see abstract art as a kind of visual jazz making.

But before we get into the specifics, let's talk about the qualities and characteristics of art that had been liberated from the real and became part of what we call modern art. To clarify, modern art (usually considered to be art created from1860 into the 1970s) and contemporary art (after 1970s) does contain work made by Realists and even Photorealists. All of it is not abstract. But in this regard, even realistic work was transformed. We will look at some of these examples too, but our primary focus will be on semiabstract and abstract works.

When art is detached from the real—becomes, in other words, nonrepresentational or nonobjective—there are still echoes of the real. The artist may be liberated from the desire to imitate, but the physical world remains in his or her consciousness. This bank of images is full of references to what we have observed in our lifetimes. We have attached names to these images, and they are the alphabet of our visual language. So, when we step up to the easel to make a work of semiabstract, or abstract art, we bring this vocabulary with us to the task.

I could argue that the term "nonrepresentational" is specious, or at least requiring some clarification. An abstract work might not represent an object, but how about a feeling, a mood, an idea? Do these representations not count?

What they don't do is to copy or imitate. That does not mean we don't make use of these references. Let me tell you some of the whys and ways artists make semiabstract and abstract works and how they relate to the seen world.

LITERAL VERSUS IMAGINARY

Here are some of the synonyms for the word literal: documentary, factual, objective, true.

You would probably agree that painters of realism were attempting to make something that could be called literal. Now what is the antonym to literal? Here are some of them: imaginary, hypothetical, theoretical, apocryphal, unauthentic, chimerical, fabulous, fanciful, invented, make believe, mythical, embroidered, exaggerated. Most of these can be applied to modern art.

So, one way to describe the phenomenon of this paradigm shift is as a desire to move past the literal into the imaginary—or in the case of the Impressionists, who still made recognizable scenes and portraits, to the fanciful. You might also argue that the Impressionists amplified the definition of "truth" itself as they concentrated on how the specific light impacted the color used to illustrate it.

Finding a deeper truth, so to speak.

This shift involved making the literal, or what was thought of as "truth" about more than portraying a subject. It involved a revelation of not only what the subject looked like, but what the artist thought was important or interesting or personal about it. Modern art puts the artist front and center. The artist brings his or her feelings and thoughts into the picture, and this transforms the way we see it. Modern art is uniquely individualist; one might say this is the emblem of the modern era itself.

The artist Clyfford Still was born in North Dakota and spent his childhood in places featuring prairies or other wide-open spaces. He became a color-field painter. Do these swaths of color perhaps hearken back to the environment he grew up in? It is difficult to see how they cannot.

Likewise, consider the Ocean Park paintings of Richard Diebenkorn, whose oeuvre evokes the glorious light of the California coast, which inspired his abstract compositions.

Did the urban settings the neoplasticist Mondrian encountered influence his interest in the grid? Undoubtedly so, as this is all evidence that what artists observe plays an important part in what they choose to focus on in their abstract work.

The abstract artist may not be referring directly to a subject as he or she paints, what we call **working from life**. That does not preclude having done so at a previous time, working from sketches made directly from a subject, and then modified. Sometimes artists make an original study from life, then many subsequent studies from the original one, like a game of "telephone," in which little by little each study changes, and the final work may have morphed totally from realistic to totally abstract.

It is a misnomer that abstract work just pops onto the canvas, *al primo*, without any reference or source. Many works are what we call **abstracted** and have their foundation in specific subject matter. This is not always the case, as some artists work more directly and allow one stroke to lead to the next without having a subject in mind as a starting point. However even with this methodology, sometimes a stroke or shape that develops may suggest a subject or reference, and the artist may then embrace that subject and lead it to its natural conclusion.

Since I, as a working artist, have personally taken these routes to creating artwork, I will point out how the works discussed may have developed and come to fruition. There is no magic involved; one idea naturally leads to the next. But sometimes we are not able to read the road map.

One of the ways to describe modern art is that it has moved from the literal to the imaginary, from the universal to the individual, and from the traditional to the revolutionary. But human beings are still human beings. They see the same oceans, trees, animals, sun, and moon. And these images fill the memory banks of twenty-first-century artists as much as seventeenth-century artists. Though the references in abstract work may be obfuscated or hidden, they are there, and you can have fun looking for them and asking what the influences might have been. Sometimes the title will suggest an answer. If not, digging a bit into the life of the artist may give you some clues. Think of it as a bit of a treasure hunt.

From an artist's point of view, I want to give you an idea of what an artist might be thinking of when he or she makes an abstract work and how these may jibe with those references I spoke of previously. These are just some clues as to how an artist gets from point A to point B and what he or she is actually doing:

1. SIMPLIFICATION

One way artists compose an abstract or semiabstract work is to have an actual subject in mind, and perhaps in front of him or her, and then choose only certain details of that subject to portray. Artists can extract elements of an object or group of objects into a work of art without necessarily identifying the object(s). I refer to this as simplification, but by no means is it necessarily consonant with simplicity, though it could be.

Look up *Woman Reading*, a Cubist work by Georges Braque painted in 1911. Sometimes the artist will give a clue to his reference in the title, as here. As you look at the work, you don't see a woman or a book or a chair. You see straight and curved lines and shapes, and a limited palette of neutral colors.

There is no illusion—in fact the space depicted in the work is very shallow. You see a nearly flat design. But hunt a bit and you will find curved lines that suggest part of the reader's body and the arm of the chair, perhaps a leg shape. Braque must have wanted you to know his inspiration was a woman reading or he would not have mentioned it in the title. He is not interested in reproducing the woman in the chair; he just wants you to see what he finds interesting about the subject.

I cannot think of an artist who more beautifully exemplifies the manner in which simplicity is both the doorway to modernity and its heart than the marvelous Milton Avery, whose lovely paintings mark the first half of the twentieth century. Avery worked from life and never abandoned the representational, but he stripped it to its essentials, creating flat, simplified forms and radiant color, if perhaps in a minor key.

Here is a work from 1944, called simply *Female Artist*—even Avery's titles were stripped of unnecessary frills. We see an artist at work with her back to us. She is composed of areas of flat, unadorned color (in this painting a bit more primary than many of Avery's more somber compositions).

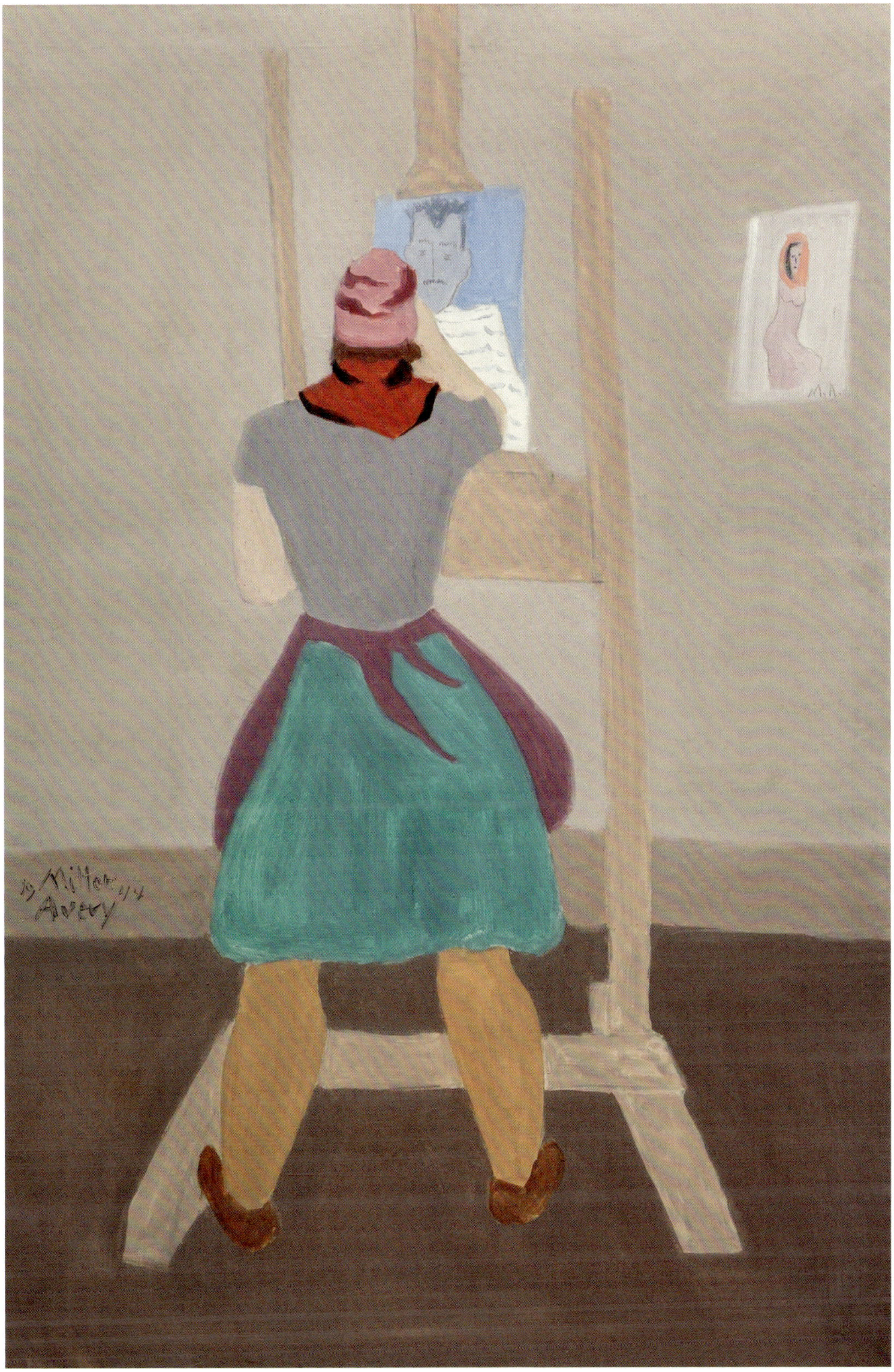

Fig. 56. Milton Avery, FEMALE ARTIST.

There is no attempt to fill the canvas with colors and shapes, and indeed Avery has allowed the composition to breathe—his quiet spaces are decidedly important. He gives us the essential, the facts, and nothing extraneous. It is a frugality, a reservation, that serves the painting and the viewer well. Nothing but what is needed.

Avery was friendly with some Abstract Expressionists—notably Barnett Newman and Mark Rothko, the latter of whom spoke at Avery's memorial service in 1949. He acknowledged Avery as "the poet of sheer loveliness . . . where the poetry penetrated every pore of the canvas to the last touch of the brush."

Like Cézanne, Avery was a painter who was recognized and regaled by his fellow artists—a "painter's painter" if you will—though not as celebrated by the public as he perhaps deserved. Not only was his work recognized by his colleagues, his place in the history of art is also well warranted.

As Avery discarded linear perspective—replacing it with color that spoke of space in flat application—and unnecessary detail, often painting faces without features, he was drilling down to only what was needed, in his careful and determined methodology. This clearly was a harbinger of abstraction. The journey is clear. The simplicity exhibited in the important work of Milton Avery marks a definite cornerstone of modernism.

2. LOOKING FOR ESSENCES

Another way to explain this is to suggest that the artist is looking to depict what he or she finds "essential" about the object. This is another extraction process. Here is an example from the painter Piet Mondrian, an abstraction of a church.

Here the artist has forgone any resemblance to a building, and given us vertical and horizontal lines, some crossing, that express what he felt was the essence of the church. A visualization of lines that by their placement, size, and intensity, say "church," without describing a building. In other words, they express "churchiness" or "spirituality," without depicting anything that resembles a church. Many modern artists wrote about the spiritual name of their work, and the meaning of "finding the essential" in the object. We will discuss this more fully in later chapters.

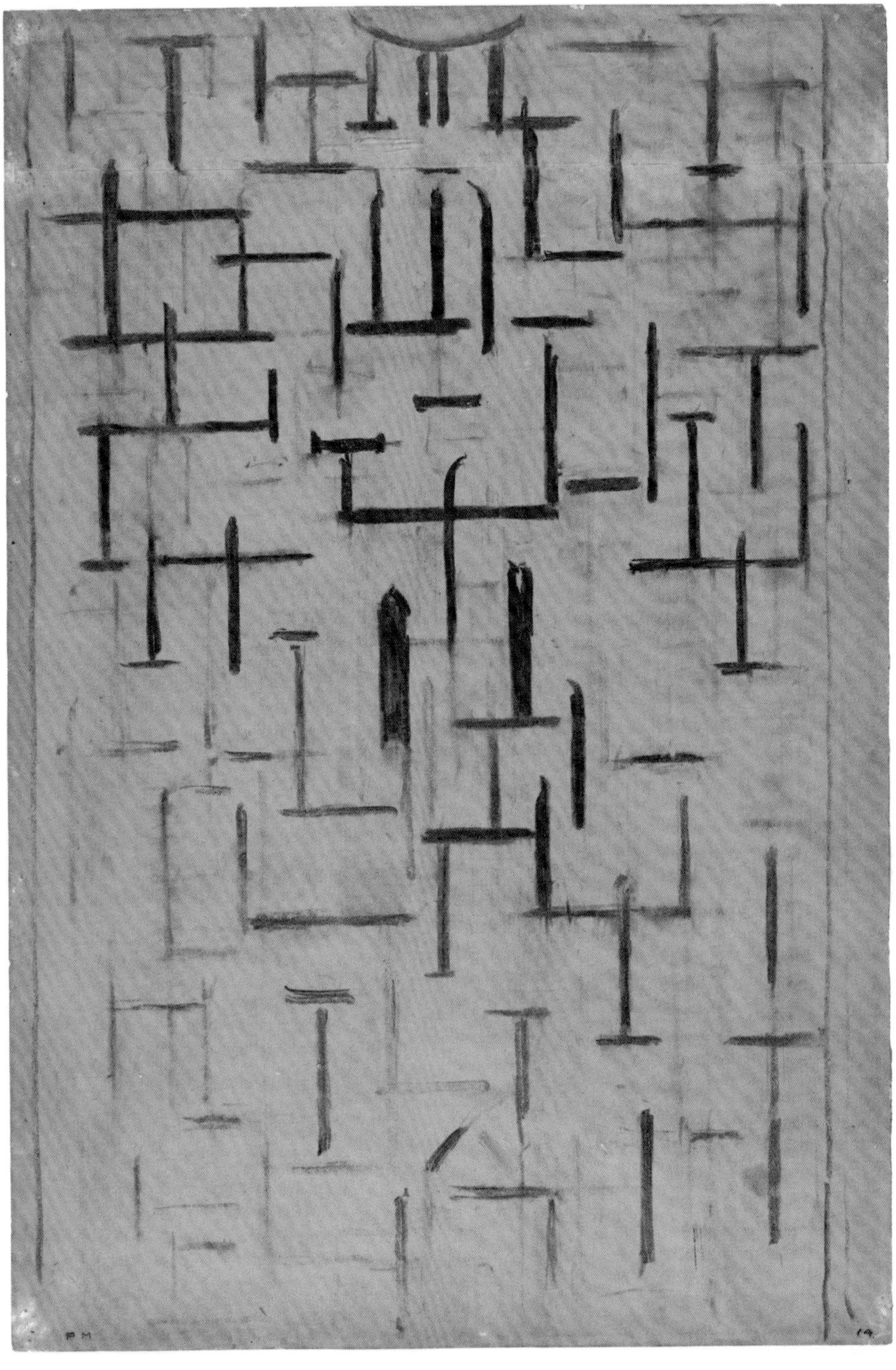

Fig. 57. Piet Mondrian, CHURCH FACADE 5.

3. PATTERNING

When the need to reproduce is eliminated and the artist is free to do as he or she pleases, many choose to highlight patterning, or structural elements, which, divorced from the skin that covers them, reveal the armature the artist finds beautiful or interesting. Here is an example in a painting by the playful Paul Klee. We care not whether his reference is to a particular building or group of buildings or the time of day. We see it as an elegant pattern of lines and areas of color. Locality or temporality is simply irrelevant in this early work of modern art. In this case, we might say that the "decorative" has usurped the "descriptive."

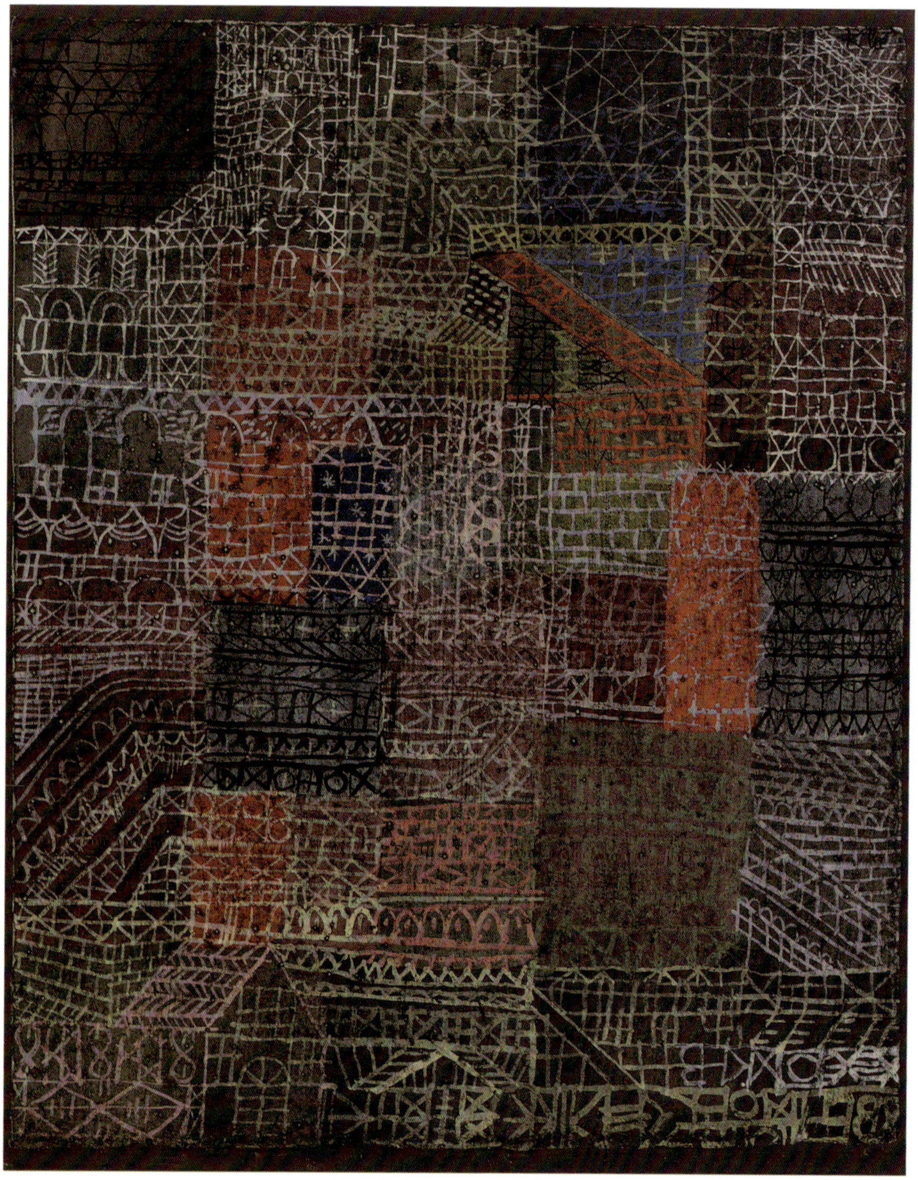

Fig. 58. Paul Klee, STRUCTURAL II.

4. DECONSTRUCTION

Another way to express this is to say that the artist is deconstructing his or her subject. This is very evident in Cubist works where the painter works from an actual subject, like a still life, but, instead of reproducing the components, he or she takes it apart and then reassembles only certain of the elements to create a composition. The artist is choosing, from the assortment of colors and forms he sees, only those that are of particular interest. Creating the illusion of the collection of objects is not the primary goal, and, in fact, the space captured in these works is often abbreviated so the composition appears almost flat—or as if its planes (like boards or cards) were stacked one on top of the other.

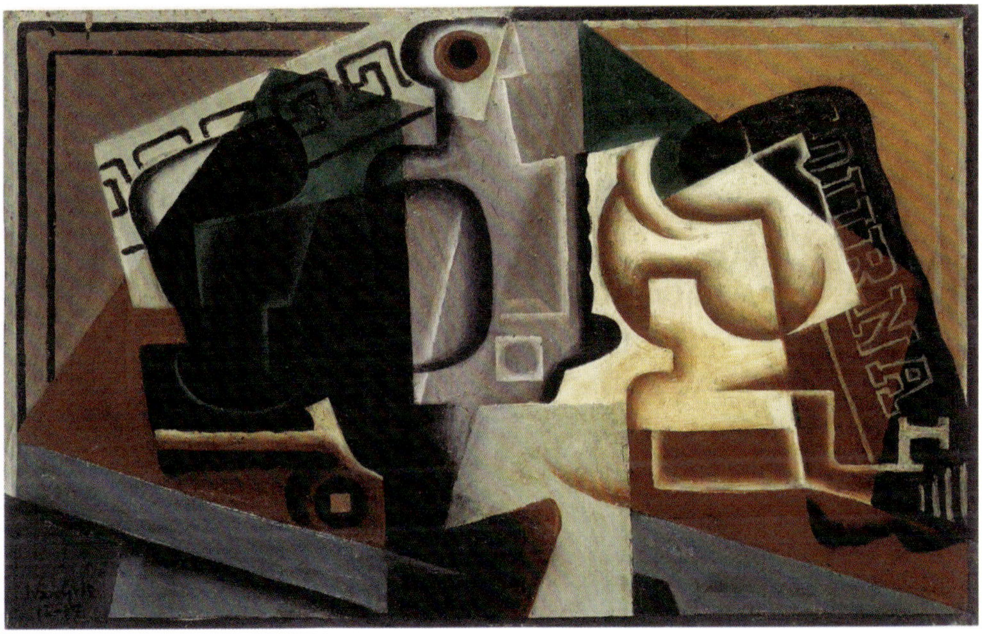

Fig. 59. Juan Gris, GLASS AND CARAFE.

5. SHAPE MAKING

We describe a three-dimensional object as possessing "form," that is, length, width, and depth. A **shape**, on the other hand, is imaginary. It is a flat, enclosed area created by making a line that returns to its starting point. It can be geometric, like a square or circle, or organic or free-form. There are an unlimited number of shapes possible.

Many abstract works of art are composed of shapes. Sometimes these shapes are reminiscent of objects and indeed, artists may take an actual subject—still life, landscape, or figure—and extract out of it a collection of shapes. The resulting work may suggest the objects and be semiabstract or not. If the actual forms are not alluded to, the shapes on the canvas appear as flat, decorative rather than representational, and we would call it abstract. Often, shape-filled paintings will also contain lines in various thicknesses.

Here is another Cubist work by a lesser-known painter, Georges Valmier, which is composed of stacked planes and flat shapes. The work is called *Tulips*. The artist was obviously more interested here in a composition of interesting shapes rather than a bunch of pretty flowers.

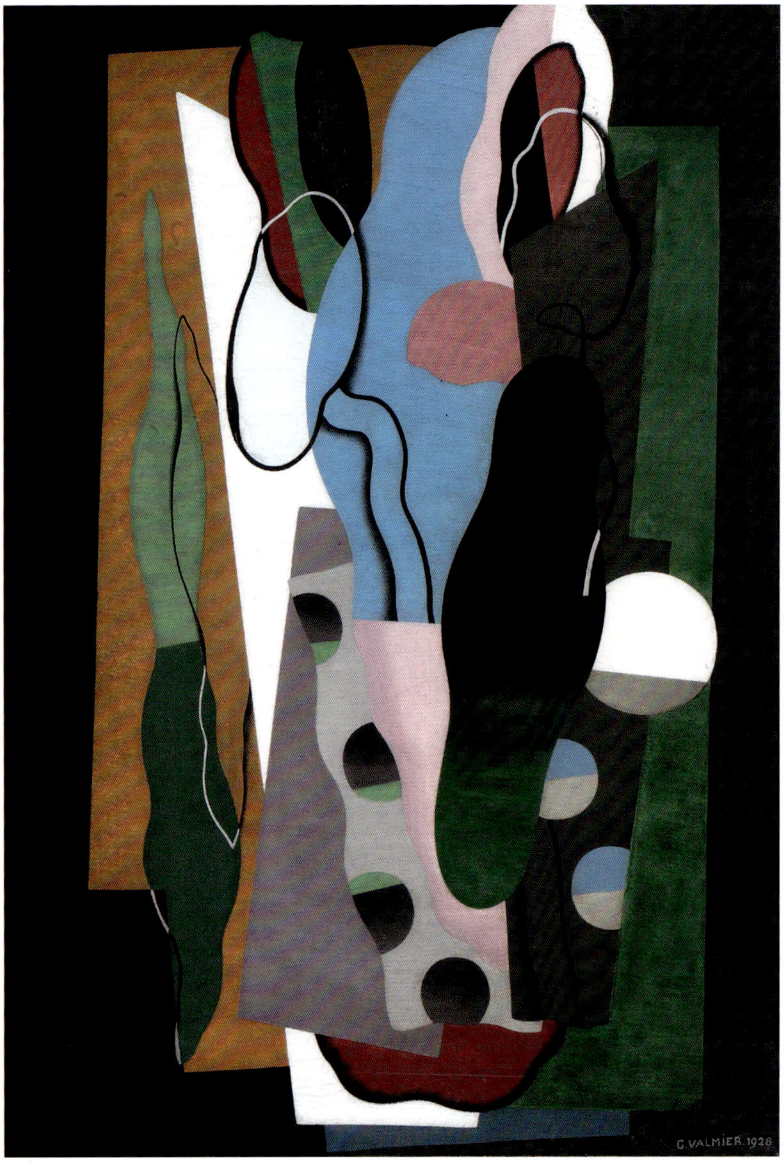

Fig. 60. George Valmier, LES TULLIPES.

5. THE FEEL

Painting is a very sensual exercise, or it can be. The paint itself is a wondrous medium that—based on the way it is applied, the surface used, the hue's opacity or translucence, and how all this is combined and orchestrated—can be a feast for the senses. Many painters are enthralled with the sensuality of the medium and find it more captivating and important than the subject itself and the rendering of said subject.

In *Joy of Art*, I devoted an entire chapter to discussing the polarities of artists in general, from a variety of scale and criteria, one being the spectrum from most romantic to most classical. To reiterate, the classicist strives for harmony and symmetry and is probably more formal and careful, cooler and more controlled, than his cousin the romanticist, who is looser, more subjective in his/her approach, and probably more informal and emotive.

When these personalities take to modern art, you would be more likely to find the classicist in the Cubist or geometric abstraction sphere, and the romantic letting the paint flow in an expressionist manner. These are generalizations, of course, and most artists fall somewhere in the middle of the spectrum and their works have attributes of both.

Nonetheless, sensuality is one of the main drivers for abstract painting and for one so inclined, the possibility for creating interesting and magnificent applications of paint itself (what we call texture) may be the point. Some of these painters fall under categories labeled Lyrical Abstraction, Gestural Abstraction, or Color Field Painting. These styles will be elaborated in future chapters.

As you read more in this volume, you will be able to identify painters who are so driven by the incredible juiciness, vivacity, and grittiness of the paint and other materials that it has become the raison d'être for their very work. In this regard, in the section of living artists, pay particular attention to the work of Malcolm Liepke.

6. SYMBOLISM

A cousin of "essences" is what we might call symbolism, something that stands in for something else. This is another characteristic and way to look at many works of modern art.

A good example prized by many modern artists is Picasso's *Guernica.*

This is not an abstract work, but it is a modern painting. Exhibited in 1939, it made a huge impression on museum audiences and on many modern painters. The size, neutral colors, and particularly the expression of the theme of the horrors of war using symbolic allusions in such a dramatic fashion stirred and inspired many modern painters. I have read that Jackson Pollock (who we associate with his dense pour-and-spill paintings) was so enthralled by *Guernica* that he made many variations on the theme.

Anyhow, look for symbolism in modern works of art. And refer to a discussion later in this chapter about Mondrian's theories on the subject.

7. FROM LANDSCAPE TO ABSTRACTION: ONLY A SMALL STEP

As I mentioned, any subject can be treated in an abstracted fashion, and it is my contention that every work of art begins as abstract, regardless of the subject. Building any object-based figurative work requires in its early steps just putting down paint, and before any specificity is achieved, we have an abstract work.

Given that, there is no subject more adaptive to abstraction than that of landscape. What is any landscape composed of? Imagine a simple seascape: sand, sea, and sky. Three bands of color. Now if I paint it in the local colors—tan, green and blue, you will say it is a landscape. But what if I change up the colors? Make a band of purple to represent the sand, red for the sea, and yellow for the sky. Do you still see it as a landscape or not?

Going further, what makes those bands of color interesting? Perhaps it is the way I apply the paint, by the texture, by color variations within the masses of color? Are you conjuring up a memory of a Mark Rothko? Do his colored triads now ring a bell?

Have a look at this painting by Degas and tell me what you see. Mountains, a Valley, Rocks, Sky?

Yes, perhaps. But could you not as easily answer and say I see a purple piercing green, a band of white, a sumptuous design? This painting is just a breath away from being an abstract composition.

Landscape is an easy lob into abstraction, and many abstract paintings are reminiscent of specific places without being descriptive of them. Abstraction from landscape or expressive of landscape is usually referred to as lyrical abstraction or gestural abstraction or color field. We'll get into those fine distinctions in a later chapter. Suffice it to say, landscape and abstraction are the very best of friends.

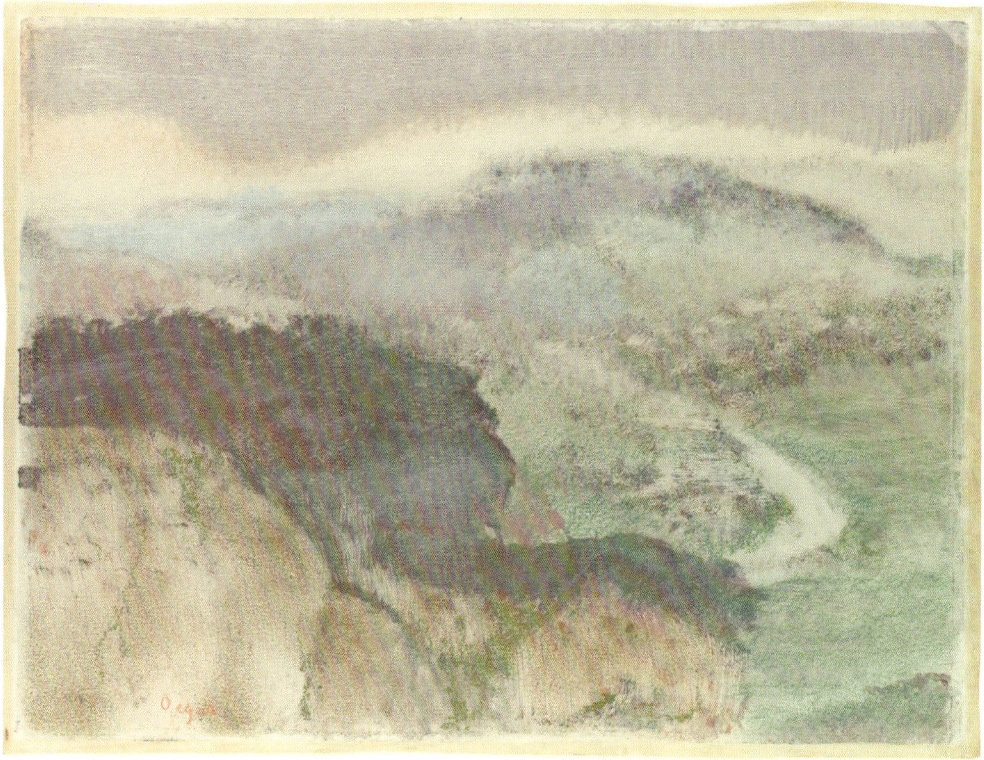

Fig. 61. Edgar Degas, IMAGINARY LANDSCAPE.

Here's a good example of how with a bit of reductive painting, an apparent landscape can morph into an abstract painting. We are lucky to have two Richard Diebenkorn works to compare and contrast. The first is called *Ocean from a Window* from 1959, and the second, *Studio Window Ocean Park*, created in 1970.

In the first work we clearly see a perspective of an interior view—notice the cup on a table—to an exterior one. Richard Diebenkorn was a follower of Henri Matisse, who painted many interior-exterior window views. This theme is particularly resonant for a colorist as it encourages the artist to find sunlit tones for the exterior while simultaneously choosing more tonal colors for the portion of the canvas representing the interior. This theme also makes for an interesting composition.

In this Diebenkorn work, we see clearly marked horizontal divisions—earth, water, and sky—that remind us of the traditional rule of thirds, a division of landscape paintings into three horizontal areas. Diebenkorn adds a linear element to this work to identify the window. The color is fairly local.

When we view the second work, we see that the interior and exterior have become one—instead of in and out, we have just a composition of shapes and though one

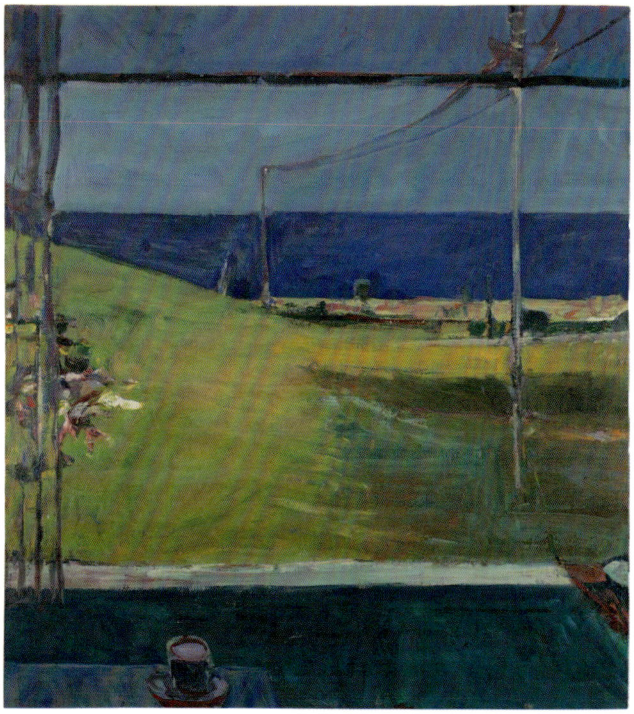

Fig. 62. Richard Diebenkorn, OCEAN FROM A WINDOW.

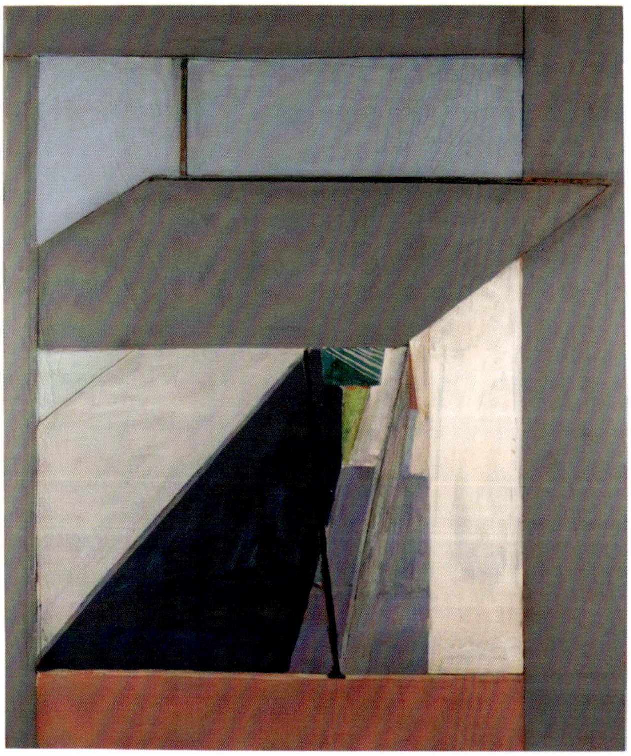

Fig. 63. Richard Diebenkorn, STUDIO WINDOW OCEAN PARK.

might identify a rectangle that is the window, one of the planes of color violates that shape. What we have now are flat areas of color, simplified shapes, and straight lines. The window itself and the view from the window have now morphed into an abstract design.

As is the wont with many modernist painters, once the process of simplification begins, it is likely to continue. In the case of Diebenkorn, he proceeded to make a whole series of even more rarefied and reductionist works from his studio window overlooking Ocean Park, where the painting of the light in gleaming and tonal mixtures fills even fewer and simpler divisions of the canvas.

I encourage you to look online at this series. It will show you a great deal about how the artist in a sense plays that game of "telephone." In each iteration of the subject, the message gets reduced even further until it barely resembles in any concrete fashion the original inspiration. That is, in a nutshell, the very story of abstraction.

8. VISUAL PRIORITIES

In an earlier chapter we referred to the expression "art for its own sake." Most modern artists will tell you that realistic painting makes use of pictorial elements like color, form, composition, and texture, but these are in the context and for the purpose of representing a familiar object, like a person, animal, mountain, rocks, flowers, etc. The pictorial elements are present, but they are not primary. In abstract painting, and even in looser representational work like Impressionism, the focus is on these elements primarily.

For Monet, who painted the haystacks at all times of day, his subject was not haystacks. It was the color of the light.

For Picasso, who painted the woman's face from the front and side in the same work, the subject was not the woman. It was the interesting shapes that defined space.

For Klee, who painted all kinds of things in the most whimsical way, the subject was not the things. It was the whimsy.

Modern artists want you to see the pictorial elements as primary. Their subject is the light, color, shape, composition—not the subject, e.g. the woman, landscape, or building. These are only premises or prompts the artist uses to display his true interest. In other words, art for its own sake.

9. MAKING A STATEMENT

When we think of making a statement or expressing an idea, writing is the art form that comes first to mind. We can express ideas with such complexity with words, can't we? Can we express as well in pictures?

Well, the saying is that "a picture is worth a thousand words." But is it really?

The answer is, it can be but doesn't have to. We can read a lot into a picture that may not necessarily be there, can't we? And a great deal can be inferred about what the artist might have been thinking, but we can be wrong about this. We usually need more information to know for sure.

I am excited in upcoming chapters of this book that we will have the opportunity to ask the artist, "What were you thinking when you made this work?" It will be edifying.

But remember that sometimes when you read a book, find something in it, and tell the author what it has made you think of, he will say, "I didn't think of that, but I can see what you are saying."

In other words, the artist may not know himself what his work conveys.

There are pictures that aim to deliver a specific message, and that message is pretty clear. Picasso's *Guernica* surely delivers some undeniable truths about the horror of war. Cartoons can deliver a very concrete message, though many of them use words to enhance and make that message clear.

Modern artists also sometimes use words in their pictures, and we will be looking at some examples, and also studying this whole facet of modern art—the desire to make a statement, be it societal, political, philosophical. Sometimes the statement is just the very point of making the artwork at all.

RECAP

I hope these nine examples give you the first inkling of the motivations that led to the many, many iterations of modern art that were to come flooding out of artists' studios once the beast was released. We will go into a lot more specificity as we look at the artist's intentions and processes in depth.

Sometimes the reasons to do something are not the first apparent. Instead, **what not to do** is the driving force that propels one into a new direction. This is very much true in the creation of modern art. Artists knew they *did not want* to copy, make realistic pictures. So, what did they *want* to do?

Well, it took time to arrive at the replacement.

Here are a few of the things modern artists **DID NOT WANT**:

1. They did not necessarily want to be neat.
2. They did not want to make pretty pictures.
3. They didn't want to paint what other people wanted.
4. They did not want to use formulas.
5. They did not want to be perfect.
6. They did not want the work to look "finished" (in other words, dead).
7. They did not want to do what others were doing.

Now, here are a few things modern artists **DID WANT**:

1. They wanted above all to express themselves.
2. They wanted to do something that was personal.
3. They wanted to be authentic.
4. If they had to choose truth or beauty, they would choose truth.
5. They wanted to experiment and improvise.
6. They wanted to extol the pictorial elements.
7. They wanted to create something "sublime."

Did they succeed? Was modern art the answer? Was it all worth it?

That's where we go now.

FORERUNNERS TO MODERN ART: REALISM AND ART NOUVEAU

In our last chapter on originality, we took a glance at Courbet, who was a leader in the Realism movement from 1848 to 1900. Focusing on devotion to subject, authenticity, and the common man, this period was a kind of purification of representational art. It was followed for a short time by its antithesis, the playful and decorative Art Nouveau period, which took the stage from 1890 to 1910.

Both Realism and Art Nouveau were forerunners to modern art, each in their own way, Realism for its purity of intention and Art Nouveau for its willingness to import the decorative into art and also to legitimize other art media, which would certainly play a much more prominent part in modern art.

I introduce you to an Art Nouveau-influenced painting of this period made by a not-too-well-known British painter and sculptor, Frederic Leighton. He was an individual born into privilege, not a starving artist by any means. In fact, he was paid a family allowance through his life and was granted a peerage—and became a baron—for one day only, as he passed away one day after this distinction was granted.

Leighton was rather an academician, having studied at the Accademia in Florence, but this particular work—*Flaming June*—is a jewel, absolutely stunning. Leighton's

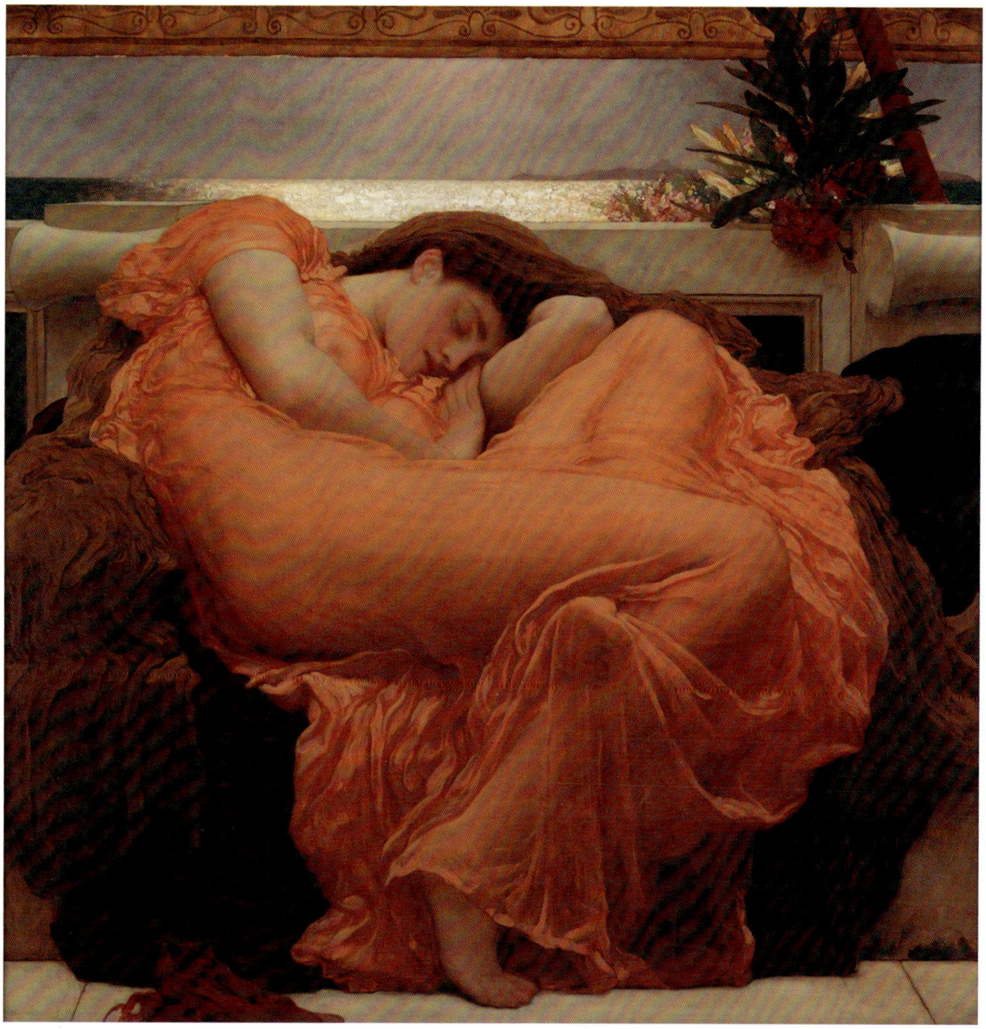

Fig. 64. Sir Frederic Leighton, FLAMING JUNE.

studiousness comes to bear in this beautifully drawn figure of a young woman crouched in sleep. What makes it so extraordinary is the orange "flaming" dress he has created, remarkably in gooey oil paint, the meticulous folds of the fabric so exquisitely detailed.

Though I am not a particular fan of academic work, finding it often stiff, I bow to the achievement here. It is a triumph in painting, luscious and a party for the eyes. Do you find it as splendid as I do? Once again, I remind you, reader, not to become overly enamored with any period or style. In every era, every time, every manner of work, there is something that will pierce your preconceptions and shine as the extraordinary human accomplishment that it is. Look everywhere to find these jewels.

We now turn to some of the major movements that followed, where modernity flowered like some phantasmagorical garden fed on supercharged plant food. The decades from the late nineteenth century into the early twenty-first have produced some remarkable works of visual art and we will hit some of the highlights here.

IMPRESSIONISM: TURNING ON THE LIGHT (1865–1885)

The movement that begins to catapult art into modernity is Impressionism. Impressionism took hold in Europe, predominantly in France, from 1865 to 1885, and then spread its wings and morphed into several significant movements that modified its focus.

We have already mentioned the Claude Monet work that catapulted Impressionism into consciousness. Visualize, if you will, Monet and his pals—Renoir, Sisley, Bazille, Manet, Pissarro, Cézanne, and others—hanging out in a Paris café and sharing the details of their daily work. How excited they must have been with their glorious new experiments in plein air painting.

They had discovered the light and what fun it was to take the paintbox outside and just paint the great outdoors. Can you picture the easels all set up in the poppy fields of France? I have had the extreme pleasure of painting those poppies and sunflowers in the little villages a short distance from Paris, and in the south of France, and it is a delight. Add to that the elegant gentlemen and damsels in their nineteenth-century finery, what a subject indeed. But remember, we have already seen those Impressionist paintings; these artists were creating them for the first time.

And nothing quite like this had come before. There were intimations from other painters: perhaps Turner with his quasi-Impressionist paintings of stormy seas, or Delacroix, with his vibrant color mixtures. These Impressionists went all out and made a number of innovations that together comprise the menu of this movement. Let's enumerate them here.

Firstly, as I have mentioned, they went outside to observe the light and paint al primo, not, as their forerunners had accomplished by virtue of memory. Imagine, if you will, being in a dark house for a long time and then one day, opening the door and stepping outside. The light would strike you as absolutely blazing, and you might even unconsciously raise your hand to your eyes to protect them.

Portraying this blazing light accurately demanded some changes in painting procedure. You needed a light ground to start, not a dark or mid tone previously employed by painters. Since you were no longer working from the shadows up, you needed very few dark paints and a predominance of light mixtures. Your value gamut would be relatively short. Impressionists eschewed the use of black paint (with the exception of Manet, who was the master of black and used it convincingly) but could add a little black into their light mixtures to create more tonal colors if they wished.

They did not view the scenes they painted as painters of old—with a primary image in the foreground and a less realized, and therefore more insignificant, background. No, this would not do because in Impressionist thought, there was no background—every note was equally important.

In the spirit of al primo painting, direct building up of paint, they did not paint sequentially, allowing the paint to dry and then adding additional layers or glazes. They painted wet paint into wet paint, laying the color mixtures side by side, and not blending them. They believed that the eye of the viewer would do the blending and feel the vibrations these notes of color created. In what was rather revolutionary thinking, they set out to create visual effects, not representations or copies of objects.

Understand that creating an effect rather than making an object is like playing three-dimensional chess. It is a form of advanced thinking. That is why, in a nutshell, Impressionism is the first real foray into Modernism. The Impressionists are not painting things. They are painting a "play" of light, which is active (rather than passive), connotes movement and change, and requires one to think ahead, planting a foil for the notes to come.

My painting teacher, Norman Raeben, taught this in his classes. He explained that if you were attempting to paint a red flower, say, in a certain kind of, let's say, bluish light, you had to prepare the canvas to receive that red. Instead of putting down the red, you would hunt for the color that would make that red pop—maybe it would be a sour green. The green is the foil. When you finally add the red into the green environment, it will sing. He called this process "indirection," taking the long route to "arrive" at the destination.

One of the features of Impressionist works that I love are the shadows, which are not dark holes because they are portrayed as part of the light, are painted tenderly, and include color. Notice the color of the shadows when you look at Impressionist paintings. I am particularly fond of reflected light softening the shadows in many lovely Impressionist works; Degas was a master of these.

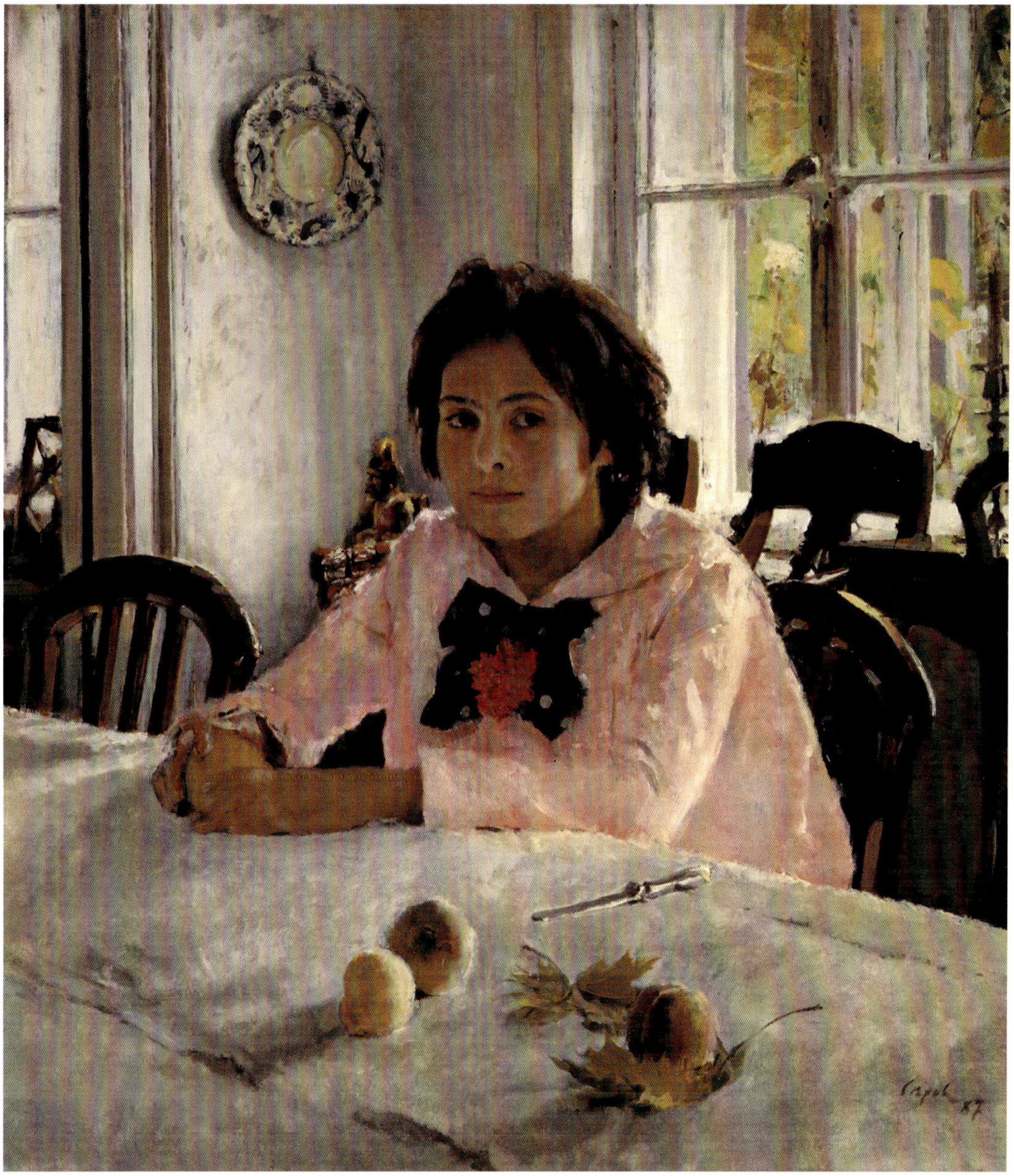

Fig. 65. Valentin Serov, GIRL WITH PEACHES.

Be reminded that the camera was a relatively new tool to this group of painters. Now that a camera could make a representation of a scene or figures, artists had to wonder what they could do that the camera could not. Just being accurate or making a believable rendering was no big accomplishment anymore.

The cameras of this era could not do one thing that the painters realized they could. With new colors available to them like cobalt and cerulean blue, viridian, different yellows and roses, and a new and improved way of applying them on the canvas, artists could create not just lifelike resemblances, but instead, beautifully subtle symphonies of color. Gorgeous surfaces that vibrated are the signature of Impressionism. A veritable visual feast of light and color.

We associate Impressionism with France, but the movement spread around the world. Here is a painting by a Russian painter, Valentin Serov. It was painted in 1887 and is not a plein air work, but exhibits some of the lovely qualities of Impressionist painting, particularly the reflected lights. I love the composition with the window reflecting its light on the back of the figure and on the items on the table, the back of the chairs, and the wall. It is unusual with the light coming from the rear of the figure.

Impressionism is a movement that will never die. In later chapters we will look at living artists who employ Impressionist thinking and protocols in their work today.

POST-IMPRESSIONISM: PERSONALITY ENTERS THE PICTURE (1885–1910)

Impressionism was a revelation, and it opened the door to modernism. But artists are ego-driven and have the desire to put their own take on everything. It was inevitable that once the door was opened, each artist would want to assert their personality and drive the movement in a different direction. And that is exactly what happened.

There were many commonalities. No one was going to forsake color now that it had become a star player. Some had a yen for more structure and form, lost in the blur of the Impressionist's atmospheric color. Some craved a more interesting subject. Each artist wanted to put their stamp on the genre and accomplished just that. A natural progression, the next step.

Some memorable art was created in this period. We've already had a look at a few: the dreamy Henri Rousseau and singular Vincent van Gogh. In each case we will be looking at the singular contribution that informed each artist's work and advanced

Impressionism into other movements down the line. Every artist has much more to recommend his work, but we are isolating here their individuality which made their work unique.

Paul Cézanne (1839–1906): Shape and Form

This is an excellent moment to consider how the illusion of solidity is created on a flat surface. Think of a geometric shape, like a square or rectangle; it is flat. If I want to turn the rectangle into a three-dimensional form, I can accomplish this by imagining planes—flat surfaces—and combining six of them to create a box. Likewise, a three-dimensional circle is called a sphere, and other three-dimensional geometric shapes include the cylinder and the cone.

Paul Cézanne sought solidity in his life and in his art. He wanted the figures and objects he painted to have greater solidity and to be more three-dimensional. To accomplish this, he laid his brushstrokes of paint in such a way that they represented planes (surfaces) and together these strokes created the illusion of form.

He created the illusion of objects by visualizing them as three-dimensional geometric shapes. He took complex forms found in nature, simplified them, and attached his pieces of paint to the imaginary forms. In a sense, he was building the forms with the paint.

It is easy to see how Cézanne's concentration on geometric forms could be a bridge to Cubism, in which painted planes were not just the foundation for painting the object, but remained as flat shapes that described the space in an entirely new way.

Cézanne's pictures still defined figures and objects, but in a new way that would influence and give permission for other painters to dispense with the illusion altogether. He was a seminal artist and an artist's artist, much admired by his contemporaries and descendants.

Here is an example of a landscape painting by Cézanne. Can you see how his notes lying side by side construct this image in such a craftsmanlike fashion? He was like a carpenter of paint. Each dab of paint is applied in a different direction of the stroke, with consciousness of what it represents, the plane that it defines. These planes or surfaces create the illusion of form.

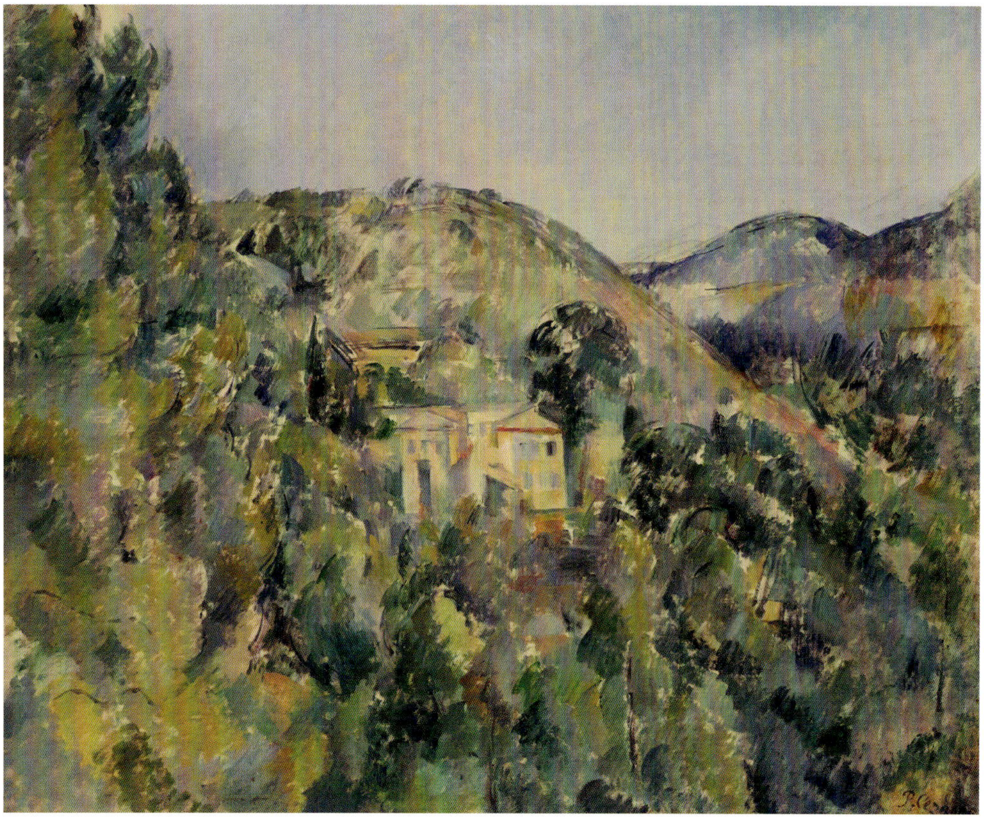

Fig. 66. Paul Cézanne, VIEW OF THE DOMAINE ST. JOSEPH.

Georges Seurat (1859–1891)

What Cézanne is to form, Seurat is to color. We all know his wonderful work, *A Sunday Afternoon on the Island of La Grande Jatte*, which may be the most famous work executed in this period by a post-Impressionist painter. It took two full years to complete, and this in the life of an artist who only lived to be thirty-one. This was not a work that was painted al primo, from life. It was concocted from numerous preliminary drawings, some sketched from people in the park, reconfigured and refined to create this remarkable tableau that seems to reverberate. It is a huge work: 6.6 feet by 9.8 feet.

Seurat was a scientist of sorts, and studied theories of color by various thinkers, most particularly the American physicist Ogden Rood, who promoted the idea that complementary colors placed in pairs would vibrate and create a sensation of rich color. This idea led Seurat to apply this theory to his technique, doing meticulously just what Rood suggested.

Seurat entertained theories by others as well. A French chemist, Michel Chevreul, wrote that the eye could do the mixing for the artist: two colors close together would produce a third color. Another color theorist, Charles Blanc, advised a scientific methodology, suggesting painters plan and strategize the effect each color would have on the whole. Taking color theories a step further, mathematician Charles Henry lectured on the symbolic meaning of color. Seurat purportedly attended these lectures.

Most artists use color intuitively. They know that warm colors come forward and cool colors recede. Red complements green, orange complements blue, and yellow complements violet. But Seurat took this a step beyond. He applied the formulas consciously, with deliberation. He had a name for this process; he called it *chromoluminarism*.

Seurat posited that if he used warm colors and directed lines upward, he would achieve a positive emotion of happiness. If he balanced light and dark tones and warm and cold colors and used horizontal lines, he would conjure peacefulness or equilibrium. And if he used cold and dark colors and lines veering downward, he would connote sadness. The application of the notes of color that replicate vibrations of light is referred to as **pointillism.**

This seems very formulaic and obvious now, but no one can deny that regardless of his reasoning, he created some memorable works of art.

Let's have a look at a Seurat painting in which *La Grande Jatte* is featured in the background.

This painting has an interesting history. In making it, Seurat was thumbing his nose at critics who disparaged his now-famous *A Sunday Afternoon on the Island of La Grande Jatte*. Critics found that work, now lauded, not to be sufficiently realistic for their tastes. Apparently to challenge that view, Seurat made *Models* in a large size, previously reserved for paintings that depicted religious figures or celebrated people, instead of so-called genre paintings, usually much smaller, of common folk. He made sure to include an image of the famous painting in this descendant.

The same pointillist technique is utilized here, and you can clearly see how the dots of color seem to make the surface shimmer. See that effect on the wall of this painting, which appears purple but is actually made of dots of pink and blue. There is a static quality to the figures, as there is in the *Grand Jatte* painting. These paintings have

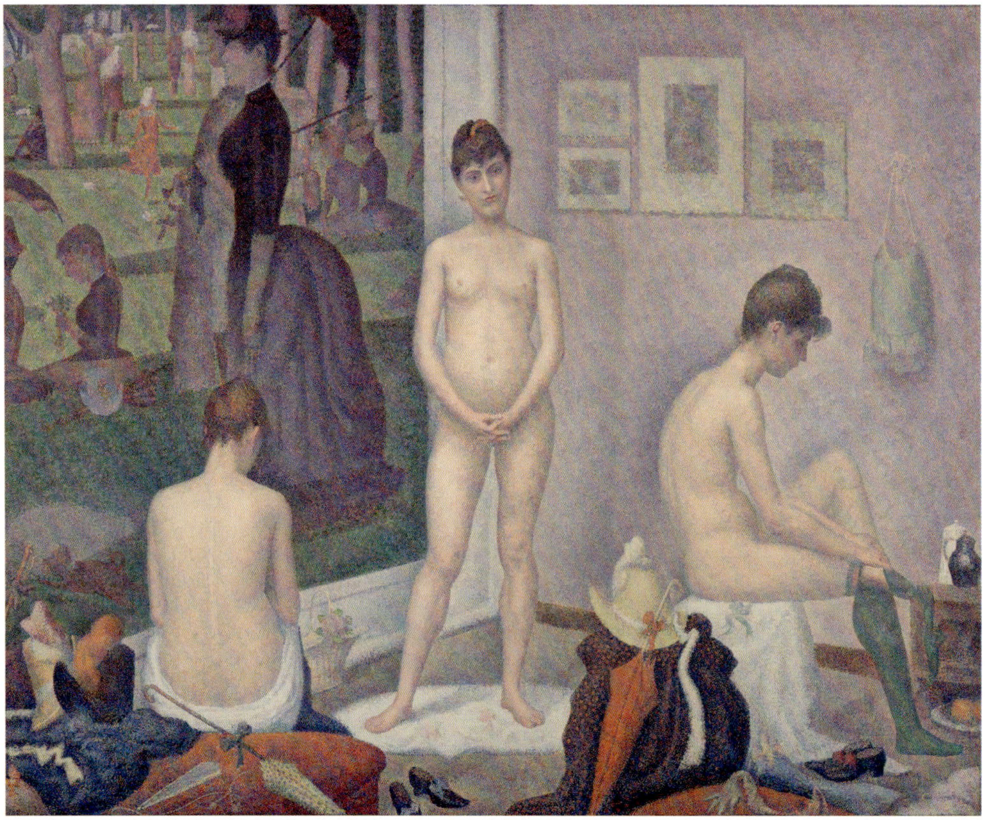

Fig. 67. Georges Seurat, MODELS.

always made me think of the child's game where everyone is told to move and then someone yells "freeze" and everyone becomes still, frozen in place.

If you have the opportunity, look at other pieces by Seurat, in particular his circus series, and you will find the same effect, which is really quite curious. But he gave us beautiful images in his short spin around the sun.

The Nabis: Edouard Vuillard (1868–1940) and Pierre Bonnard (1867–1947)

I confess. Though I have vowed to avoid judgment and applaud all visual art, I have a particular favorite in these two artists. I absolutely adore the work of Bonnard and Vuillard and consider them my personal mentors. I even created a painting in which I am sitting at the table with these two artists in my studio. They are with me as I stand at the easel. Here is that painting of mine, made in 2015 at the one-hundred-year anniversary of Bonnard's painting *Coffee*. In my painting, I am drinking coffee with my mentors.

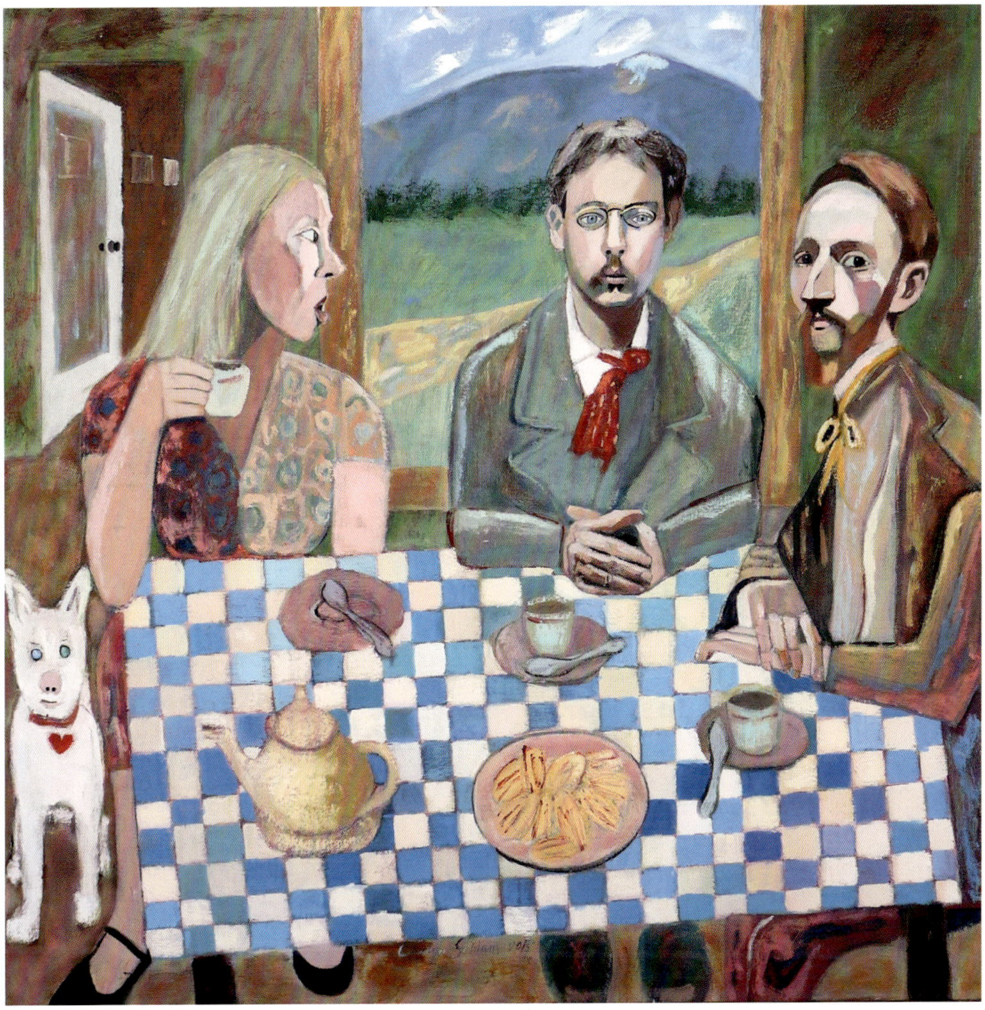

Fig. 68. Carolyn Schlam, COFFEE.

I love the work of Pierre Bonnard and Edouard Vuillard for many reasons. I am delighted to tell you why. I am not suggesting they should be your favorites, because we are all different and resonate to all manner of artworks.

Jean-Édouard Vuillard (1868–1940) was a quiet man who lived with his mother, a seamstress; she appears in many of his works. He and Bonnard were a special branch of the Nabi group (*Nabi* means prophet) referred to as Intimists, for the intimacy of their subject matter. This is one of the reasons I love their work. It is soaked in emotion as their subjects were objects of deep meaning, even love.

The Nabis were a post-Impressionist group of painters who followed the very extravagant Paul Gauguin, a symbolist. The Nabis too found symbolic meaning in their use of color, which was not scientifically based like Seurat but intuitive and deeply felt. This is another reason I love this work. The color palette is more sophisticated, not formulaic, and arises from deep sensitivity. Vuillard in particular used a limited palette, often tonal colors that are deeply satisfying and exquisite.

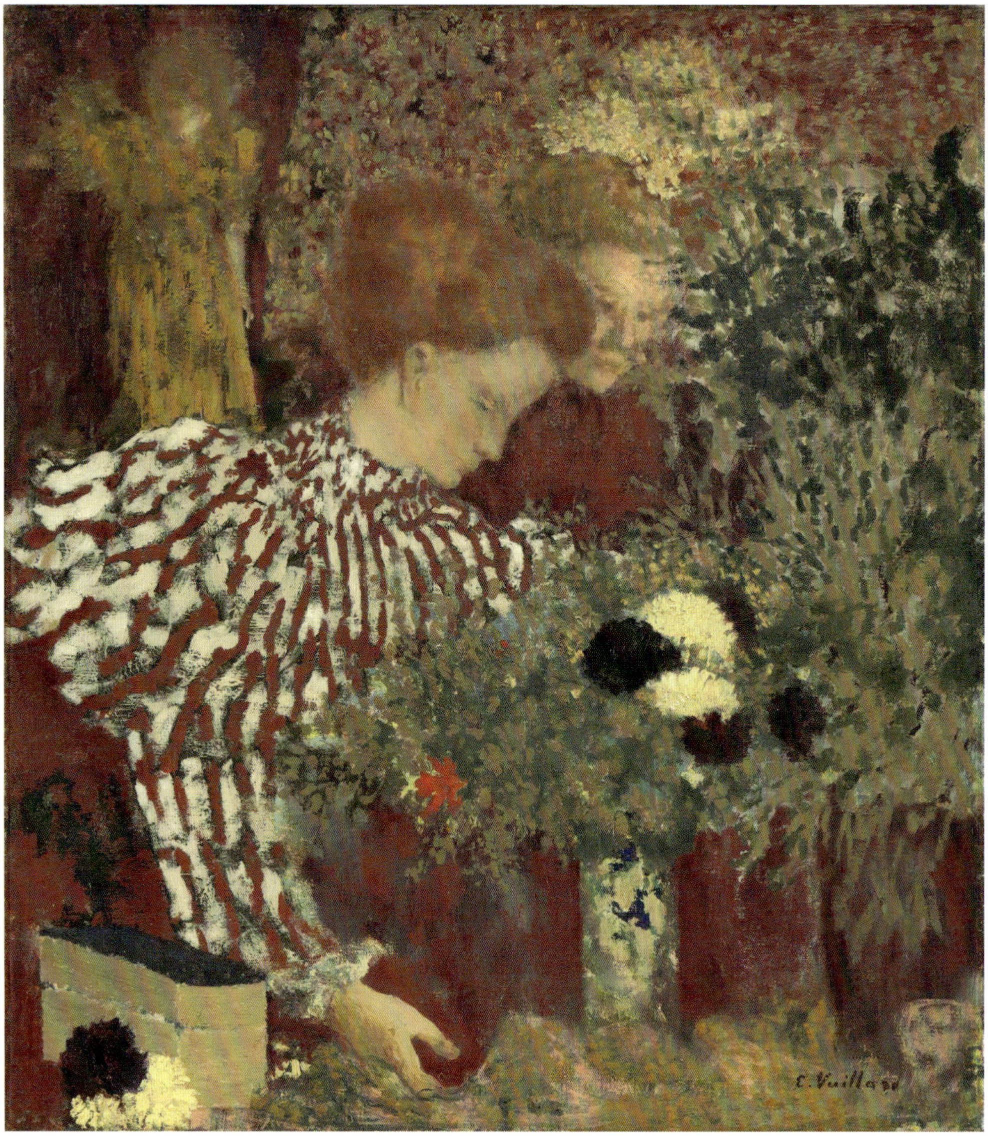

Fig. 69. Édouard Vuillard, WOMAN IN A STRIPED DRESS.

This work is a veritable tapestry of color and design. There are two women featured in the painting, but they are no more important than the flowers or the wallpaper. They are a part of the whole, blending together, so you cannot say where the flowers end and the woman's blouse begins. The predominant shades of alizarin and green are magnificent together, punctuated, as they are, by the light yellow of the flowers and the gold and flesh tones.

There is nothing here that is accidental. Vuillard has such an intuitive understanding of color that he predicates each color with a subtle tone. This creates a vibration of color—see this in the blouse and the leaves. I could look at it forever.

Vuillard excelled at many other things, including designing theater sets, murals, stained glass and ceramics, and graphic art. He was a designer as well as a painter, and it shows in his compositions. Cézanne was obsessed with form; Seurat a technical colorist, so how would you classify Vuillard and Bonnard?

Vuillard told us what mattered to him: relationships. The relationship between that alizarin and green recognized by the senses, the compositions that impart a satisfying and elegant design, the patterning that brings the notes into harmony. Every part, every note, chosen for the sake of the whole.

Both Vuillard and Bonnard were influenced by Japanese prints, and you can see why. Vuillard collected these prints and loved them for their simplicity. He also loved the way they incorporated designs, especially from nature, florals and vegetals, into their works. Bonnard shared this affection for Japanese style and was also on the same page as Vuillard when it came to the "whole painting conception." The figures he included in his works were also just part of the whole, as in this painting.

Paul Bonnard (1867–1947) used his wife as a subject in much the way Vuillard featured his mother; they had much in common. But Bonnard's work is sunnier, generally, and less tonal in color than that of his contemporary. It is interesting that I categorize his work as sunny—his colors are so light filled—because he did not paint en plein air. He was a studio painter, working from drawings and then calculating how to use the drawings in making a painting. He also worked on many pieces at once and did not determine their overall size in advance. He had canvas tacked up on the wall and only framed the work when it was finished.

In Bonnard's memory bank were the beautiful sunlit colors of gardens and flowers and he brought them with him into the studio. His color was extraordinarily rich, as evident in this painting where the women's faces are vividly red and frame that crack of blue water. I am getting a sunburn just looking at it.

These two images I have shown you are figurative, yes, but can you see that once the painter becomes enchanted with the light and color, the subject pales in importance? And once that happens, we are only a breath away from abstraction.

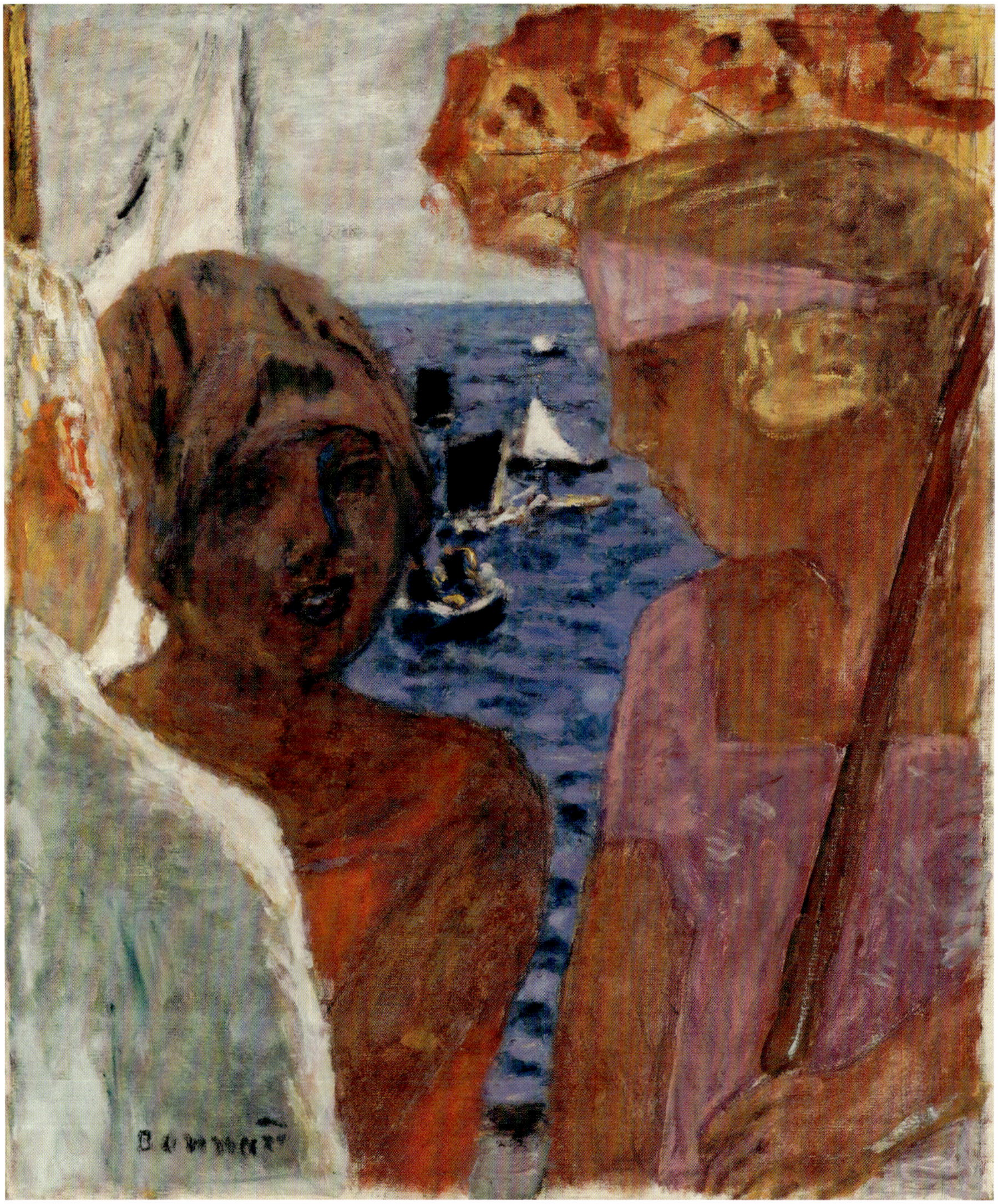

Fig. 70. Pierre Bonnard, CONVERSATION IN ARCACHON.

Though I recognize this and can celebrate the abstract elements, I personally prefer this stage to any other. I am happy the figure is visible even though it is in the context of a supercharged symphony of light and color. My predilection is for what I call "near abstraction," finding and seeing the abstract in the real and the real in the abstract. But that is just me.

I think of Bonnard as the father of my own painting. He died in 1947, the year I was born. In a strange way I feel he passed the baton to me. This is not unusual. All painters feel this way when they look at art that they love and admire. These painters are our ancestors, in essence, and they have thankfully left their legacy so we may carry on and move the art form forward.

FAUVISM: GOING WILD WITH COLOR (1900–1935)

It was perhaps inevitable that artists would decide to punch up the light-filled, sweet colors of Impressionism and so they did, in this stage of post-Impressionism called Fauvism. The "beasts" include Henri Matisse, André Derain, Maurice de Vlaminck, and to a lesser extent Henri Manguin, Georges Braque, Raoul Dufy, and Georges Rouault.

We will take a short peek here at two of these, Henri Matisse (1869–1954) and Georges Rouault (1871–1958), two artists in the movement but actually polar opposites in theme and mood. It is instructive to see that a similar technique can be utilized but still demonstrate a totally different perspective.

We have the joyous Matisse, a prodigious talent, who is regarded as a giant in modernism, a true colorist, whose simplified forms and exuberant color influenced many modern painters, principally the marvelous Diebenkorn. He worked with unbridled aplomb and his works exude vibrancy, gusto, and positive energy.

Even after Matisse became ill late in life, his creative life force persisted. Unable to stand at the easel and paint, and with the aid of assistants, he created his famous cutouts, work that opened an entirely new page in modern art. The cutouts (an art form also referred to as decoupage) rarefied Matisse's graceful designs as they eliminated any distracting details. This was presaged in his 1910 work *La Danse* in which the figures are like cutouts arranged on a simple colorful screen. These works, which I think of as Matisse distilled, have received wide acclaim from the public; a 2014 show of Matisse's cutouts at the Tate Modern was the first to attract more than half a million visitors.

On the other side of the spectrum, Georges Rouault took a bold turn away from the Impressionists by utilizing vibrant color and especially strong outlines in black, a verboten color to the light-obsessed. This may partially be explained by his interest and work with stained glass.

He was rather a serious figure, favoring religious subjects and the existentialism promulgated in his day, an emotional man whose work leaned toward expressionism. Those strong black outlines were to find a following in Abstract Expressionist works to come. See the work of Robert Motherwell and Franz Kline for the resurgence of those powerful black lines, now without the subject and color of Rouault.

As a sign of his intensity and commitment, would you be interested to learn that at the end of his life, he purposefully burned three hundred of his works of art? His reason: he did not believe he would live to finish them and would not leave them unfinished.

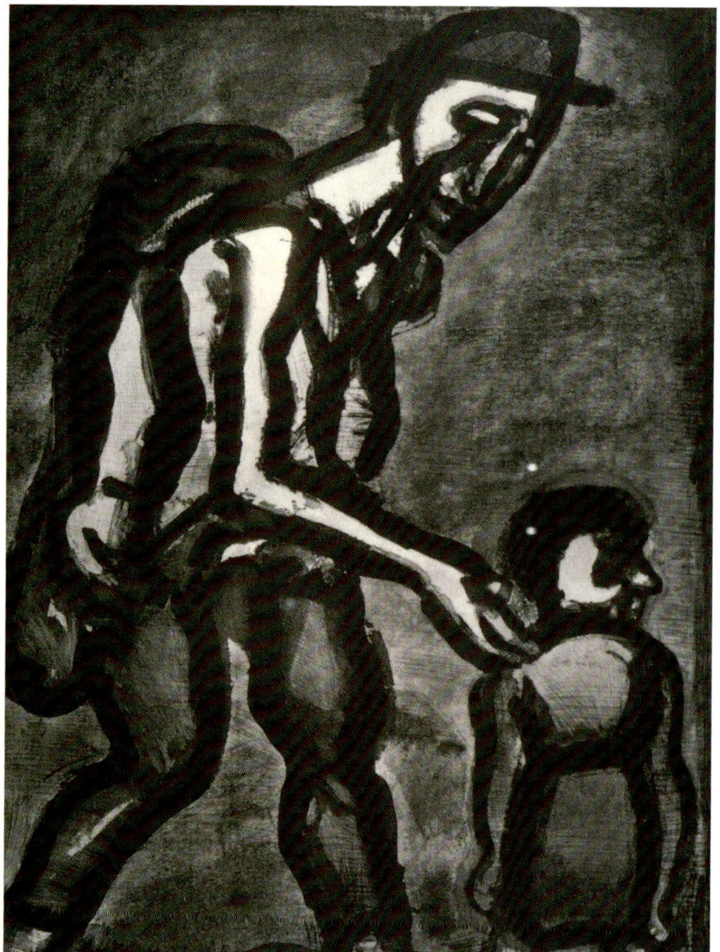

Fig. 71. Georges Rouault, SE RÉFUGIE EN TON COEUR.

EXPRESSIONISM: TURNING INWARD (1905–1920)

Artists, though usually forward looking, are of their time, and their experience as human beings is reflected in their artwork. The turning of the twentieth century was a turbulent time in which World War I (1914–1918), a devastating cataclysm, affected all who endured it. We may now forget that over 14 million people lost their lives in the conflict.

It is not surprising then, that the art movement that flourished during this period, especially in Europe, was Expressionism. Rejecting representational art, this was an avant-garde movement that focused on emotional expression, and in large part, negative emotions, or the "angst" so dominant in society.

This was a time of upheaval and distress. Sigmund Freud (1856–1939) was delving into the human psyche. Edvard Munch (1863–1944) had revealed his now-famous *Scream*. The emotional Vincent van Gogh had chopped off part of his ear. Fyodor Dostoevsky was examining the mind of a murderer.

Some of the new Expressionist paintings were fully abstract; many were not. But all were transmitters of deep emotion. Familiar names include the French Rouault, who was classified as both Fauvist and Expressionist, the latter because of the fervor of his bold religious work; and the Italian Amedeo Modigliani (1884–1920), whose paintings of lovely, sorrowful, long-necked women are memorable.

In Germany, where the movement began, we had the Blue Rider artists Franz Marc, August Macke, Paul Klee and Russian-born Wassily Kandinsky, the latter of whom did turn to full abstraction and influenced many artists to follow him. In addition to Kandinsky, Russian artists Chaïm Soutine (1893–1943) and Marc Chagall (1887–1985) also were considered Expressionists, though they worked after this initial period of Expressionism had ended.

Soutine and Chagall were both wonderful, individualist artists, and their work is full of feeling. Soutine is known for his loose painterly style, very animated surfaces, and lack of interest in anything remotely classical. He was a true romantic and Jewish, as was Chagall (and also Modigliani, by the way), and a larger-than-life figure. He is known for his paintings of animal carcasses, of all things, which he purportedly painted from life, having been inspired by a Rembrandt treatment of this inelegant subject.

Soutine's figures of unbeautiful women are precursors of the work of many figurative artists who would be called Expressives. Think the American Alice Neel (see one of her works in the Perspectives chapter) and the contemporary British artist Jenny Saville.

Though brimming with emotion, Chagall's work was the very opposite of the angst-driven early expressionists. He was a happy man who celebrated life in his art. His subjects were lovers, goats, the circus, musicians, flowers, all taking flight in a colorful whirlwind of happiness and gaiety. If he felt anxiety, he banished it from the world of his art. He must have loved the town where he was born and raised called Vitebsk, where Jews were then in the majority. He portrayed it in a beloved folk art manner.

So the Expressionists were champions of emotion, mostly negative, but in some cases, like Chagall, just the opposite. It is art dedicated to expression, regardless of origin or quality. We will have a look here at a work by a German Expressionist who is not as well known, Käthe Kollwitz (1867–1945). The drawing on torn paper absolutely reeks of emotion.

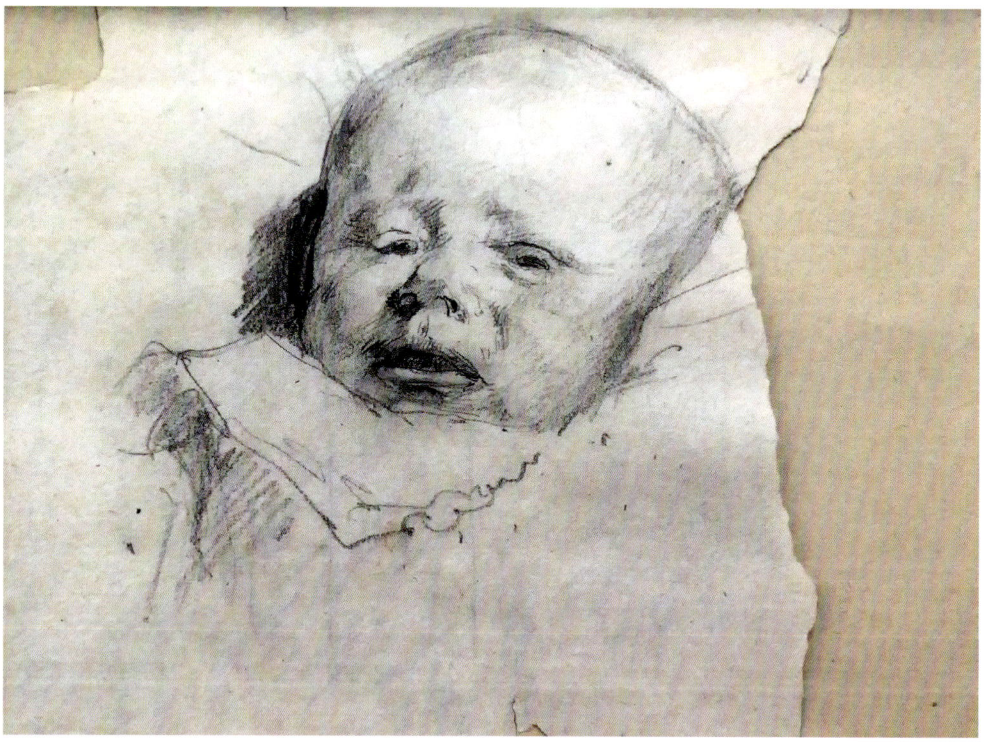

Fig. 72. Käthe Kollwitz, SLEEPING CHILD.

How poignantly she has imbued this drawing of a child with so much emotion. With very few strokes of the pencil, she has delivered so much—you can feel the child's discomfort so readily. It is truly remarkable. Can you pinpoint artists who are led by emotion? Can you see a difference in the quality of their line, the way they portray the subject?

CUBISM: LET'S BE SQUARE (1907–1914)

We have already looked at Paul Cézanne, his fascination with form, and his later simplification of forms into geometric three-dimensional figures. It was only a small step then to Cubism, a movement in which form was further deconstructed and presented as flat planes from different points of view in an attempt to visualize the object in the round. This deconstruction and reconstruction had an enormous effect on modern art, catapulting it away from the object totally and into many nonrepresentational directions.

The initial Cubism practitioners include, most notably, Pablo Picasso, Georges Braque, Juan Gris, Fernand Léger, Robert Delaunay, and Jean Metzinger. We have a perfect window into Cubism and how it was such a huge step into modernity in *Portrait of Mme Josette Gris.*

You can clearly see here how any verisimilitude to nature has vanished. Instead, we see a flattened image comprised of planes or surfaces where shapes have been superimposed. Think of a stack of cards, one atop the other, and on each we see a fragment of a picture. The three-dimensionality has been altered; see for instance how the chair rail of the wall is askew, as it lies in two different planes.

Other aspects of realism have also flown out the window. The eyes do not match. There is only one ear. The hair appears in one plane and disappears under another. There is only one shoulder. The leg held by the arm is stunted. There are interesting shapes that do not describe anything.

This is no longer a painting of a figure. It is drawn from a figure, but the artist has taken the elements he likes, left out those he did not, and made a composition that he found pleasing and interesting. Geometry for its own sake. You can clearly see how a few more hops and we are into totally abstract, geometric painting. We will see examples of this in later chapters.

With permission granted by Cubism to deconstruct the subject, artists could go in many directions based on their bent. More organic shapes. Semi abstraction. Full abstraction. Abstract Expressionism. Color field. Minimalism. It all follows out of

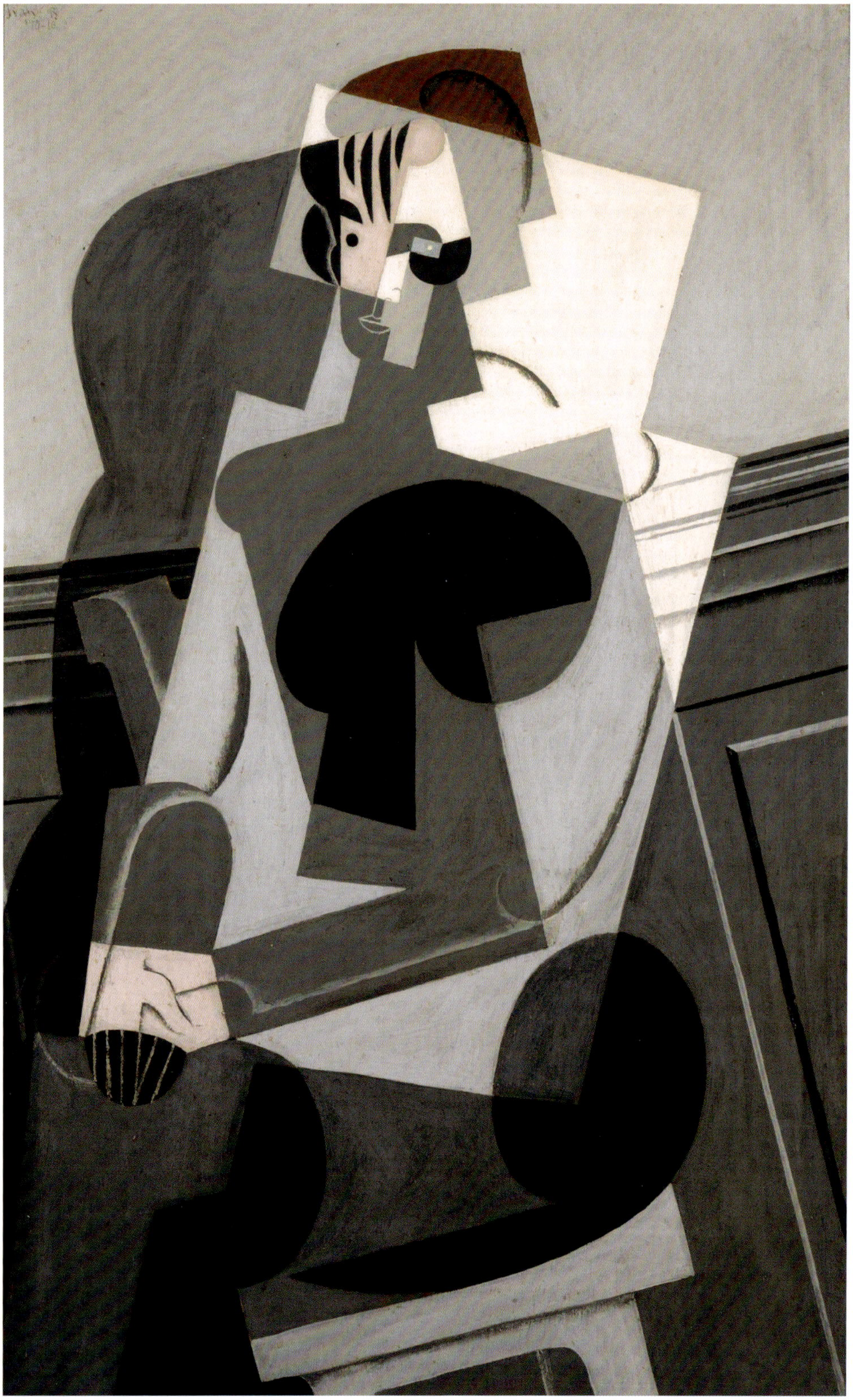

Fig. 73. Juan Gris, PORTRAIT OF MME JOSETTE GRIS.

this departure from representation, which itself had many iterations. We visit some of these departures now.

SURREALISM: I HAVE A DREAM (1916–1950)

Point. Counterpoint. Thesis. Antithesis. This is the story of art. Just as one group goes in one direction, i.e. the annihilation of realism, another goes to the opposite, hyperrealism or Surrealism. Exaggerated, fantastical realism. The dream. The nightmare.

This, and also another concept—that history repeats itself. Remember Hieronymus Bosch—we had a look at him in our chapter 3. A genius of the fifteenth century. Well, here we are again arriving at this juncture in the twentieth.

So, Surrealism that arose between World Wars I and II was not new, just reborn. It was a movement of people who clung to a kind of realism, but not in the naturalness of the subject, just in the treatment. The subject was something new, the stuff of dreams, fantastical combinations and impossible situations. You've seen them in all probability. All are under copyright and I cannot show them here but allow me to list some of the highlights. Just google the titles and have a look at these.

After you see them, you can psychoanalyze the artists if you wish. These works were created during the period that Sigmund Freud and his dream theories were in their heyday. It was a time when the subconscious seemed like a much more valuable source for the artist over the logical mind. These artists made these dreams/nightmares manifest:

Rene Magritte

GOLCONDA (1953): It's literally raining men in this well-known work. Magritte's signature bowler-capped men are falling from the sky.

THE TREACHERY OF IMAGES (1928): In this work we have a drawing of a large pipe and the words under it clearly say, "This is not a pipe."

What is this about? Is Magritte playing with us, trying to test our grasp on reality? This introduction of language, actual text into visual art is a modernist phenomenon, and you will find it a part of many later conceptual works.

Joan Miró

HARLEQUIN'S CARNIVAL (1924): More things falling, crazy shapes, squiggles, fish, monkeys. Supposedly, this does not come from an actual dream, just a made-up one.

Giorgio de Chirico

THE SONG OF LOVE (1914): This Italian precursor of Surrealism made this combination of three unrelated items: a bust, a rubber glove, and a ball. What was he thinking? We have no idea to this day. It is a never solved metaphysical puzzle.

And of course, last but the most recognizable Surrealist work of all:

Salvador Dalí

THE PERSISTENCE OF MEMORY (1931): If you are familiar with any Surrealist work, it is probably this one. The dripping clocks in the wasteland. What could Dalí possibly have meant? It is obvious he was making a statement about time, perhaps its undependability—or rather, our mortality?

Dream analysis is subjective, so I will leave these questions for you to answer as I move on to another art movement entirely.

ABSTRACT EXPRESSIONISM: AMERICAN EXCEPTIONALISM (1940s AND 1950s)

Most of the art movements we have looked at heretofore arose in Europe, particularly in France. But now we turn to art that is decidedly American. When you think about the characteristics of this movement, the qualities we usually assign to the ethos of the United States come clearly into focus.

The United States is a big country with quite a bit of square footage as compared to the countries of Europe. "Wide open spaces" is the term we use to describe it. And this is exactly what the Abstract Expressionists working in the mid twentieth century in the United States were re-creating on their canvases. And the canvases themselves were larger than those utilized by the European realists, romantics, and Surrealists, for that matter.

Taking a suggestion from the Surrealists' playbook, these American abstractionists were engaging in a kind of improvisational thinking. Freed from any need to make recognizable objects, they were led by psychological forces, not logical thought, favoring the unconscious, as the Surrealists attempted to accomplish with their "automatism."

On their large canvases, the Abstractionists got into the sensuality of the paint itself, with some, not only freeing themselves from the object as subject, but also from the brush, electing instead to pour and drip and splatter and throw the paint at the canvas. An exemplar of this technique was Jackson Pollock, who also did away with the easel, dropping the paint right onto the canvas on the floor. His style of work was called **action painting**.

Whether or not the Abstract Expressionists dripped the paint, they all got very interested in the paint itself, its properties and sensual qualities. When there is no object, ask yourself, what is left?

The answer: Color, shape, line, and texture. It makes sense that the artist would aim to deliver excellence in these areas.

Artists like Mark Rothko became aficionados of paint, applying it ever so subtly, so it shimmered and glowed. Barnett Newman (1905–1970), another color field artist, eschewed brushwork and made simple compositions made of flat color that invite serenity and meditation. Helen Frankenthaler (1928–2011) discovered a way to use unprimed canvas that absorbed the oil in the paint, allowing the surface to sing with pure pigment. Robert Motherwell (1915–1991) and Franz Kline (1910–1962) employed large swaths of black line to great effect.

Each elaborated an individual style and signature given the parameters of abstraction. Robert Rauschenberg (1925–2008), a prodigious innovator, introduced other materials into his "combines," creating a turn into mixed media and Pop Art.

Painting is very much about application, and each artist has a different "touch" in much the same way that each person has a different recognizable signature. No two artists apply the paint in exactly the same way, and when you become an engaged student of painting, you will be able to identify an artist not only by his imagery, but by the feeling of his or her paint. Is it dry or oily? Is it spread like butter or washed? Thin or gummy? Transparent or heavy? Flat or layered? Is there an under painting? Can you see layers peeking through? Is the paint speckled? Dotted? Brushed? Dabbed? Sanded?

You may not realize it, but a large part of the reason you prefer one artist over another is the way he or she applies the paint. It is like the preference you have for a certain clothing designer, or shoe fabricator, or ice cream. It is made the way you like it.

I enjoy traveling over the work taking in the offbeat color mixtures, and the general topography—the hills, valleys, and crevices that my eyes encounter. It is a pleasant excursion and I look forward to visiting when I next get the opportunity. I encourage you to look at abstraction in this way, to stand back and look at the work as a whole and see what it conjures in your imagination.

Note the title for a clue to what the artist either strove to evoke or found in his paint. Then let your eyes wander to and fro, as I do. If you look at the work this way, even if you are not a fan of abstraction and prefer visual works that are reminiscent of objects, you will get a lot more out of the work and probably enjoy looking at it. We hearken back to our statement that art is communication, and it takes two parties to make the connection.

Abstraction is a study of space itself, and Diebenkorn and his fellow American Abstract Expressionists took advantage of the "space" following World War II in America when a new life seemed possible, and opportunity was around every corner. These artists had the ability to think big, make large works, and take chances. Remember that this is not a common occurrence in history when restriction, deprivation and loss curtail the ability for liberal thought and action. Artists, for the most part, are of their time. It is important to keep that in mind and note the associations and aesthetic preferences.

OP ART AND POP ART: EYE CANDY (1950s AND 1960s)

Visual art has often been viewed as an elitist enterprise, one accessible to the aristocracy and professional classes but not relevant to the society at large. This is truer of certain art movements, like Abstract Expressionism, which may be difficult to understand, and where artist intentions and impulses seem far-fetched and abstruse.

In reaction to Abstract Expressionism, characteristics and categorizations of which were ridiculed by critics and reviewers, there arose in the 1950s and 1960s the phenomenon we refer to as Pop art, particularly in the United Kingdom and most emphatically in the United States. Pop art returned visual art to the vocabulary of recognizable imagery after the amorphous abstractions of color field and action artists, and utilized imagery from mass culture—advertising, comic books, and other commercial sources—importing it into the fine art realm.

Employing humor, irony, parody, and satire, these Pop Art works are an attempt to level the playing field, erasing the division between the high culture of visual art and the often-haughty condemnation of commercial applications. Can you see Pop art as backlash to the pretentiousness of Abstract Expressionism?

Where Abstract Expressionism focused on personal expression, Pop art highlighted popular culture. Where Abstract Expressionism centered on the sensual, spiritual, and rarefied emotions, Pop images were cool, drawn from the material and commercial worlds. Abstract Expressionism was about poetry; Pop was all prose. Abstract Expressionism was abstract and stimulated by the imagination, subtle and evocative; Pop was unambiguous, down to earth, generic, and common.

MINIMALISM: JUST THE FACTS AND NOTHING BUT (1960s AND 1970s)

I am guessing that you have already gone to a modern art museum and seen a work on the wall that you thought was there by mistake or said something to a companion like, "I could do that."

It may have been a work that falls into the category of minimalism, another movement that arose as a reaction to the feverishness of Abstract Expressionism. The truth is, they did it, and you didn't. And why they did is significant.

Abstraction was a distillation, a subtraction of extraneous visual elements, in an attempt to arrive at some kind of pictorial essence and liberation from the object. How this "essence" was to be proved or evaluated, however, was questionable. Though a critic might wax ecstatic over an abstract composition, how would anyone know it was crafted by an artist and not a trick, say, made by a child or an elephant's trunk? Reading abstract work is not a cakewalk.

It might be a noble goal to try to arrive at something "essential" and to that end, to eschew all decoration and extraneous frills to get down to utter basics. Of course, like all seemingly good intentions, this worthwhile endeavor can go overboard. And land us at the proverbial question mark.

If you take this reductionism to its natural conclusion, paring away pictorial elements, what is left? In 1915, Kazimir Malevich gave us a clue when he exhibited his work *Black Square* in Petrograd. When you eliminate all traces of reference to objects, all aesthetic elements like color, shape, and line, you arrive at nothingness, blankness, zero.

And then where do you go? It is one thing to simplify and quite another to "throw out the baby with the bathwater." If you believe art is too focused on superficiality, aimed at the making of so-called "pretty pictures," perhaps sentimental, overly concerned with emotion, and short on meaningful content, what can you do? What can you make?

Fig. 74, Kazimir Malevich, BLACK SQUARE.

Was minimalism a dead end? Not exactly. Artists are persistent and loath to give up. When art had distilled itself down to this natural conclusion, the black square, something had to give. And it did. What came to mind was yes, the mind, i.e., what we now refer to as Conceptual Art.

THE BRAIN TAKES OVER: CONCEPTUAL ART (1960s AND ONWARD)

According to Paul Wood in *Conceptual Art* (Delano Greenidge Editions, New York, 2002), the artist Duchamp purportedly said that he was bored by the "limitation of art in thrall to the senses" and wanted to return art to the service of the mind. Others agreed art could serve thought more productively by taking it a step further and merging it with action.

The reaction against the object and the search for a reasonable replacement arose in a process, and was concentrated mostly from the 1950s onward. It started with artists experimenting with their medium and beginning to incorporate myriad additional elements. The dissatisfaction began with this manipulation of the traditional media and then morphed into a rejection of it.

Wood tells the story of Robert Rauschenberg who, in the 1950s, asked Willem de Kooning for one of his drawings and then proceeded to erase it. The point was to deconstruct the original piece and in so doing, to unmake the artist's purpose and substitute his own. He claimed that he was returning the artwork to its "primordial" essence.

Traditional visual art can be seen as the making of objects for the purpose of aesthetic reflection and enjoyment. In this worldview, the artworks are concocted by a selective class of exceptionally skilled individuals we call artists. They are believed to be endowed with a peculiar faculty we call talent, which enables them to create these works. Not only are these makers deemed to be exceptional, but their work is also collected by another, higher class of mostly wealthy individuals, and the possession of these exceptional works of art convey favor and status on collectors.

When viewed in this context, art itself may appear to be class related—made by specialists for the most entitled members of society. This is partly what engendered a reaction against traditional art-making practices, a rebellion of sorts, and a challenge to art for art's sake.

Conceptual art is also a rejection of Abstract Expressionism and minimalism, art forms that were themselves rejections of traditional art. Abstract Expressionism got rid of the object but still was sensory based. Minimalism got rid of the object and the sensation—but was deemed empty, devoid of meaning. Alas: resurgence of thought-based art!

We refer to these new attempts to substitute thought-based works, performances, and other activities under the broad category of "Conceptual art." Conceptual art is an attempt to find meaning and to move beyond the preciousness and class-based nature of art.

Here's an example of conceptual art that may clarify this. Wood tells of the English artist John Latham, an art teacher at the time, who invited his students for what he called a "chew-in" in 1966. He took the book *Art and Culture* out of the library, tore out pages, and asked the students to chew a page and then spit the masticated page into a receptacle. Latham then added chemicals and yeast to the mixture, distilled it into alcohol, and then returned the test tube containing it to the library.

The artist/teacher got fired but a suitcase containing a copy of the book, the test tube and chemicals, and Latham's pink slip became a work of conceptual art, now in the Museum of Modern Art in New York. In 2000, it was displayed at the entrance of the museum during its survey exhibit of the art of the late twentieth century.

So what is the art? The art is the act, and the idea that led to the act, not the objects. That, in essence, is the meaning of conceptual art.

IN SUMMARY

Modernity took art into new dimensions. No longer attached to the object thanks to the camera, and schooled in new movements that championed light (Impressionism), personality (Post-Impressionism), color (Fauvism), emotion (Expressionism), multiple perspectives (Cubism), the imagination (Surrealism), the sensuality of space (Abstract Expressionism), the audaciousness of popular imagery (Pop Art) and essences (Minimalism), where were artists to go next?

They went into the mind (conceptual art), deriving imagery that arose from ideas or made a statement. They incorporated text into their imagery. After realizing the canvas didn't have to be a square or a rectangle, it occurred to some that they didn't need a canvas at all. And moreover, they didn't actually need paint, or any other traditional art medium. They could just be, just act, and that could be art (performance art). Or they could fill a room with stuff, organized or not, and call it a day and a work of art as well (installation art).

But wait. Maybe they didn't need a room at all. They could just go outside and use some land-moving equipment and create something. This wasn't garden-variety gardening. It was land art or earth art. Remember Christo, who made the environment his canvas? He not only decorated our environment, he also changed our thinking about art, didn't he?

Other media rose to the fore. The former craft media—ceramics, glass, welding, woodwork—moved into fine art applications. Artists had fun combining them both in two- and three-dimensional creations. The categories began to blur. Two- and three-dimensional spheres of influence, painting, and sculpture, were no longer absolute. Painting could be sculpture, and vice versa.

(Continued on next page)

Our quick tour of modernist movements has illustrated how kinetic visual ideas became once the process was initiated. The rules had been broken, remade, and broken again. It was all art. They could just do whatever spirit moved them to do. An artist was not just a person who made things that could be named and hung on walls. He or she was a creative being who could do just about anything, with anything, and call it art.

Photography became a large part of two-dimensional art, and photo fragments began showing up in painted work. Art became more and more personal, and the passions of artists formed subcategories: feminist art, LGBTQ art, trans avant-garde, body art, projection art, and, of course, digital art.

I encourage you to look up all the new movements for more clarification on their dynamics and to familiarize yourself with the practitioners. But before we leave this chapter, we need to discuss Digital Art making in a bit more detail.

I was born in the mid twentieth century when art making was absolutely hands on. I still like the feel of working with my hands and using the myriad tools that have been developed to perform a specific function in art making. I love to use materials I find at Home Depot and incorporate them into my work. I use fabric, papers, and found objects too.

Somehow, though, using a computer to make art just seemed like a cheat, and I avoided it. Then in one of the live drawing sessions I like to attend, there was an artist working on his laptop, drawing from the live model. Though I still prefer the feeling of the pencil on the paper, I had to admit that he did some interesting work, and like magic, was able to refashion these efforts into countless iterations with the click of a mouse or touch of a smart pen. This was pretty cool. I admired his work and changed my mind about the computer.

Now we find ourselves poised at the doorstep of artificial intelligence, which may take us into entirely unforeseen dimensions. I know too little about this to comment on it at present and, of course, am a skeptic, but in the spirit of this book, I will remain open. Onward with art!

These are tools created by humans. The art is made by the hand that holds the tool, and the brain that directs the hand, not the tool. That is the story of modernity and the story of art.

WHEN THE OLD IS NEW: TRANSCENDING THE CLASSIFICATIONS

I have recently become acquainted with very old paintings that have appeared in the context of something frightfully new: video games. Before we leave the topic of modernity, we absolutely must have a look at these works, painted by Pieter Bruegel the Elder in the sixteenth century depicting the Tower of Babel. The artist made three works on this theme, and here are the first two; the third, a miniature, has been lost.

Religious themes were common at this time and these paintings refer to a story in the book of Genesis about Babel, a city built by the descendants of Noah after the great flood. Nimrod, the builder, was ambitious and exhibited inordinate pride in his effort to build a tower that would reach to the heavens, this in clear violation of God's authority. In the story, God punishes the sin of human hubris by making people speak so many languages that they cannot communicate with one another.

It is ironic that in the story Man is reprimanded for his attempt to use his resources and technology to achieve this lofty goal. The tower is only part of it; in the story, it is to be the center of a community where people can find connection with one another.

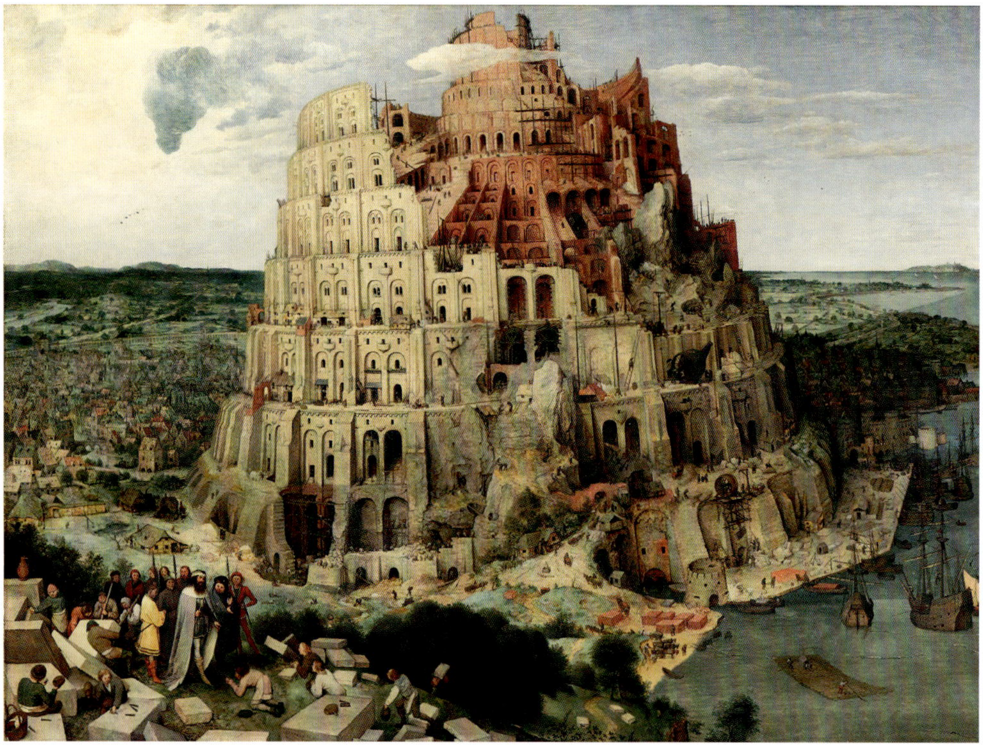

Fig. 75. Pieter Bruegel, THE GREAT TOWER OF BABEL.

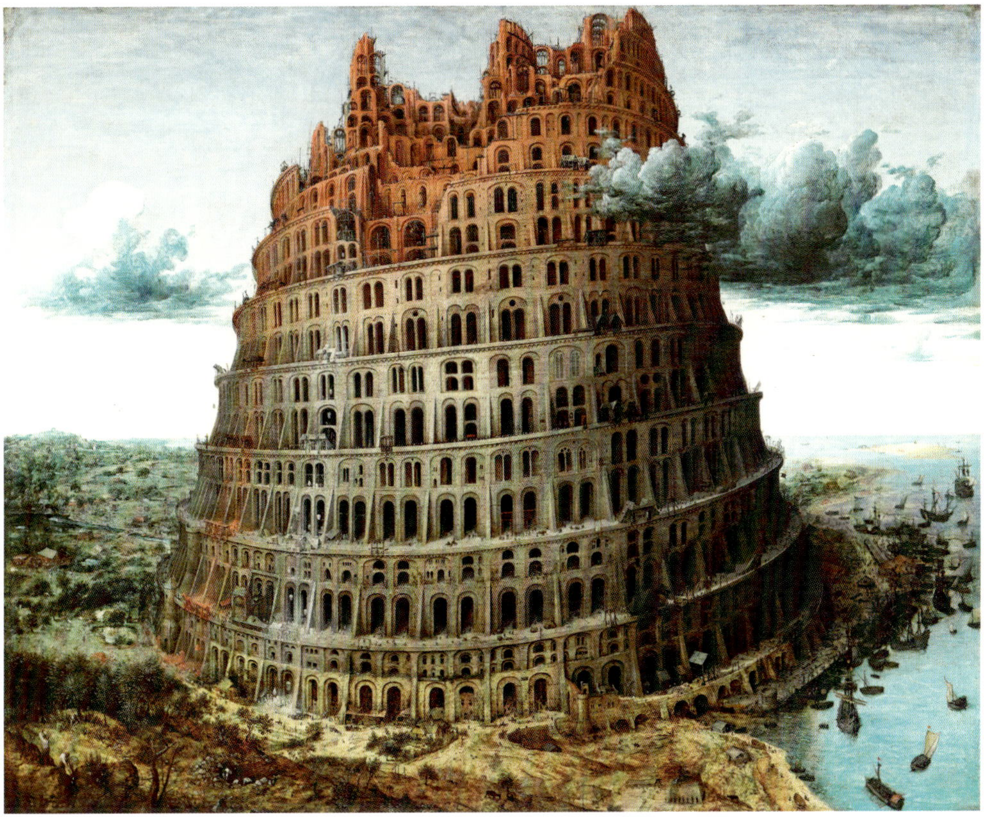

Fig. 76. Pieter Bruegel, THE TOWER OF BABEL.

Now let's look at these paintings. When I saw them for the first time, I was struck with how compelling they are, and how strangely modern. When I did some research, I found that I was not alone in this thinking. In fact, images of these paintings have appeared in video games created in the twenty-first century, in a 2012 video game depicting a zombie survival mode, and in *Let It Die*, a 2016 game. Uncanny, isn't it, as the twenty-first century gamers can be seen as a community where people find connection, can they not?

These paintings are more than half a millennium old, yet they are as relevant today as they were then. Both works refer to the Roman Colosseum in the imagined design of the structure. I am especially struck by the smaller of the two paintings, in which the tower punctures the clouds as mentioned in the Old Testament. It is a dark work, and there is a menacing quality. I can see why it appealed to video gamers.

I offer these paintings to you in this chapter on modernity to suggest that you do not make assumptions about what is old and what is new. In spite of what I have said here about the qualities of modernity, there are always exceptions. Some old works are new, and some new works are old. Tastes morph and change and what was discarded can become chic again. The best way to deal with this is to evaluate every work on its own and find in its integrity what it has to offer.

When our minds are open and nothing is absolute, we can discover all the amazing works that jump their categorizations and classifications, and we can see them as unique and marvelous works of art. As the great explorers of the fourteenth and fifteenth centuries remind us, discovery is possible when we don't know where we are going.

Apropos, here is a photo of Lisbon's beautiful *Monument of the Discoveries*, which depicts the explorers who discovered the New World. As they are enshrined here reaching into the unknown, we are inspired and charged to follow their example.

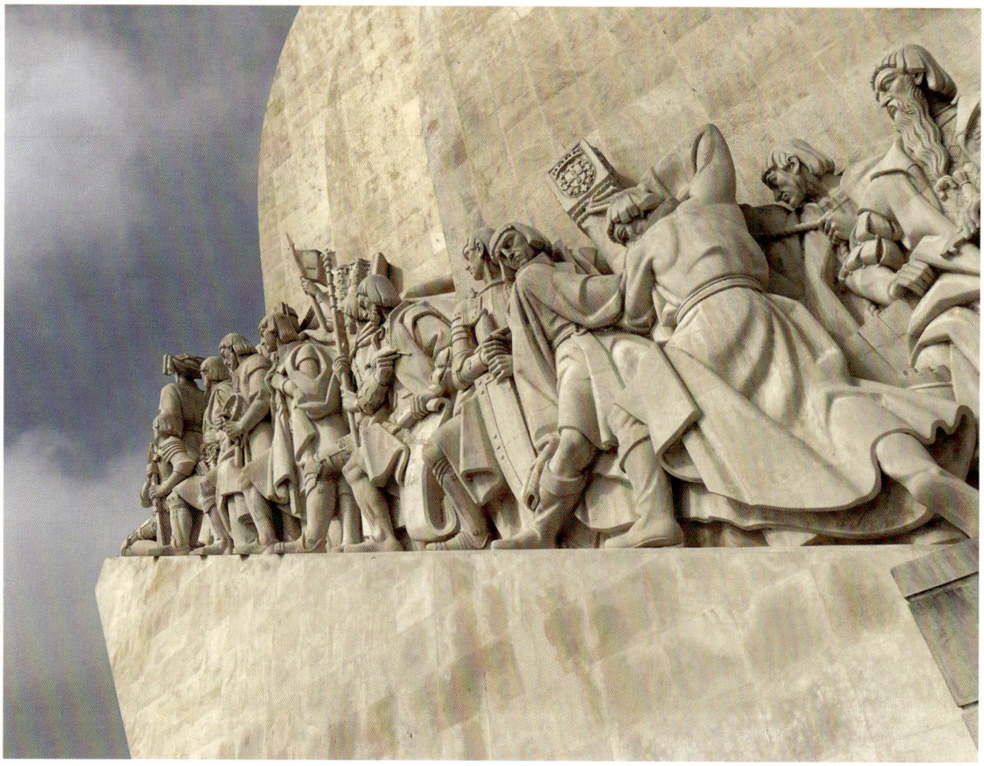

Fig. 77. MONUMENT OF THE DISCOVERIES, Lisbon, Portugal.

Chapter 7
Perspective

Imagine, if you will, a group of ten artists at a life drawing session sitting around a model. Each artist has his worktable set up. Some are using charcoal only; others charcoal and pencils. Another has a box of pastels, and the woman on the side has a palette with acrylic paints. I am there too, with my own collection of favored tools—a bottle of ink, oil crayons, and some pencils. One artist is using a computer.

In addition to our media, we each have a different surface to work on. Some are working small in a sketchbook. Most have large sheets of paper, but some are using a cheap newsprint brand and others expensive watercolor paper. We all have different ways to sit and work. Some sit on stools, others in comfy chairs, and a few are standing.

Why am I telling you this? Because I'd like you to imagine that after twenty minutes of this pose have elapsed and we are on a break, you can go around and see what all the artists have done. Now, mind you, we all are working from the same model in identical clothes in the scenario we all agreed to, though each from a slightly different point of view. This will be fun. But wait, every picture is completely different. How did that happen?

It happened because we each have a totally different point of view and intention. The fellow working with the cheap newsprint is a cartoonist, and he is always going for gesture. The woman working on the watercolor is obsessed with impressionistic soft color—she was the one who set up the scenario because to her, the figure is just a bunch of notes of color. The digital artist has flipped out his background six times—he's into composition. And the realist in the corner has done a study of the right leg and all its musculature in detail. I've got an inky movement with some rubbed-in painting of her face.

We all see the same thing and see it totally differently. Why? The reason is that we want to see it in the way that interests us, that speaks to us, and that is why we have come to this place on Wednesday morning. We come every week with the same intention. To do our thing.

It's a matter of perspective.

I was thinking of how I could give you that experience of walking around the room and seeing everyone's work. It would be so useful in helping you understand what you are looking at and why the artist chooses and then develops his or her approach, elects which materials to use, and effectuates how to realize his or her artistic intention.

Instead, I decided to choose a common subject, select a bunch of artists who worked from that subject, and show you their work, while elucidating what, in my opinion, is driving them. I decided to choose the theme of Mother and Child—a popular subject, and one more complex than a simple portrait.

So, we will pretend that time does not exist and that I have gathered the various artists in an imaginary studio in the present, where they are about to make works of art on the theme of Mother and Child. This is, undoubtedly, a very sentimental subject that evokes the tender feelings most of us have toward children, and the very favorable way we think of maternal love.

You might think it is easier to work from a subject such as this, one that engenders feeling, but it is not necessarily so. Sometimes a subject can be so evocative that it is overwhelming. Think of trying to paint a magnificent sunset. You may feel inspired as you gaze upon it but daunted in your attempt to duplicate it. It may be so beautiful that you are led to copy it, rather than interpret it, and you may get frustrated that your work does not hold up to nature. In my humble opinion, nature always trumps art.

So we already know we have a challenge here—to deal with this emotional subject in an honest and not overly corny or vapid matter. Also, because the subject is one of the most commonly attempted, we will be challenged to create our work in an original and personal way.

The subject has a long history, partially because of religious references to the Madonna. We will be going back with our examples about a millennium. Our imaginary class of twenty artists come from as early as the thirteenth century, and there are two from the fifteenth century and two from the eighteenth, but the bulk of our group hails from the late nineteenth century. We have mother and child works from fourteen artists who were born in the latter part of the 1800s into the early 1900s, as this was a fervent period when representation, and this subject in particular, was still prized.

Unfortunately, since I am limited to public domain images, I do not have many recent iterations that can be replicated here, and so have added one of my own. I also offered a challenge to the living artists featured in this book, to create a brand-new Mother and Child. An artist I studied glassmaking with years ago, and one of the most original living artists working in stained glass today, Judith Schaechter, offered a most unusual work of hers on the theme, which is now on view in one of the most prestigious museums in the world, the Hermitage in St. Petersburg. You will find these examples in the Appendix to this book. As you view them, you can refer to this chapter to see their forerunners and analyze how modernity has or has not altered the perspectives on this subject.

So let's begin. Some of these artists are exceptionally famous; others are obscure. The only thing that matters is that they have attempted to make a work of visual art on the subject of Mother and Child. Let's see how they all did.

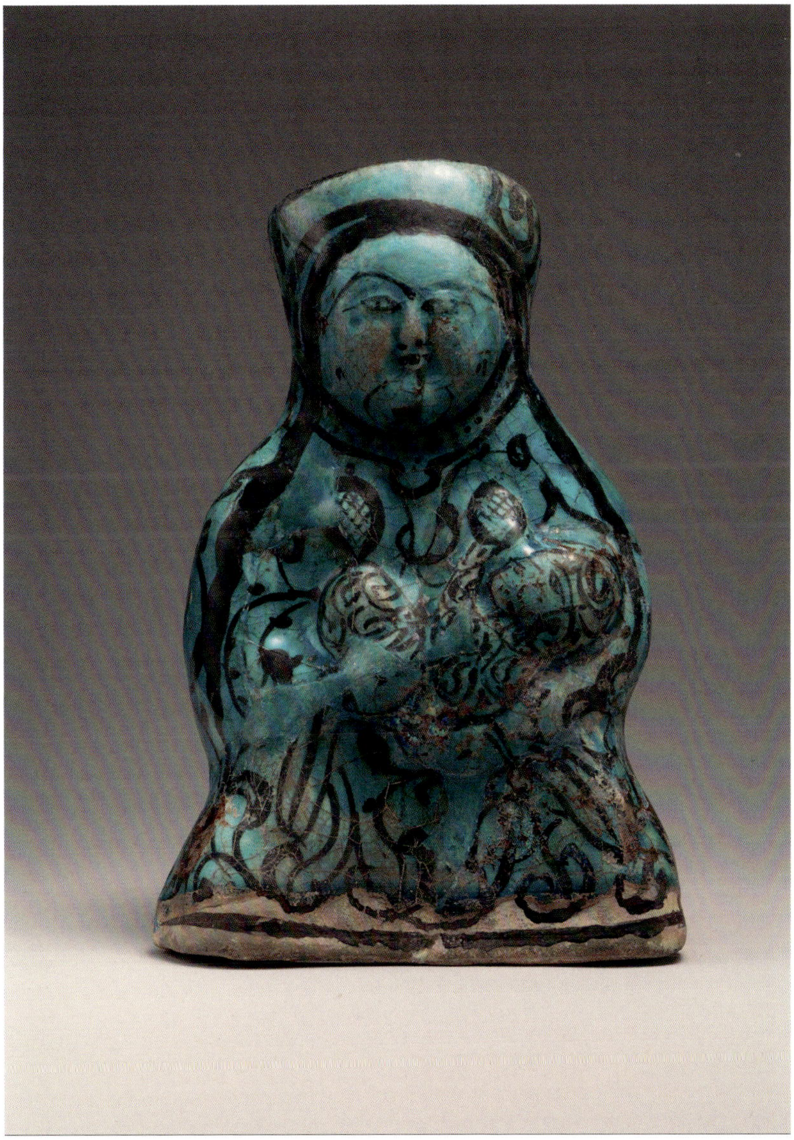

Fig. 78. THIRTEENTH-CENTURY MOLDED VESSEL.

1. UNKNOWN ARTIST, MOLDED ISLAMIC VESSEL, CERAMIC

Here's an interesting thought: Sometimes the oldest artworks will resemble the newest, as this ceramic sculpture. Why? You ask. Because artists of old (this is a medieval work), with their lack of information, often made simplified, iconic forms, while modern and contemporary artists, with a great deal of knowledge, admire this simplification and want to return to it—not because they have to, rather they wish to get down to essence, eliminating distracting details that take away from the direct experience of the artistic message.

In this lovely little ceramic, which is so beautifully painted with turquoise glaze and black lines, the baby is just barely suggested and is clearly a part of the mother. Don't you also think that the turquoise color is extremely modern? Wouldn't you expect an artist of this time to use a more naturalistic color as a glaze? Brown or tan or red?

I look at this work with amazement. It could have been made in my favorite ceramic studio in Ojai, California, in 2022 instead of over eight hundred years ago.

2. LEONARDO DA VINCI, *MADONNA LITTA,* TEMPERA

3. SANDRO BOTTICELLI, *VIRGIN AND CHILD WITH ANGEL,* TEMPERA

These Renaissance artists, both masters, lived at the same time, so it is not surprising that these artworks, both tempera paintings, are so similar. They both feature mother and child in a like posture in the foreground, with a stage set kind of background, well-painted yet perfunctory.

As we've mentioned before in this book, leaving work unfinished, raw, or textured is a feature of modernist work. In the Renaissance, leaving the painting in this state would be anathema. The paintings are perfected to such a degree that they veer toward unreality. The skin is so smooth without lines or imperfections that it looks like it is made of rubber.

Likewise, though the figures are assuming a posture of loving embrace, these works do not impart any affection. The babies, in particular, are decidedly unlovable. The painters are incredibly accomplished and skilled, superb draftsmen, yet their paintings are surprisingly dead. They pay more attention to exactitude of fabric and drapery than human expression. What is missing?

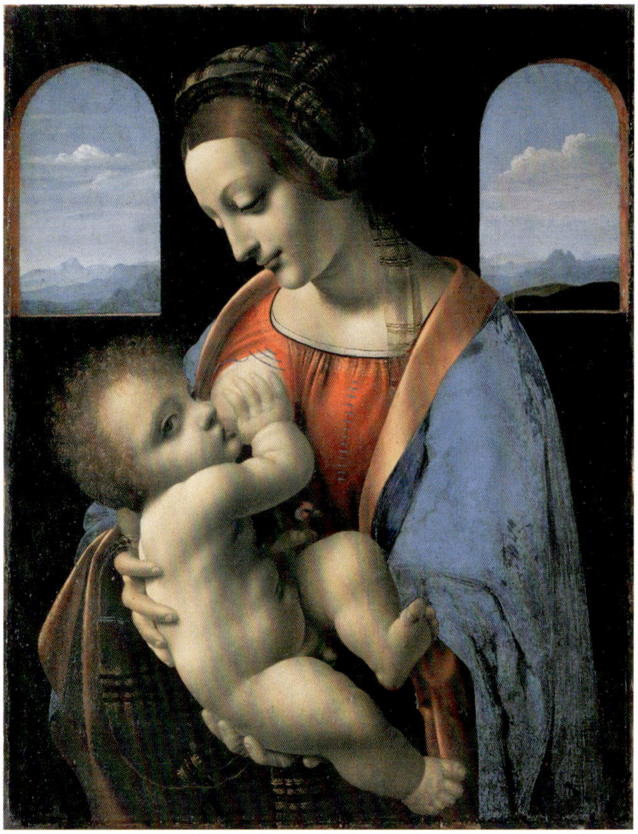

Fig. 79. Leonardo da Vinci, MADONNA LITTA.

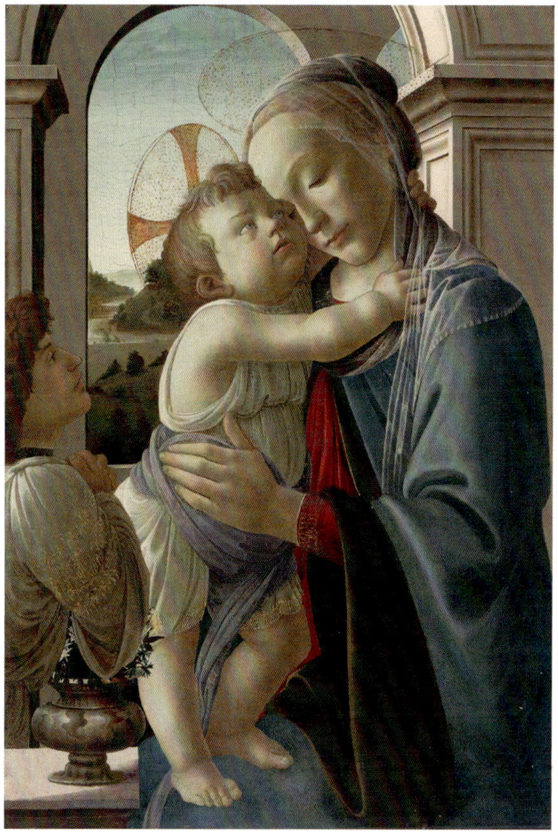

Fig. 80. Sandro Botticelli, VIRGIN AND CHILD WITH ANGEL.

My contention is that they are so concerned with the correctness of their efforts that this imparts a falseness to the works. They are constructed by formula—that is why they are so similar—and the personality of the artist, and therefore of the subjects, is just not present.

Ironically, allowing a more naturalist feeling and letting the work breathe is actually a much more sophisticated way of creating art. It would take centuries for artists to allow themselves to let their work just be, faults, blips, pimples, and all.

Compare these works by masters to some of the less-famous artists here, and you will see that mastery of effect and technique may not be sufficient to create a masterpiece. More on this as we proceed.

4. GEORGE ROMNEY, *MOTHER AND CHILD DRAWING*, PENCIL

Why have I even included this tiny drawing by a not very well-known British portrait painter whose paintings you might just skip over when visiting the museum?

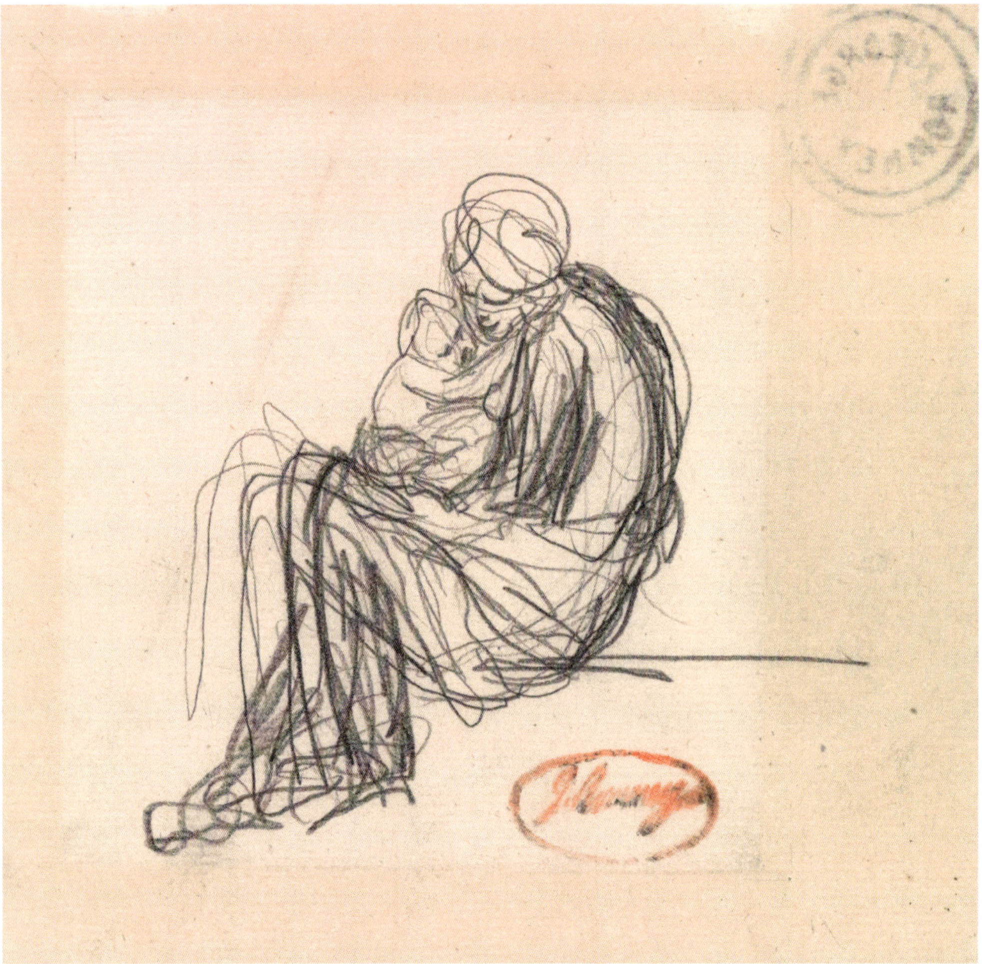

Fig. 81. George Romney, MOTHER AND CHILD.

First of all, it is kind of good to remember that artists of every era do all kinds of work that you never see, because they only show you what they believe is their best. I often long to see the throwaways and mistakes as well as the successes—don't you? We would feel we had more in common with artists and identify with them more.

Romney was an eighteenth-century English portrait painter of the fashionable folks of the day. His work is capable yet uninspired, and most of the portraits are fairly traditional, with the figure posing and a dark background. This is a drawing by the artist, and I don't know whether it was a sketch for a painting or just a scribble.

It's a far cry from his very polished portraits, but it's interesting to see nonetheless. It's unlikely that it's a plan for a painting because there's no context, no composition suggested, just the two figures. But it's good to remember that even artists who make very elaborate paintings must start somewhere.

5. KITAGAWA UTAMARO, *MISTRESS AND SLEEPY CHILD*, WOODBLOCK

If you think you have seen this work before, it is probably because this artist is emblematic of Japanese style. He is known for his over two thousand prints and achieved fame during his lifetime. Though he worked in the late eighteenth century, his work became known in Europe in the nineteenth century, when it was discovered and imitated by the Impressionists. Later we will look at a print by the American Impressionist, Mary Cassatt, where the influence of Utamaro is quite evident.

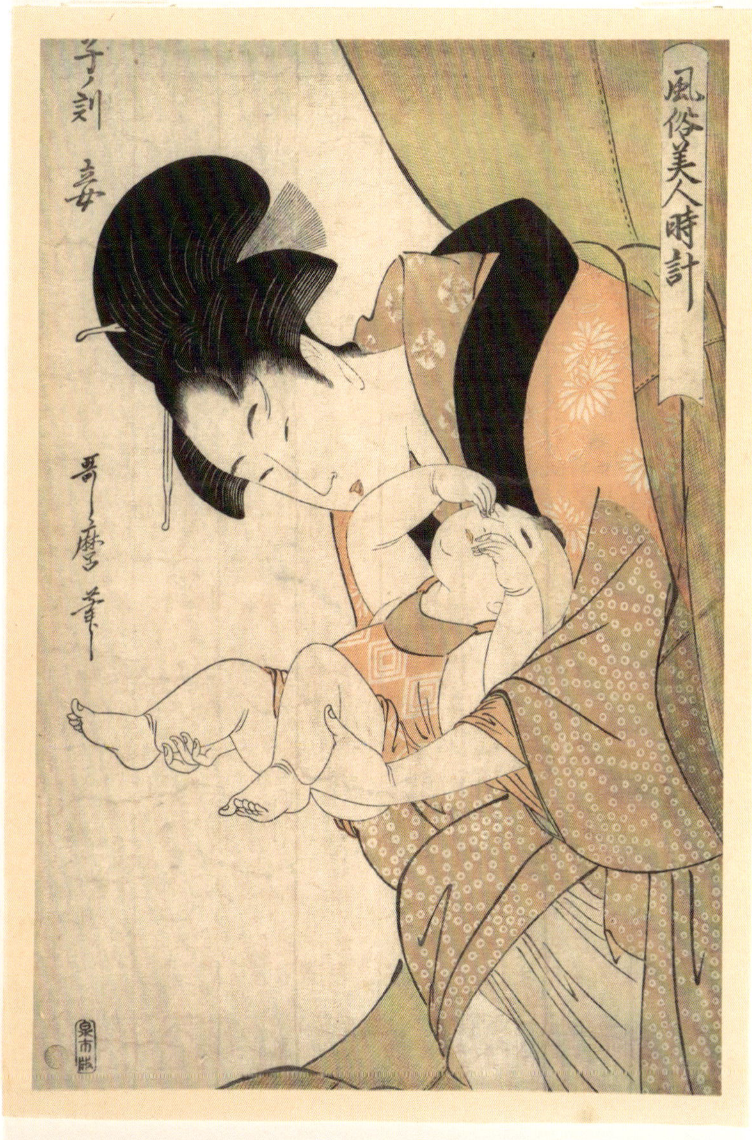

Fig. 82. Kitagawa Utamara, MISTRESS AND SLEEPY CHILD.

Utamaro presents us with his version of feminine beauty which is characterized by the oversized head and coiffure, eyes painted as slits, long nose, and tiny bud mouth, repeated in the drawing of the baby. This is an illustration, not really a painting, and it is highly decorative, with excellent compositional values.

It is a stylized work, and since style trumps substance, there's not much here we can relate to. It is decorative, and we can admire it, but it does not touch us emotionally. The Impressionists loved Utamaro for the simplicity of his design and gracefulness of his line. They also appreciated the way he placed the figures, only partly inhabiting the picture, not in the center with background surrounding them. This is a more modern approach to composition. Also note the addition of the lettering as a design element. This was new to European eyes in the eighteenth century.

Make sure to flip back to the Utamaro when you view the Cassatt and compare the two.

6. BERNARD BLOMMERS, *MOTHER AND CHILD AT SEASIDE,* OIL

Here we have a relatively obscure Dutch painter and lithographer, who painted mostly genre scenes. Let's have a look at his little painting of Mother and Child:

This is a modest work, but I like it a lot. Surprised? It's not a terribly original work, the color is tonal and somewhat drab, the composition is nothing extraordinary, the figures in the distance seem irrelevant, just placed to fill space—and yes, all of that is true.

I like it because of its tonal naturalistic color, which is atmospheric and believable. You can feel the weather, which is a good sign. I like it because it is all of a piece; all the notes fit in the schema and belong. There is nothing that is discordant. I like the textured paint, especially the impasto on the woman's headscarf. I like the drawing of the relationship between the mother and the child. I like the specificity that the child is lifting her foot out of the water—I can guess that the water is cold.

This painting is a success. It is as humble as can be. I am following it with the extreme opposite—a painting by Klimt, an artist moved to extravagance, with big ideas and as flamboyant as can be. It is good to see both sides of the spectrum. Here with Blommers, we have authenticity in the quotidian, and it is very satisfying. Klimt goes for the extraordinary, the outré, the other worldly, and the fantasy.

Which do you prefer and why? If you wish, you can love both extremes for different reasons.

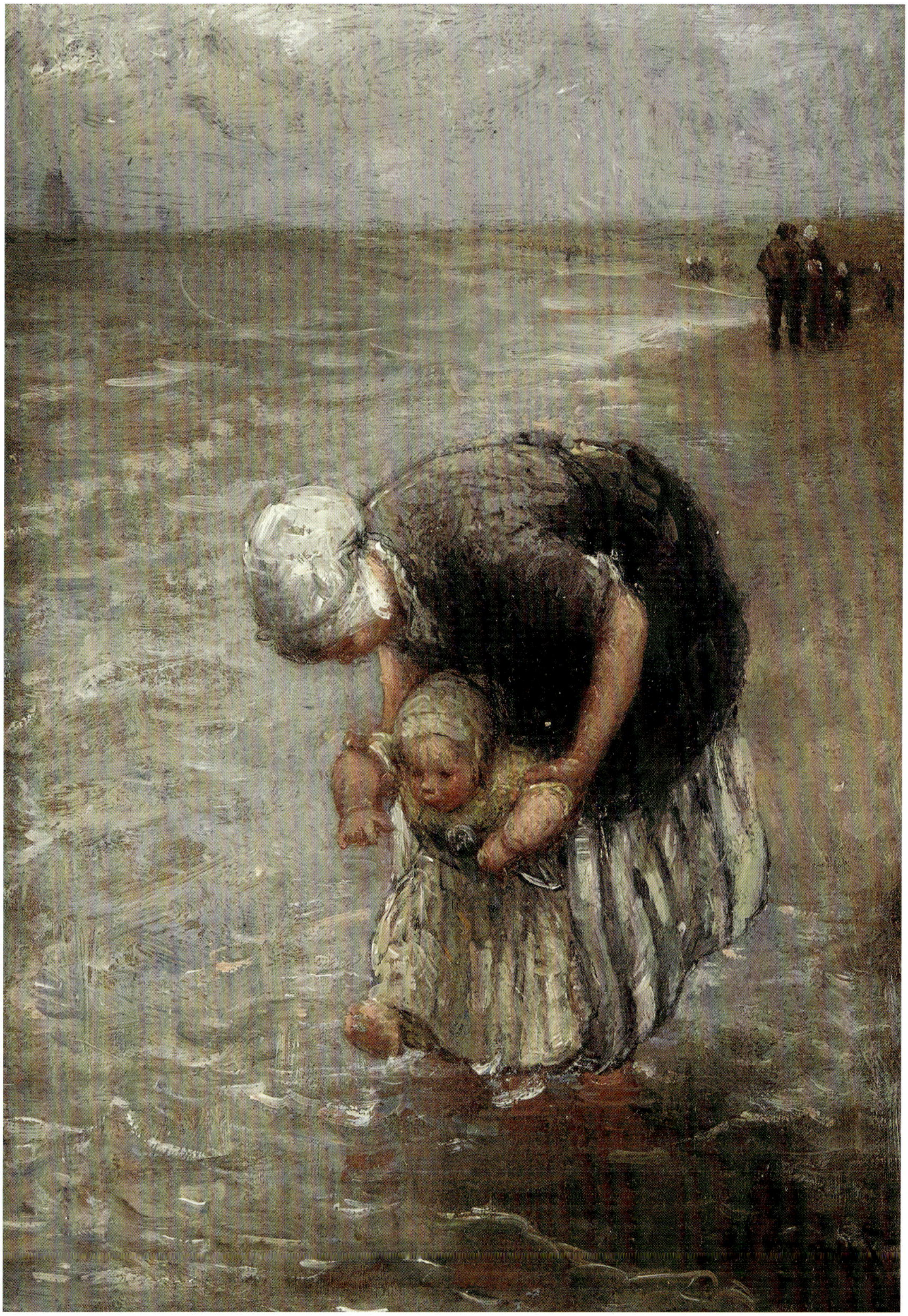

Fig. 83. Bernard Blommers, MOTHER AND CHILD AT SEASIDE.

7. BERTHE MORISOT, *MME. GOBILLARD ET SA FILLE*, WATERCOLOR

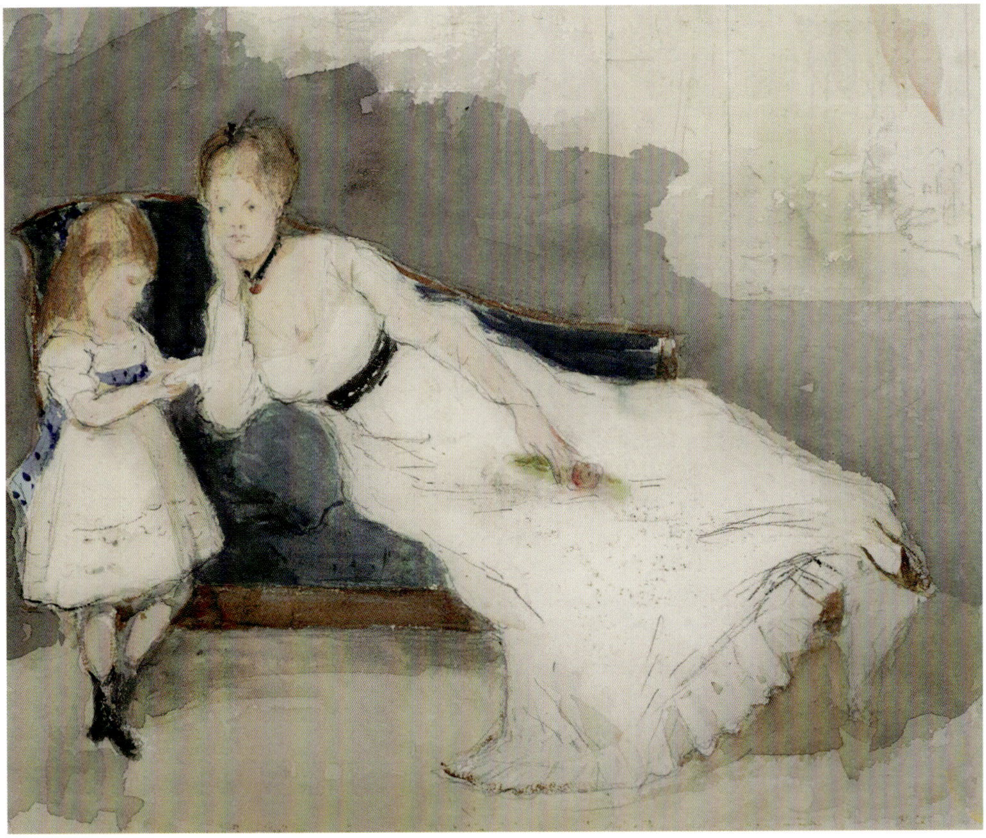

Fig. 84. Berthe Morisot, MME. GOBILLARD ET SA FILLE.

Here is a little watercolor by the French Impressionist Berthe Morisot (a portrait of her by Manet is in the first chapter of this book). Morisot was considered one of "*les trois grandes dames*" (the three great ladies) of Impressionism and exhibited in many of their exhibitions.

Here is a small watercolor by Morisot—she worked in oil, pastel, and watercolor—and it has the delicate touch she became known for. Her critics disparaged her technique with the verb *effleurer* (to touch lightly), and it is noted that Morisot interpreted this as anti-feminist commentary. She was actually quite unique and experimental—using unprimed canvases and loose brushwork—something that would later be utilized by color field artists like Helen Frankenthaler to achieve a glowing surface.

Morisot often worked on a small scale, as here (I wonder if that had anything to do with a diminished sense of self or status) but her success is a testament to her talent. It is much more difficult to achieve clarity on such a tiny work. But here you see it, the figures clear, enunciated, unpainted with a few simple lines, and emerging out of a wash of color. A lot said with little effort. She shows us how understatement can speak volumes.

8. GUSTAV KLIMT, *THREE AGES OF WOMAN*, OIL

Ah, Klimt, he was a character. A larger-than-life egotistical artist (the derogative "artiste" even comes to mind) who "swung from the chandeliers." He exhibits this even in the size of the work—the large canvas speaks of his self-confidence and aplomb. I have read that, though Klimt's work is much applauded and quite popular, he is not considered an important artist in the history of art. This is totally due to the fact that he was such a complete individualist, with a unique perspective, style, and set of skills. He is pretty much copy proof.

Decidedly, no one has ever made a Mother and Child like this one and no one ever will. It is exquisite.

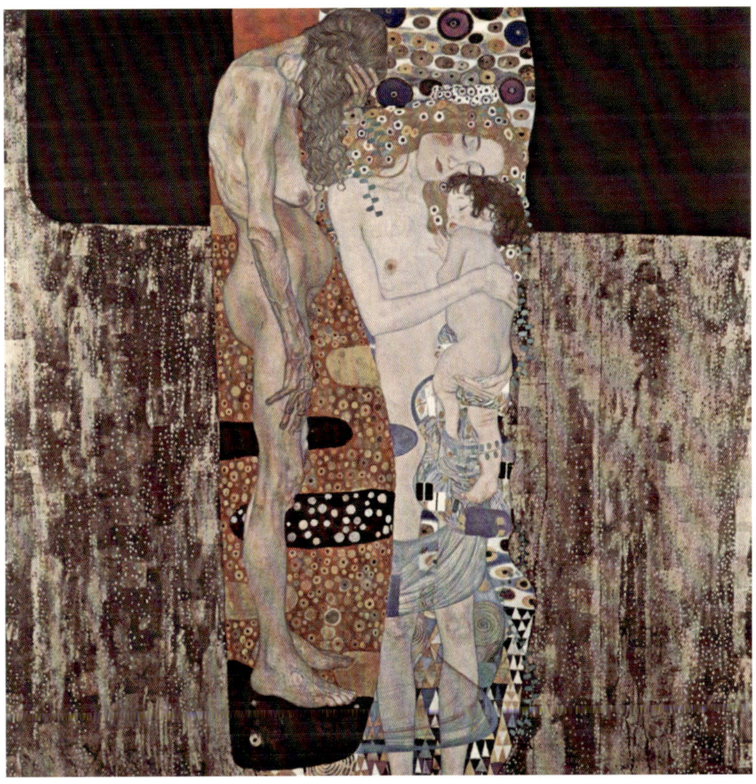

Fig. 85 Gustav Klimt, THREE AGES OF WOMAN.

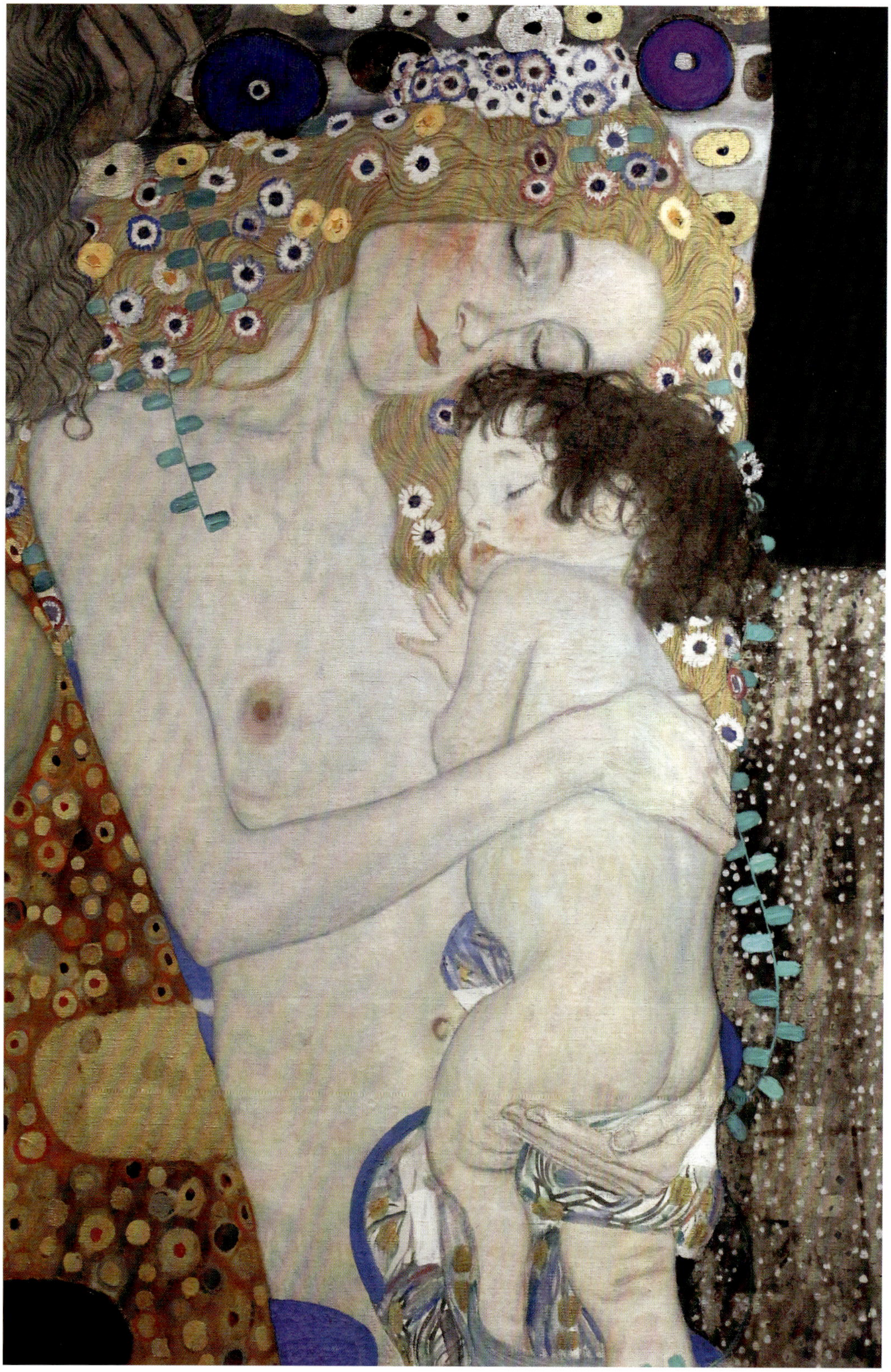

Fig. 86. Gustav Klimt, THREE AGES OF WOMAN, detail.

The painting depicts three ages of women—a mother and child, and a third figure to the left, an aged woman. This is a large square canvas, but the figures are crammed down the center with a large part of the canvas, both right and left, just background. I am not sure why Klimt composed the canvas this way.

I provide you here with an additional photo showing just the young mother and baby cropped out so we can really appreciate the beauty of this painting. Mother and baby are locked in a passionate embrace, both with their eyes closed and roseate cheeks, showered with flowers. We can appreciate Klimt's incredible ability exhibited here in the painting of the hands as they cradle and support the baby. All of the patterning and design elements only serve to augment the beauty of these figures and their relationship.

Turning back to the full painting, notice the superb painting of the old women, her distorted belly, and her feet and hands. This is a painting tour de force. I can quarrel, as I usually do, with Klimt's overdoing of the patterning as a distraction, and here with the composition, but the quality of the painting is undeniable.

What do you think of it?

9. HAROLD GILMAN, *MOTHER AND CHILD*, OIL

Post-Impressionist painter Harold Gilman's *Mother and Child* is notable for a number of reasons. The color is vivid, broken as it is into planes. But it is the texture of this work that makes it exceptional. It feels like fabrics that have been sewn together, with some of the fabrics rough in texture and others smooth.

Study the face of the mother, in particular. The bands of pink and blue, with the neck shadow represented by a sage green. Harold's color is not what we call local—it is unusual, imaginary color that somehow works—the blue head of the baby, the green and ink hands of the mother, the red light on the pillow, and the gold background field holding it all together. This is color we would expect from Paul Gauguin, and here it is on a mother and child from an Englishman.

I think this is a wonderful piece. The composition is satisfying as the mother and child fill the space beautifully. There is patterning in the way the paint is applied. It is integral and not purely decorative. And there is tenderness in the relationship between the mother and baby. All in all, an equilibrium and balance, in spite of the very lively palette.

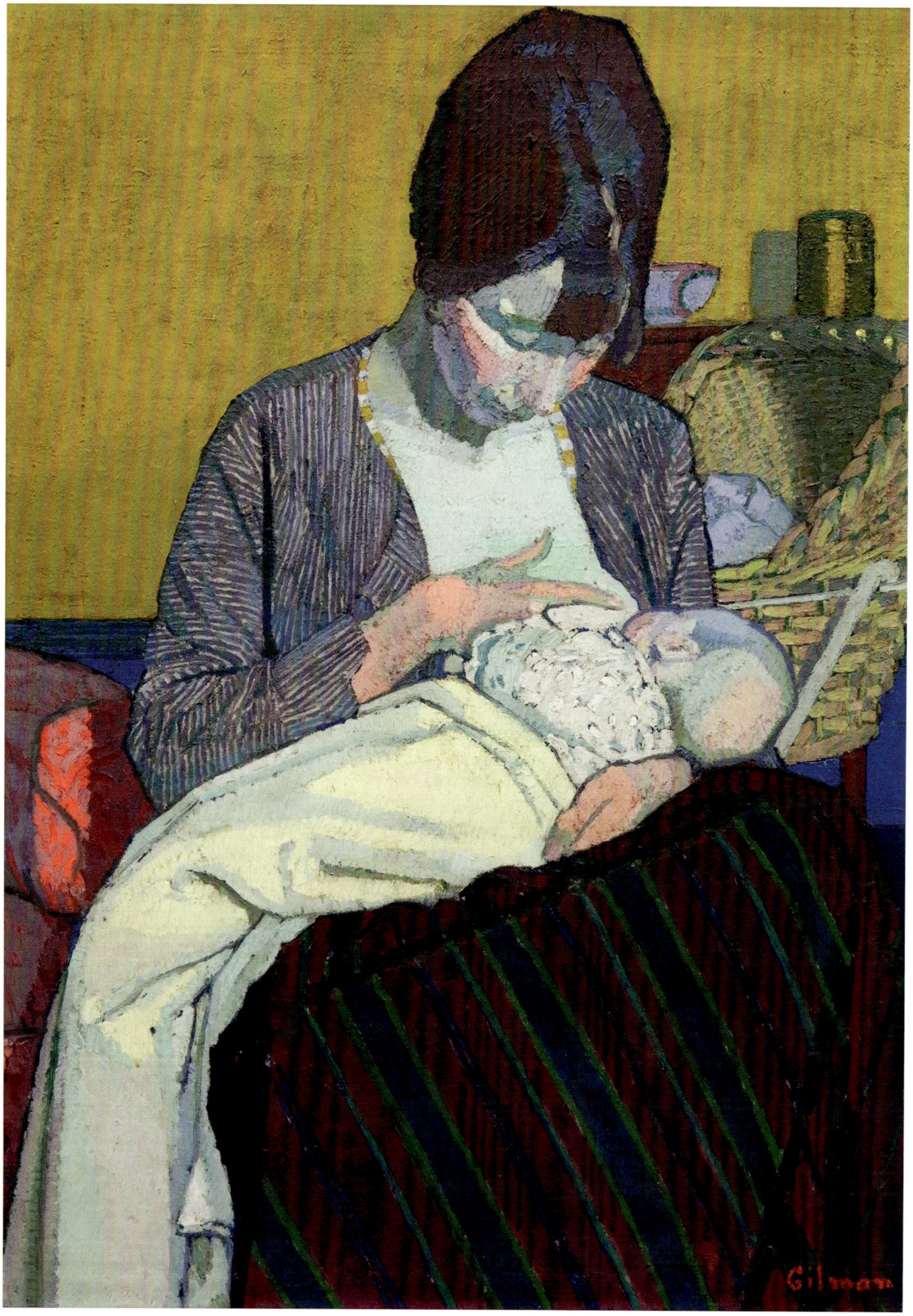

Fig. 87. Harold Gilman, MOTHER AND CHILD.

10. JANIS ROZENTALS, *MOTHER AND CHILD*, OIL

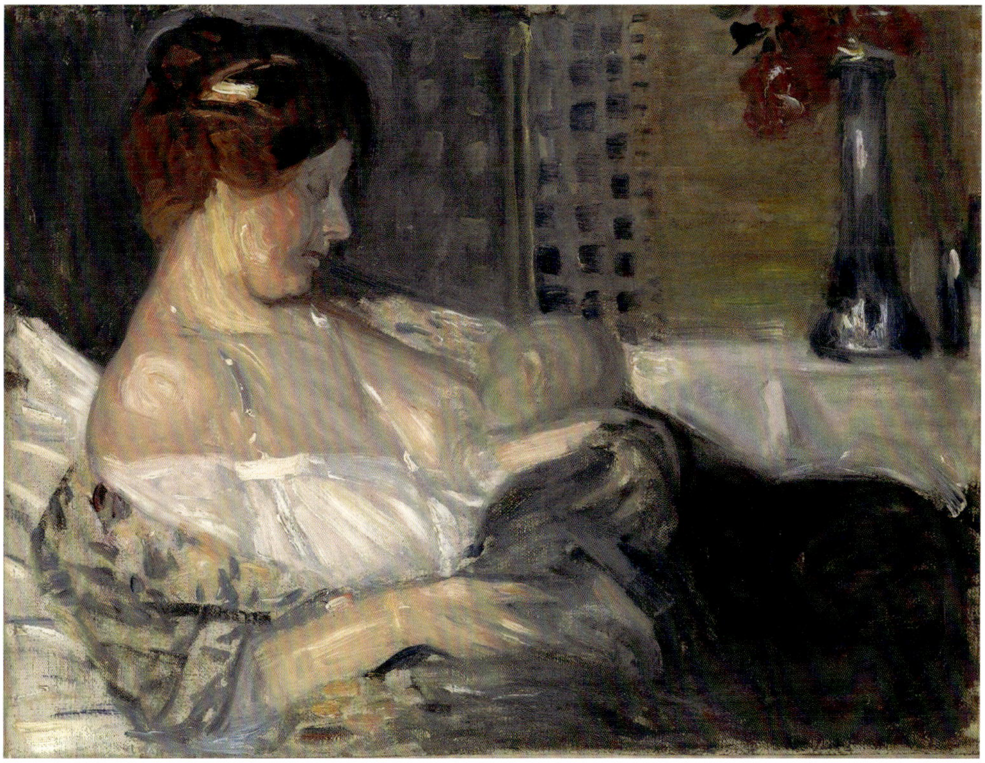

Fig. 88. Janis Rozentals, MOTHER AND CHILD.

The oil paint here feels wet while the Gilman is just the opposite—very dry, even dusty. This painting was created in an al primo manner, wet paint into wet paint. I admire the loose paint and the unceremonious way this painting has been made. There are some excellent notes; the shadow of the face is particularly well painted and feels real. Some of the highlights, like the white on the shoulder and the yellow on the lit side of the face could have followed the form and been more effective.

All in all, this is a terrific effort. Rozentals was a Latvian portrait painter who achieved renown in his native country. This work is not typical of his better known works, as they are considerably more finished, some quite lovely. But this little painting is a good example of a technique of loose, wet-into-wet oil painting, and so I am happy to include it here.

This might be an opportunity to opine the idea that "less is more." As you become more expert in looking at art and knowing what to look for, this idea may come in handy. Artists often tend to overwork their art in an attempt to perfect it. There often comes a point when the artist arrives at an inflection point. He or she has achieved something truly excellent on the canvas, and he takes a step back to admire it. If he or she is wise, the artist may leave the work at this point, let it rest, and come back to it at a later point with fresh eyes.

If something nags, he or she may take the opposite course to try to make it better. This decision often, though not always, ends in disaster. Why, you ask? Because pursuing past this point has an intention the work did not possess until this point, the intention to improve, fix, or beautify. Not the same intention that took him to this point—the intention to *create*. Invariably, this will take the artist down a road he may not be able to return from.

As you look at art, try to get into the mind of the artist. Did he or she go too far? Overreach perhaps? Or, is the work like this one by Rozentals, of a piece? It is going to make art a lot more interesting as you make these distinctions with your educated eyes.

11. MARY CASSATT, *MATERNAL CARESS*, DRYPOINT

When it comes to the subject we are discussing here, Mother and Child, there is no artist who loved and pursued this subject more beautifully than Mary Cassatt. I could have filled twenty slots in our imaginary class with Cassatt works, and I encourage you to take one afternoon to google Cassatt and study her renderings of this subject. One is more beautiful than the next.

Mary Cassatt was an American who spent most of her life in France, working and exhibiting with the Impressionists. She was a dear friend and colleague of Degas. They often painted together, and Cassatt and her sister even modeled for Degas. Though she embraced the theme of mother and child above all others, she never married and had no interest in being a wife and mother.

Is this surprising? Her works show such devoted love and affection between mother and child; they are filled with emotion. How do you explain that this feeling was not personal to her? Perhaps she just viewed it as a fascinating subject, something beautiful to explain in paint? As Degas admired his dancers, Cassatt admired this special relationship, and found joy in depicting it.

I have selected this particular work because it shows the influence of Japanese art on Cassatt. Make sure to look back to the Utamaro after you've reviewed this work.

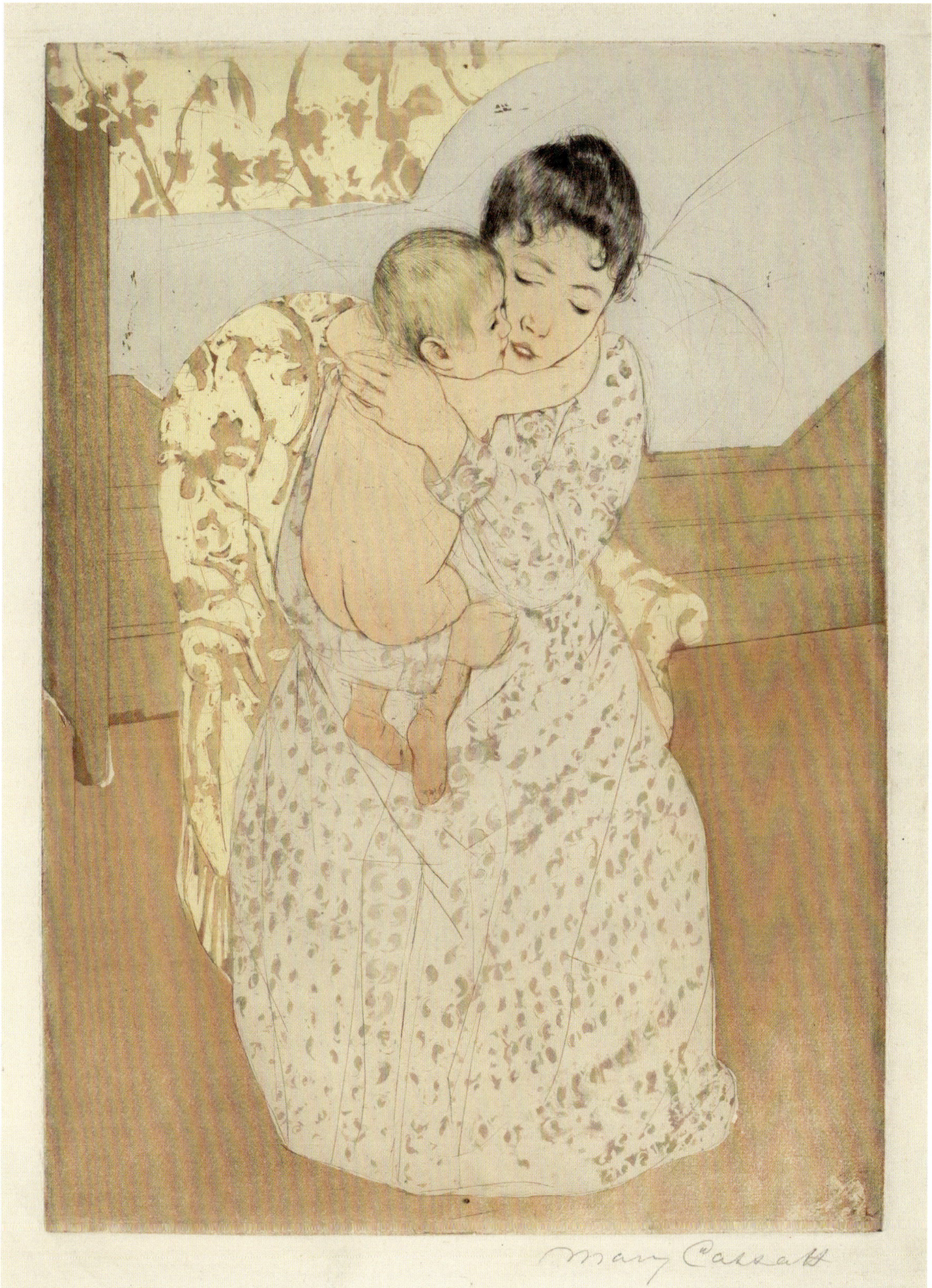

Fig. 89. Mary Cassatt, MATERNAL CARESS.

What has Cassatt borrowed from Japanese works, and what is hers? Let's take this work apart. She has borrowed the color scheme—it is almost identical to the Utamaro—and also the patterning on the robe. But the figures are front and center, not partially offstage like the Japanese print. Cassatt's is softer, has no significant black with the exception of the mother's hair, and even that is softened.

Most significantly, the Cassatt—though similar in color and also a kind of colored drawing, rather than a painting—much like the Japanese print, is not stylized. It is abbreviated with a simplified drawing of facial features, but they still suggest an actual woman and child. There is also more narrative in the Cassatt. The baby's arms are draped around the mother, and we can feel the emotion in the caress.

The latter is not found in the Japanese print, which is more decorative than emotional. So, Cassatt has borrowed the design elements, but she has imbued them with affection. May I also say that her pale yellow with patterning is just stunning in this context.

It is a treat whenever we have the opportunity to see a work "after" that of another artist. Cassatt saw in the Utamaro characteristics that inspired her and that she wished to personalize—express in her own fashion. Faithful to the original in terms of color and subtlety, Cassatt adds the emotional connection between mother and child—the embrace. Both are worthy in their own right.

12. EGON SCHIELE, *MOTHER AND CHILD*, DRAWING

A student of Klimt, Egon Schiele lived a short life, only twenty-eight years, but was prolific in his drawings, drawing continually, through his conscription in World War I, while in a jail cell, and even in the three-day period between his wife's death and his own. He was decidedly an Expressionist, throwing all his emotional drama onto the canvas. The overt sexuality of his nudes was derided by his contemporaries, but his work stands alone today in its expressive power and personal originality.

Here is a mother and child from Schiele. Crude and intense, mother and child share a body. There is no attempt to apply the paint with finesse. You can see the Klimt influence in the mother's hand, but Schiele was much wilder than Klimt, who made many embellishments in a very tailored manner. Klimt wasn't throwing paint on a canvas.

Nothing was buttoned-up about Schiele. He did many self-portraits, nudes, and figurative pieces; you will find all manner of distortion in his work, but it is interesting, bold, and worth studying.

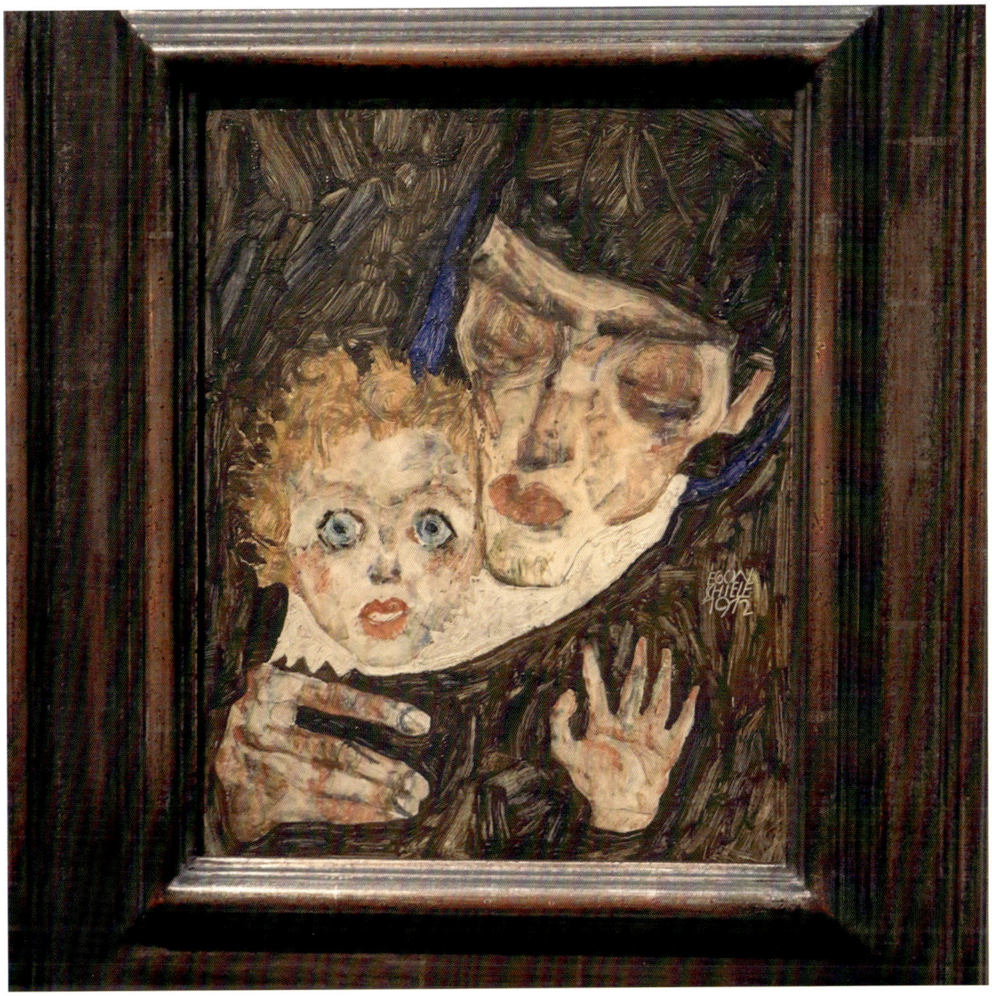

Fig. 90. Egon Schiele, MOTHER AND CHILD.

13. JOAQUÍN SOROLLA, *MOTHER*, OIL

I was not familiar with this Spanish artist's work when I came upon this painting. I absolutely adore it. It is utterly different from all the other iterations of this theme.

This is a painting the artist made of his wife and newborn baby. He sees them in a sea of white, encased in light which bathes the canvas and makes this scene so very special. The poignancy of this painting is palpable. Do you see the mother reaching her hand to touch the baby? The father has captured the intense emotion of his viewing this miraculous scene. We are viewing it with him.

This is truly an amazing feat, to create such a minimalist work that is so affecting. Again, it reminds us that "more" is not "better," and that "less" can be so powerful.

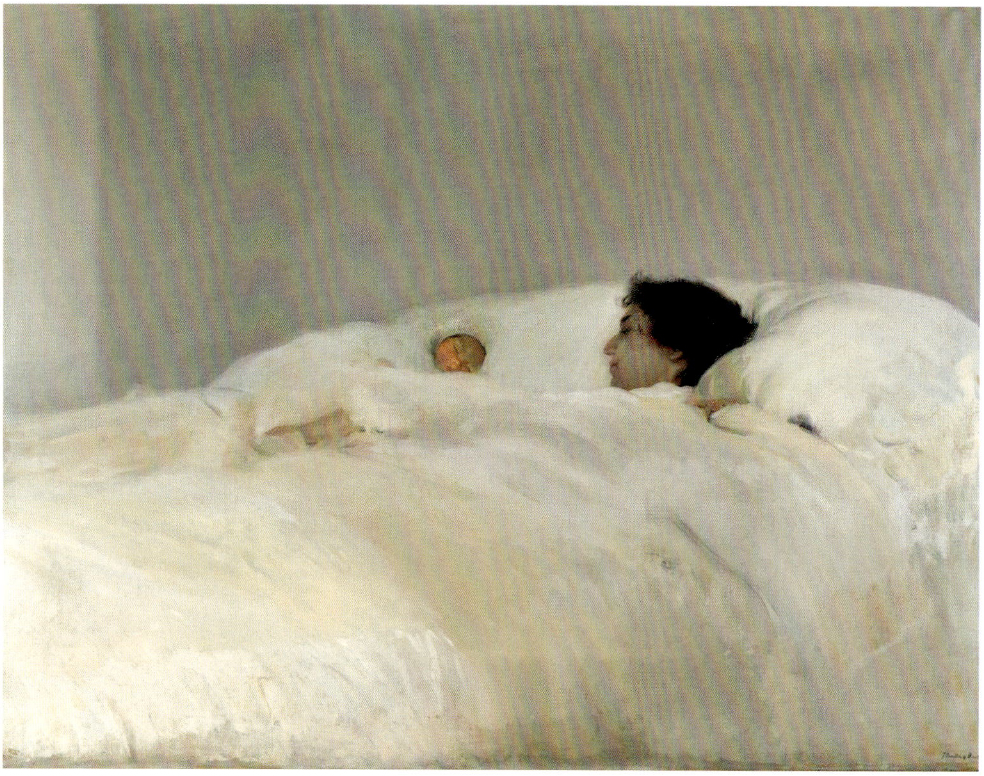

Fig. 91. Joaquín Sorolla, MOTHER.

Look for areas of quiet when you look at art. This work would not be as potent if the figures were larger. It is their smallness that allows us to feel this tenderness.

The gradations of soft gray on the walls and colored whites on the bed are just magnificent. Study how Sorolla used the slight variations in notes to create the form of the bed. It allows your eye to feel its three-dimensionality. You just can sink into it.

Magnificent painting! Remember that an artist like Sorolla is the equivalent of a character actor. Not as known or revered as the leads, these artists often do work that is even more compelling than the stars that all know and recognize. Kudos to Sorolla for this memorable work of art.

14. SANTERI SALOKIVI, *MOTHER AND CHILD*, OIL

We travel to Finland to find Salokivi and view his version of mother and child. It is a painting with thick oil impasto, mostly midtones, carving the form with little notes of color. Nothing startling here, just a pleasant work with the figures backlit. There are some unexpected hues, like the red on the child's face, the green on the

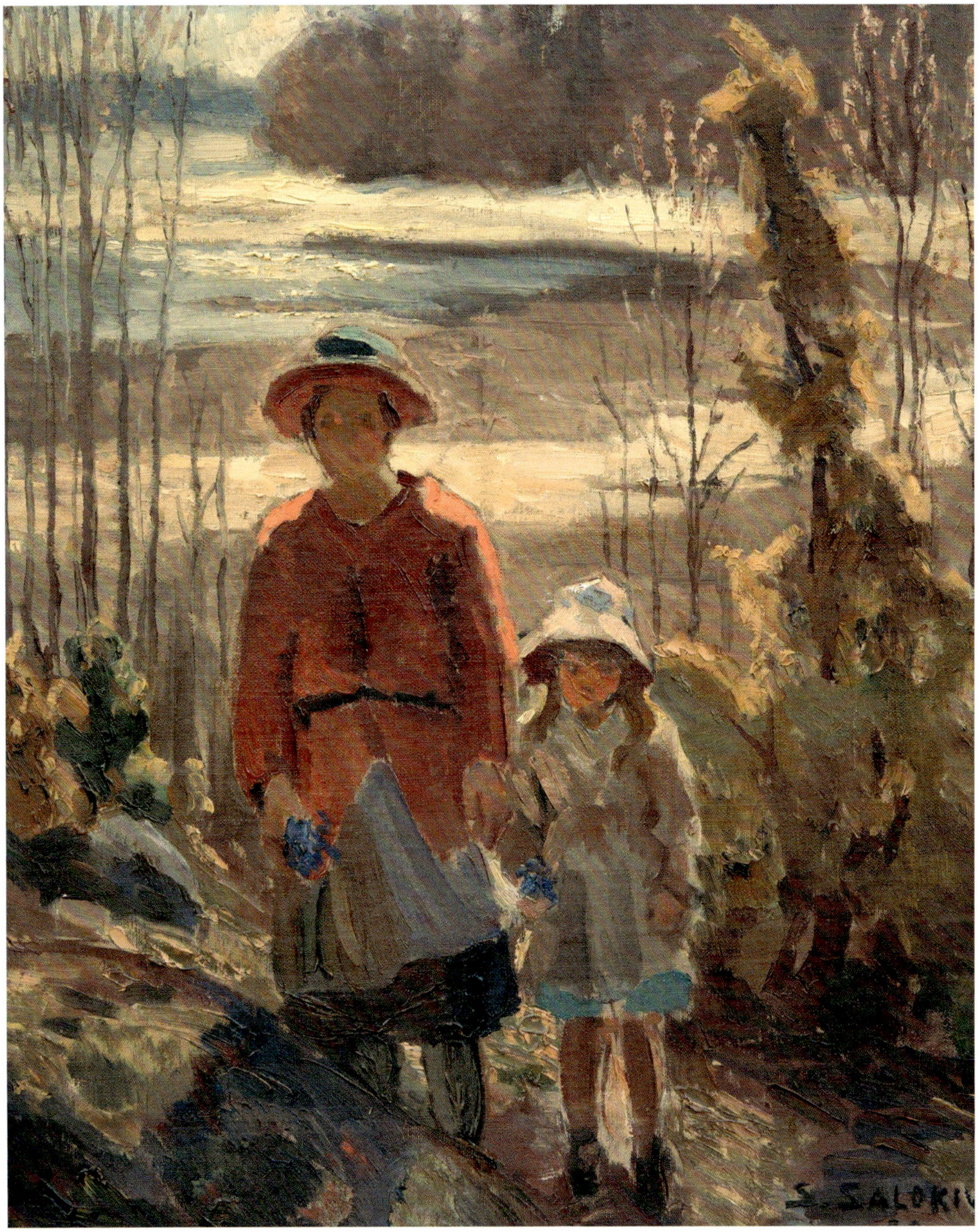

Fig. 92. Santeri Salokivi, MOTHER AND CHILD.

mother's hat, but otherwise, just an attempt to build a representative scene utilizing pieces of colored paint.

The illusion of distance could have been enhanced with thinner or lighter paint mixtures in the background. The hills behind the figure are slightly too prominent and confuse the eye. There is no attempt to individualize the figures or to create any emotional relationship in this work.

It is a capable, though not extraordinary effort to paint a scene that is integrated so the figures are part of the whole, and in that it is successful. When you view a work such as this and compare it to a master like Monet, you can easily see why one is capable and the other is a master. The eye of Monet is not only more alert but more affective; it is filled with emotion, which elevates his work.

We need to look at all levels of work, though, to truly recognize mastery. If you only view the highlights, this level of achievement is normalized, and the highlights cease to be remarkable. Looking at many attempts at art making is the only way to truly appreciate art. This goes for the greats of art as well, as not every work by an artist is successful. It is so useful to see what is not and understand why.

15. EDVARD MUNCH, *DEAD MOTHER AND HER CHILD*, DRAWING

When we talk about emotion in art, there is probably no artist more associated with the phenomenon than Edvard Munch, known around the world for his instantly recognizable *The Scream*. He was the very definition of "Expressionist," baring his unhappiness in this and other works.

In this painting, he gives us the dark side of motherhood, loss, which Munch experienced personally and profoundly with the death of his own mother when he was

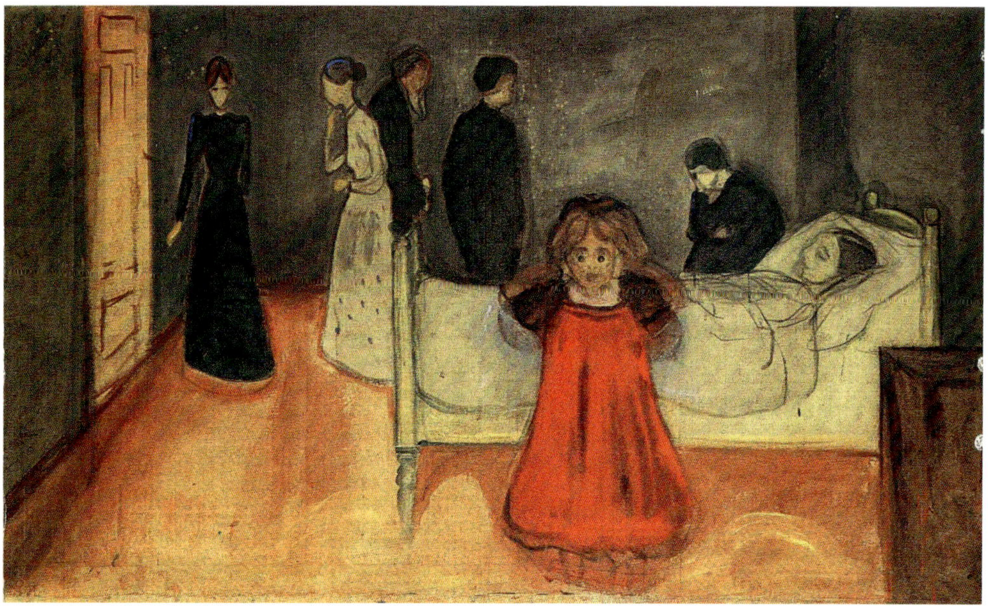

Fig. 93. Edvard Munch, DEAD MOTHER.

five and with the later demise of his eldest sister, probably another mother figure, as well as other losses he was to suffer in a difficult life.

So here we have a mother and child where the mother is dead, another opportunity for Munch to portray if not a scream, the inner embodiment of one.

What can one say about a work like this? There is no point in opining on its aesthetic values.

I can only point to visual art as the great outlet for humans to express their deepest feelings and horrors, all the emotions that haunt them, make them manifest on paper or canvas, and perhaps help to heal, or at least release the devastating feelings.

This is the greatest argument for making art available to everyone, especially children, so all may enjoy this expressive outlet. Would we have a more peaceful world if we all were able to be "expressionists" through art? I believe the answer is yes.

16. CHRISTIAN KROHG, *MOTHER AND CHILD*, OIL

Now we turn to Norway, a country we don't ordinarily associate with visual art, to look at a mother and child from one of this country's exemplars. Christian Krohg was a prominent person, and in addition to his painting, he was a journalist and author. His work falls into the realist category, and he stayed true to naturalistic values, choosing subjects from daily life. Let's have a look at how he realized the mother and child theme.

Well, here Krohg stays true to his mission and gives us a tired mother. She is not romanticized in a reverential pose cradling her newborn as in other iterations we have looked at (Klimt, Cassatt, and Gilman, as well as the Renaissance works). She is shown in her exhausted state, and Krohg has been true to the scene, even leaving in the window cord in the upper left (I have no idea why).

His mission is verisimilitude, and he achieves it quite well. I am a fan of his texture and application of paint, which is superbly applied. His color is local—the wood is red-brown, the bed cover is tan and white, and the dress is gray, but because the paint is so well applied, we accept all as true.

The artist is not painting the light with the figures as only a premise. He is giving us the authenticity of a scene, and he achieves his purpose as effectively as he can. There is no need for fanciful color—it would be discordant in this context. There is no need for expressive distortion as it would be irrelevant here.

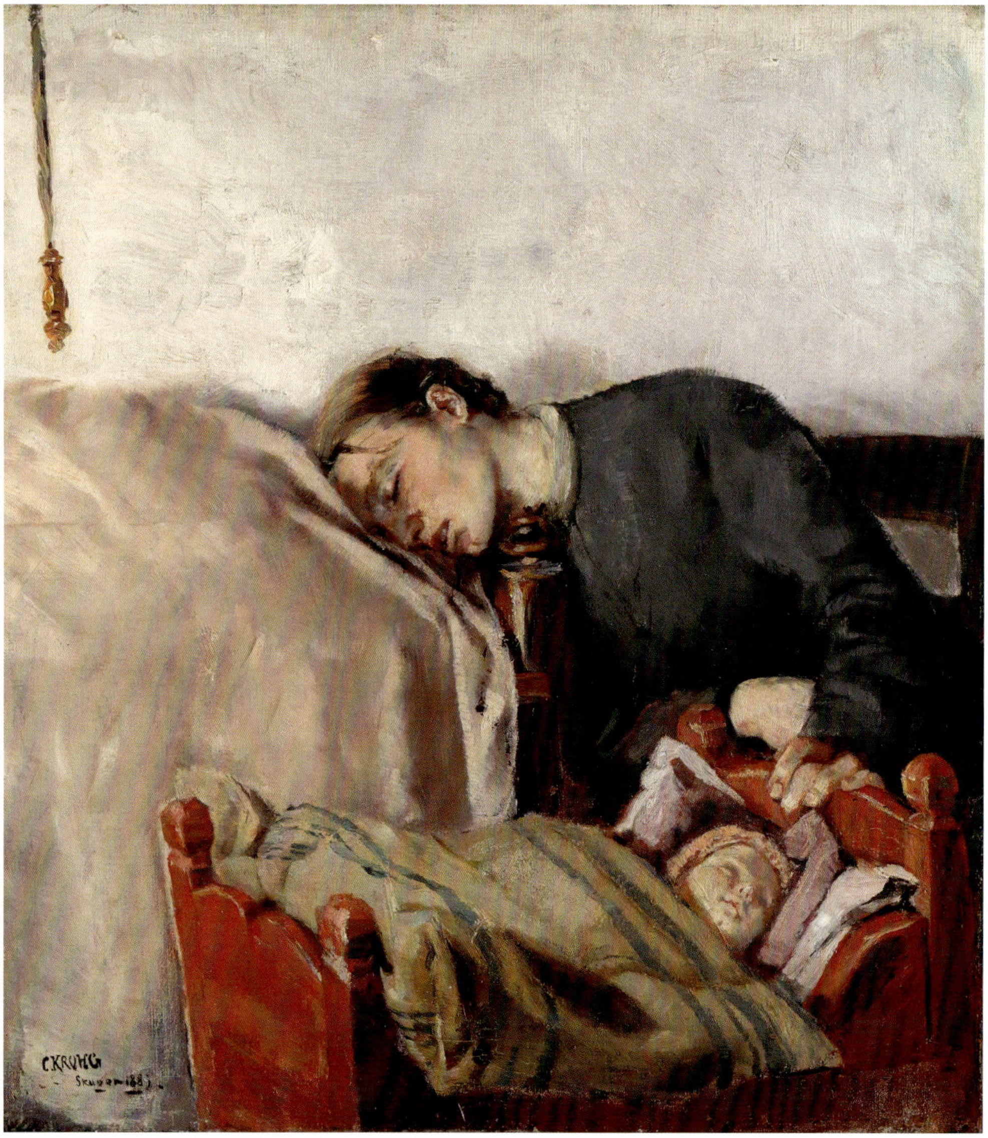

Fig. 94. Christian Krohg, MOTHER AND CHILD.

This is a painting of a day in a life, and an excellent example of a humble, realistic work of art. I was not surprised to learn that Krohg was a journalist, as this painting is actually a journalistic work of art. Much like one of his articles, it aims for truth, and truth is what it delivers in spades.

17. BELA PRATT, *YOUNG MOTHER*, WHITE MARBLE

We haven't looked much at sculpture but cannot neglect this important art form. I am introducing you here to a traditional work on the theme by a Connecticut sculptor, Bela Pratt, to discuss and admire, but also as a liftoff point to discuss the

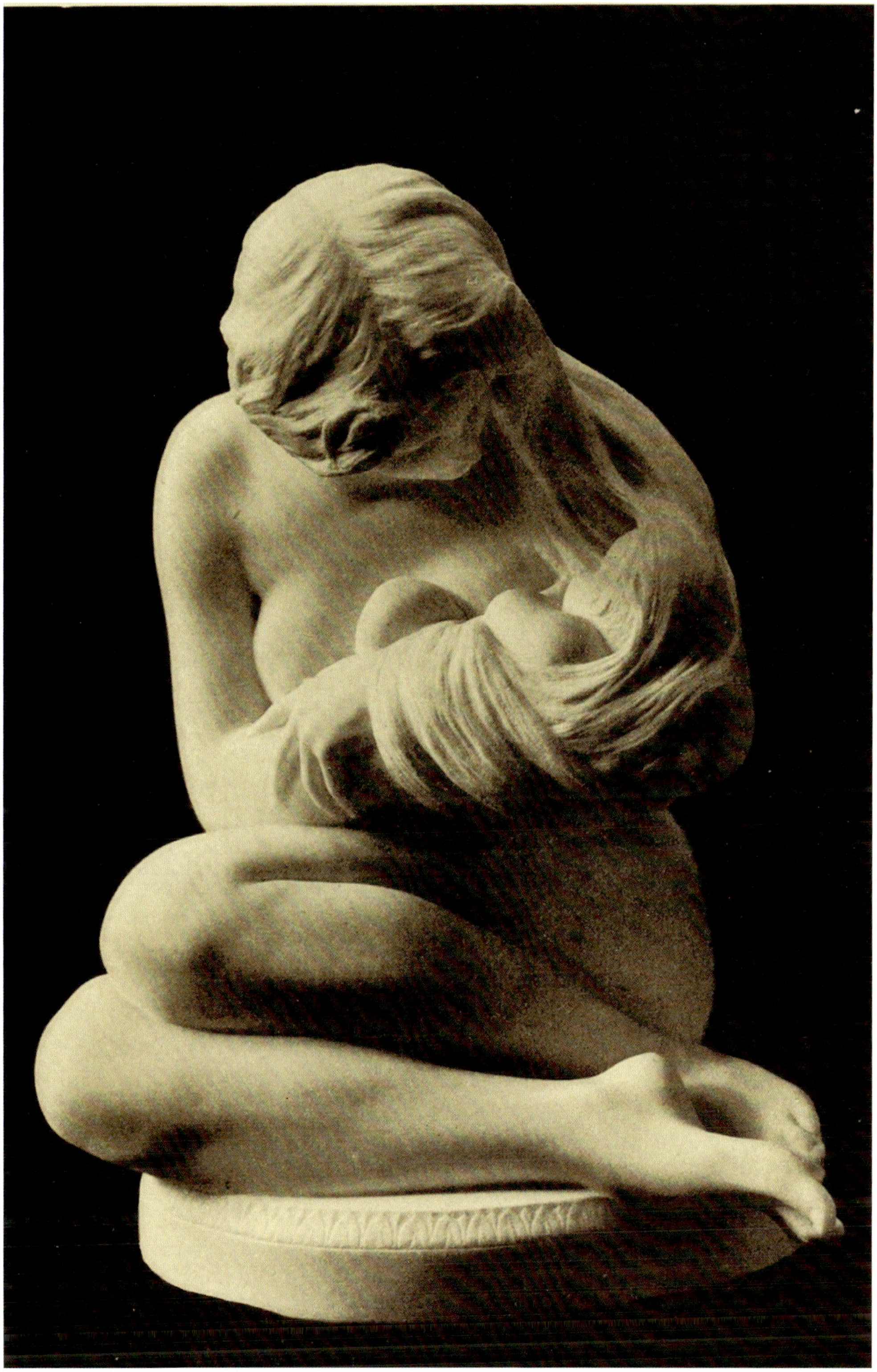

Fig. 95. Bela L. Pratt, YOUNG MOTHER.

sculpture of our next artist, Henry Moore, who introduced a modernist approach to sculpture that I'd like to discuss in more depth.

The Pratt *Mother* is an absolutely beautiful work. Is it a statue or a sculpture? A statue is a subcategory of sculpture. It usually depicts a representative figure, real or imaginary. It may have been created to memorialize a person or group of persons, and though the sculptor may use his best efforts to do so effectively, his intention is not necessarily to create a work of art. A sculpture may be made of any material, is three-dimensional, and may be of any subject, or no subject at all. It can be realistic, semiabstract, or completely abstract, and is created as a work of art, not for any other purpose.

In some cases, as in this work by Pratt, the designation is ambiguous. The work does not commemorate any particular person, as a statue might, but it does depict a person. I think it is clear that it was made with the intention of creating a work of art, so I believe we can properly refer to it as a sculpture.

What makes this sculpture so lovely? It is called *Young Mother*, and the artist has created a beautifully proportioned female in a pose in which she is wrapped around her baby with her head turned in total devotion. He has captured the gaze of love between the two figures. It is compelling and one can't stop looking at it and enjoying it.

The intention of the artist was to create beauty and he succeeded. In the tradition of the Greeks, who excelled at figurative sculpture, he has configured a vision of idealized figures, perfect in their exceptionalism.

18. HENRY MOORE, *MOTHER AND CHILD: HOOD*, TRAVERTINE MARBLE

When we now turn to look at Henry Moore, we are looking at modernist sculpture that has a different intention totally. There is idealization in modernism too, but not the idealization of physical beauty, rather a more complex, symbolic approach to the beauty of form itself. Let's get into what this entails.

Henry Moore was an immensely popular and renowned sculptor who achieved fame and fortune during his long life and influenced many to follow him. He is simply synonymous with modernist figurative sculpture.

His work is found around the world in many public spaces, as well as museums. He was inspired as a child by Michelangelo, and like the master, all of his work is anchored around the subject of the human being—the singular figure, mother and child, lovers, and the family. He explored relationships in his work, the relationship between parts of the body, between individuals, and between groups of individuals. He made ample use of voids—negative spaces that created the relationship of the solid parts that encase them. He also made integral sculptural bodies and laid them in relation to one another.

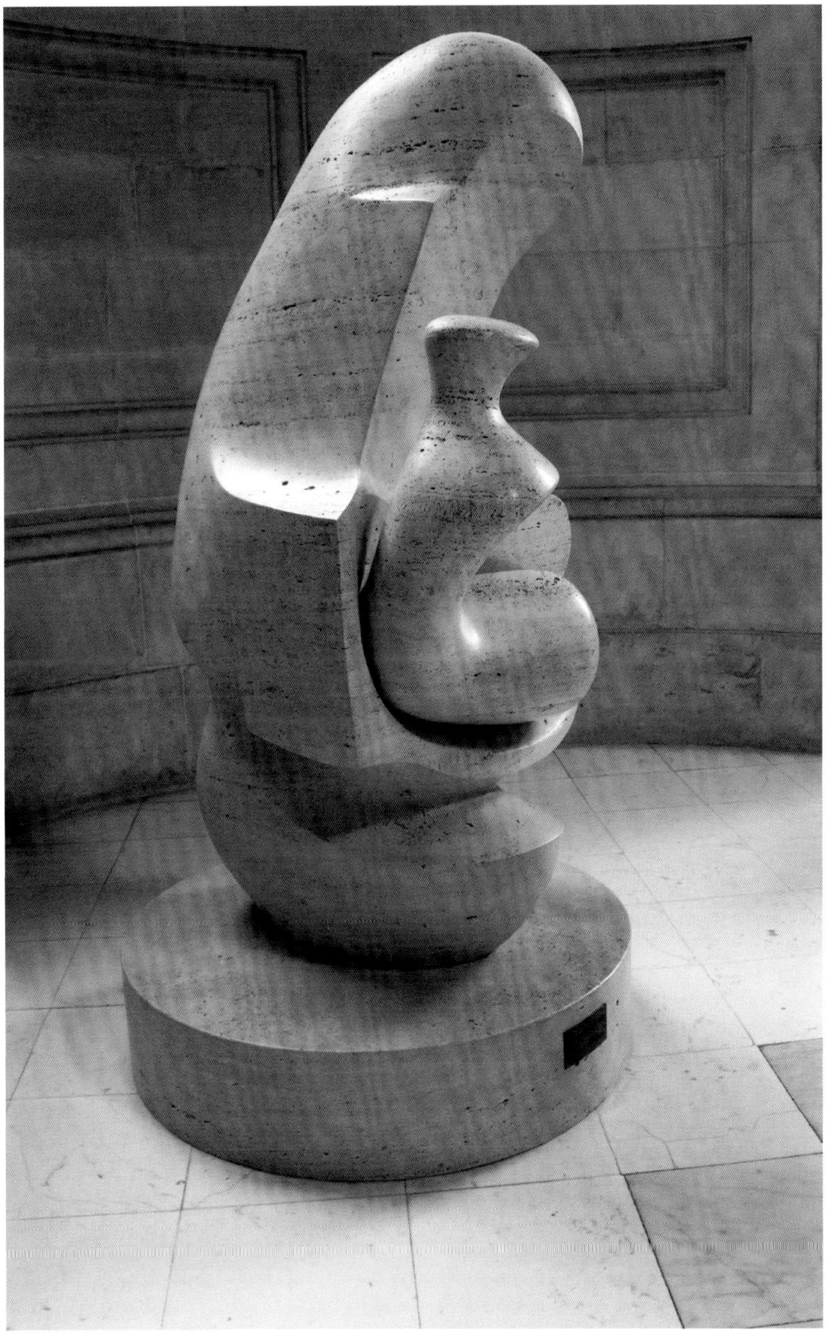

Fig. 96. Henry Moore, MOTHER AND CHILD: HOOD.

He used simplified forms to represent the individual parts, but the sculptures remain semiabstract—we can still recognize them as figures. By simplifying the forms, realistic detail fades into irrelevance, and we can focus on the spatial relationships and the beauty of the forms in and of themselves. We can also appreciate the medium itself, as we do in this mother and child.

Because of the lack of specificity and the perfection of the simple shapes, the work rises from that of a particular mother and child, to a universal mother and child. It becomes an iconic, symbolic work, rather than a portrait. Modernist sculpture as created by Moore takes the art of sculpture to a new purpose and aspiration: to rise from personality to transcendence.

Here was Moore's 1967 statement as to why his work became increasingly simplified: "My sculpture is becoming less representational, less an outward visual copy, and so what some people would call more abstract; but only because I believe that in this way, I can present the human psychological content of my work with the greatest directness and intensity."

19. DOROTHEA LANGE, *MIGRANT MOTHER*, PHOTOGRAPH

This photograph that the documentarian and journalist Dorothea Lange took of an impoverished mother and her children during the Depression became at the time the most reproduced photograph in the world, according to the photographer Martha Rosler. Lange did not know the woman's name, but she was compelled to take the photograph, hoping that it could help the woman in some way.

It is a powerful image, haunting even, and I am including it here because though every photograph is not a work of art, any can be, and the medium is as valid as any other. The camera is just a tool, like a brush or chisel, and it is the hand that holds it that determines whether the resulting work is a snapshot or a photographic work of art. Time also is the arbiter, in that master works from any period seem to live on. But this is not absolute, as many masterpieces are buried in dumpsters and never see the light of day, and works less worthy are extolled.

I am a great fan of black-and-white photography, especially, and I apologize for not including more examples in this book. My favorites are Brassaï, André Kertész, Henri Cartier-Bresson, Alfred Stieglitz, and many others.

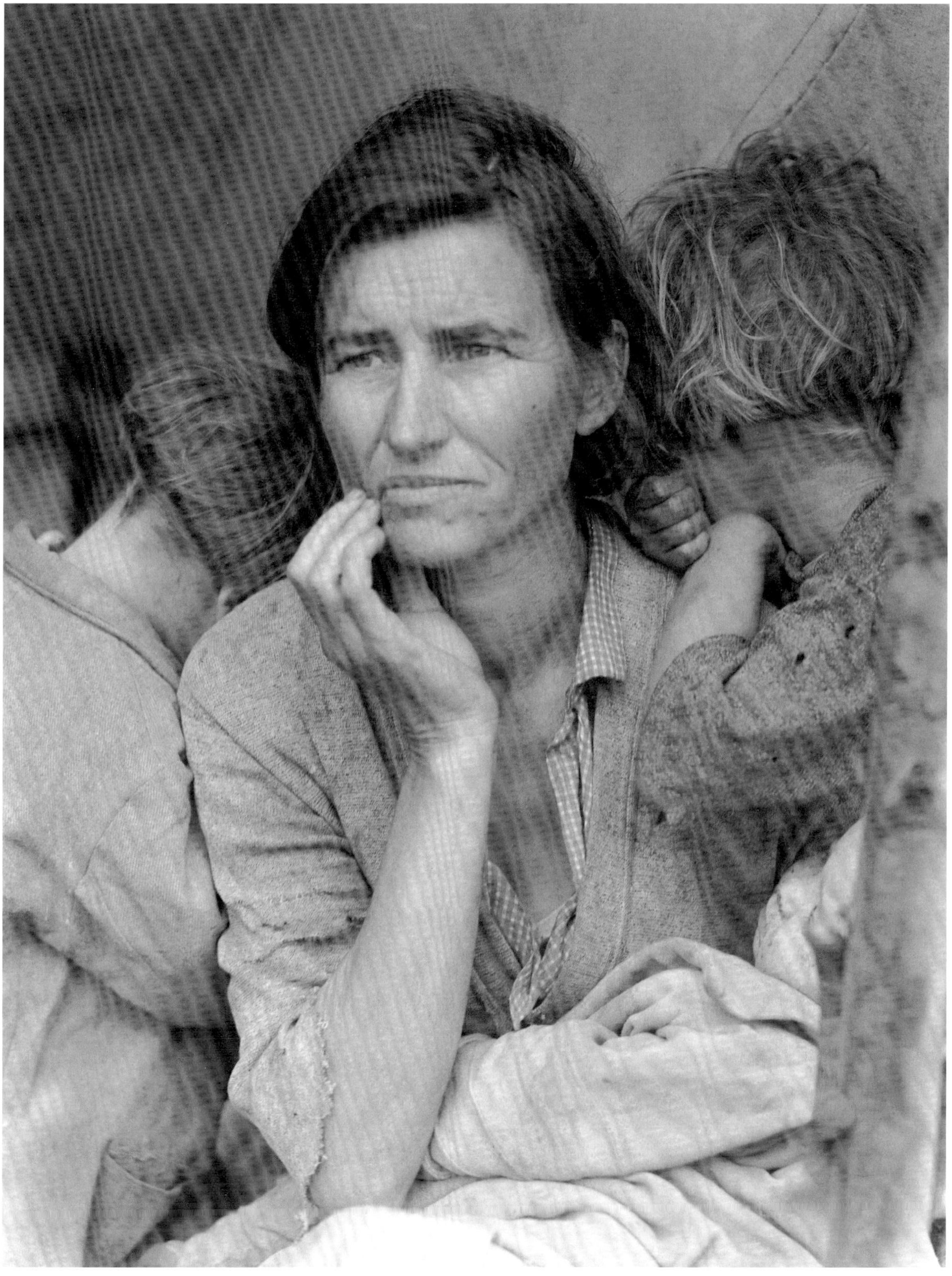

Fig. 97. Dorothea Lange, MIGRANT MOTHER.

20. ALICE NEEL, *MOTHER AND CHILD HAVANA*, OIL

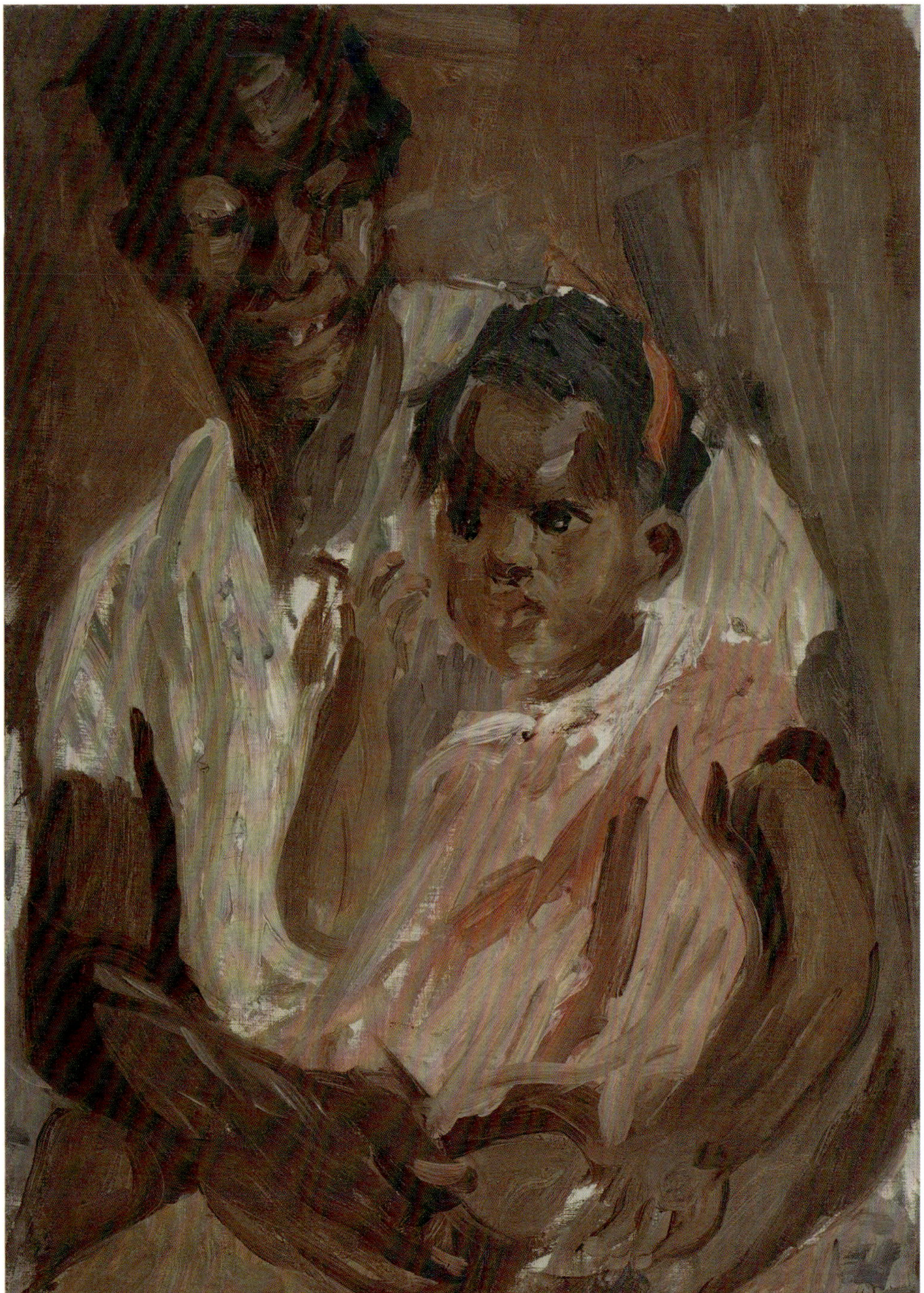

Fig. 98. Alice Neel, MOTHER AND CHILD HAVANA.

Born at the very turn of the twentieth century, Alice Neel was a feminist in her life and in her art. Working during the time when Abstract Expressionism was the rage, her devotion to figurative work put her at the back of the pack. But she persisted and is now praised as an original, eschewing the objectification of women in art and substituting an image that recognizes and celebrates an authentic female perception.

We are looking here at an early work by Neel that she created while living and working in Havana, Cuba. In her student days she had come under the influence of Robert Henri, who coincidentally was the master of my mentor, Norman Raeben, who I wrote about in my first book, *The Creative Path.* Henri and Raeben were proponents of a rather loose style of painting characterized by active, lively brushwork (the Ashcan School). The whole canvas was so enlivened and driven by feeling and sensation.

We see this influence in the mother and child by Neel. It is as if she started painting and did not pause until the entire canvas was complete. The work has a spontaneity, lack of self-consciousness, and freedom that is unmistakable. This makes for a very consistent and harmonious image, really quite remarkable as you continue to look at it.

Neel suffered greatly in her life, yet she is revered, and rightly so, as a free thinker, an explorer and adventurer, and as a great artist who strove to speak truth to power and resisted convention, artificiality, and the dominant male art establishment. Someone worthy of further study for sure.

21. FRITZ STUCKENBERG, *MOTHER AND CHILD*, OIL

I was not familiar with the work of this German Expressionist but was happy to discover this abstracted and stylized mother and child work. With a series of colored curved planes, Stuckenberg has hidden the elements of his two figures. You can admire the work as a colored abstraction without even noticing the hands and heads of the figures.

I am confused by the little stairway lines in the lower right, not having any idea of their significance. I don't find the rainbow of colors interesting, but the manner in which the figures are found in the shapes is excellent and hearkens back to Cubism. The Stuckenberg was an excellent find in illustrating how a very specific subject can be treated from an abstract perspective.

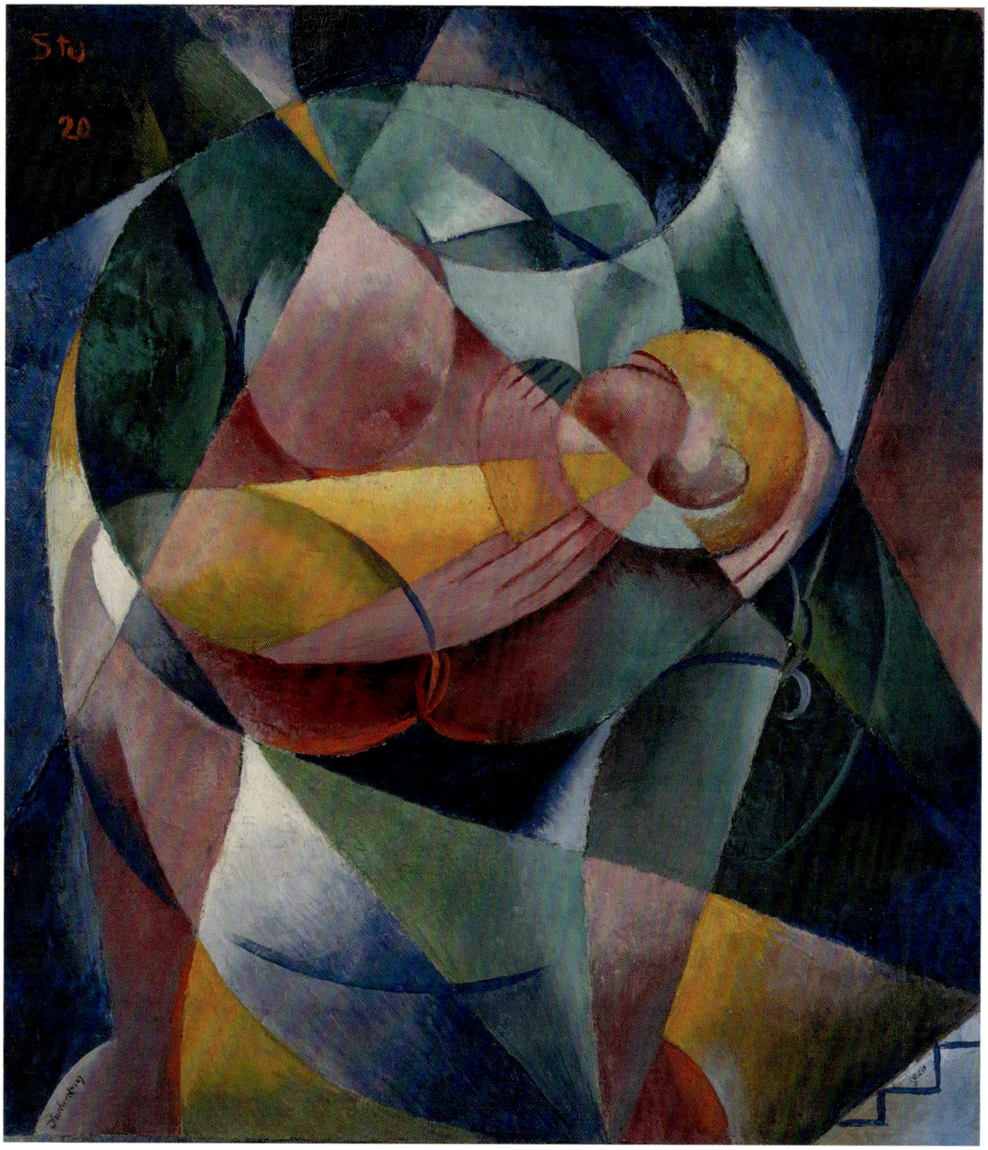

Fig. 99. Fritz Stuckenberg, MOTHER AND CHILD.

22. MILTON *AVERY, MATERNITY*, OIL

This is a work made in 1950 by Milton Avery on a subject he favored. A scan of his works on the theme includes many paintings with considerably more detail. But I chose this one because it is a distillation of the idea of mother and child to its essence. Paring down the shapes to the minimum, Avery eliminates all distraction, all decoration, anything that might displease us. Each flat colored shape announces itself and declares its meaning. Each color seems carefully chosen and deliberate—and these are not the timid, airy colors we associate with this artist. No faces are needed—the colored shapes tell us all we need to know about the relationship between mother and baby.

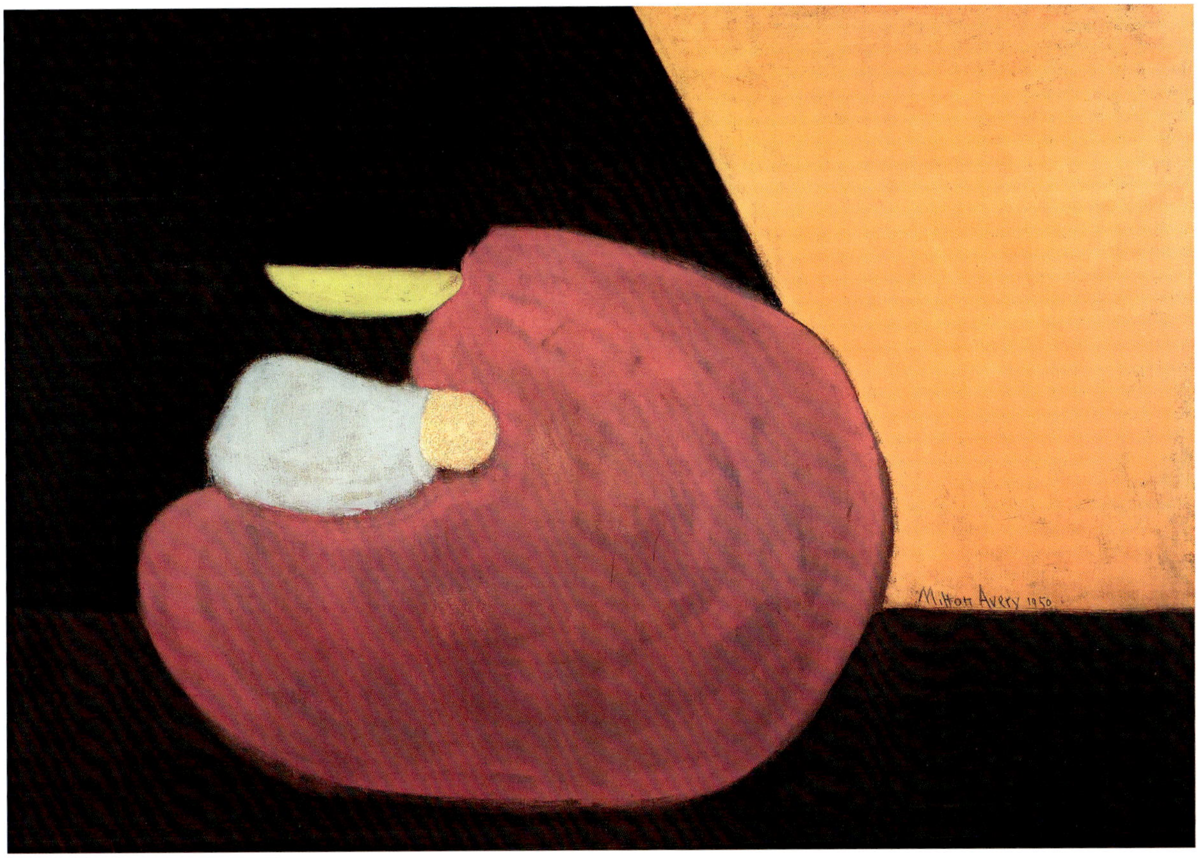

Fig. 100. Milton Avery, MATERNITY.

I want you to recognize that it takes courage for an artist to work so simply and to forgo detail in a work. In such a simple work, every element must be correct for the artwork to be compelling. In a way, it stands naked before you. Milton Avery was a man of courage who was willing to put his visual ideas down on canvas truthfully, clearly, and without obfuscation of any kind. This is commendable. Don't you just adore the wonderful composition and palette in this work?

I do.

23. CAROLYN SCHLAM, *MOM, CHILD AND DOLL*, COLLAGE

As you have probably already guessed, the theme of Mother and Child is a favorite one of mine and I have made a number of versions during my career in a whole variety of media.

I like the subject for the same reasons I have outlined here in our discussion of these artists. It is a sentimental subject, one for which we have definitive emotion. It also poses the dynamic possibilities of relating two figures, which is always interesting. It can be interpreted using pretty much any approach and any medium. So it is an excellent challenge for any visual artist.

The artwork I am sharing with you is on theme but it is not one of the many romantic pieces I have done, attempting to put into paint my emotion for this emotional bond. No, this is a constructed work, which is more focused on design, patterning, and composition. I have included a current and more endearing Mother and Child in the Appendix so you can compare and contrast.

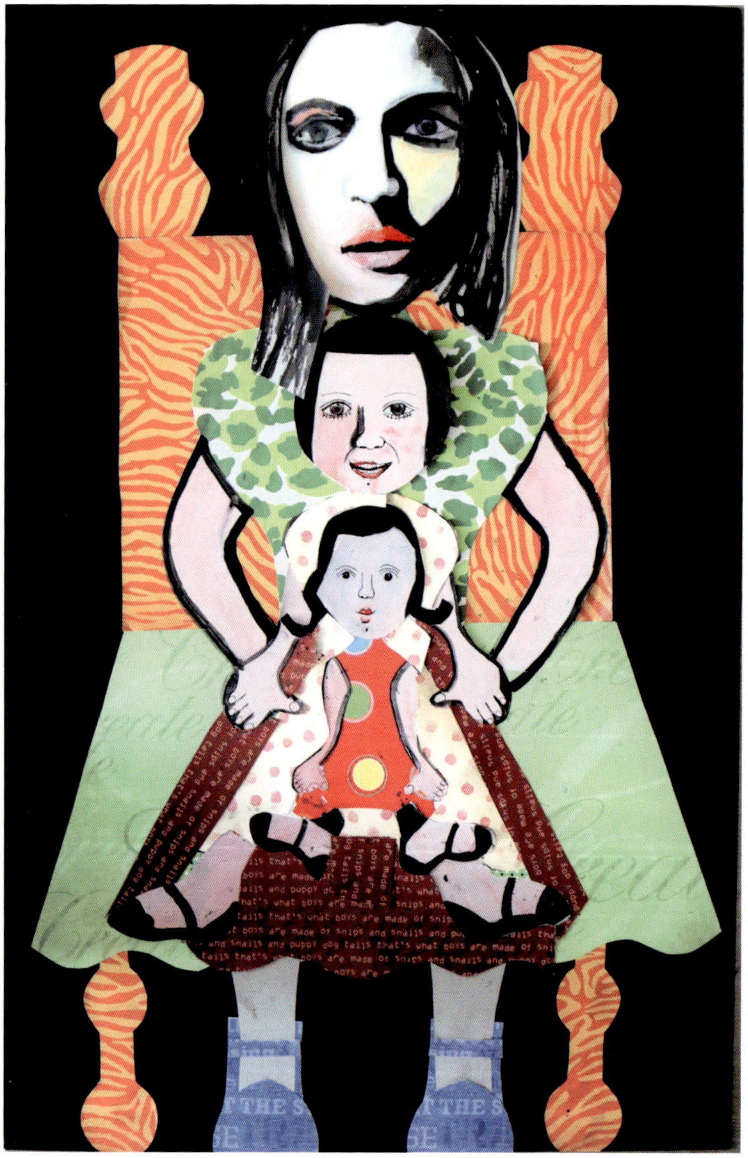

Fig. 101. Carolyn Schlam, MOM CHILD AND DOLL.

This work is a collage. I painted the faces and cut and pasted papers to make the composition. It is just the result of an idea that popped into my head one day and which I worked to realize. Nothing too serious, just kind of fun to look at.

Artists explore many moods and states of mind in their work and often flip back and forth. In my case, I am a bit of a tinkerer, I love puzzles, and putting things together—ideas, books, dolls, found-object sculptures, all kinds of oddities. My art practice allows me to play, experiment, and try to manifest what are often contrivances that occur to me in dreams, while I am swimming, or walking the dog. I have made people into little glass chairs, pillows into all kinds of creatures, a woman in a box, pots with arms and legs, all kinds of creative bursts and treats. My studio is a playroom, a facsimile of Santa Claus's workshop, a kindergarten where I get to be both the teacher and the child. Lucky me!

IN SUMMARY

I hope this review of twenty-three works on the same subject has given you a sense of perspective and that you now have an inkling of just a few of the myriad ways there are of looking at this subject or any other. And it is never-ending, as artists continue to come up with new ideas, new materials, new ways of visioning and making art. Make sure to visit the Appendix to this book to see the modern renderings on this theme.

The miracle of life is the foundation of art and I daresay the subject of Mother and Child will continue to interest artists as a worthy avenue for their minds and hearts. I am wondering what artificial intelligence will make of it, don't you? Let's stay tuned to find out.

Chapter 8
Essence

If you somehow could put all the artists in the world together for a Zoom meeting to discuss the meaning of art—what they were all after, what made them get up in the morning and want to rush to the studio—there would be one word that kept coming up. That word is *essence*.

Artists—people who have a burning need to express themselves regardless of the medium, style, or subject—by their very nature and intent, drill down into their hearts and psyches to find that kernel of meaning, that intrinsic nature, that indispensable quality, that ***IT*** that is the *essence* of what they seek.

I know this not only because I have read many books about art, or looked at lots of works of art, or talked to many artists, which I have, but because I know, as one of them, that this is the engine that keeps us going, canvas after canvas, disappointment after disappointment, joy after joy. This is the **quest** I spoke of in *The Joy of Art*. This is our North Star, our raison d'être, our reason to be who we are.

So what is it exactly, this essence? What is this one thing we want to find, to create, that we will surely know when we see it. Is it the same for everyone? If not the same, is it similar?

My answer: It is a something—a quality, a shape, a rhythm, a dance, a color, a style, whatever you want to call it—that is, to the very closest degree, the embodiment of who that artist is. If the body and soul and consciousness, the totally individual DNA of that artist could be bottled, this would be the perfume that emanates.

Sound crazy? Wacky? Fantastical?

That's what we are trying to put on that canvas or in that sculpture. If it's a flower, it's the artist if she was a flower. If it's a figure, it's how we want a body to look and feel. If it's abstract, it's the way we like to move. It's just ourselves, not the way we appear to others, or the way we look, or how we sound or act. No, it's who we are down deep, where no one can quite peer. Our identity.

We're bringing it out for the world to see. It is, yes, our essence. The unspeakable that we recognize instantly. The nitty-gritty.

Now that I've said this, what can you do with this information as a person who is interested in art? Will it help you to understand and appreciate art?

It absolutely will if you begin to treat your viewing of art likewise as a quest. A quest for what? A quest to uncover the nature of the artist's essence and identify it.

Here are questions to ask:

What makes this artist tick?

What matters to him or her?

Why does this artist create what they create?

Where did that style come from?

Let's look at the work of a few artists with this in mind and identify their raison d'être, their be-all and end-all, okay?

Here goes.

Part of the essence is physical.

When I look at the way Picasso drew the figure, I see him. He was a short, stocky man; if you chose his spirit animal, it would be a bull. His work has a decided physicality too; there is nothing filmy or fey about it. He draws with authority, bullishly, if you will. The figures are generously proportioned, and he is determined and strong; he puts on the paint definitively, not delicately.

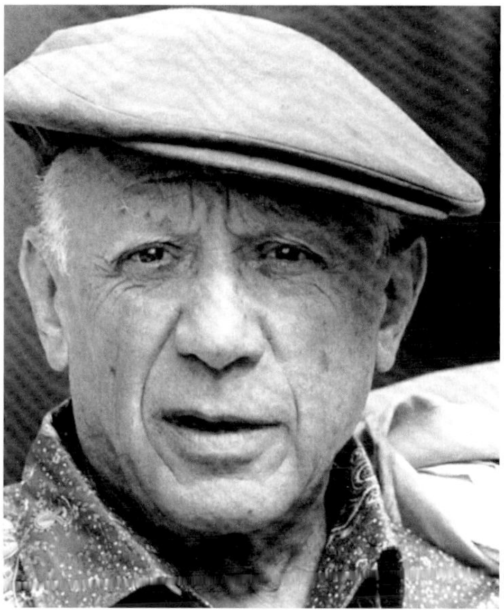

Fig. 102. PHOTO OF PABLO PICASSO.

Then you have Giacometti, the artist who sculpted overly elongated and thin sculptural figures, some with those overly large feet that grounded them. His aesthetic, his message, is embodied in these fragile, breakable yet rooted forms. And then you have his opposites in Aristide Maillol or Fernando Botero, with their swollen figures. Why these choices, these obsessions, this specific physicality?

We project ourselves into our work. A lot of it is unconscious. We have a certain way of drawing, a definite rhythm, a heavy hand, or a delicate one. We sweep or we are dainty; we are ferocious or tamed.

We stand at a certain way at the easel. We move in a very repeatable fashion. We hold the brush in our own way. We mix the paint in a unique fashion. We favor particular colors. We don't necessarily mean to, but it becomes a habit. It seems instinctual, the way we hold ourselves and move while we work.

Modigliani's women are immediately recognizable. They are languorously splayed on the canvas, heads tilted to the side, eyes a solid pupil-free color of the Mediterranean Sea. Their arms are folded in the curve, the curve is everything. The Italian S curve, he must have it.

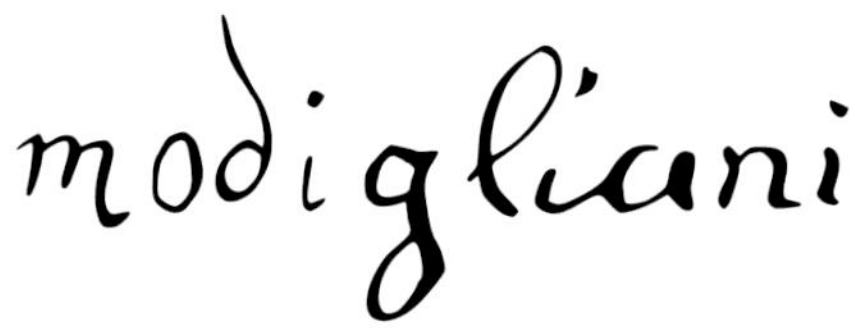

Fig. 103. SIGNATURE OF AMADEO MODIGLIANI.

Renoir is oh so sweet, I wonder why. There is sugar in every mixture. Bonnard puts sunshine in his colors—he is positive, but in a different way. Vuillard is so tasteful, adding a little black to give us those subtle tones. Take note: Every artist spins a different symphony of color, and their palette has a decided taste and tone. Listen.

For the artist, the way the elements of art that we elaborated in our first chapter—light, color, shape, and form, space, texture, line—are elaborated is very, very personal. The ingredients may be the same, but the recipe and proportions are unique to each. Together, in concert, they speak to the essence—what the art is about and its one-of-a-kind signature.

People who see my work comment: all the women look the same. Did I intend this? No, it just comes out that way. Do they look like me? Not like my image, no, they do not resemble my countenance.

What do they resemble then? Perhaps an inner reflection, a selfie of the self, how we look on the inside. Does this make sense? I know it to be true.

Artists may compete to gain favor, to win prizes or competitions, or to be selected and have their work well reviewed, prized, and purchased, but we know that in truth, there is no competition. Each of us can only be ourselves, so we can only be better at revealing our essence and taking it to the nth degree. In truth, there is no competition that is meaningful, except that which we undergo with ourselves.

After a while, as we repeat and redo and try again, this search for the essence takes shape and we get to own it. People recognize it. They call it our style, our signature. We get to claim it.

No one can take it, and if they imitate it, we will call them inauthentic fakes, or even apply the dreaded adjective "derivative." If you are a bona fide artist, you've got to drill down into the formula that is you and turn it into that unmistakable something. People will pay good money for that eau de parfum.

As followers and readers of art, it is the multiplicity, the infinite variations that we can enjoy, that provides us with joy. This is augmented when we recognize what each artist is going after. How can we know if he or she has arrived, if we have no understanding of where they were going with their work?

Part of the essence is psychological. Also sociological. And philosophical.

When I was in Paris in 2023, I visited the Musée Carnavalet and chanced upon a painting by an artist I was not familiar with. The painting was a portrait of the feminist journalist known as Séverine, the first French woman to run a newspaper, also known as Caroline Rémy. Here is a photograph of Séverine for reference.

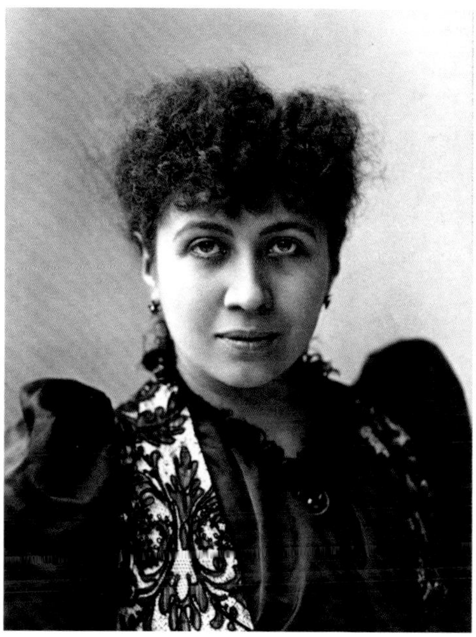

Fig. 104. PHOTOGRAPH OF SÉVERINE.

The creator of this portrait was Amélie Beaury-Saurel (1849–1924), a French artist born in Barcelona. I was not formerly familiar with this artist, but I was struck by this portrait. What was interesting about it?

It is a beautiful work with many fine attributes I can point to. The drawing is first rate, with the figure in the foreground and a good halo of deep space behind her. Her form is prominent but subtly wrapped in a revealing fabric with expertly painted folds and draping. Her two hands fall well with their weight well defined. The palette is limited, neutral even, but satisfying. The work is harmonious and not overdone, very pleasing to look at.

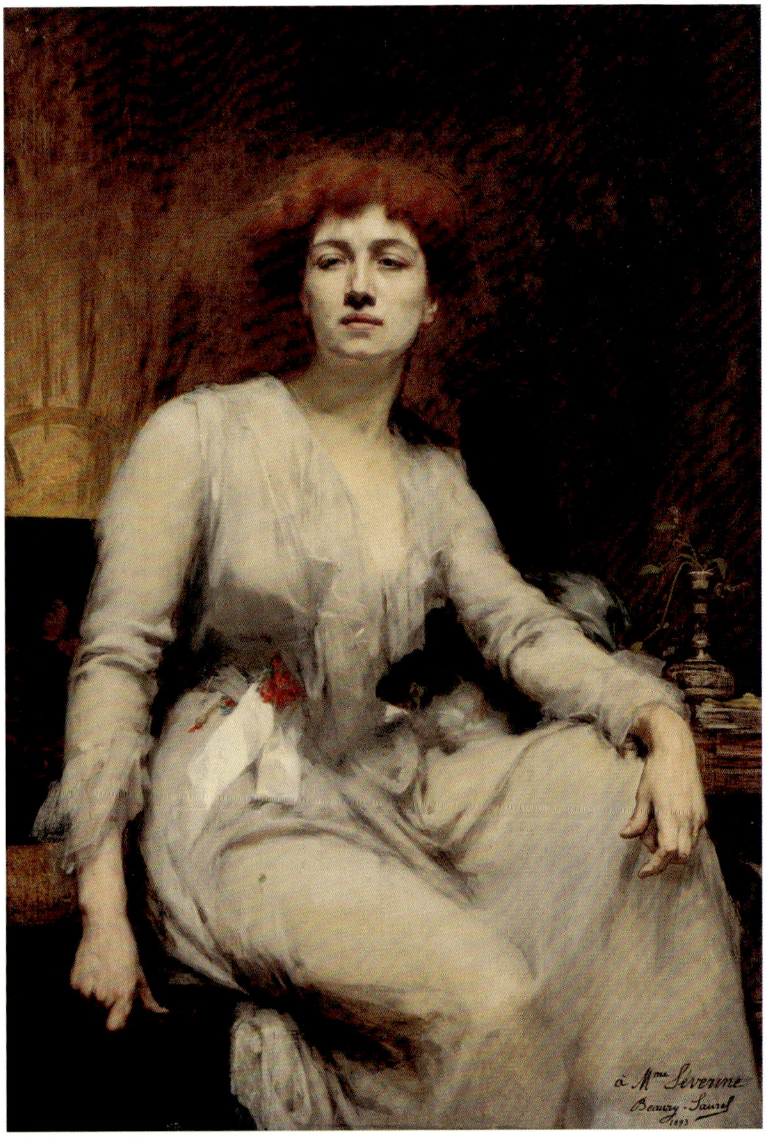

Fig. 105. Amélie Beaury-Saurel, PORTRAIT OF SÉVERINE.

All true. Aesthetically masterful. But what makes this work so compelling that it stopped me in my tracks? Above and beyond all the attributes that make this an act of superb painting, the artist has captured something extraordinary. Study the expression of this figure. Despite her obvious beauty as a no-longer-young woman, I feel her fatigue, resignation, struggle even. Disappointment? Perhaps.

Intelligence? Definitely. Skepticism and Wariness? Yes, surely.

Perhaps we can attribute this to the fact that the artist is a woman, and she has identified with her subject. The model is a famous woman, and much is known about the facts of her life, if not her psychic status. But the artist has found a way to reveal more than her appearance or her character. She reveals her state of mind, her emotional state. Perhaps artist and model are simpatico. The artist is not famous, at least not as famous as her male contemporaries. Maybe she has put this reality into the paint.

Whatever the reason, the result is a quite extraordinary work of art, and a true homage to the subject. It is an accomplished woman's portrait of an accomplished woman. With the recognition that in spite of the accomplishment, both artist and subject still lag behind their male counterparts and have to work three times as hard to get where they are. This certainly had a bearing on the manner in which the subject is portrayed, her comportment, features and expression.

But this is not all. In researching this painting and the subject, I found another artist who decided to paint Séverine. The Impressionist Renoir was a fan and did several versions of this subject. Let's keep in mind that we are now looking at a portrait of a female subject created by a successful male artist.

This portrait is painted in a looser, Impressionist style. Perhaps you may view it more as a painted drawing than an actual painting. It shows a woman from the waist up, dressed in feminine finery—headdress and flower neckwear. She sports a demi smile, posing attractively for the artist.

The artist was surely interested in the subject, as he painted her four times. But why? In all four iterations, we see just this pretty woman, with little hint of her status or role, and no reference whatsoever to her state of mind.

She is hardly a person, almost a foil for the flowers and decoration, revealing nothing at all, an excuse for the artist to try out his painting prowess. Am I being too harsh? Am I showing my own biases?

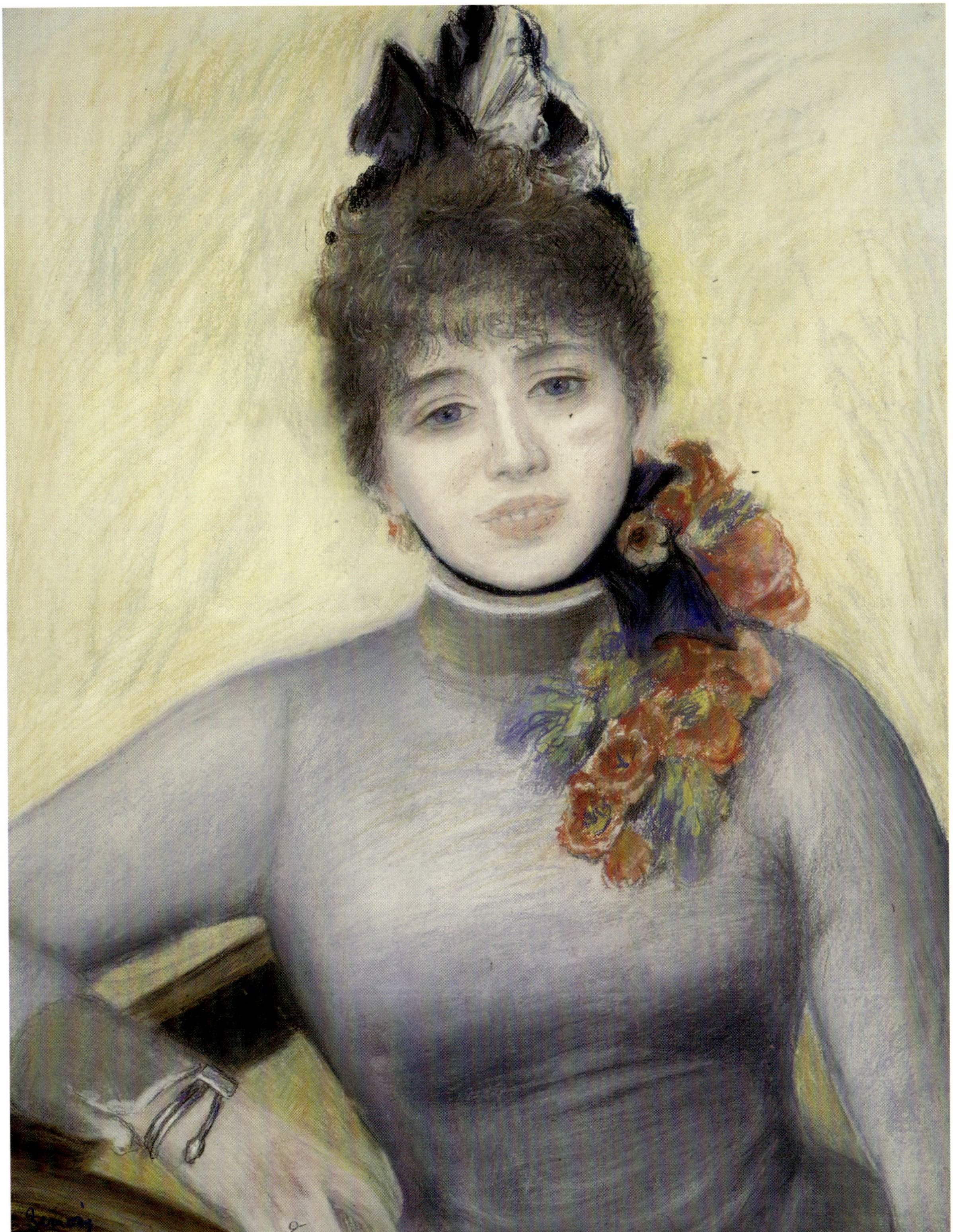

Fig. 106. Auguste Renoir, PORTRAIT OF SÉVERINE.

Do we attribute this lack of content to the fact that Renoir disparaged the subject? That he failed to see her and to portray her as a person of substance? That, for whatever reason, he failed to read her state of mind and chose to paint her merely as a pretty woman? Do we assume he was a misogynist or are we reading too much into this work? Do we conclude it was Renoir who was shallow?

Just as the artist sees the world from his unique vantage point and chooses subjects that are meaningful, and in so doing reveals what energizes and inspires him or her, so does the viewer see the work from their individual point of view, prejudices and biases included. I plead guilty; you can surely read my bias in this analysis. Remember, though, that does not necessarily make it incorrect.

Essences are sought and revealed both for the artist and viewer, and the nexus of these judgments goes a long way to determining what is culturally relevant and what is applauded and respected, both in terms of praise and monetary value. These judgments are always in a state of flux, as the myriad factors that affect human perspectives are constantly changing.

I encourage readers and viewers of art to search to uncover artists' essence through their works while at the same time staying cognizant of their own preferences and biases. There is no way to be pure in our thinking, but in being aware of where we are coming from and what is important to us, we can do the best job in understanding works of art.

Part II

The Art of Today and Tomorrow

Introduction
Artists of Today

I am very excited about now having the opportunity to share with you the work of living contemporary artists working and exhibiting their work today. It is a privilege and I thank them all for their participation. I have sought out artists who work on a variety of subjects in their own inimitable way. They come from places all around the world. Each has their own song to sing. Some are well known, others not as much. They are all superb practitioners of their craft.

There are more people engaged in the arts than ever before and many of them are supremely talented. I could have selected dozens more. It is so easy to discover new art as most working artists either have their own websites or post their work on general sites or artist representatives' sites. You can probably google any phrase or category and go on an art hunt. That's how I discovered many of the wonderful artists that are featured here.

I wish that I could say that I have given you a representative sample. Truthfully, there is no way I could have accomplished that for a number of very good reasons. First, there are just too many people making art, and what they make is incredibly diverse. The possibilities are endless, and the way people find to express themselves, within any genre, is truly mind-blowing. I could only truly offer a paltry number of these many points of view.

Another reason, of course, is that I am selecting them. Though I endeavored to choose work that I found interesting and expressive, my own limitations, prejudices, and preferences invariably influenced my selections. Add to that the fact that the world is vast and I am in a mere corner of it, with limited access to those in faraway cultures. Another reason is that I am old, and I admit my proclivities probably lie in more traditional arenas. Those working in modern iterations that may involve artificial intelligence, performance-related work, and other avant-garde iterations leave me scratching my head.

Though I did not intend for this to be the case, I see that I have a preponderance of figurative artists represented. As a figurative artist myself, this subject is most interesting to me, and I guess led me to gravitate to my compatriot artists who also enjoy the subject. I certainly do not mean to suggest any superiority for this genre. My personal interest just serves me here, in that I can explain it in more detail and with more assurance.

I apologize for this. It is said that the music we relate most to in our lifetimes is the music we listened to when we were adolescents on the verge of adulthood. Perhaps something similar is true for visual art. I studied art with an individual born in the year 1900 who had no knowledge of many of these forms, media, and approaches. I, two generations ahead, have become somewhat more familiar, but probably not enough. I will leave it to a younger author to continue this inquiry where I have ended it.

So, this is not a representative sample of the art of living artists. It is not comprehensive. In fact, it just offers a teeny glimpse at the work of just a very few artists who chose to participate in this endeavor. Others I contacted declined, for one reason or another. As you might expect, most of them were already well known. They were not seeking any more exposure.

Now that I have given you that disclaimer, please understand that, although this is a small sample, it is nonetheless a good one. Our purpose is to utilize the keys we have discussed in the first part of the book to look at these works and apply what we have discussed. So these works are as good as any for our purpose. That being said, I am not minimizing their excellence in any way. In fact, they were selected because each is a superb exemplar of their intention and craft.

A caveat. I have asked these artists to place themselves into one of three artificial categories I have created, to choose one that best describes their intention. I had a feeling when I decided this that they might balk at these classifications, saying they cannot limit themselves to any one category. And they are surely right, as no one can truly be characterized in this artificial way.

Why have I made these distinctions, then, you ask? My answer: to isolate and highlight the various motivations artists may have in initiating and following the creative process. I am hoping that these categories will assist the reader in understanding the genesis of a particular work of art and thereby find a pathway to interpreting any word of art they might encounter.

The three categories are:

1. **Beauty**, i.e., the way it looks: technique, design, and composition
2. **Truth**, what it says: message, narrative, statement
3. **Emotion**, how it makes us feel: resonance, passion, the personal

Just as we have seen artists fixate on an intention and purpose only to see the next generation seek an opposing view, these categories might seem artificial, yet still offer an elucidating framework. The distinctions may not be definitive, but the journey should be an interesting one.

So step with me from modernity onward as we look at the artists of today and think about tomorrow. I guarantee it will be an engaging and revelatory trip.

Chapter 9
Living Artists Whose Focus Is on Beauty

BEAUTY—THE WAY IT LOOKS

Every visual artist is concerned with the way their work looks. This goes without saying. Firstly, he or she has endeavored to put the work in visual form. It is something the artist wanted you to look at. That is a certainty.

That does not mean that the artist necessarily wanted to create something that was attractive, or any of the synonyms you can think of—beautiful, pretty, pleasing, lovely, stunning, etc. He or she would be concerned that whatever was created was well presented—that it delivered, to the best of his or her ability whatever the artist's intention might be. It might be to make a statement about something, to convey the quality of something, to engender a feeling or sensation, to be funny, or clever, or intelligent, or whatever.

Regardless of the intention, how that intention could best be realized in visual form is a crucial element in the effort of every visual artist. Every artist has a certain bank of skills to apply to the task. Some have excellent photographic recall of objects and can draw realistic renderings easily and well. But not every artist is so endowed. Some refer to source material, like models and photographs, for guidance and counsel. Some eschew drawing or painting objects at all and express themselves exclusively with abstract geometric or organic shapes, or other abstract elements such as linear treatments and fields of color.

Some artists work in a systematic fashion, preparing sketches and planning their works, applying materials sequentially and realizing their ultimate goal in a well-thought-out routine. Others work totally al primo, and let their imagery occur in an unscripted manner. Either way, though, as the process proceeds the artist is minute by minute asking, *Is this what I want to do? Does this look right? Is the paint too thin, too thick, too red, too blue? Am I on track?*

They are measuring their work against what, you rightly ask? A standard of excellence perhaps? An expectation? A hope? A fantasy of making the most amazing piece of art ever made? An imaginary scale of beauty?

We don't know exactly. What we do know are things like this: *It isn't good enough. It's too dark. The paint is too thick. It looks dead. It's not what I wanted to say. Wow, I love that mark on the upper right. The feet are too small.* These are the kind of thoughts that enter an artist's consciousness while we are working. It is a stream of qualifications and judgments we make that propel us to make changes, make choices, and proceed.

Here's a question for you: Does anyone want to make an ugly painting? That's very difficult for us to imagine, isn't it? What if I said our intention was to express a negative idea or emotion, like corruption, greed, the ugliness of war? I would have to impart ugliness, wouldn't I? Can you impart ugliness as something that is beautiful? Certainly not.

I hear you quoting my own talk about expressiveness. Yes, if expressiveness is the goal, and the artist has achieved that, he or she has created beauty *in* ugliness. Not the beauty *of* ugliness. The beauty of artistic authenticity. The beauty of expressive form. The beauty of creative power. The beauty of courage. Every artist wants to put forth that kind of beauty.

I told you these three distinctions were artificial, and that, in fact, every artwork has elements of each. But breaking them up in this way allows me to talk about them in an interesting way and to assist you in deciphering visual art generally and specifically.

Now there are some artists who strive to make beautiful surfaces, drawings of beautiful women, landscapes of scenes they deem beautiful, lighting that is startling and wondrous, like sunsets and sunrises, and the like. That does not mean that these works do not also convey a message—make a statement about nature, perhaps, or move us to a strong emotional reaction. To tears even. Beautiful scenes and people can engender enormous feeling, in both the artist and the viewer.

So, I could take every living artist who is participating here and put their work into any of these three chapters, couldn't I? But I have selected a few that I consider standouts in one or the other and have thus allocated their placement.

But remember, all artists have it all. We all have eyes to see, hands to make, head to ponder, and heart to sigh, and we apply them all in everything we create. Perhaps in different measure. But all present, interacting, and working together to produce the total effect—the look, the message, and the feeling. ART!

This is not an original idea. There is a quote by St. Francis of Assisi that dates to the thirteenth century on this very subject. Keep it in mind as you read and review these three chapters:

> He who works with his hands is a laborer.
>
> He who works with his hands and his head is a craftsman.
>
> He who works with his hands, head, and heart is an artist.

Let's now meet some of these artists of today.

MALCOLM LIEPKE: A PAINTER'S PAINTER

As a painter, I have long admired the work of the artist Malcolm Liepke for his unrestrained gusto in applying paint to canvas. His facility with the paint is just stupendous, and as a result, his canvases are vibrantly alive. Since his subject is the figurative, that means he has injected lifeblood into these visions of mostly female models. They literally pop off the flat surface and make you believe they will next be stepping out to greet you in person.

I spoke to the artist about what drives him. He told me that he's after the emotional quality in his portraits, and the particularities that mark their humanity: the tilt of a head, attitude, stance, that show who they are. Noting the resemblance in many of these paintings, he told me he paints them the way he wants to see them, in his words, "I make them mine."

I noted that I thought of Manet when I looked at the work Liepke contributed for this book, *Lady in Black*, and we got on talking about black, which he loves, and some of the other color favorites like rust and green that you will find in his work. That led us to talk about some of his favorite artists like Sargent, Hals, and Velázquez for the virtuosity of their paint; Degas for his cropping; Whistler for compositional excellence; and the marvelous Vuillard for his color subtleties. He is influenced also by Japanese works, another clue to his love of black. Suffice it to say, I agree with all of his choices.

Liepke is a painter's painter, which means that his works are what we call tour de force, truly masterful. In this work, you can clearly see the ferocity and skill he is able to bring to bear. He mentioned that he strives for a feeling of monumentality, mentioning the great Klimt, and we can see this in this very statuesque portrait. Have a look and just take it all in. I am also showing you a closeup of the cropped head so you can zoom in on the painting. The gleaming eyes, the weight of the head apparent even though it is swamped by the black hair, the sculptural paint that defines the nose so you feel its structure—this is sensual painting of the figure at its finest.

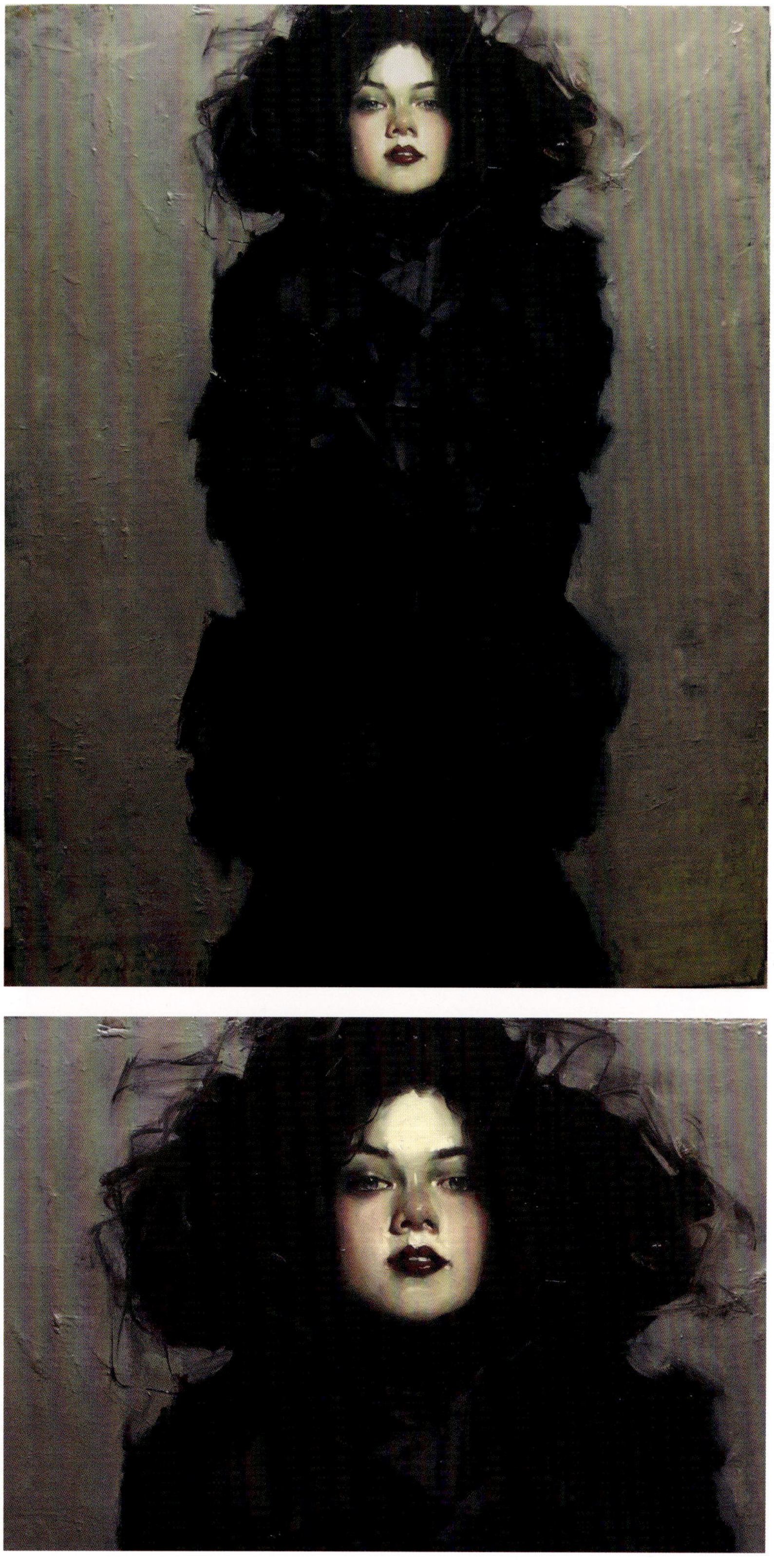

Fig. 107. Malcolm Liepke, LADY IN BLACK (with detail).

VIKTOR BUTKO: LYRICAL LANDSCAPE

Viktor Butko is a painter and his primary genre is landscape. He describes his treatment as "romantic landscape," and like many landscape painters, is attracted to the conditions where nature presents at its most emphatic or intense, perhaps those moments that are fleeting or short lived, as Butko specifies, "before or after the storm, the first snow, the spring flood, the moonlight, twilight, dawns, etc."

These are the treasured moments that the artist brings to the viewer through the medium of his artwork. They have moved and inspired him to make them permanent on the canvas, hoping the viewer will share that inspiration. Butko describes this desired reaction as "making the strings of his soul sound in a certain way."

Let's have a look at Butko's painting. I selected this out of many of his lovely works because of its simplicity and directness. Many landscape painters like to paint sunsets, and this is a daunting subject indeed, as is any extremely beautiful or notably dramatic moment. Many artists fail at it because they cannot, with the miserly tools of paint and oil and turpentine and canvas, begin to capture the magnificence of sky as the light of day reaches its crescendo and transforms the land in a glorified moment until it succumbs to darkness. It is challenging indeed to undertake such a grandiose subject and to do it competently, let alone brilliantly.

The simplicity of this work aids in this effort. Butko made this work on Shelter Island in the Village of Dering Harbor. He says that he painted it in what he refers to as "a state of altered consciousness," in which his observation is tinged with memory. We have discussed this phenomenon before in this book as I have explained how the artist imparts his emotion into his "eye." He is not only painting what he sees, he is adding into his strokes and color choices what those observations make him feel, and not only in the direct moment of execution, but in all the moments of his life that have brought him to this point.

We, the viewers, can relate to this as well, as we carry with us in the banks of our own memories the many sunsets we have witnessed, and the feelings they have engendered. Viewing Butko's painting brings us back to our own experiences. It is familiar to us. We have surely at some time watched the sun sink over water, on a cloudy day when the light was diffused. We have been there; we enjoy a moment of recognition. It may bring sadness or happiness or just nostalgia. Butko has awakened our emotions.

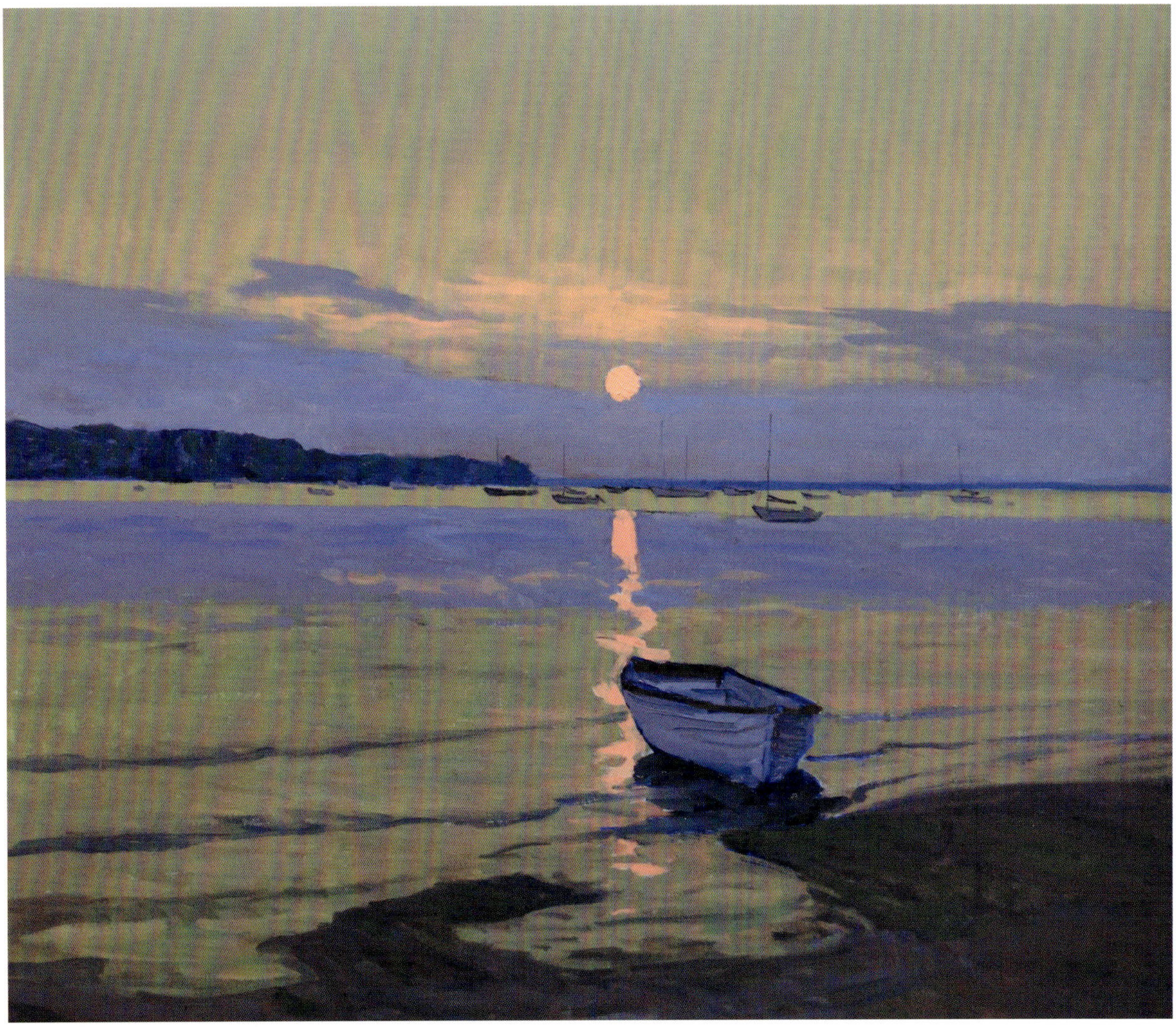

Fig. 108. Viktor Butko, CLOUDY SUNSET AT DERING HARBOR.

The artist achieves this feat with his tender application of subtle tonal color that is punctuated by the vibrant pink ribbon of the sun's dying rays. It is his restraint that makes the work so effective. The soft understated color and the preponderance of just a few colors is what makes that punctuated color so effective here. It is not overdone, and we appreciate that as we look at it. We can easily imagine that in a few moments, the darkness will descend, and the moment will have vanished. This gives a poignancy to the scene.

CHUCK FISCHER: GEOMETRIC ABSTRACTION

Now we look at an artist who speaks in the language of abstraction, and geometric abstraction at that. Are you thinking that he is making a design? The word *design* when used in this context with the article *a* as "a design" is commonly thought to mean a decoration. And what is a decoration? It is commonly thought of as ornamentation, something that imbues an artistic accessory quality.

But when I asked Chuck Fischer to explain his work, though he clearly named it as geometric abstraction, his intent was certainly not to make an adornment or attractive design. He had a much more developed source and inspiration.

Here is how Fischer described the impetus for this work of art:

> I landed in Paris on my first trip to Europe and was picked up at Charles de Gaulle airport by friends who drove down from Denmark. We first drove to the Loire Valley and toured some chateaus then continued our drive south. It is the memory of driving along the Côte d'Azur, having a picnic overlooking St. Tropez, and arriving in the village of Villefranche-sur-Mer that inspired me to create this piece. The watery blues rendered on aluminum, both literally and figuratively, reflect my experience of looking out over the Villefranche harbor to the Mediterranean Sea from my balcony at the Hotel Welcome. The counterpoint of the terracotta accents in the piece represents my memory of the terracotta-colored facade of the hotel and the fourteenth-century Chapelle Saint-Pierre across the street, where Jean Cocteau decorated the walls with frescoes.

It is unfortunate when we look at art that we don't always have the kind of information about the artist's experience that Fischer provided us here. That backstory enables us to see this work of art in an entirely new fashion, not just as an interesting design or masterfully made construction, but as a work of the imagination that resonates with his experiences and plays into ours.

I see the blue of the Mediterranean Sea, the twists and turns of the Côte d'Azur, that marvelous coastline which defines this fabulous place. You can picture yourself taking those turns in a tiny sports car with the wind in your face. The work expresses the energy and feeling of fun this place connotes. I can picture the exuberance Fischer experienced in driving through it. He gives us whirls and twirls and petal-like shapes and textured nooks and the many shades of blue that represent the sea. I like that he broke the square and gave us that little extra piece with the two circular shapes. The structural terracotta pieces too. It just works and is fun to look at.

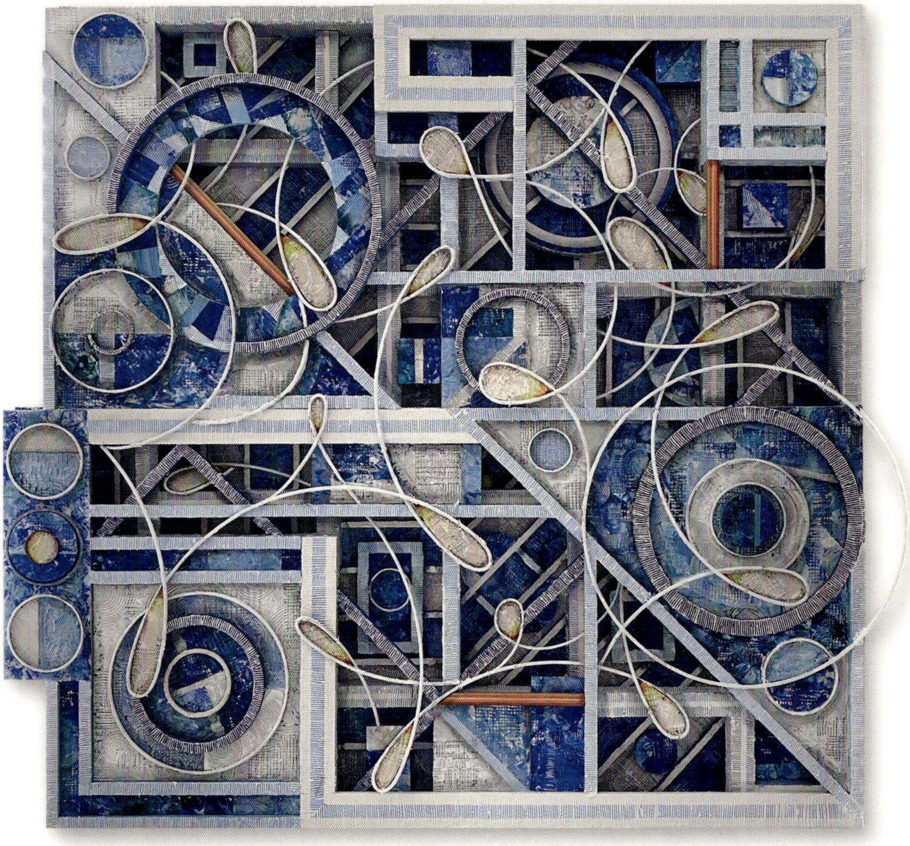

Fig. 109. Chuck Fischer, VILLEFRANCHE-SUR-MER.

Inspiration is everywhere and regardless of the style or subject matter the artist feels most comfortable in exploring, there is much more that goes into it—and that we, the viewer, know very little about. There's a reason Chuck Fischer translates his feelings into geometric abstraction, but we're just not privy to it. He could have stood at that window at the Hotel Welcome and painted a landscape, a couple of figures cruising the beachfront, the church across the street or a bird flying. Instead, his brain and heart devised *Villefranche-sur-Mer*. He translated what he saw and how it made him feel into this very handsome and ingenious construction.

VERONICA CAY: MIXED-MEDIA EXCURSIONS

Veronica Cay is one of the artists who would not specify which of the three categories I provided were her primary focus—look, head, or heart. I have to assume that all are equally relevant to her and that perhaps they are all rolled into one overriding incentive.

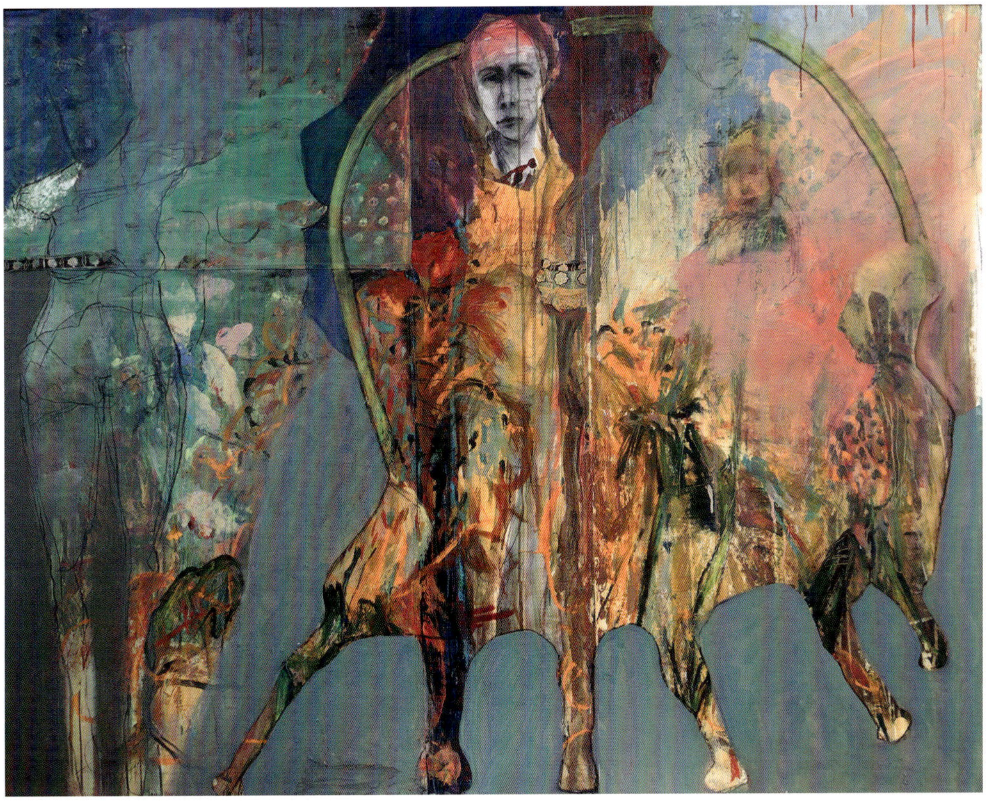

Fig. 110. Veronica Cay, BREATHING DEEPLY INHALING COMFORT.

She is a mixed-media artist, both painter and sculptor, creating drawings, paintings, assemblages, and works utilizing textile and ceramic. She has advised that her artwork arises out of regular sessions with the model in weekly life-drawing sessions, where she uses a variety of tools and even works with both hands. She eschews perfection, choosing instead to concentrate on expressive freedom and spontaneity. Then she brings these inspirational works back to her studio for further development.

The work we have chosen for this book is part of her "Bed" series. Veronica explains the meaning of the bed as part of the household that is our resting place, our "safe haven" where quiet talks are often undertaken with children, and as the transportation venue for our nightly excursions into inner space in the shape of our dreams. Let's have a look at how that meaning is delivered in this artwork titled *breathing deeply inhaling comfort.*

The work is on a horizontal format and resonates as a fantastical place, a landscape or environment, if you will, not necessarily on Earth. Perhaps it is an imaginary or dreamed world. We see three figures in this environment, one a woman looking out at us, and two others—one a young child and the other a bit older. They are on a surface which may be a bed except for the fact that it appears to have horse hooves as bed legs. I note this is no ordinary horse—there are six legs.

Just as an experience or thought on a particular day can result in a dream dimension that night, I imagine that Cay's experiences in the life-drawing session may spark a similar happening as she steps into the studio to take that experience and reconfigure it—dream it to a new reality. The impulse has transported her to this new dimension, and even she will be surprised by the result.

We cannot know our dreams until they happen, and in a similar fashion, the artist becomes acquainted with her unconscious in the making of her art. The beauty of art is that it makes this dream world available to the viewer as well. Just looking at it may very likely spark our own imaginations.

Here is how Cay comments on her artistic inspiration: "My work is a way of making sense of transitory moments in time—an energy transfer that is never repeated, like a shadow flickering across the ground is fleeting. I am reminded of running through beach scrub as a child with the intense heat of the sun burning through the treetops and the shadows are deep and liquid." Poetry in word and image!

Make sure to look at Veronica Cay's sculpture in our Appendix exhibition.

DAN MULLER: SHAPES OF MEMORIES

Our memory is a depository of images we can draw from when we make art. For Dan Muller, whose memories of childhood were rich and satisfying, his is a vivid storehouse for inspiration he can dip into and resource. He explains how he has done so with the joyous image *Houses at Night*.

Muller's mixed-media work reminds me of Chagall, whose childhood memories also came alive in his artwork. For Chagall, a Russian village, and for Dan, southern Wisconsin, but both capture the spirit of a happy childhood. Muller explains his work this way:

> Lines and shapes weave together to create an interesting pattern of weighted colors that accumulate to evoke childhood memories of night—a magical time when shapes and colors emerge out of the dark and there is a silent, soft glow from the moon and stars. During the day, your sense of perspective allows you to take in vast expanses; at night what you see is more constrained. Everything

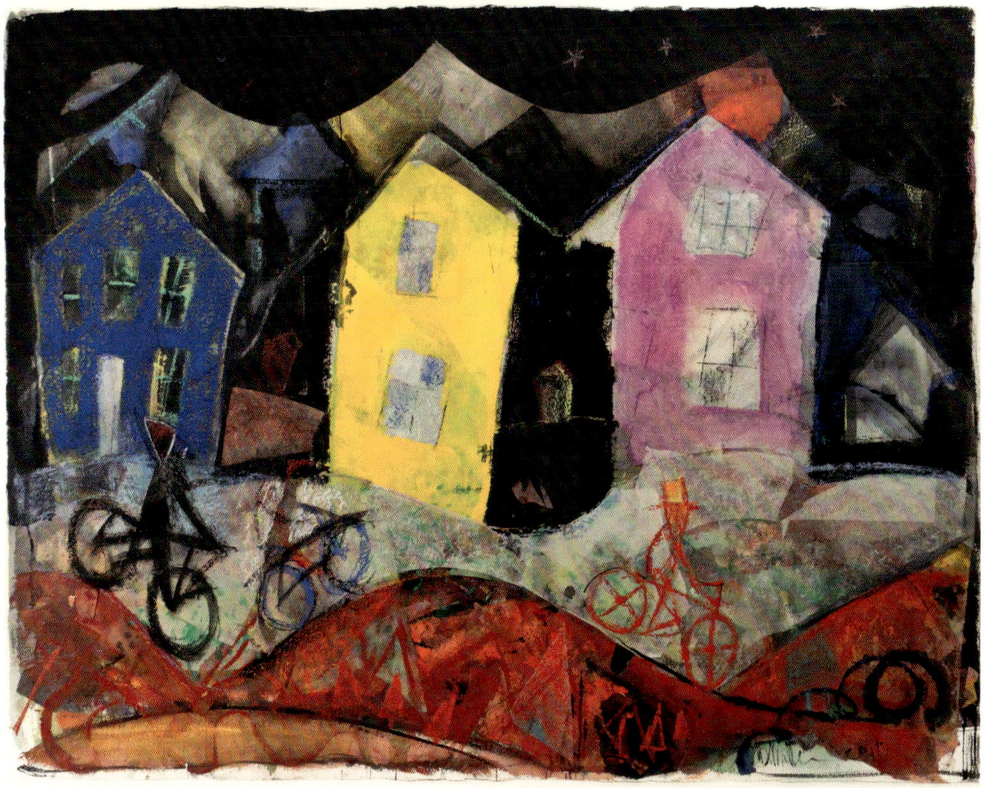

Fig.111. Dan Muller, HOUSES AT NIGHT.

seems closer, even the night sky. The darkness surrounding the houses has gradations adding to that sense of mystery and wonder as objects appear. The houses seem to grow out of the ground. The group of bicycle riders act as bridge between the starkness of the houses and the rolling shapes of hills in the foreground.

There is an exuberance and simplicity here that evokes the best of folk art. I like especially the rendering of the bicyclists riding up and down the hilly roadway; they give a feeling of energy and zest to the work—and also a bit of whimsy, especially with the front rider wearing the top hat. Very Chagall-esque, indeed!

Muller told me that as a child he enjoyed visiting the Milwaukee Public Museum and viewing the dioramas exhibited there. Each is a little world one can enter and he enjoyed popping from one to another. In a sense, that is what he is continuing to do with his artwork as each becomes a new world he can pop his attention into.

Muller likes to take a lot of photos as he goes about his days, driving and trout fishing. As he is looking about, he is observing patterns in nature that become the building blocks for his compositions. Here's how he frames it:

> There's a certain richness to the colors of the waters where the shapes emerge and the rolling hills seem to interlock, which inspires my work. When I start a mixed media piece, there's not a set image in mind; I start with large shapes and through adding and subtracting an image/concept begins to emerge. Ultimately I am creating a visual environment where the objects live—a fascinating place in time that draws you in with the richness of colors and shape and triggers memories of the fleeting magical moments experienced in life.

Thank you, Dan Muller, for sharing your happy memories with us.

REGINALD K. GEE: INSIDE OUT, OUTSIDE IN

The art gallery that represents the artist Reginald K. Gee refers to him as an outsider artist. But what does it mean to be an outsider? Outside of what exactly? The art establishment? The prevalent zeitgeist?

Those deemed outsider artists are often thought to be unschooled, outside of the established route to becoming an artist. But many well-known artists did not attend traditional art schools. And those who are unschooled can become quite adept at their chosen art form once they work a while. Do we then still consider them to be outsiders?

I declare that Reginald Gee is *in*, as this work clearly illustrates. According to the gallery, his work explores a wide range of subjects including "playful musicians, surreal vistas, mystical dreams and fantastic visions," and his expressive vocabulary is large. His biography states further, "He borrows from his heritage as an African American and Native American incorporating historical images, symbols and numerology into his artwork."

In *Footwork*, we see two dancers joyfully engaged, their arms enlarged, displaying toothy grins, hats prominently perched. I love the background divided into four sections, each colored differently, as a foil to the dancers. I love the decorative notes like the speckled feet and patterning on the clothing. But above all, I adore the absolute freedom and exuberance of the imagery. It makes me want to start dancing.

If there is anything to say about "outsider" art, it is this: Without the conventions of more traditional art, and the strict training that often curtails creativity, talented "outsider" artists like Reginald Gee point the way to what is important about art: the joy of self-expression. If there is a poster child for "The Joy of Art," it is Reggie Gee.

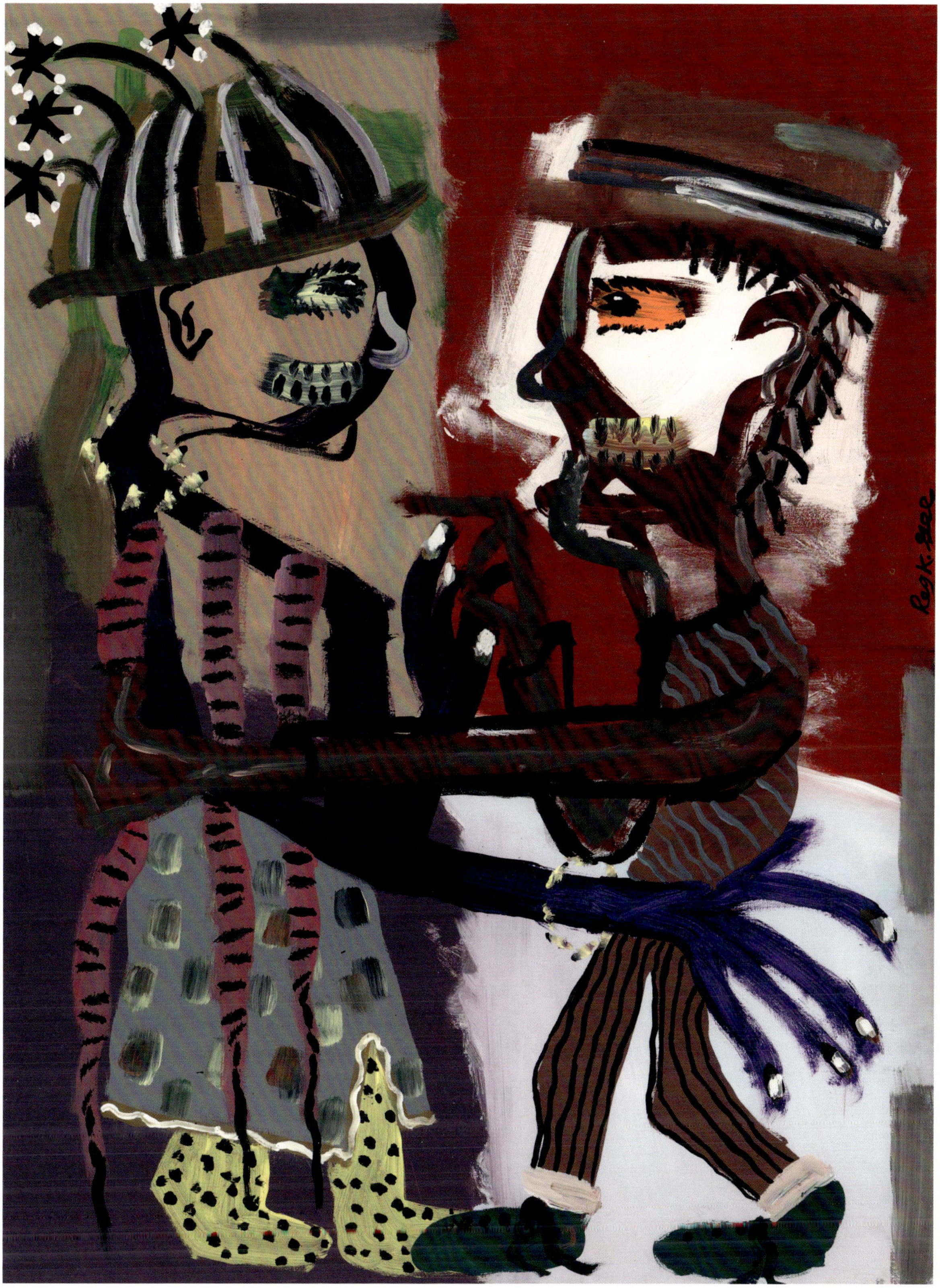

Fig.112. Reginald K. Gee, FOOTWORK.

BERNICE SOKOL KRAMER: WHIMSICAL REFLECTION

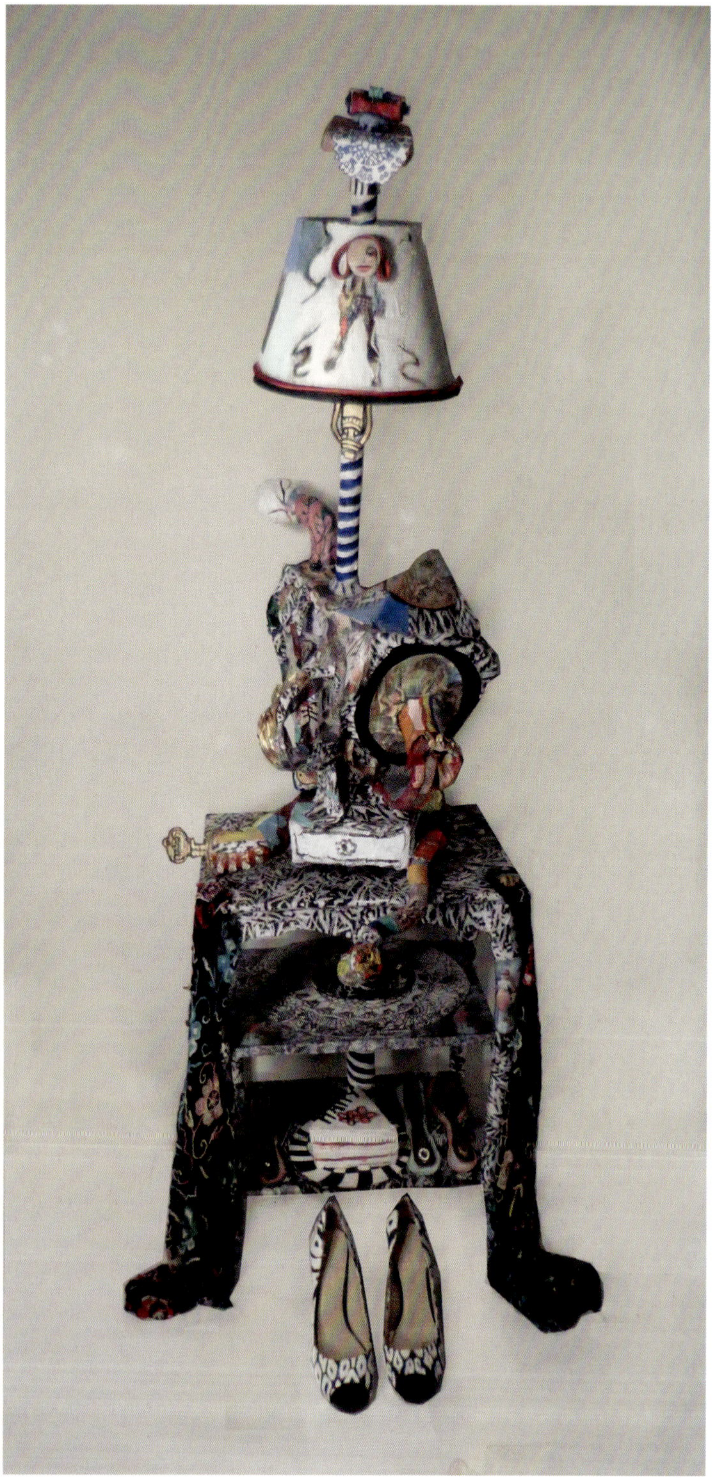

Fig. 113. Bernice Sokol Kramer, SAID THE TABLE TO THE LAMP, IT'S A PIECE OF CAKE.

There are many ways that visual art can speak and make an impact on the viewer. For the sculptor and collage artist Bernice Sokol Kramer, stopping the viewer in their tracks can be a satisfying intention. Her sculptures and collages offer the unexpected, the startling, the whimsical or humorous, in often contrarian combinations that force you to take a second look.

Challenged by the gallerist, Sokol Kramer created a work for the exhibition "Over the Sofa" at the Carter Burden Gallery in New York City. Her method is elaborated here:

> A piece of furniture—either an end table or coffee table was to be used. I found an end table at my neighborhood thrift shop the next day. The only other object I purchased was a lamp shade, which sat atop a vase-like collaged structure I made from discarded cardboard items from a sculpture awaiting construction were a better fit for this piece. Painted paper plates, a painted pair of shoes, paper-mache knives and forks, my sister's embroidered scarf, and a paper-mache slice of birthday cake achieved my desire for a fanciful companion to a sofa.

Artists like Sokol Kramer love to create works out of found materials, repurposed and reassembled in interesting ways. Finding these discarded, seemingly obsolete objects and then giving them new life and meaning in a work of art is the result of a very satisfying creative visualization. It also serves to awaken the viewer's imagination.

Sokol Kramer's title also provides humor. Lest we forget, art making is as much about entertainment as deep thought, and an important function of creative visioning is throwing us off the familiar, the ponderous, the correct, and engaging us with something fresh and new and yes, even lighthearted or frivolous. It is all part of the picture.

PHYLLIS HAMMOND: A LIFE IN SCULPTURE

It is not easy to create sculpture and it takes an extraordinary person to persist in this art form. Making sculpture, especially large works, requires not only imagination. It involves a grounding in engineering, logistics, and physical prowess. Having tried it myself, I can tell you, making sculpture is hard work.

So when I met the extraordinary artist Phyllis Hammond and saw her petite frame and met her impish gaze, I admit I was intrigued. Then I became acquainted with her lifetime of sculptural accomplishment, from her engaging work in ceramic to the large metal works she conjured in recent years. Wow! I had to learn more.

Creative people are blessed with an uncanny attentiveness. Many people receive pings from the universe offering a new idea, but to an artist these little voices are a call to action to turn something they have seen or heard or imagined into physical manifestation. Phyllis Hammond is such a creative whirlwind, having worked a lifetime taking these messages and turning them into fantastic works of art.

A sojourn in Japan as a young person prompted her to begin to work in clay, which absorbed her interest for many years. The sight of Japanese dolls who have neither

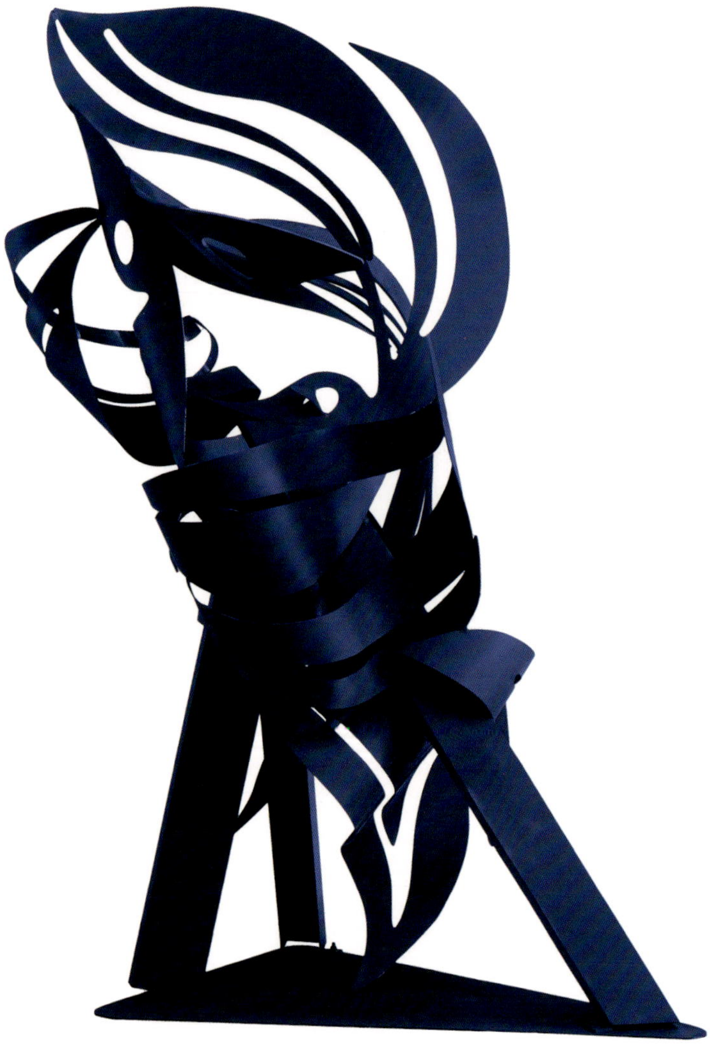

Fig. 114. Phyllis Hammond, BIRD'S NEST.

arms nor legs inspired her to make her own figurative sculptures. Unfortunately, I cannot feature them in this book, but I encourage you to look them up.

It was a lesson she gave students—to draw lines and shapes on paper, cut them out, and fashion the cutouts into paper sculptures—that birthed a new direction. She decided to take her own lesson to the next level and convert her drawings to metal sculptures.

Technology is her partner. The drawings are scanned, then converted to a program that allows a water jet machine to cut the shapes from four-foot by eight-foot sheets of aluminum. But that's only the beginning.

Imagine Hammond defining these cut metal pieces with a hammer and anvil and then having them fed into a rolling machine. The finished works are then powder-coated in primary colors.

Hammond contributed *Bird's Nest* for this book. It is typical of her soaring expressive forms, many of which remind her of the ability of birds to "cut through the air." This required, in her words, "a lot of variety and playfulness and bending and turning and twisting and mainly the experimenting, experimental forms and color."

Now that you've imagined this remarkable and delicate woman creating these works, imagine them sitting in the landscape, in counterpoint to their environment, punctuating it, enlivening it, defining the space. They are absolutely marvelous, but more marvelous than the art is the artist, a font of creative spirit, grit, determination, vigor, and vision. I can't wait to see what she comes up with next!

CAROLYN SCHLAM: SELF REFLECTION

I am always trying to give my renderings of women some emotional heft, to try to make them come alive. They are not alive, of course, just a pile of paint, but they were created by someone who is, and that's what makes it possible. I have learned that aliveness is not created by copying; in fact, copying will assure failure at the task. One cannot copy life—that is a contradiction in terms.

So because I know this, from years of trying, I no longer try to use local color—skin tones and the like—and just endeavor to make the most expressive painting I can, and not too carefully, or in a prissy way, because then for sure it would not feel alive. You must be kind of free and daring with the application to get life. Too exact and it's a flop.

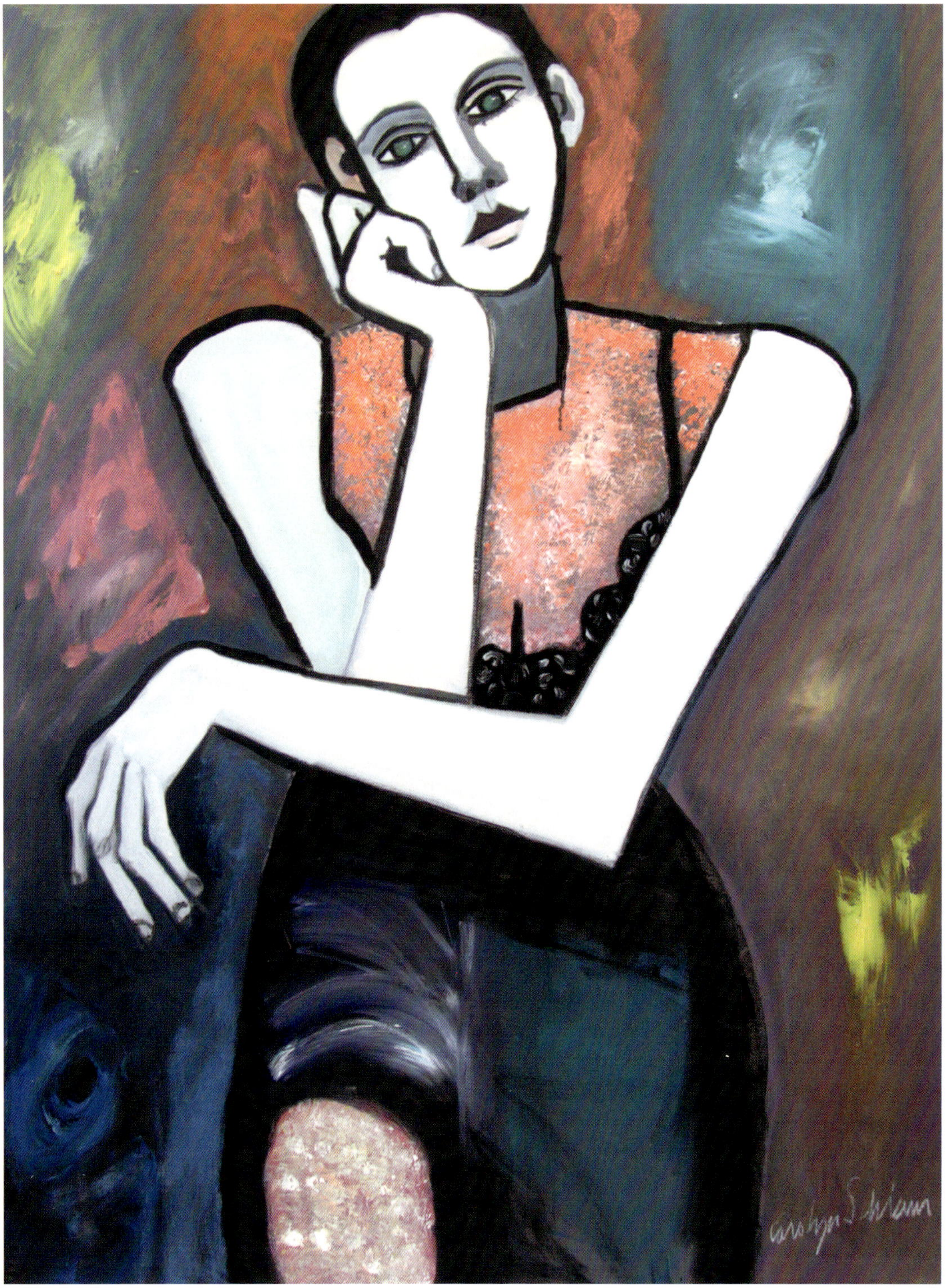

Fig. 115. Carolyn Schlam, WISTFUL.

I have painted images of women in a variety of ways, some quite naturalistic, others more abstract, utilizing shards of colored light. I worked in stained glass for some time, so I guess it makes sense that I see things this way—broken up into these fragments. A puzzle of light and shadow.

Other artworks I have created, both in oil and other media, like the work shown here, are more stylized, more like symbols than portraits. I chose this work because to a large degree it contains a quality I see reflected back at me when I look at my body of work. An expression, a look, a state of mind.

The definition of the word "wistful" is "having or showing a feeling of vague or regretful longing." I find that longing expressed in many of the characters I create, and probably none so much as here. I do not necessarily intend to portray it, but the emotion comes through my fingers and enters the paint and lives on the canvas. It is a potent driver of my aesthetic and personal expressiveness, the essence I spoke of in chapter 8.

Look for the personal message, the secret message, each artist imparts through their imagery. It is a miracle, really, when you think of it, that humans can create lovely and expressive things, that they can make art. That they can build skyscrapers and rocket ships and robots that move and think, and also can do such terrible and ugly things.

I often wonder if people who do terrible things could know what it feels like to make something truly captivating like a work of art, or something wondrous like a robot or spaceship, would they forsake the terrible things? I think so, don't you?

We can only hope, and make art available to everyone. To try to neutralize that feeling of being unloved that causes so much distress in the world. Expressing those feelings through art and hopefully feeling proud of what you have done has to help assuage the hurt. I know it makes me feel like I've done something worthwhile and consequential. What's better than that?

You will find my Mother and Child work in the Appendix exhibition.

Chapter 10
Living Artists Whose Focus Is on Truth

TRUTH, WHAT IT SAYS

All art is a form of communication, an exchange of ideas and feelings in visual form. Every visualization in art is a statement and conveys a message. But what is that message and how is it delivered? This is the aesthetic question we are dealing with. In this chapter we are looking at art in which an idea, thought, message, or statement is the precipitating intention of the artwork. The artist set out to say something in the work; that is its primary purpose.

This does not mean that other purposes were not realized, that feelings or emotions did not play a part or were not made evident in the work, or that aesthetic concerns did not compute. The characterizing quality is that the work is driven by the desire to convey an idea, regardless of what other elements are at play. Each of the artists we will discuss here interprets this in a different manner, and I will attempt to clarify the idea, how the idea is communicated visually, and what it means.

Since we are talking about ideas, we must discuss the term *conceptual art*. I am not asserting that the artists we will look at here are conceptual artists, only that their intention is to strongly convey an idea. This does not make them conceptual artists per se.

Conceptual art is a movement that arose in the 1960s and 1970s. The first work of conceptual art was determined to be *Fountain* by Marcel Duchamp, which was actually a urinal. The artist submitted it to an art exhibition for the express purpose of challenging the art establishment, and it worked: an entire movement sprang up to applaud him.

The movement arose as a reaction to the grandiosity of the art movers and shakers and the art movements of the time, such as minimalism, Abstract Expressionism, or photorealism, which, though having different values, were still traditional in the sense that they produced material things—paintings and sculptures—that were designated as "art."

Why, they asked, did art have to be these special things, and why did they have to be physical at all?

Art could be a performance, an experience, an utterance, a scribble. Did art have to be made by a skillful hand, promoted by an art gallery, something on a pedestal considered extraordinary?

"No," said the conceptual artists.

Conceptual art was a form of dematerialization—taking apart the material and the materialistic aspects of art making. It was more minimalist than "minimalism," because though minimalism reduced the elements of visual art to the essentials, conceptual artists went even further and threw away the canvas itself.

Artists, for the most part, are questioners and questers. They are always questioning what they are doing and searching for new ways to express themselves. Conceptual art arose in this fashion. I wanted to give you this context before we moved on to look at this group of artists who do not identify necessarily as conceptual artists, but whose work exhibits definite *concepts* that are important to them and which we will elucidate.

These are fine distinctions, but remember that Art, with a capital A, is a big umbrella that includes the myriad ways creative visual artists have found to express their concerns, interests, obsessions, ideas, definitions, emotions, and approaches to this activity of self-expression. There is no real way to isolate thought from feeling and from expressive form. It is all present simultaneously.

These artists highlight an idea in their work, using their own artistic language to communicate it. Let's have a look.

LOLA DEL FRESNO: MULTIPLE MEANINGS

Lola del Fresno's work delivers a layered effect and a layered meaning; we read the layers contextually, like a game of three-dimensional chess.

She utilizes media like graphite, acrylic, inks, and oils to compose her drawings over Mylar paper, and then installs them to overlap on other images or photographs or to be displayed in a sequence.

As you look at this work, you may wonder why there is an absence of color. The artist explains that she works in a monochrome to focus viewers on the meaning of the works, so they are not distracted by aesthetic enhancements. Her restraint is purposeful and provides a window into the artist's primary intention to inform, to awaken, and to educate.

Her own words state her intention best:

> In my practice as an artist, and in my work, I bring a psychological study of the multiplicity of realities, exploring the integration of the landscape in the urban environment and the human figure in relation to these spaces. Long interested in issues of identity and inequality, my work directly relates to my desire to create spaces in which the average person can reckon with and come to terms with their cultural heritage and economic conditions.

Let's take a closer look into this work, *Girl Running*. Before you examine it, take note of its size. The work is quite large, over 12 feet wide by 6 feet long. This is not a work to hang over a sofa; it is more like an installation and meant to live in a public space and seen by a larger audience. It contains a message for many.

We see a drawing of two children; one is running. We note how expertly drawn they are, how they feel alive and in motion. They are drawn on a transparent sheet, overlaid on a photograph of a typical suburban house. What is meant here, we wonder?

Del Fresno tells is that her investigation in this piece is about our relationship with home, this most important place where we seek security, refuge, where we feel we belong, and which identifies us. In particular, she refers to our childhood home, which lives in our memories for a lifetime. She explains, "*Girl Running* tackles deep-rooted fears and desires that many citizens face. The word 'home' transcends the physical dwelling place. More than a structure built to provide relief to the elements, it is the womb of our societal being."

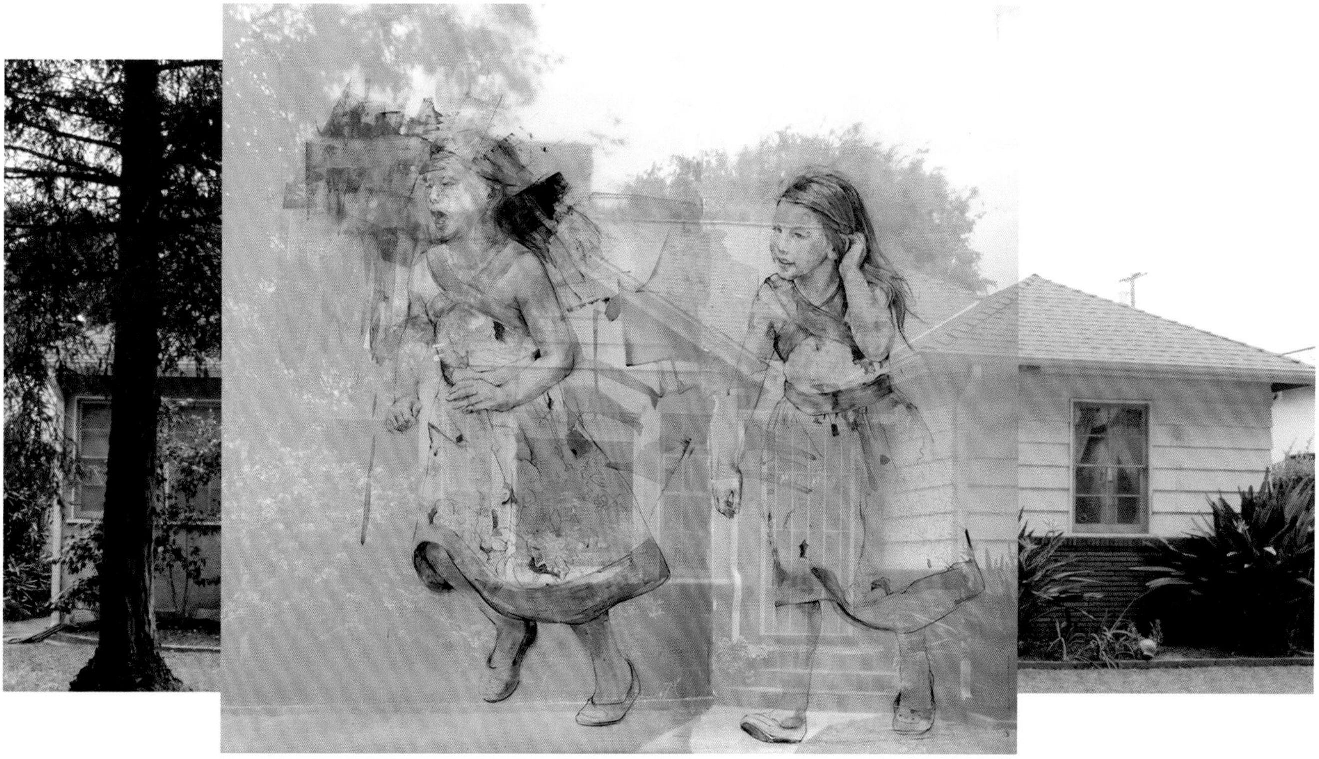

Fig. 116. Lola del Fresno, GIRL RUNNING.

Through this work, the artist is challenging us to consider our own relationship to home and more broadly the potential trauma of the immigrant's separation from that source of safety and well-being. By placing the image of these children in the context of home, the artist is exploring her main concerns of cultural heritage, economic exclusion, and integration into society. Her work asks of us that we explore these important issues as well. Lola del Fresno offers us a brilliant and original way to accomplish that through her art.

Make sure to view Lola del Fresno's work in the Appendix exhibition.

BOB CONGE: DREAMSCAPES

The artist Bob Conge is a night owl. Not only does he find the wee hours of the night a particularly advantageous time to make his art, but also the subject matter that inspires some of his recent work is the nighttime realm—the stuff of dreams. Though he is not what we think of as a conceptual artist, he is very much driven by concept and content—he is definitely speaking to us through his

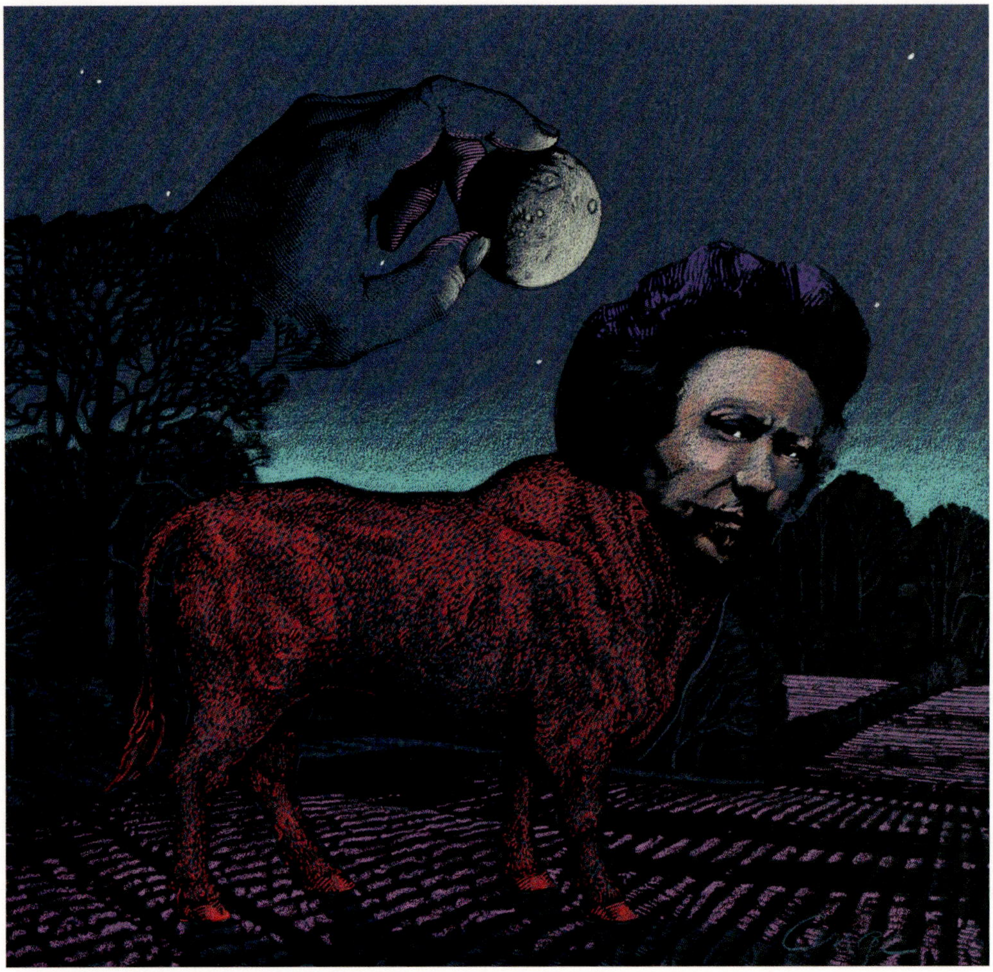

Fig. 117. Bob Conge, A REMBRANDT NIGHT.

art and his art encourages us to think and to ponder the meaning of his dream-soaked imagery.

Artists often have a lot to say about other artists they admire, and there are many examples through art history where artists have reinterpreted the work of a favorite—think of Picasso's myriad versions of the Velázquez masterpiece *Las Meninas*. In Conge's case, he has chosen to convey his admiration in a different fashion—by composing a visual virtual dream that represents an artist, as here.

And what is this dream he has imagined for Rembrandt? He articulates his symbology in this way:

> I chose the body of a bull for Rembrandt to convey his tenacious individualistic strength. He never compromised his expression even in commissioned

> pieces and his work is as fresh today as it was 400 years ago. Rembrandt's head is turned towards the viewer as he sees right through you. It is Rembrandt's hand arranging the moon in the night sky because he has earned the right to put it anywhere he wishes.

I asked Conge to decipher this image, and he was kind enough to comply, but one does not need a map to experience this work. The face of Rembrandt resonates with a piercing assurance and experiencing it in this surreal environment presses us to search for meaning. The joy of the work *is* the mystery and the challenge to penetrate it is what it is all about.

The artist defines himself as "a tinker, a follower of muses, day dreamer, night owl, purveyor of magic, high wire act," and then adds "and maybe not."

As viewers, he has gifted us with a puzzle, a head-scratcher, a visual conundrum. Good deal, I say. We are fascinated with the dream realm morphed into art.

JIMMY WRIGHT: CULTURAL RECORD

In part 1, we looked at one of the lovely floral paintings by this artist. But artists often go through many stages in their creative lives, dedicating themselves to one subject or another, as accords with their life experience.

In this section, we are looking at a work Wright created in 1975, taken from a series of works on paper he created in the 1970s about the gay subculture before HIV/AIDS.

Here is how he describes that period in his life:

> Jimmy Wright moved to New York in 1974, following a period of graduate study at the Art Institute of Chicago in which he engaged with the emergent group of Chicago Imagist artists. His work from the Chicago period reflects his upbringing in a religious family in Kentucky, with serene and mystical scenes of baptisms and other non-Christian spiritual imagery. Upon arriving in 1970s New York, he immersed himself with the same fervor in the thriving gay scene of the period, frequenting the bathhouses, discos, and sex clubs that flourished in that heady post-Stonewall, pre-AIDS moment. The drawings, done from direct observation and personal experience, evince a sense of immediacy similar to that of Toulouse-Lautrec in fin de siècle Paris

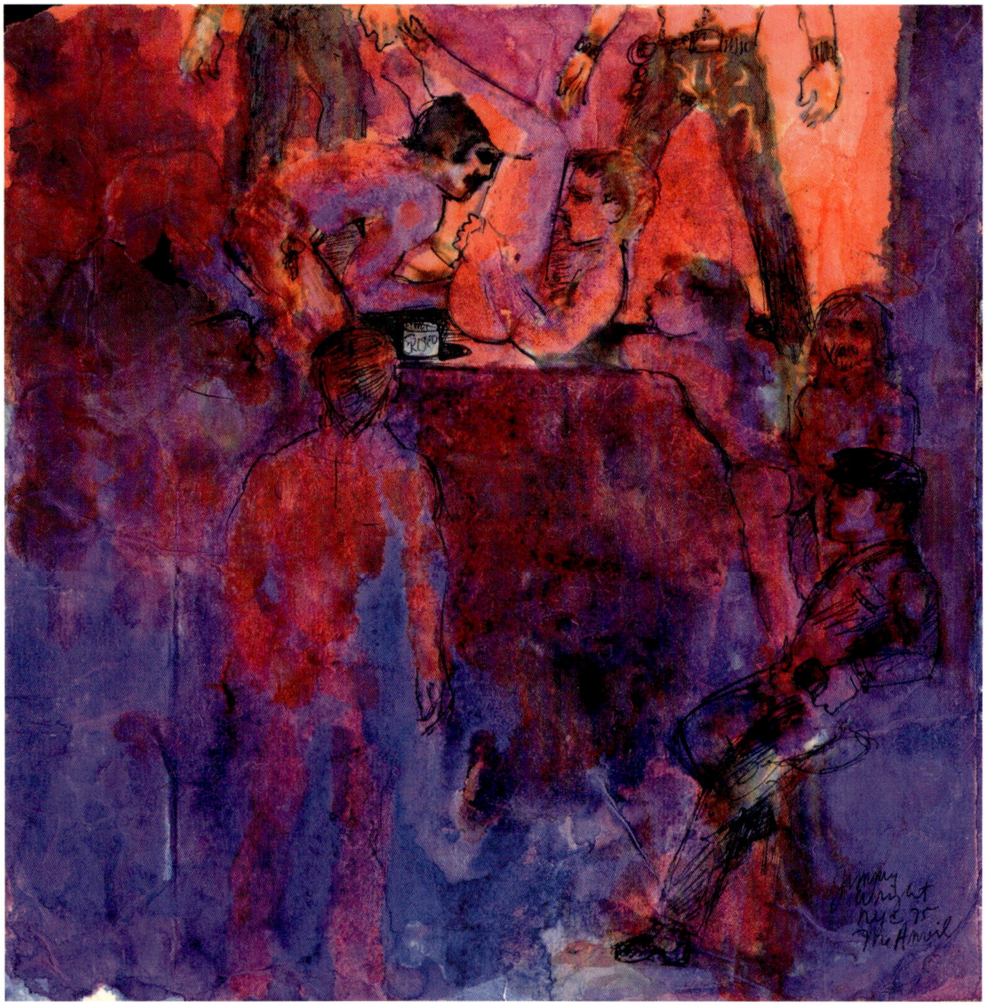

Fig. 118. Jimmy Wright, NIGHTWATCH: THE ANVIL.

> or George Grosz in Weimar Germany. The technique is varied, with some works in a sooty, smoky graphite, some quick and cheeky in pen and ink, and others tenderly rendered in gouache and watercolor. The sex club drawings are raw; the bathhouses romantic.

We have discussed here how art chronicles in vivid and indisputable ways the time and ethos of culture in which it is created. Here is a perfect example in this "romantic" work. We, who have lived through this time, and know what havoc and heartache was to follow when AIDS took hold in the gay community, can view these "documents" of their time as virtual dreams. And they have a particular poignancy as they speak in innocence of what was to come and befall these individuals.

Works of art function as memories and as historical records. That makes them more than pictures; they are experiences and reminders of the unexpected exigencies we face as human beings.

Jimmy Wright's work is also found in our Appendix exhibition.

DAVID PROVAN: SCULPTOR OF OTHER DIMENSIONS

David Provan creates his artworks in a variety of media: steel, bronze, aluminum, clay, wood, watercolor, ink, and acrylic paint. They are abstract for the most part, but he has a clear intention. The work he submitted for this book is *We Live Within Each Others Wounds*, which he describes as a "matrix of holes held together by a web of steel bands that represent our responsibility to, and interdependence upon, each other.

If you are perplexed by the title, Provan further clarifies that the holes are evocative of our human and "intertwined" vulnerabilities, our wounds so to speak.

Once again, it is helpful to have the artist speak to us of his intention, as abstract sculpture can be difficult to read, and we may interpret it as a design or composition, not being cognizant of the artist's references. In his writing to me, Provan enunciated his philosophy of existence, which is made manifest in his sculptures.

He explains:

> I've come to understand that we inhabit a universe that extends far beyond the grasp of our five senses. These extremes evade us because they are, for the most part, too microscopic, too cosmically huge, or too glacially slow for us to comprehend. Through my art I've tried to construct objects that model and resonate with that world that lies just beyond our understanding.

Does it make more sense now? The positive pieces and the vacancies in the sculpture are not arbitrary; they represent those realms that we are unable to access from our human vantage point.

In that other universe, all of this would be as clear and obvious as could be. They also, as in this work, represent the dynamics of human interaction—relationships and phenomena that the artist is projecting into sculptural form quite intentionally.

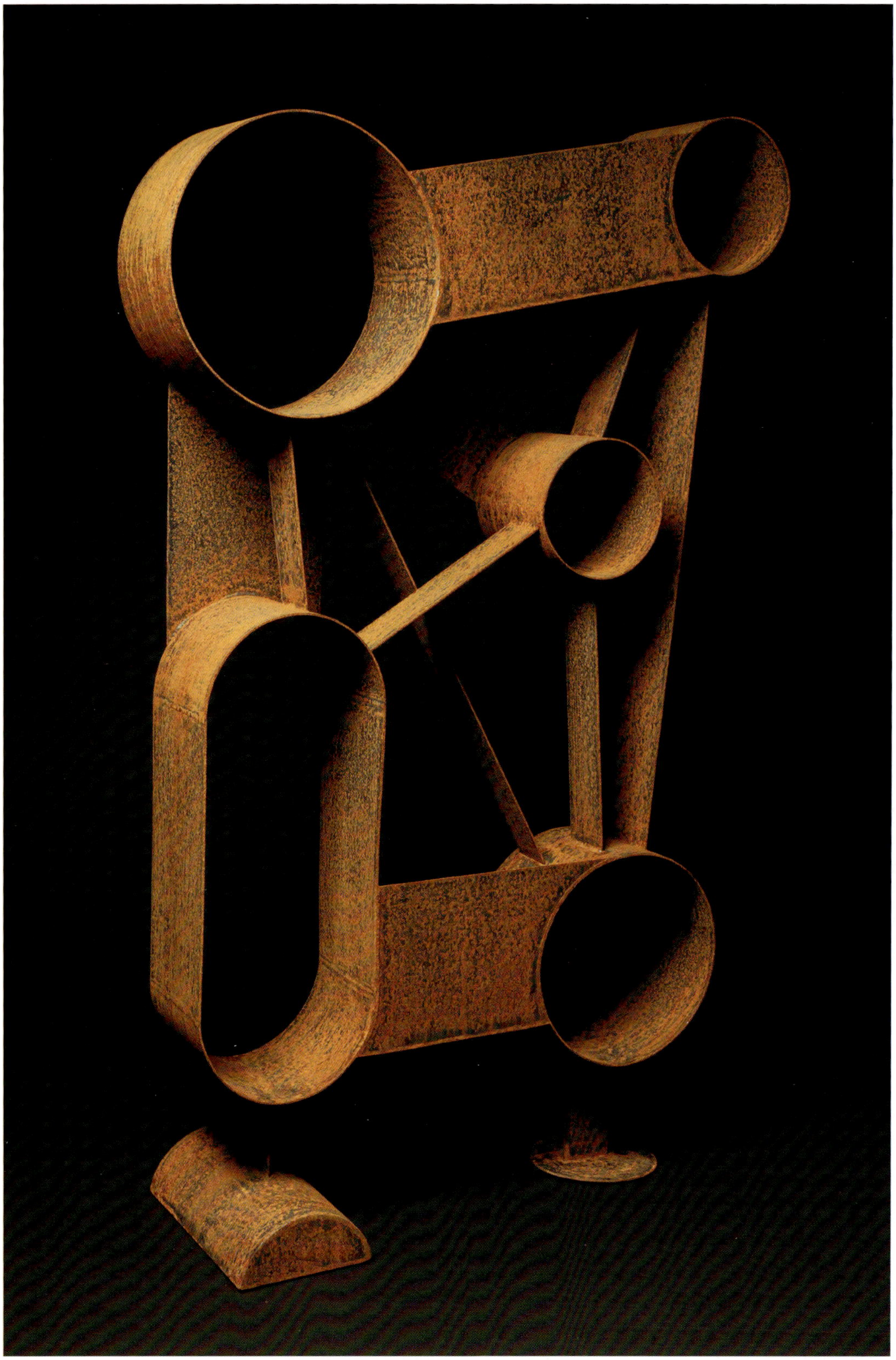

Fig. 119. David Provan, WE LIVE WITHIN EACH OTHERS WOUNDS.

Provan, like all the artists introduced here, had a choice as to which category best represented their primary focus, and he chose this one: works that make a statement. All we need do is to read it, or perhaps more aptly, to let it speak to us.

MICHAEL LEBOWITZ: NARRATIVE PHOTOGRAPHY

Pictures tell a story, both what they obviously say, and also what is unsaid. The unsaid has to be read, too, but doing so requires that we open ourselves as viewers to receive. Photography is a particularly apt medium for narrative, and Michael Lebowitz declares his mission to be just that.

His words: "There is a story in every image. My job is to capture it. and let the moment live, unchanged by me or my technology."

The black-and-white photograph displayed here appeared in Lebowitz's book *Tarmac Meditations*, along with this poem, titled "I DID NOT GO TO THE WAR."

> I never went to the war,
> Seemed like the right thing to do.
> I was wrong.

First, what we see, the obvious: mist rising out of a body of water, a dock, some reeds, a slide. No people, a seemingly lonely spot, not much going on. What does this have to do with war?

But wait. It seems like a forsaken place, a leftover place, far away from anything or anybody. And all that mist, suggesting things hidden, feelings bubbling up perhaps, maybe regret?

These are my feelings as the reader. But I know they may not be the same as the artist's who created it. I come to it with my history, he with his own, and as I look at the photograph I may not be privy to his experience. I am just taking information from what I see. I do not know why he took this photograph, but it speaks to me, nonetheless, and refers to something in my own psyche.

Lebowitz notes: "Childhood's end, miles from home, the end of season, end of things, decisions made in the moment that last forever."

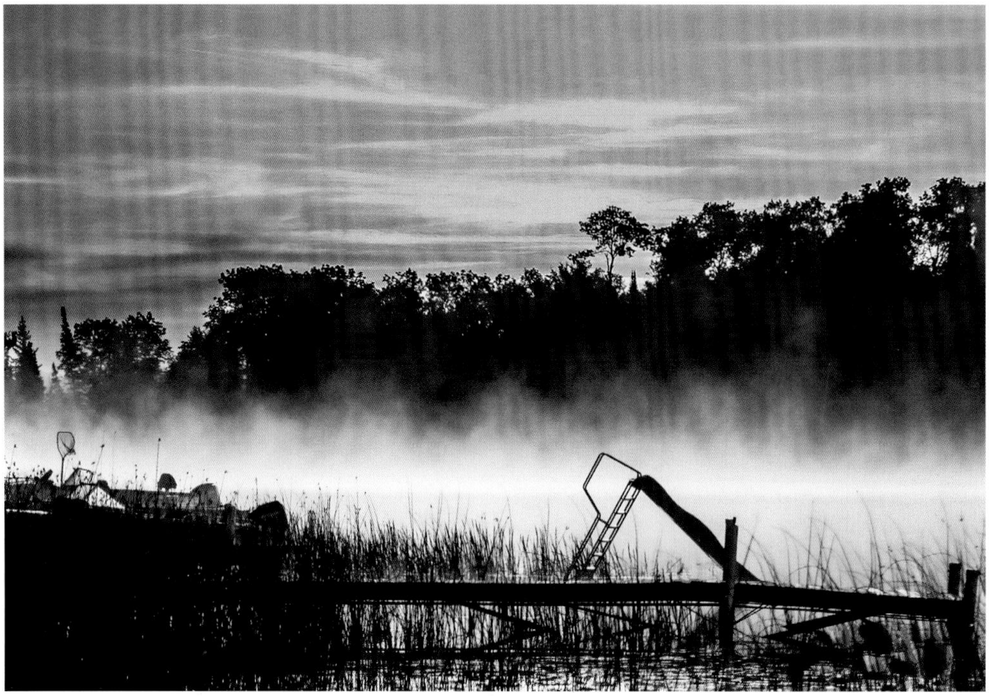

Fig. 120. Michael Lebowitz, I DID NOT GO TO THE WAR.

Your reading may be entirely different. But no matter. It is the artist's job to present, to stir the pot. The rest is up to you. Art is a story and a dialogue.

Check out another of Michael Lebowitz's photographs in the Appendix exhibition.

DB WATERMAN: ARTIST ACTIVIST

I refer to DB Waterman, a Netherlands-based artist, as an activist artist because quite literally, her medium is her message. Her work is concerned with the current state of our world and the issues that plague it like our deteriorating climate. Her statement is not only contained in her imagery but embodied in her practice. She literally applies her concern for the environment in the materials she chooses—she is not only expressing her values but living them.

Waterman explains it thus:

> I see everything as a potential canvas. Works of art can be made on canvas, paper, or cardboard. My first mixed media technique to create a basis for my paintings consists of newspapers, magazines, pieces of paper and packaging

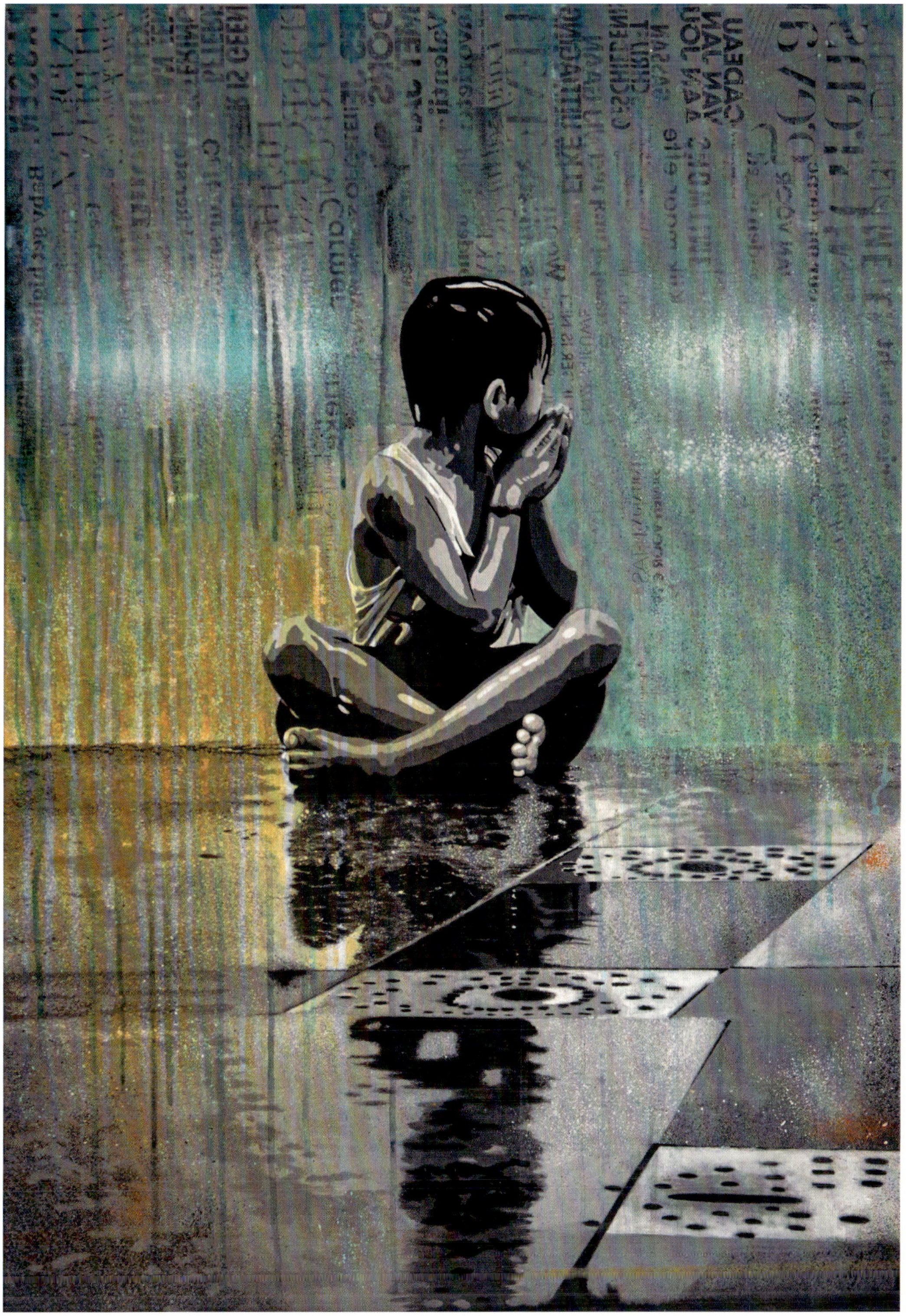

Fig. 121. DB Waterman, FOR A BETTER FUTURE.

> material. I mix these with acrylic paint in different layers. This creates a lot of depth and structure. . . . The technique is intended to imitate old, weathered walls with torn off posters and peeling paint. This creates an urban, street art look.

She explains that in the effort to create a transparent collage, she developed a technique that involved the layering of various materials so each remains visible—her list of materials is exhaustive and includes household items in addition to standard art supplies. Her process delivers a surface the Japanese refer to as *wabi sabi*—a weathered appearance that is true to nature and applauds the aging and decay inherent in that naturalness.

Many artists find the local hardware store, junk lot, home improvement big box store, thrift store, and dumpster to be excellent sources of art supplies. Rural or urban, the artist is a hunter and digger, with the stealth of an eagle seeking out those "found" items that will bring their artwork to the next level. I can totally relate to Waterman and her creative practice. Let's look at her work for the book in this context.

The work is double edged. We see a child depicted in a downpour. The work speaks to us about the threat to our environment from climate change. And it simultaneously makes us ponder the fate of the children of the world who are innocents in this pending catastrophe. The depiction of the innocent child serves to make the message even more potent. We cannot help but wonder what we have done to destroy his future.

Waterman uses her art to make a statement about children, their innocence and resiliency in facing the world we have created for them, and their ability to both find joy in the mess and to strive to create a better future. By repurposing materials in her artwork, Waterman is living her values as she integrates and inculcates sustainability into her message.

Waterman's art is not only beautiful and resonant—it perhaps may have the effect of calling its admirers to action. This is another important way art can not only educate and enlighten us—it can actually motivate us to change and to use our understanding to change the world.

CARRIE PEARCE: VISUAL DELIGHT

All artists, regardless of style or subject, find some variant of pleasure or satisfaction in the process of creation. For the mixed-media artist Carrie Pearce, the sheer sumptuous delight of concocting her very tangible and potent imagery out of paint and found objects is palpable. It is also decidedly original and fabulous, a treat as much for the viewer as for the artist.

Here is Pearce exclaiming her joy in her own words:

> I have eliminated the things I don't enjoy doing and have added things I do enjoy. I do what I like, which is, painting the portrait, finding "stuff," embroidery, construction, and woodcarving to name a few. I am equally inspired by a multitude of things like fabrics, fibers, jewelry, toys, books, and other ephemera.

Here is her magnificently crafted mixed-media work *Dolly*, where the painted doll is embellished with many dolls and ephemera. This might be considered an assemblage and is quite close to falling into the realm of sculpture. It is a phantasmagoria of dolliness: the doll of dolls, absolutely over the top, and marvelous! Enjoy it!

You may be surprised that Pearce chose this particular category, declaring that her primary intention was to deliver a message, not to express her emotions or create a beautiful work, although most assuredly, she has managed to deliver on all of these foci. What then is the message?

Pearce tells us that for her, "art is play," and that her intention is to "create a visual treat," a feast, both in the making and the viewing of the art. She describes the process of making *Dolly* as "a blast," the embellishment of the wigs as "ridiculous." But she also catalogs the extreme effort, craftsmanship, devotion, and care in painting the head with renaissance techniques, implanting the bejeweled background with calibrated precision, and in every sense striving for excellence.

We can't help but question: Is this play or is it work? The answer is that it is both, joyful work engendered by a playful spirit. And this surely is the message Dolly delivers: *I am delight.*

The bonus for the artist is that this found delight is also a window into self-awareness. Pearce tells us that "figuring out who I am as an artist has been a long road. I feel that, by finding my process, I found my art. I am still discovering myself everyday

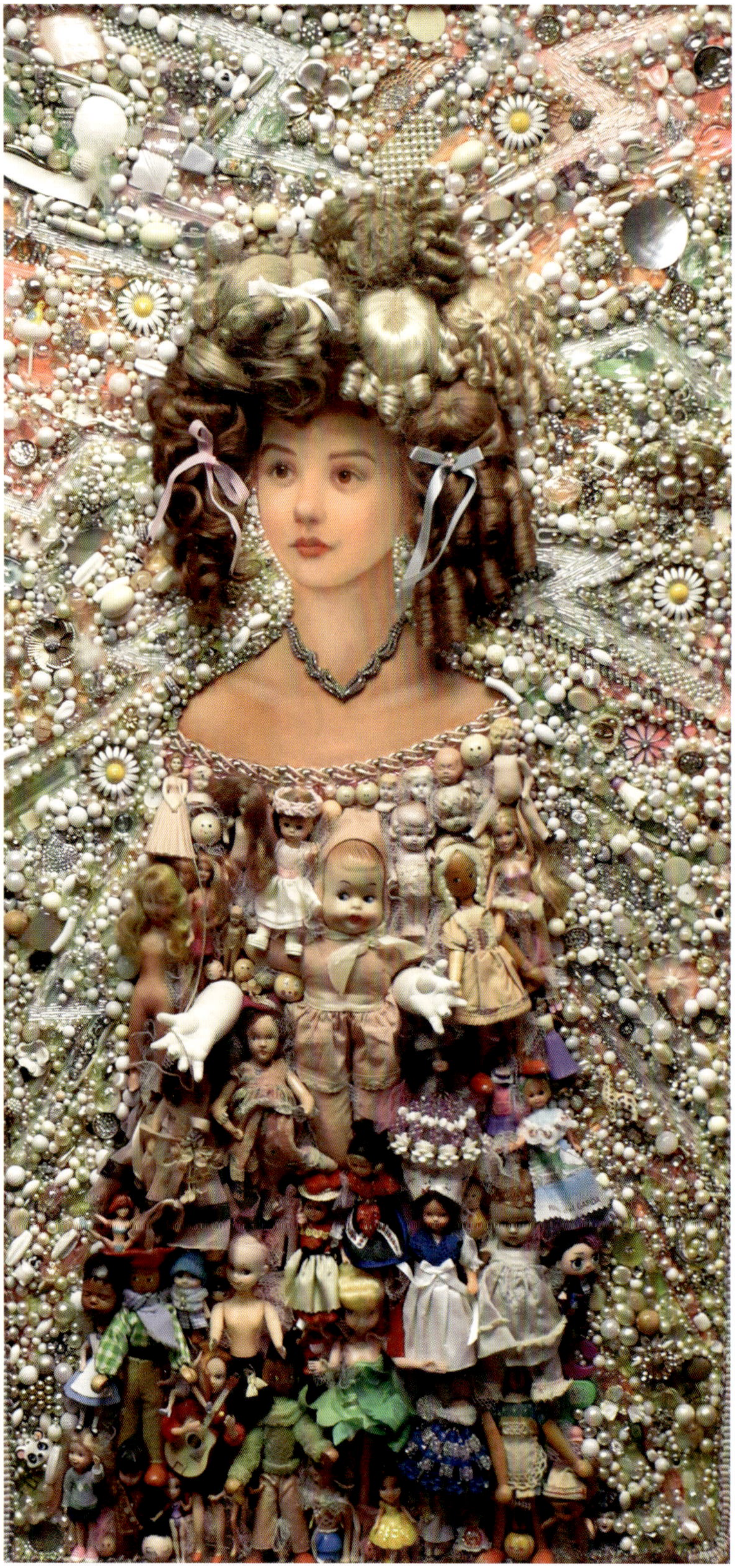

Fig. 122. Carrie Pearce, DOLLY.

and probably will the rest of my life. The uniqueness of me is the only thing I can offer, that someone else can't do. It's really simple, I am following my bliss."

We who are privileged to make and view art can join in this reality: artistic expression and appreciation as a pathway to self-realization. Any subject, any style of expression can offer this reward as the artist finds their own source of meaning, identity, and pleasure through the process.

Chapter 11
Living Artists Whose Focus Is on Emotion

EMOTION, HOW IT MAKES US FEEL

Of the three categories I laid out for artists to highlight their artistic intention, this one was the most popular. It is clear that most artists, most creative and expressive people in fact, designate the heart (especially if pressed to be specific) as the source of their intention and inspiration. Their art, regardless of style or subject, is driven by the desire to communicate human emotion, and to impart the subject with empathy, love, passion, whatever you want to call it.

The artist is called to put his heart on the canvas, so to speak, whether he or she wants that heart to appear beautiful or haunting or compelling or whatever other quality. Mere description will not suffice for most; the artist is not a reporter of facts. He or she is an interpreter of information and ideas that come to his or her consciousness for one reason or another but are then transformed into material form—an artwork that has been imbued with emotion.

The artist is a messenger. He or she is propelled to communicate something to someone and he or she deems the message to be significant. Otherwise, why would the artist expend so much effort in shaping it? It is not a scribbled message, notifying the recipient to know something or directing that recipient to take an action. No, the message is this: "Look at me; this is what I have made—can you feel it?"

It is also true that these same artists are clearly making a statement and using their brain to do it. I have asked the living artists shown here to define their intention and many of them speak quite distinctly and eloquently of their very conscious purpose in making the work. I don't have to reiterate the obvious again, that we need our whole organism to function and certainly to make art.

So now I am happy to bring you the voices and images of some of these artists who contributed one of their works and specified that the expression of emotion was a driving force in its design and execution.

I note an interesting fact, though, that gives me the opportunity to talk about gender roles in the making of art. All but two of the artist respondents to my questionnaire who specified that "the way it makes you feel" is the most direct motivating force for their artwork, are women. A few of the artists, including one man, refused to make a choice and checked all the boxes. But only two male artists checked the emotion box solely. Interesting?

I certainly do not assume that women are more emotional than men, and that female artists express more emotion in their artwork than their male counterparts. It is more likely that women are more open to attributing their inspiration to emotion, in admitting this as the operative component, than men are. But remember that most of the art we are familiar with that has been made over the centuries has been made by men. Women were excluded from the art makers club until only recently. And even today, they have a more difficult task in bringing their work into the public eye as men still outnumber them in museums and galleries. Hopefully, this is changing—slowly, indeed, but surely.

I am an artist and a woman, and I am trying, in my way and in my purview, to correct the imbalance and present to you some of the truly wonderful female artists I have discovered. With my small sample here, I had hoped to present to you a wide diversity. I do not believe I have been able to include a transgender artist, and I apologize for that. There are also many ethnicities I have undoubtedly left out and, hopefully, if I have the opportunity, I will correct that in future.

In any case, here is a selection of some excellent artists who work from their heart and proudly declare that for all to see and enjoy.

ANN-MARIE BROWN: NARRATIVE FIGURATION

The painting of Ann-Marie Brown's selected for this book was stolen from the gallery where it was shown in Montréal. *Desi in Her Mother's Dress* is from a series of works called "Hey Girls" that chronicle the critical moment in a girl's life when her body brings her to womanhood. Just like the landscape painters who choose moments of heightened drama like sunsets and storms, figurative artists often pinpoint dramatic human milestones or events that are soaked in drama and consequence.

What is the meaning of narrative in this context? As opposed to a portrait that offers a rendering of an individual's appearance, which may highlight not only the physical resemblance, but also the character, posture, and even suggest the inner life of the figure, a narrative work goes beyond the "look" to create a story, an experience, a kind of interaction between subject and viewer.

Brown describes a dangerous encounter she had with an individual who threatened her and the fact that, in that moment, her vision was distorted so that she saw the perpetrator's eyes and mouth in clear focus while the rest of his face was a blur. In a similar fashion, at the easel, she selects visual data that goes beyond description to evoke an experience for the viewer that is a match for actual experience.

Utilizing a difficult medium like encaustic, she describes her process in this way:

> There is a slickness to imagery that I'm resisting, both in the figures I choose to paint and the methods I use to paint them. Encaustic is tricky and the marks that build up on the canvas while the painting is being fought for have a value, like scars and wrinkles on a person. They are the story of becoming, written on the body. There's an unpredictability to the encaustic process which disrupts my intention for a piece and opens a dialogue with the emerging image.

Every artist builds their own methodology to suit their goals. In her attempt to create a feeling of aliveness in her figurative work and to avoid a posed or static image, Brown defines her method thus: "I work to affect this by layering contradictory expressions over each other to imbue a sense of motion and texture."

We see this in the work presented here. The figure seems to be thrusting herself out of a miasma, in a state of transformation, as she pushes through to define a new persona, shape, and reality. This is Desi's story in this moment when she is wearing her mother's dress and morphing into womanhood. The painting is about metamorphosis, and the murky mixtures and application suggest the process the

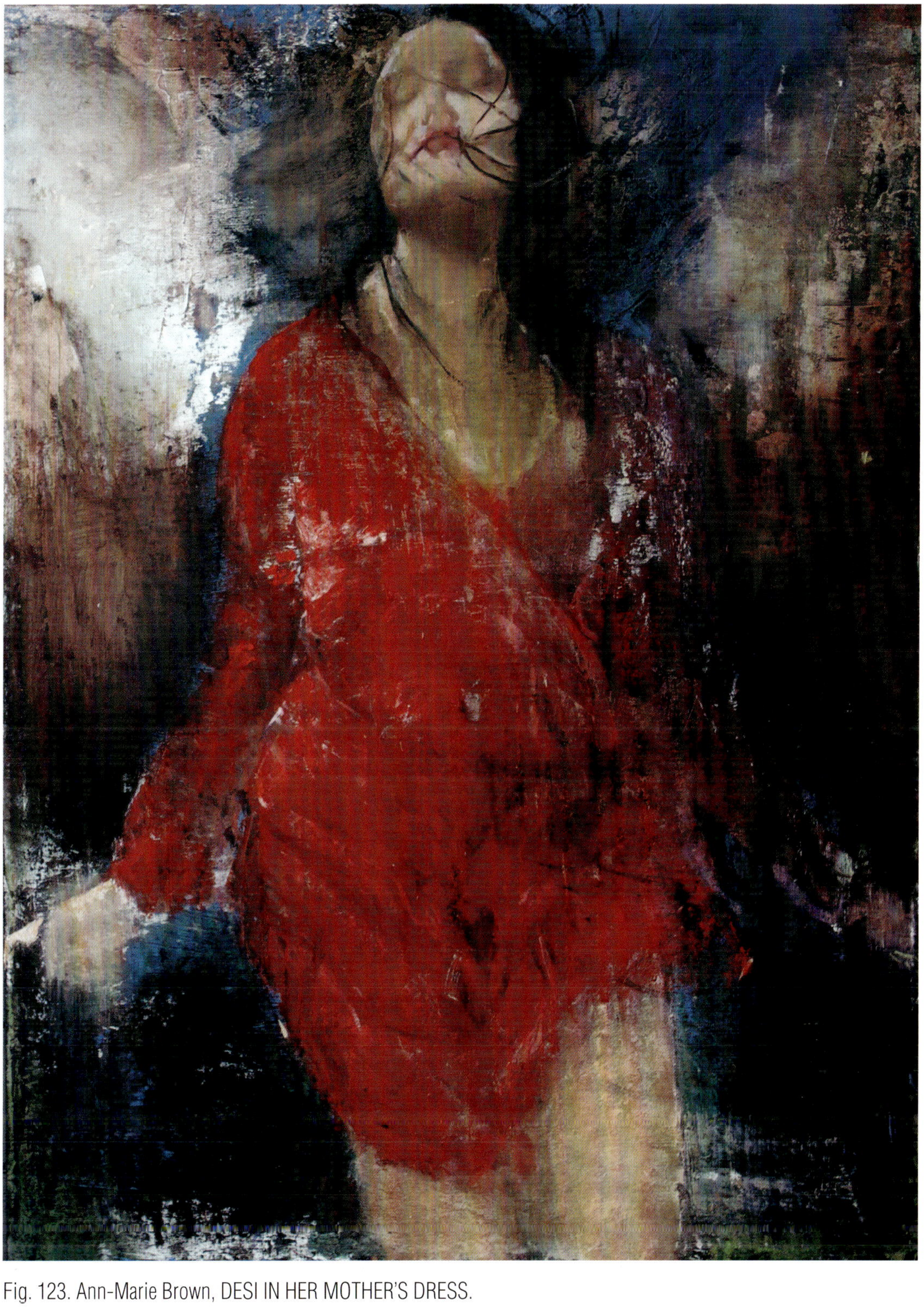

Fig. 123. Ann-Marie Brown, DESI IN HER MOTHER'S DRESS.

figure is undergoing. Brown says her paintings function as Rorschach tests. We read the visceral paint searching for meaning. She quotes the reviewer Joseph Rosen for *Blank Spaces* magazine who, upon viewing her work, said, "The longer you look, the less certain you are of what you see."

In this way, as the viewer searches for the message of the artist, he or she brings his own experience to the task of interpreting it. The artist acts as facilitator; the viewer as co-creator. We all see things differently; we read the narrative and get a different meaning out of it. That is what art as experience is all about.

Ann-Marie Brown has also made a contribution to our Appendix exhibition.

ANNA BOOTHE: FIRE AND ICE

Anne Boothe is a sculptor working primarily in the medium of *pâte de verre*, a form of kiln-fired glassmaking; the English translation is "glass paste." This is a complicated procedure where the artist creates a positive sculpture in wax or clay; then creates a negative mold, fills it with a paste of glass particles called *frit*, fires the mold in a kiln until the glass particles coalesce into a solid mass, and then cools the form so it can be removed from the mold.

What motivates an artist to choose to work in a medium such as cast glass? Boothe said that glass is appropriate for her "because it can convey the simultaneous strength and vulnerability, as well as translucency (or degree of visibility)" of her primary aesthetic inquiries: identity, perspective, relationships, and communication on both conscious and unconscious levels. She also notes, commenting on the technical difficulties and vagaries of this medium, that it delivers an excellent "medium through which to practice humility."

Creating these works is a demanding process indeed. Boothe creates assemblages that "are meant to be icons, pseudo-mirrors, or even prosthetics that aid in self-comprehension, and, for her, provide objectivity for issues or feelings that are often difficult to articulate."

She uses certain recognizable forms symbolically: hands that represent holding on and letting go, hearts and brains as representing emotion and ideation.

The piece we have selected for this section is *Growth* and was created in her early glassmaking years. Let's have a look.

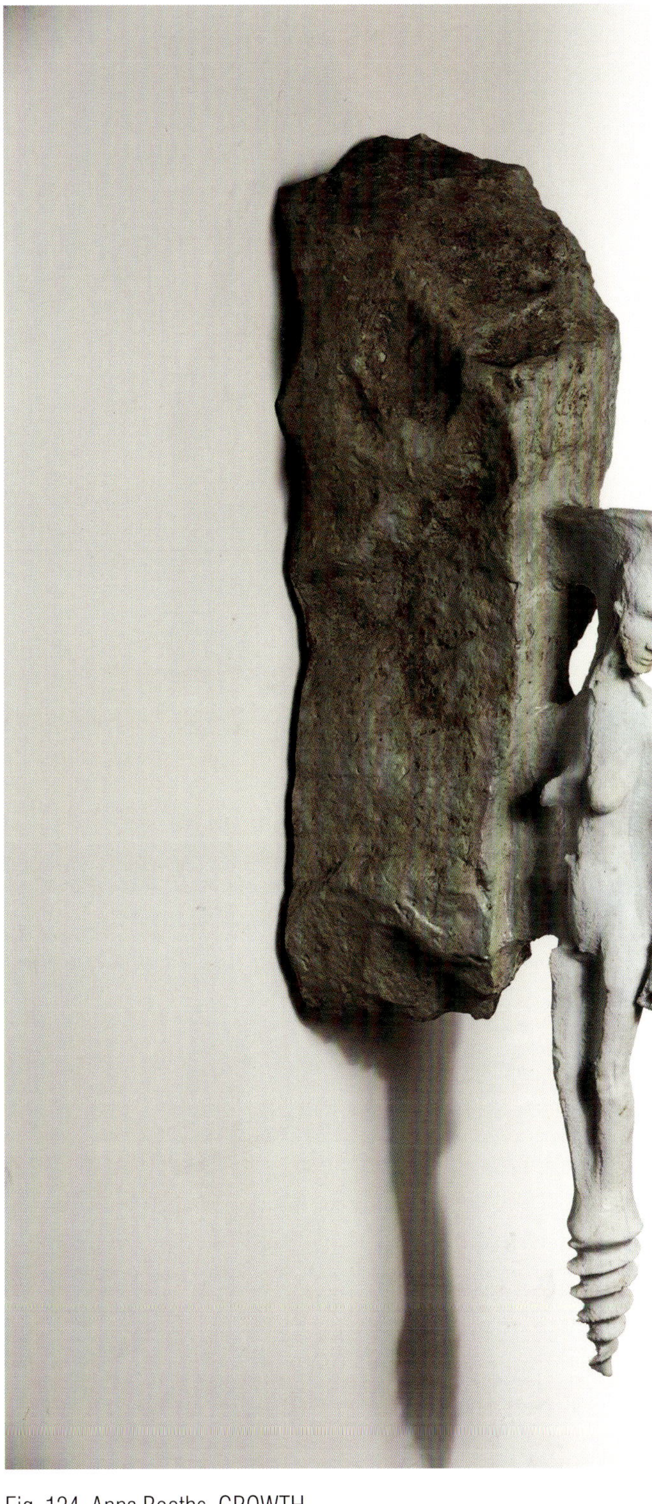

Fig. 124. Anna Boothe, GROWTH.

We see a female figure buttressed by a large rock form. The figure looks ancient, but we see a screw-shaped structure in place of a foot. The figure is attached to the rock, which represents the earth, but also seems to be pulling itself away from the rock. The glass is an ice-blue color, chosen to represent serenity.

When we are in doubt about an artist's intention, we can take information often from its title, as the artist has given us a clue to her meaning. Boothe tells us the work is about what she refers to as a "sense of calm fortitude."

The growth of which she speaks is the ability to manage one's own life in an adult way, creating balance and holding on, while remaining independent. The meaning of the screw in this context is a similar equilibrium—a screw can go in both directions, to connect and to disconnect. That is another aspect of growth: the ability to exercise free will.

Sculptural media like glass and ceramic are indirect methods that the artist executes in distinct stages and require the use of kilns that often surprise the artist with an unintended result. There is a significant learning curve in mastering the technique and bending it to the artist's will. But the material itself is so appealing texturally and visually that it can be especially effective when all goes well. Kudos to artists like Anna Boothe who continue to create emotionally resonant works in this demanding art form.

Make sure to look at Anna Boothe's sculpture in the Appendix exhibition.

SHEILA FEIN: ARTIST ILLUSTRATOR

There is nothing ambiguous about Sheila Fein's artwork. She is an artist and illustrator with a rich vocabulary of imagery who has the ability to present in expert fashion. Here is her painting of two little boys, probably siblings, at play.

Fein here exhibits the illustrator's ability to concretize events and happenings. As a result, her work not only shows two children at play, but it also tells you about their relationship. The older child with the bucket is obviously directing the play for the amusement of his little brother. We can probably deduce this will be their lifetime relationship and that dynamic is the true subject of this work.

Fein says she focuses on the "here and now of popular culture." Her ability to draw and paint so expertly is what makes this possible. Her very graphic style is able to

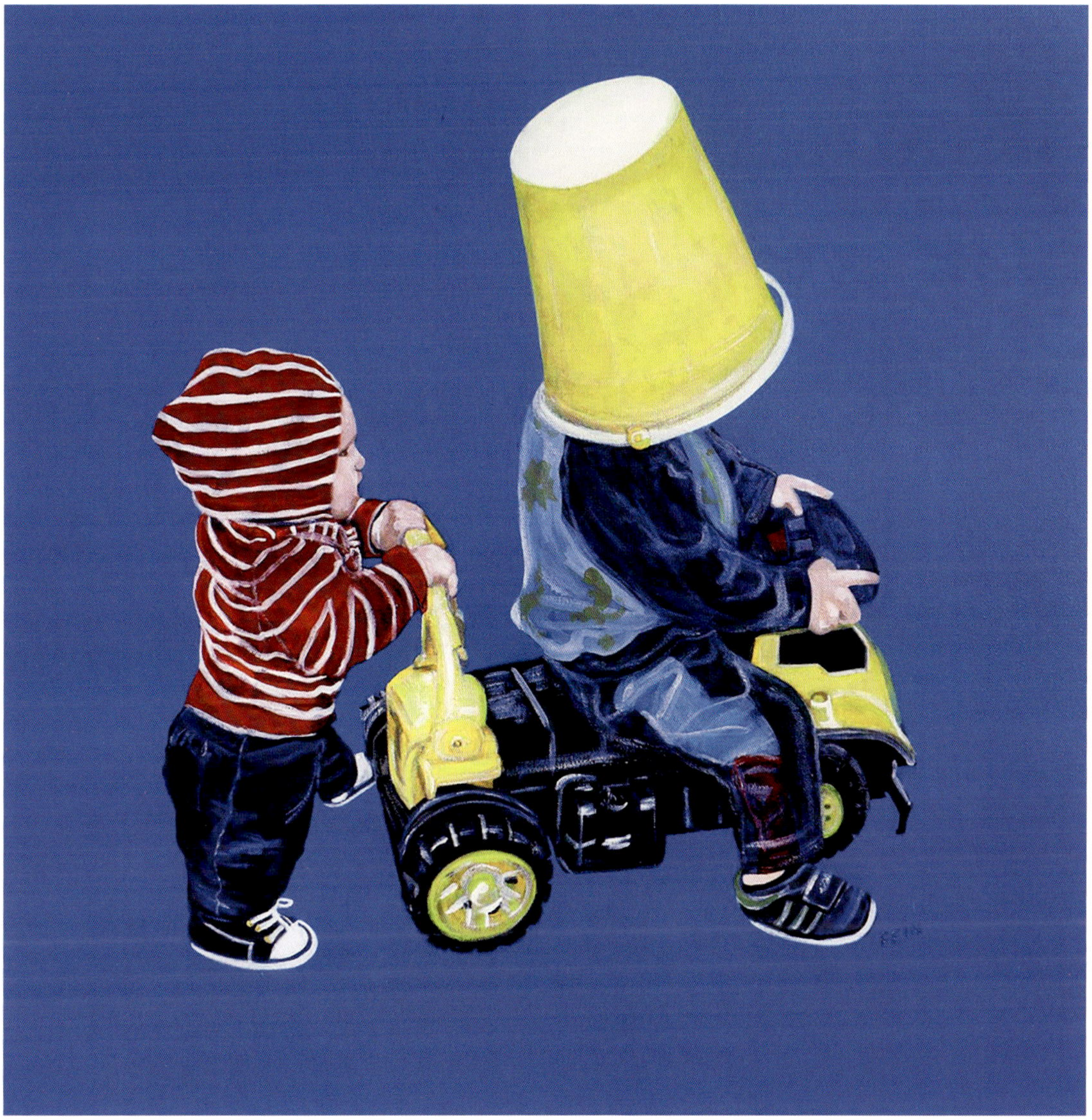

Fig. 125. Sheila Fein, BUCKET HEAD.

deliver a message in a no-nonsense manner, made possible by her choice of subject and ability to render it so convincingly. Something like this only works because of that expertise—try to imagine the same subject with a mis-drawn or sloppily crafted bucket.

I love the rich blue background of this work and the short gamut of primary colors that seem so appropriate to the subject. The flat application of color is also essential to the efficacy of the piece.

Fein is an image maker of the everyday and of today. She is an astute observer and works directly from life with a deep connection to her subjects, rendering them with devotion. Though she does so in realistic fashion, she writes that she "hopes to inspire and provoke thought" with her work.

Like every artist, Fein tells us how she sees the world and what matters to her.

Make sure to view Sheila Fein's colored pencil work in the Appendix exhibition.

STEPHEN MAFFIN: FRAGMENTED FIGURES

Stephen Maffin is one of two male artists who indicated that his primary focus was on emotion, giving his portraits an emotional reality. He has developed a rather interesting technique utilizing plaster and burlap to create a unique painting surface that imbues it with a crackled, aged appearance.

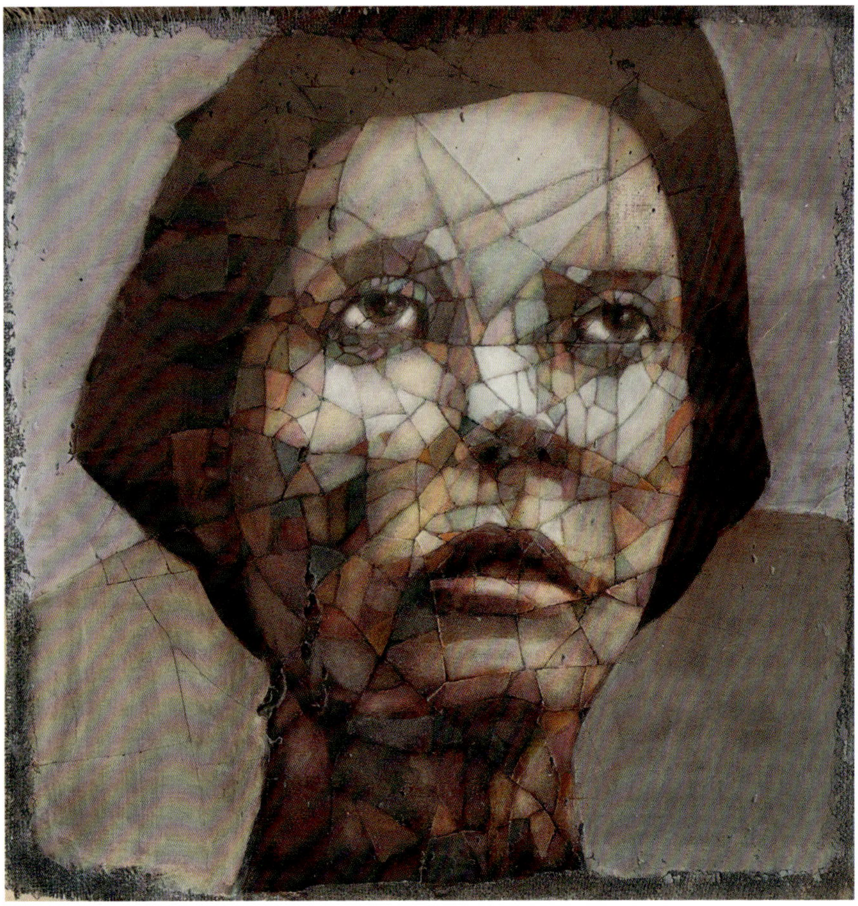

Fig. 126. Stephen Maffin, LORE.

We have discussed how each artist not only has a particular and very personal perspective, but that this perspective is matched by a very specific "touch"—a way of applying the paint that will allow the artist to achieve his desired look. This is strongly evident here, as Maffin's work is instantly recognizable by virtue of this surface he creates. The divisions are not literally planes, as in Cubist works; they break the human face as if it fell on the floor and shattered.

Perhaps it is this shattering that holds the meaning of Maffin's work. The multiple facets of the human face symbolize the complexity of the personality and inner life. They also suggest the precariousness of existence—the fragility of the human being after all.

In this work, the limited palette is especially effective, as the tonal fragments coalesce to form a riveting portrait. Seeing the face broken this way undeniably lends an emotional quality to the work.

Human beings are complex, this rendering seems to assert, composed of many aspects and contradictions.

MAGDALENA MOREY: ABSTRACTED MOVEMENT

In this section we are highlighting a figurative work by the artist Magdalena Morey, but you can find one of her landscapes in a previous chapter. She is able to create a feeling of deep space in her abstracted landscapes that allows us to travel visually in and out of the canvas. This facility is evident in a different way in this figurative work.

I love that you can first enjoy this work without even finding the figure, with the fields of beautiful color and textured, pinpointed areas creating a vivid abstract painting. As your eyes travel around the canvas you find first the linear hand and then trace it back to what now appears as a body in motion, a tilted head reaching into space and the other arm and hand, having been painted more faintly as is appropriate to its position in space. You then realize we are looking at a dancer and that she is in movement, the white lines behind her sufficient to give us the wall of the room she moves in.

I see the figure as a dancer, but the artist told me she visualizes her as a symbol of self-empowerment, navigating the difficulties of life and striving to attain balance and perspective. It is not uncommon that the viewer will see something in the artwork

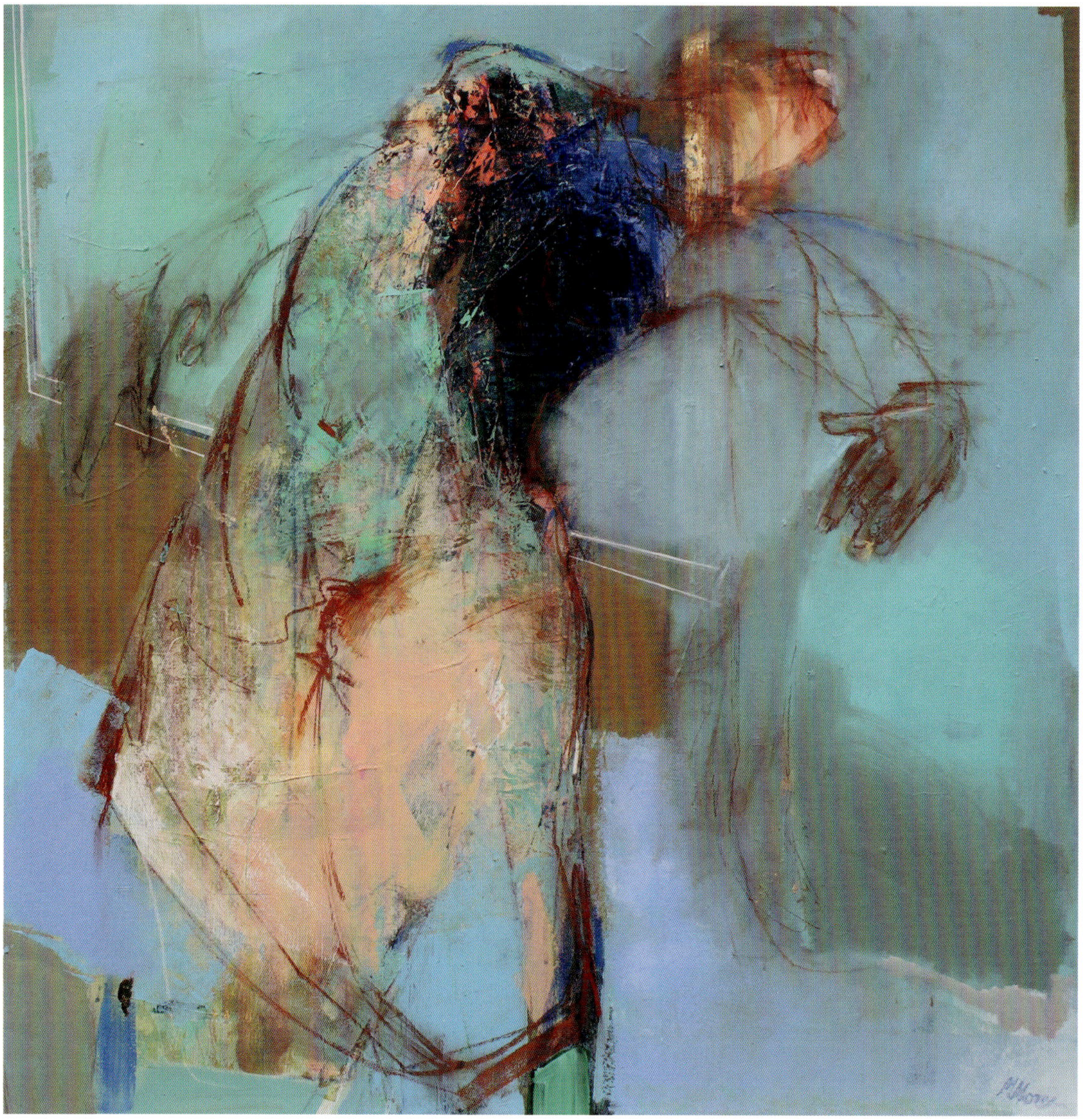

Fig. 127. Magdalena Morey, FINDING BALANCE.

that the artist did not necessarily intend. We read art from the perspective of our own experience and in the light of our own values and visual ideas.

Morey is utilizing abstraction for a distinct purpose. Not only does she savor the beauty of color, light, and texture, she recognizes that these elements work together to give life to her imagery and prevent it from feeling static, just a trapped moment. To avoid creating what might be viewed as a kind of snapshot, where the figures are frozen, she utilizes the large swaths of color, to de-particularize the moment, and materials like gold leaf, to highlight and dramatize elements and inject energy and dynamism. We are delighted to find the figure in movement and can imagine her next steps. The work is vividly alive.

As you look at figurative work, keep this in mind and search for how the abstract elements enliven the work. They remind you that regardless of the degree of verisimilitude, what you are looking at is a composite of strokes, pools of color, lines, saturations, and textures, that together trick you into thinking what is before you is a person. It is not; it is an apparition conjured from these potions and the wizardry of the artist.

JUDITH SCHAECHTER: CONTEMPORARY STAINED GLASS

Stained glass is an age-old practice which we associate with churches and religious themes, but the remarkable artist Judith Schaechter has turned those traditions on

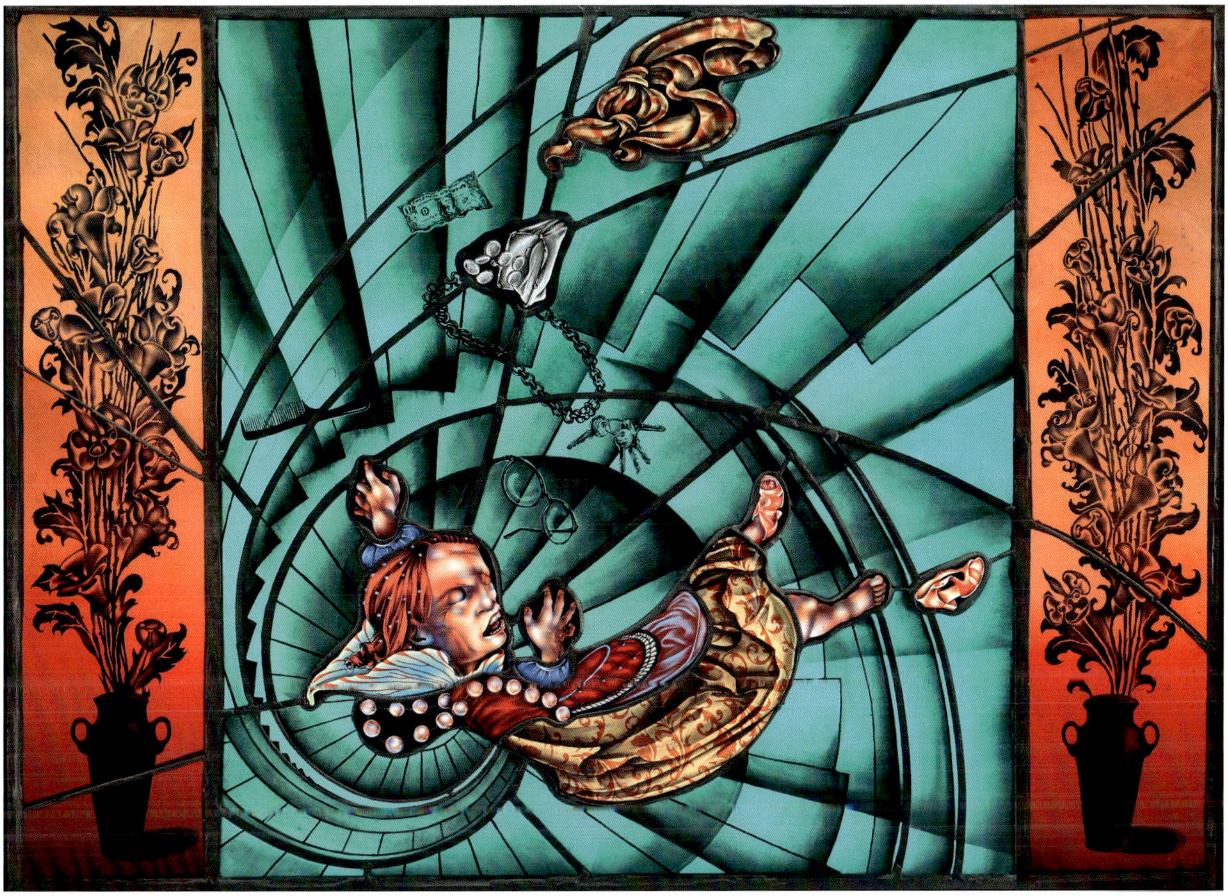

Fig. 128. Judith Schaechter, DE-LUXE.

their head and taken the possibilities of this medium to the next level. She was the first artist-instructor I met when I began my study of glassmaking at Brooklyn's Urban Glass, and I was utterly amazed with how she was able to turn her own iconography into this rather intransigent medium.

Her work *De-Luxe* depicts, per Schaechter, "a woman who appears to be falling down a spiral staircase. Her personal belongings (glasses, keys, money, scarf, shoe) are free falling with her. The piece is flanked by two urns of silhouetted flowers, which may or may not suggest a poor outcome of the fall."

This composition arose in a process of trial and error, with several dozen compositions attempted before Schaechter arrived at this final version.

Schaechter said that though she has been engaged in art making for many decades and has gone through the process of creating a work of art countless times, she still "has no idea how that is accomplished."

I can totally identify with this feeling. Where one finally lands is the result of many unplanned excursions and trials, some that succeed and move us forward, others that fail and lead us in different directions. The final destination may be as much of a surprise to the artist as to her viewer.

In the case of this work, Schaechter said:

> It began as a woman slipping in a puddle of her own urine. It became something considerably less physically repulsive. I was thinking about falling and how as we get older it gets even more frightening and consequential. It's sort of a remake of one of Holbein's woodblock series "The Dance of Death," several of which feature women characters and were intended to point out that we all must die, male or female, rich or poor etc.

The creative process can lead the artist on a path to her own unconscious mind, and it can prove revelatory, a kind of therapeutic trip into our own psyches, as our pictures reveal to us their origins. Here, perhaps, a recognition of mortality, epitomized by the fall. Note, by the way, the expert enameling to create the illusion of that spiral staircase.

Just hold in your mind the care and dedication required to make those two dozen compositions and to finally devise this very expertly crafted work. This is an example of what we mean when we speak of the artist's calling. "Getting it just right" is no simple matter.

And why do we do it? Because speaking from the heart, trying to communicate our truth, is not a casual matter; it is as difficult as living and as essential as breath.

Another of Schacchter's fabulous stained-glass works is in the Appendix exhibition.

PHOEBE SCOTT: CORPOREAL SCULPTURE

Painting and drawing live in the field of illusion; they are non-corporeal media, and any implication of form is imaginary. But with sculpture, we have actual form and dimension, and this presents an entirely different set of possibilities and strictures. I introduce you to the ceramic sculptor Phoebe Scott, who is absorbed with the corporeal—the body, and in particular, the female body. She has selected the perfect medium with which to make her inquiry, as there is no more malleable and moldable medium than clay, and nothing more natural as well—it is earth itself.

Phoebe stated her interest and intention so succinctly and poetically:

> The body as an object—objectified, deconstructed, fetishized, weathered, worn, parsed, reconstructed—is a living document. Our experiences are drilled into its skin. Our memories are visceral and sensual. Our DNA holds our history and often immutable limitations. In deference to the burgeoning field of epigenetics, we are just beginning to learn that, within our bodies, we carry the bodies of our ancestors and the immediate effects of their experiences as beings, one lifetime passed to another lifetime. My work is about the body and the story it tells of its existence. I imprinted on the human life cycle, and how vulnerable the body can be no matter how indomitable we seem. I was transfixed by my own body and the bodies of others, especially those who have been marginalized by our society. I am interested in how society views women, in particular, over the span of a lifetime from childhood to fertility to infertility. I'm attracted to the tensile girding of muscle, the skin as both taut and loose, and the underpinning of bone that is most clearly revealed by the elderly. Truncation is a theme in my work because of its power and cultural relevance—what does society want to see, what does it hide and excise, how does truncation reveal how women's bodies are discussed in parts and pieces? With clay, I am able to edit and shape what is integral to the narrative. I push against the concept of the ideal body as it is shown in sculpture through history and throughout a lifetime, especially given that in our culture the ideal body seems to be the only one that is truly authorized. Even for the ideal female body, that authorization comes from those in power, not from the woman herself. Portraits of the body reflect the

world that rises up around each of our bodies, uniquely and changeably over time. The body is a commentary on the world that surrounds it.

Let us have a look at one of Scott's sculptures.

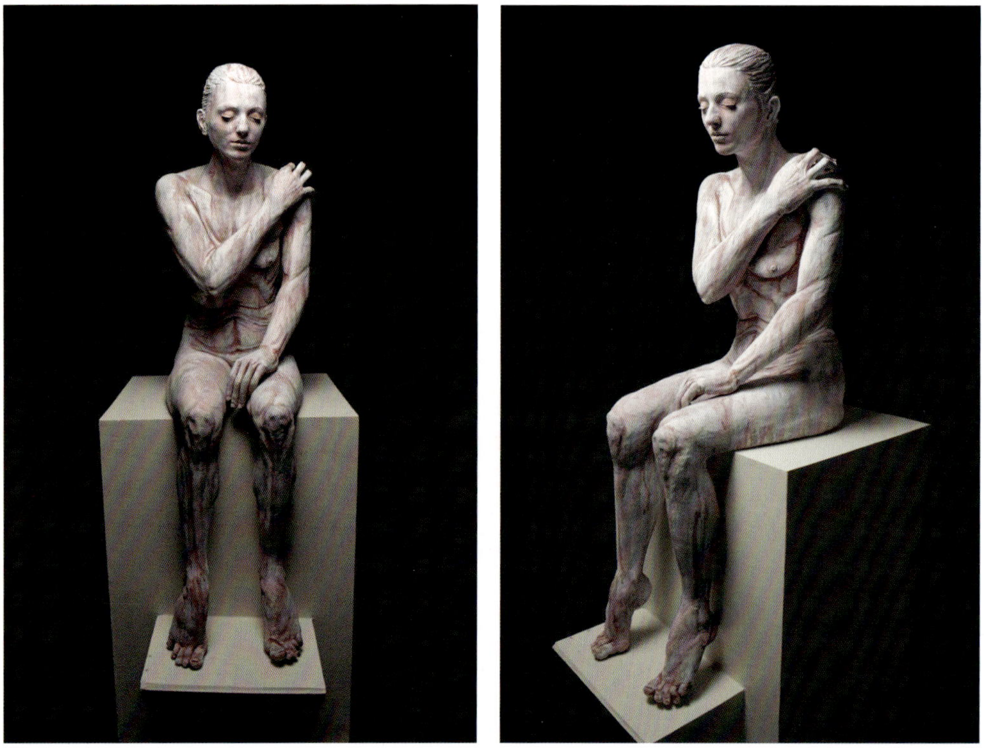

Fig. 129. Phoebe Scott, WITHIN.

Scott said that her intention in this work and in others in this series is to describe a moment of awareness, not of the self, which may include thought or consciousness, but an awareness of the person's physicality, of their body. So, she not only portrays the body itself, but the body in awareness, which will alter the look, posture, position, and features of that body.

In this work we feel that in the closed eyes and thoughtful, self-absorbed expression, the hand resting and gently touching the shoulder, the positioning of the feet with awareness of the surface they rest on. The surface coloring suggests both inner and outer realities, and the accurate creases in the stomach area and general attempt not to idealize the figure assist in creating her corporeality in a moment of self-realization. We can feel her and empathize with her. She is like us.

I invite you to take a long look at this work and to follow Scott as her work is quite exceptional.

SIRARPI HEGHINIAN WALZER: POETIC MIXED MEDIA

Heghinian Walzer uses the word "poetic" to describe her mixed-media abstractions and I believe this description is well chosen. Just as a poem's phrases and reference allude to a meaning which must be excavated, her collaged fragments and embedded drawings, working in concert, deliver to us a meaning we sense, and perhaps cannot clearly verbalize.

She explains her intention in this way:

> My poetic abstractions spring from meditations on nature and from memories that are distilled into single dramatic moments. The energetic surfaces

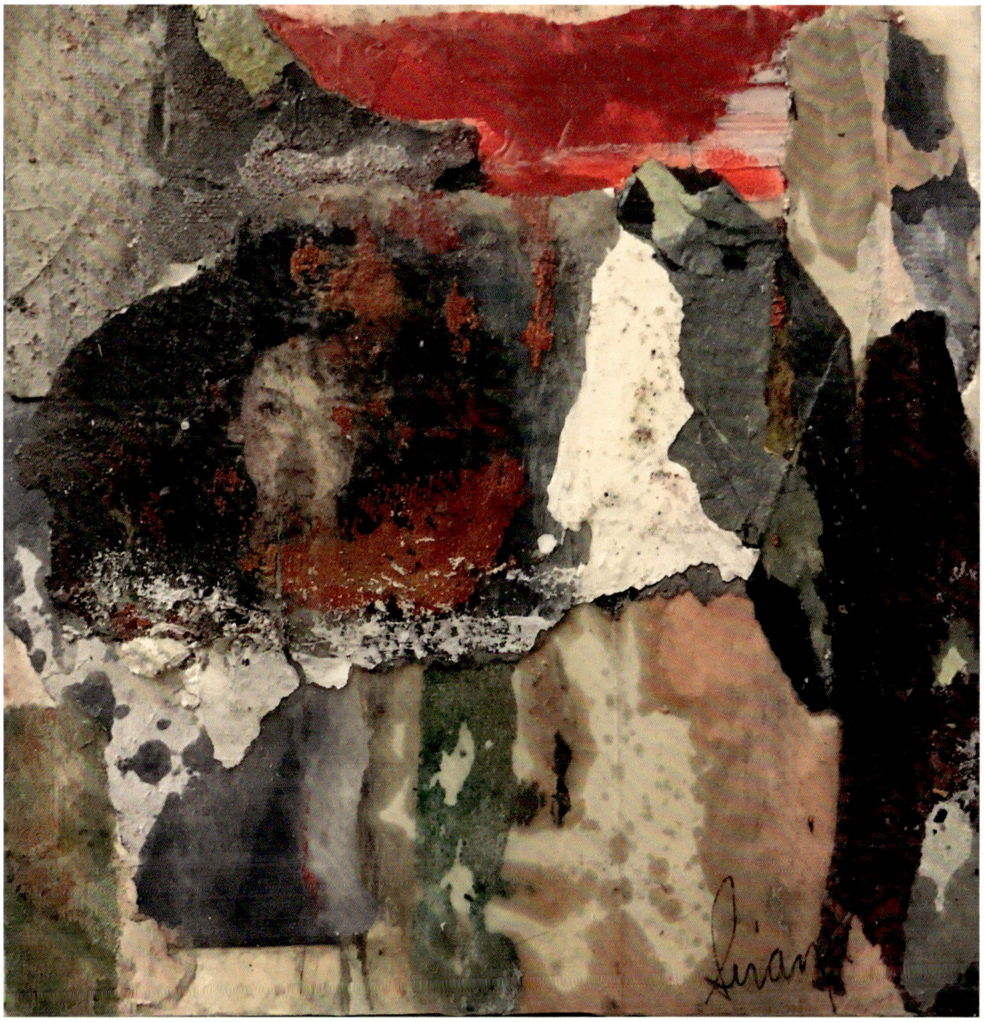

Fig. 130. Sirarpi Heghinian Walzer, PORTRAIT OF A WOMAN.

> imply an ongoing tension between freedom and containment, edging the viewer closer to that place where chaos can erupt into clarity. The deliberate juxtapositions of forms and exaggerations of color choices, provide clues to content and interpretation. The forms and exaggerations of color choices are metaphors for a search, with clues to content and interpretation, representing different layers of life, alluding both to what is present and what is missing.

So one has to be a bit of a detective, and a bit of a psychic, to penetrate the meaning of her work, but that does not lessen our interest or enjoyment in it. It is mysterious, but in a fascinating way. Here is an example called *Portrait of a Woman*. Can you understand that the portrait is not only the face of the woman, but the entire work, all the fragments, colors, and textures that surround that face, the layers and composition? The pieces are the phrases that resonate like the metaphors in a poem.

This work is part of a series called "Soulful," which Heghinian Walzer says focuses on the "ephemeral and flux of existence."

She expresses duality with her materials and marks. I was intrigued by this phrase in her writings: "The energetic surfaces imply an ongoing tension between freedom and containment, edging the viewer closer to that place where chaos can erupt into clarity."

From "chaos" to "clarity": this defines the process of making sense of a poem or visual work of art through your senses, thoughts, and feelings. It is especially relevant in the case of abstract work, which challenges us to use our own imaginations in deciphering a work of art.

See another of Sirarpi Heghinian Walzer's works in the Appendix exhibition.

KRISTIN KWAN: FANCIFUL FIGURATION

Kristin Kwan is a painter who, as she puts it, "uses elements of fantasy and allegory to explore themes of life, death, and rebirth."

Her work has a quality that takes it out of the realm of the factual or descriptive. It has an otherworldliness to it as she endeavors to depict deep emotion and states of being.

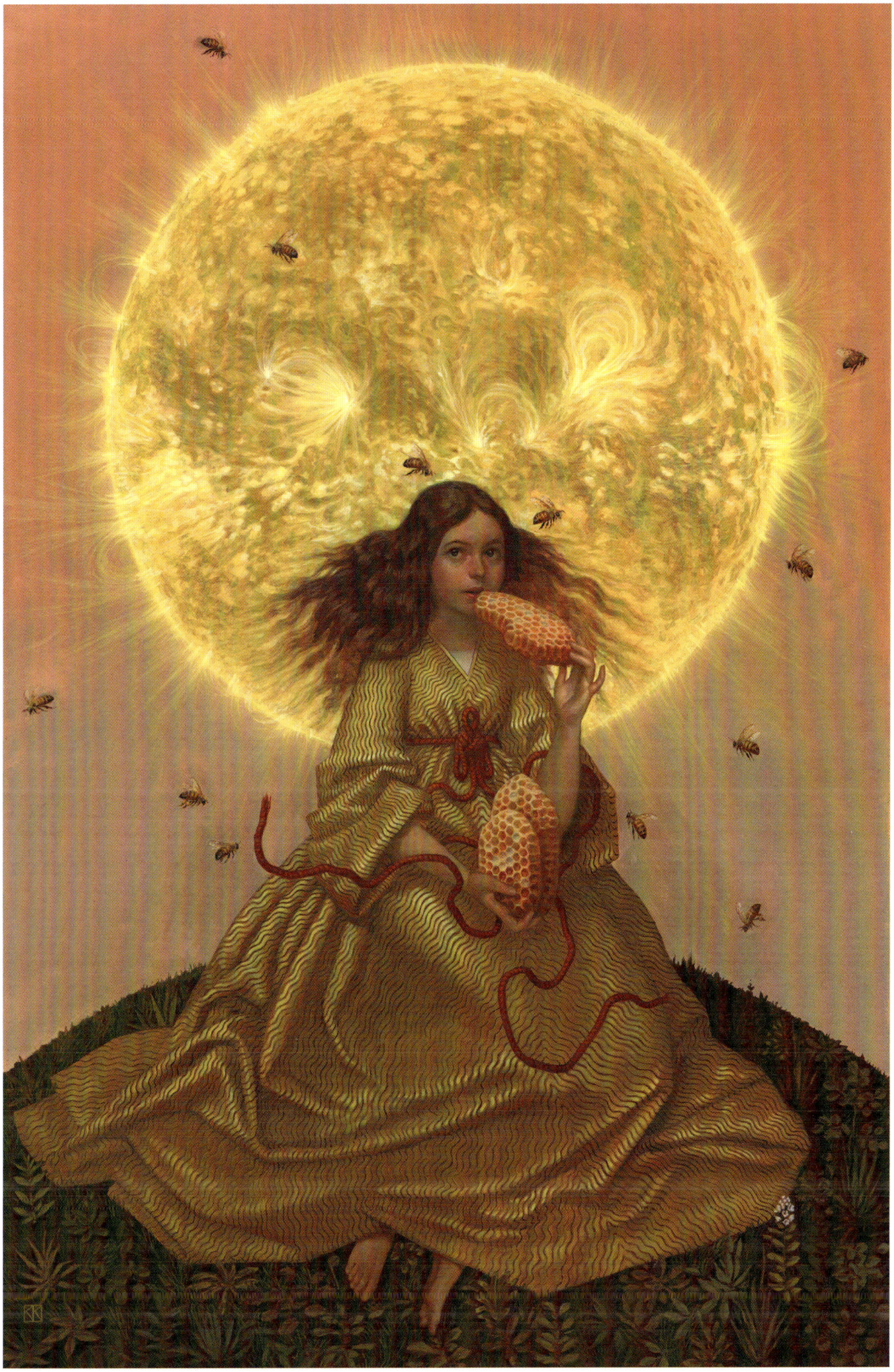

Fig. 131. Kristin Kwan, THE GOLDEN AFTERNOON.

Here we present her work *The Golden Afternoon*, an oil painting on panel. Let's have a good look.

We see a young woman feasting on a honeycomb in a swirl of bees, backlit by a giant glowing orb, the sun that is source of all the literal life-sustaining gold. Kwan says her sun resembles a "byzantine icon" and was the originating inspiration for this work—she just really wanted to paint a giant glowing sun!

Every artist's creative time periods vary: some can make a painting in an afternoon, some in ten days, but for Kwan the process is usually longer—she can think about and work on a piece for months, even years. In the case of this work, she was creating it during a time of turbulence in her personal life but tells us that through the pain and struggle, joy pushed through. Kwan defines it as "the sweetness that lies beneath buzzing anxiety above."

An apropos description: Did this suggest the bees perhaps?

In any case, the girl and bees are personifications of a state of mind, a phenomenon of our emotional lives—that in the pain of life, in the intense moments when our hearts are hurting, the very intensity may bring with it a great beauty. As she puts it, "to sit in that buzzing distraction, sweetness and beauty can be found."

She likens this state to, appropriately, the quality of light in what photographers refer to as "the golden hour," a time when the world is seemingly aglow and revelation is at hand.

This kind of very emotional painting lives in a realm of magic and myth, and the figures painted become not individuals, but symbols of life forces and realities. I am reminded of tarot cards and other evocative imagery that seems interwoven with both mystery and meaning.

ALAN POWELL: MEANINGFUL SHAPES

In semiotics, the study of signs and symbols and their interpretation, we have the concept of the icon. An icon is a simplification of an image—a shape or set of lines that represent a more complex image. Keep this in mind as you gaze at this painting by the artist Alan Powell.

What do you see? There are basic shapes—triangles, circles and squares. As Powell explains, "A triangle may be a mountain top, a sail boat, or an arrow. Circles may

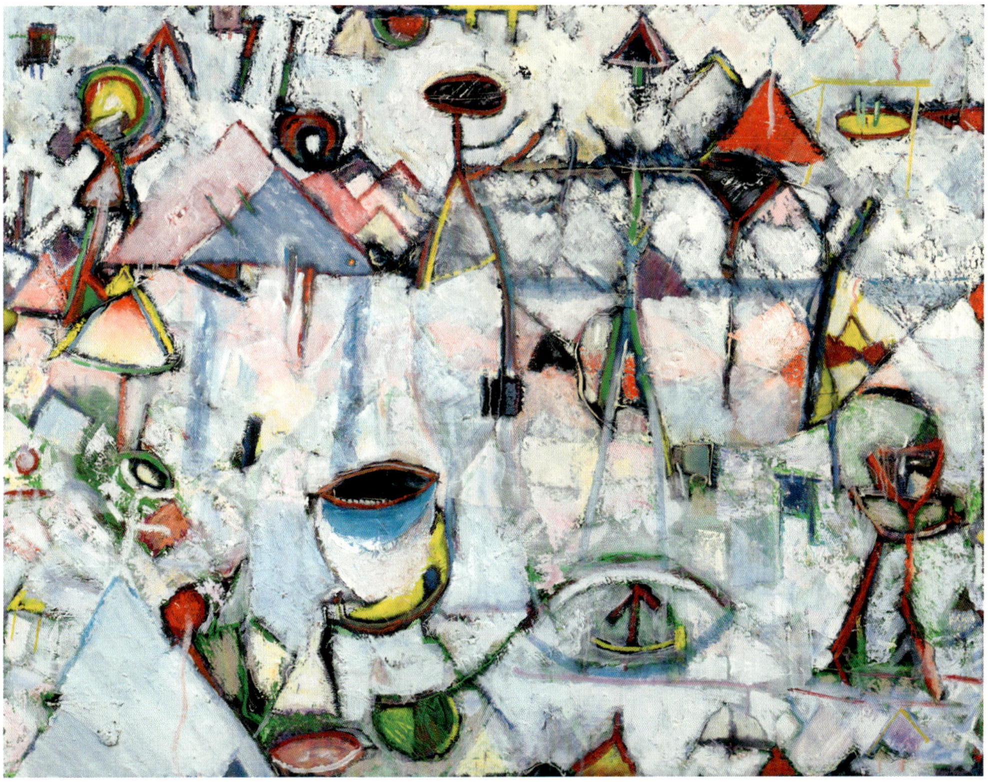

Fig, 132. Alan Powell, DANCING BY THE RIVER.

represent a target, the sun, an eye, or a bowl. Squares become doorways, windows, or walls. Symbolically, triangles can represent the flow of energy."

We don't see classifiable, identifiable people or places, do we? Yet we do get a sense of what we are looking at. We get a clue from the title of the work, *Dancing by the River*. We look for the river and find that blue horizontal line. We assume this must be a place, so we guess the triangles are mountains. We see a bunch of lines that suggest stick figures, but Powell tells us there are no real or facsimile people. Just icons, interacting.

They are interacting with each other, and with you, as the viewer. Powell doesn't want you to see people, or even rivers. As humans, we can't help but see things. We look into the sky at the clouds and see dogs and castles, but then poof, they are gone. It is kind of the same thing with Alan's paintings.

"What may look like an umbrella one day, might be seen as a road leading off into the distance the next. The stories we create upon successive viewings will differ," said Powell.

This artist wants you to participate in his creative meanderings. He wants you to look at it and see into it. He doesn't want to present a fait accompli. As Powell says, "My work needs to surprise me."

And it surprises you too. Kind of cool, don't you think?

SUMMARY: ART THAT MAKES US FEEL

Each of the artists represented here, and many others working in similar fashion, wear their hearts on their canvases and sculptures. Their driving impetus is to inject their sensations, concerns, and passions into their imagery. This takes many forms and objectives that are based on experience, ability, orientation, and creative propensities, and luckily for us, each ingredient results in a totally different look and message.

You might say that every artwork is a commentary on life in the most general sense, but each artist focuses on an aspect of life that has primary emotional meaning for them. Each artist has chosen a medium that suits them, a genre that suits their interest, and a visual vocabulary that expresses their personality. It all becomes a signature of their creative identity.

We can never reduce such a complex focus into a phrase, but if I challenge myself, I will call it this way: For Ann-Marie Brown, the moment crystallized. For Anna Boothe, a calmness and balance. For Sheila Fein, the value of relationships. For Stephen Maffin, making a whole through the sum of its parts. For Magdalena Morey, movement is life. For Judith Schaechter, confronting life's challenges and mortality. For Phoebe Scott, the body and what it tells us about the inner life. For Sirarpi Heghinian Walzer, the poetry of existence, and for Kristin Kwan, the elevation of inner reality through fantasy. As for Alan Powell, he gives you the stage and you get to write the play.

I hope you find this useful, and I challenge you when you look at art to explain (to yourself) not only what you like. That is just too easy. How about answering these questions: *What do you see? How does it make you feel? What phrase can you use to distill the artist's intention? Why do you like it?*

Think of looking at art as entering into a relationship with the artist. They have told you something. *What is it and what does it mean to you?* Answer back, even if it is only in your own mind and heart. The universe hears you.

Chapter 12
Taste

We have gotten to this point and looked at a lot of art, discussed aesthetic concepts, compared and contrasted and even drawn a conclusion or two, or at least made a summary of ideas. Now it is time to turn the camera in reverse mode and look at you, the reader and viewer. The rest of the book is about you, what you like, why you like it, and what you can do to widen your horizons, and to become a true connoisseur of art.

I have attempted to give you a cross-section of artwork—different genres and styles—but of course I am the one who has selected the works to be included here, so the book, whether I wanted to or not, reflects what is important to me and what I wanted to share. Any other writer would have selected a totally different set of works, which would have given you a totally different experience. I recognize that and accept it; it could not be otherwise.

I have tried to include not only the finest works in any genre, but also ones that may not be at the highest standard. How else could you recognize the difference? It is my belief that every piece of visual art has some virtue, something that stands out as excellent. It was created by a human making aesthetic choices, be they schooled or intuitive, who we can presume was attempting to express themselves as well as possible.

I always look to find that when I look at any work, and I suggest you do the same. First, before finding fault or criticizing, find value, that kernel of good that you have excavated like a precious stone. You are panning for gold always when you look at a work of human endeavor. In other words, look first for the positive. That's the best way to start.

Let's talk about what you like in art, and why you like it. The answer starts and ends with YOU. Who you are, where you live, and what your experiences have been. We have touched on this earlier when we discussed why artists pick a particular subject, color scheme, or style. They can relate to it, it pleases them, and it expresses who they are and where their capabilities can best be utilized.

The same goes for you as the viewer or collector of art. Let's look at some scenarios as examples. The artist grew up on a farm and loves wide-open spaces. You grew up in a crowded apartment but always yearned to live in the country. That artist's light-filled abstract work really appeals to you. You connect to it, and it inspires you.

Your sister loves blue. She's got milky blue eyes and likes to wear blue and green dresses that make her eyes appear even more swimming-pool blue. She's got a thing for landscapes and seascapes.

Some people love horror movies and don't even cringe. Others, like me, must turn off the sound to endure them. Some people like to take chances, jump from airplanes and go on roller coasters. Others prefer quiet walks down a country lane.

When it comes to discretionary items like food or other consumables, why do we need miles of supermarket shelves with countless items and myriad brands? Why?

It all comes down to taste. There are as many tastes as there are individuals, and the combinations are endless. We can give someone else a million reasons to like this or that, and it won't influence them one iota.

Taste, however, is a function of discrimination, and as we become more educated, our library of tastes tends to grow. As we collect experiences, our bank of favorables grows with interest. The more we see, the more we know, and the more we know, the more we see. It is as simple as that.

I am not only referring here to looking at art. To refine your taste buds, you need to expand your horizons: go more places, meet more people, experience different environments and cultures. You will bring all of this with you when next you visit a museum or art gallery. Whether you realize it or not, all that you have witnessed has recalculated your ability to be open to different sensations and messages. You have become more receptive, and your visual vocabulary has increased exponentially.

A caveat. I am going to partially negate what I have just expressed about exposure to myriad influences, seeing the world and widening horizons. All of us are now constantly bombarded with images on the internet and through all the media we now cannot live without. This is a different kind of experience than what I have just elaborated.

I don't even know if I would call it an experience in the sense that going to a library, museum, or a theater is an experience, something we willingly engage in as a viewer, commentator, or participant. We choose to go to the museum because there is an exhibition of an artist who has appealed to us or we have heard is fabulous and something we should check out. We don't suspect there is an evil motive in the curator's selection of this material for our viewing pleasure.

As I write this, my brain flashes a red light reminding me of recent "immersive displays" of artist's works that are aggrandized and splashed on giant screens with accompanying music to sell tickets. I take exception to this type of "show" because it is suspect. In its attempt to make art more entertaining, it distorts the artist's intention in favor of the promoter's intention, namely, to captivate us and make money. I will be extremely disheartened to learn that this is more than an aberration and that museums are turning to this merchandising of art, packaging it to make it more palatable and accessible.

Everything I am and know and have tried to impart in my books goes against this trend, which I believe could destroy ultimately what art is and the value it can bring to our lives. I am especially aggrieved to see the artist Vincent van Gogh merchandised in this fashion. He, who achieved so little recognition in his career, who was so troubled and yet endeavored to do authentic and meaningful work, would be aghast at these manipulations and denigration of his life's work—blowing up his lovely work into bloated butterflies of color splashed on walls set to music. Suffice it to say, I am not a fan.

Art is meant to be seen as it was created. If the work is small, stand close in the quiet and look at it. Stand as the artist stood at his easel and experience it as the artist did. That will be an experience you can remember.

The images coming to us on Netflix and other platforms vying for our attention and consumption are scripted and packaged by people whose mission is to influence us and capture our attention and preference. These media moguls are adept at this, and they have compiled reams of data about what we will like, what will score best in popular culture, what the top ten items will be for every possible category of goods and services they are convinced we need and want.

All this constant bombardment is confusing and is not the kind of experience of art I am extolling and hoping you will engage in. Call me old-fashioned, call me a dinosaur, but the experiences I am talking about involve personal interaction in real time with real things—people you actually talk to (I have accepted Zoom as a legitimate platform); art, which you look at in person if you are fortunate, but also in books, which you can study at your own pace; travel to the wonderful places in our world; encounters with nature and animals; in other words, direct experience, not packaged and filtered experience over-orchestrated by financial beneficiaries.

Oh, I hear you telling me to "get real," "wake up," "this is the twenty-first century" "you can't stop progress," but I counter, "you can, and you must." I watch Netflix movies too, but not too much. I keep myself on a media diet, because I don't want to become fat on falsity, greed, junk food for the masses. I don't want my eyes to glaze over and my brain to go to sleep, letting others provide amusement. I resist, and I think you should too.

You don't want taste that is prescribed, that is au courant. You want taste that expresses your unique DNA, that arises from your essential nature and authentic self. So, let's proceed with this idea of taste and answer some basic questions about it.

DEFINE TASTE

The word *taste* is both a verb and a noun. As a verb, taste means to try or test the flavor or quality of something, by some means, either taking it into your mouth or taking it in in some other way. As a noun, taste is the sense by which you perceive something as a flavor.

And what is a "flavor"? It is a distinctive experience, something characteristic to the very quality of the thing you are taking in. You may use language to label this quality, which may be positive or negative or neutral.

Some words that describe flavors: bitter, mild, savory, sour, watery, tart, sweet, spicy, robust. You can apply these to food, certainly, for example: "The meat is salty," or "the tea is minty." But they can also be applied to art: "The painting is too sweet," or "his colors are spicy," or "the application is dainty."

If something is appealing to our sense of taste, we might say it is "flavorful." If not, we may deem it "bland," "flat," or "flavorless." What about the word *tasteful*, though? That has another connotation, doesn't it? Being tasteful suggests correctness or good demeanor. Being tasteless connotes crudeness, or lacking style or grace.

So let's evaluate. Taste is discernment, an ability to perceive a flavor. It is good to have taste. Without it, we cannot understand what we see and experience. Our taste leads us to make a determination, however, that a flavor is such and such, and that we like it or not. This determination may keep us from tasting that same substance at a future time. Maybe we would discern it differently on another occasion, and like it more. In order to do so, we must not be dogmatic or fixed about our tastes.

We must use the sense, but only come to conclusions in the moment, forsaking them on future occasions. Taste is good if we use it wisely and do not foreclose the possibility of a different perception at another time. We must use taste as a verb, as something active, not as a noun, as a set thing. If we do, our taste will serve us and lead to greater understanding. If not, it may make us bigoted and closed.

Let me give you what might seem a trite example and then relate it to this idea of taste. Let's say I tried yogurt once when I was seven years old and just didn't like the taste, so I never tried it again. All kinds of new brands of yogurt have since been introduced, but I made up my mind and won't try it. Now say the yogurt is classical music or abstract painting. I listened, I saw, and it just didn't appeal.

Well, I will just be missing out, won't I? The radio will come on with an absolutely exquisite sonata and I'll quickly switch it off, or march right past the new exhibit at the museum because my mind is closed. It would be far better to have no standards of taste than these. Taste that serves is open minded and ever evolving. To develop that kind of taste, you can't just eat the yogurt once. You've got to try all the new varieties and keep trying as you become more discerning.

We must beware of the idea of "tasteful" versus "tasteless," especially, when it comes to art. Standards of what is appropriate morph and change continually, at different times, different places, and in political and social arenas. Art is a forum and a means for expression, and it needs to have the most open and forgiving environment so it may flourish.

Exercising my first amendment rights, I may make assumptions about art that I find lewd or racist and therefore "tasteless." But I have to err on the side of "free speech" above all. I firmly assert that for art to thrive, artists must be free to express themselves without censorship or restriction. Though works may offend our sensibilities, the harm they cause is minimal compared to the gift art brings to our lives. We must use our powers of discernment, our sense of taste, to recognize the differences, and to be honest and authentic in calling out objectionable and offensive expressions for what they are.

IS THERE GOOD TASTE AND BAD TASTE?

The common definitions of good taste and bad taste and my own definition are quite different. In common parlance, when someone tells you that you have good taste, what they probably mean is that you are sophisticated, like refined things that are expertly made, are unoffensive, employ excellent or perhaps expensive ingredients, are tonal and reserved in color and style, are sold at the chicest boutiques, or are collected by the entitled and wealthy scions of our society. And when they proclaim that you have bad taste, they probably mean you like cheap things that may be hastily made, are brightly colored, made of inferior materials, are overly shiny and glitzy and even perhaps offensive, and are used and sold to the masses, especially poor and uneducated people.

This definition is not about quality; it is about normatives of class that persist in the very divided and unequal society we live in. As you go about evaluating your tastes, make sure to keep these clichés of class, of good and bad taste, in your consciousness. Let's open up this discussion, shall we?

When you taste a peach that has been organically grown, without pesticides, it may taste particularly peachy. That may be because you are accustomed to supermarket peaches that are harvested too early, mass produced, and somehow have lost their peachy taste, are too hard, and taste like cardboard. This kind of taste comparison is easy for everyone to undertake; it does not take a Harvard education to judge a peach.

But when it comes to art, your ability to taste it may be challenged. Maybe you have never seen a Surrealist painting, and you can't figure out why everything looks so peculiar. You look at a de Kooning abstract painting and it reminds you of your four-year-old's finger painting from preschool.

You saw an installation at a gallery and it looked like a facsimile of your garage. You go to the museum in Spain and there are Picasso's interpretations of Velázquez's *Las Meninas*. But you've never seen that painting, and these Picassos just look like scribbles. Who the hell is Velázquez and why should I care?

What is missing in this picture? What is missing is context. References. Clues to what you are looking at and what to look for. Historical perspective. Some of the pictures are bright, some are dull, some are realistic, some abstract, but you don't know why. They are unreadable, indecipherable.

So maybe your general life preferences make you like the abstract because you like the colors, and you like billowy designs. Or maybe they make you prefer the realistic scenes because you can relate to them. Your limited experience has left you with these preferences. They become your taste. It's not good taste or bad taste. It's just lack of information, as simple as that. It's "no taste."

So what's the remedy? Get informed. Do some reading. Look at pictures online. Go to the paint department of a home improvement or hardware store and pick out the little squares of colors you like best. When you get home lay them out on your dining room table. What do they remind you of: seashore, mountain, Aunt Marge's living room? These are clues to your artistic DNA, to your sensory preferences.

If you like art and are interested in it (which you must be, because you got this far in this book), get some books on artists and study them. Perhaps you are inclined to pick up a book about Monet because you love Impressionist painting. Go for it. But also pick up or, even better, borrow from the library, a book about an artist you don't particularly like. It may prove insightful, and you may surprise yourself by coming out of it with a more positive view, or maybe a better reason for not being a fan.

Most importantly, don't reject anything. Just look. Find something and identify something you like in . . . everything. It's easy to say no—it's much harder to say yes and really mean it. To stay open.

If you do this, you will be on the road to truly uncovering what you like, and why, and ultimately, who you are. You will undoubtedly have preferences—we all do—but they will be a lot wider and deeper than they are now. Guaranteed. It will be neither good taste, nor bad taste.

It will just be taste: discernment of flavors, and before you know it, you will be able to tell the difference between the expressive work of art—the organic peach—and the not particularly expressive doppelgänger—the mass-market peach.

CAN TASTE BE WRONG?

Taste can be uninformed, but it is not "wrong." You are entitled to your preferences, and no one has a right to tell you otherwise, not even me. Your perceptions belong to you. That's a given.

I can disagree, because I have my preferences, but so what? Maybe I'll convince you, and maybe you'll convince me.

Do we want to go out and see everyone wearing the same clothes walking down the street? No way, we like variety. Imagining a world where we are all alike is a science-fiction movie about automatons. People are unique; they need to have personal taste. Nothing I have said here will take that away. What I am arguing for is that you become the best you, not that you don't "do you."

DO RICH PEOPLE HAVE MORE TASTE THAN POOR PEOPLE?

Absolutely not. The only thing rich people have more of is money. And money does not buy taste and it does not buy happiness. Unfortunately, it does buy art.

This latter fact is a painful reality to artists. That is because what we do really has nothing to do with money and the connection between our work and money is an impediment. Of course, we need to eat.

Art is and always was a commodity associated with the aristocracy. Before there were cameras, rich people commissioned their portraits from the artists of the day, and this is the main reason you find so many portraits in those dark museum salons representing yesteryear. Art continued to be the province of the upper classes throughout history, as art is a totally discretionary acquisition and only people with money to burn could entertain such a purchase.

Today artworks made by artists, some of whom were poor in their lifetimes, are traded in auction rooms for millions of dollars to the wealthiest among us, who by phone or digital connection snatch up a painting they may never even hang on a wall. I remember my amazement when I, as a young art student, found a painting by an artist I revered in the coat closet of a rich relative. Imagine that, a masterwork just left on the floor of a closet—I was amazed.

Most of the artists I have known, and I myself, never conceived of making art for money. Though of course we would like to have money, art and money just never seemed to pair. Art was something you made—and spent a lot of money on making—because you just had to. The lack of money wasn't going to stop you from doing it. It had to be done.

So it is weird to think of art just going to the rich and famous to put in their closets. If I had my druthers, I would give every piece of mine away, but I'd specify that it had to go somewhere where it would hang on a wall and people could visit it. I have been trying to do just that, to donate work to public institutions—museums, of course, but other venues too—where it would be in the public domain. If anyone reading this book would like to help me accomplish that, please go to my website and send me an email. You will make my day.

To complete this section, I will just reiterate that no, rich people do not have more taste in art than poor people. But poor people and middle-income people can become connoisseurs of art in their own right, and I encourage them to do so. They will not be able to buy the established artists sold in the fairs and auction houses and most galleries, but I encourage them to look for up-and-coming young artists and to collect their work. If collection is not your thing, let information and experience become your ticket to "good taste," your entrée into, if not the acquisitive opportunities of the rich, their enjoyment of beautiful things.

I, for one, am a major fan of "window shopping." I like to visit and rent. I do not need to own. You can visit art at public and private galleries, in public spaces, in lobbies, libraries, hotels, and hospitals, and also by collecting prints and other multiples of artists you like (they are much more affordable than originals).

Most importantly, you can become brilliantly informed and share your appreciation with the people in your life. You can become a "tastemaker" and an ambassador of the open mind and the love of art.

IS TASTE A FUNCTION OF INTELLIGENCE?

Taste is not a function of intelligence per se, but possibly of an element of intelligence—curiosity. If you have only eaten the cardboard peach and never had the opportunity of tasting the organic one, you might think it was better than it was. If you accept what you already know as truth, your perspective is limited, as a whole world of possibilities lies beyond your ken.

So, while taste may not be a function of intelligence, lack of experience is, and this can only be mitigated by curiosity—looking for ideas, images, truth, and beauty wherever it is to be found. The fewer rules you make about what is important, interesting, beautiful, or fun, the more varied and deeper will be your finds.

In art, as in life, one like does not obviate another. You can like realistic work *and* abstract work. Just because you admire the crispness of a geometric composition, there's no reason you cannot likewise dig the sweep and sensuality of more organic shapes. Just as you admire the symmetry of classicism, you can admire the irregularity of a more romantic piece. You can, truly, like it all. That is, as long as you know what you like about it. And why. Why one romantic piece is subtle while another is sentimental. Why one artist has captured the feeling and color of the light and the other has inadvertently created a moonscape.

Recognizing the distinctiveness of each work is what good taste is all about. You can get it in one easy way. Just keep looking. And using your intelligence to take notes. Easy.

HOW DO WE MAKE THE LEAP FROM "I LIKE IT" TO "IT IS GREAT"?

Big leap. Is everything we like "great"? No, certainly not. It is not great just because we like it. On the other hand, it might be . . . great, that is . . .

Here's another question: **do we like it because it is great?**

It is certainly possible, but this cannot be confirmed. Maybe we like it because it is yellow and that's our favorite color. That won't make it great.

We like to think that something we like is great. That is the vote of confidence we give it. In fact, we say it all the time.

"I love that movie. It's great."

If I am telling this to my friend who accompanies me to the theater, she might say, "It is."

Then my confidence gets a boost.

But she might also say, "It was okay, not great."

Oh, a letdown. (But I still think it was great.)

What has happened here? Subjective reality. We both watched the movie, but I really got something out of it, and my friend did not. Why?

Maybe I was paying more attention. Maybe I really relate to the subject. Maybe my friend had a stomachache. Maybe I got some good news this morning, and I'm still in a very good mood.

So, what's the conclusion? Was it great? The only answer I can give with absolute assurance is "It was great for me." Is that good enough?

I have to say not really, because we humans want to know what is great and what is just okay. We want to know it definitively. But unfortunately, there is no absolute arbiter who can deliver the final decree. We can only possibly get a consensus—a lot of people agreeing that something is great.

Let's apply this to visual art. Is there any work of art we can all agree is great? I know you are thinking what I am thinking. Who comes immediately to mind?

It has to be Michelangelo. *David*. The *Pietà*. Is there any human on the planet who would disagree that this work is great? I don't think so, but I am probably wrong, and that is because I am a Western person who has lived a privileged life, has seen a lot of art, and has a certain idea of what is good and beautiful.

Is there a person living who has had a totally different experience and visual vocabulary and would look to works like this and feel nothing? Yes, certainly there is. That is because these words—great, beautiful, art—have a different meaning to humans that is dependent on everything they are and know.

So there can be no consensus, no authority, no absolutes.

My suggestion to this conundrum. Chuck the word "great." Just *like* the art. You can catalog for yourself what you secretly think is great (in other words what you really like), regardless of who, if anyone, agrees with you. You may be right, and they may be wrong. We will never know.

IF EVERYONE AGREES SOMETHING IS BEAUTIFUL, DOES THAT MEAN THEY ARE RIGHT?

You know what I am going to say, don't you?

Our culture tells us what is beautiful, and in different cultures, at different times, those so-called things of beauty morph and change. You know this already. Round fleshy women used to be objects of beauty in the time of the artist Rubens, and now most fashion magazines feature thin and lanky models. I qualify my last statement, though, because recently socially conscious people have opened up these fashion magazines to feature women of all sizes and shapes for the sake of diversity, and this is a good thing. Whatever allows us to make our own decisions about what is beautiful is to be applauded.

Can we agree on anything, though? Probably we can get a general positive consensus on flowers, sunsets, rainbows, and butterflies. Some debate on dogs, trees, and waterfalls. Definite negative on motels, swamps, and billboards. But I could be wrong.

The answer is . . . it doesn't matter. We can each have our own beautiful. We are free to like what we like. As long as you do no harm and give the same right to everyone, enjoy your own beautiful to the max.

DOES A CRITIC HAVE TO BE AN ARTIST?

This is not an easy question. Why do I even pose it, you might wonder.

As an artist, I am extremely sensitive when it comes to criticism. All artists are. The reason is that as creative people, we take a chance and put our feelings and thoughts on paper for others to see. It takes courage to do this, and the reason is . . . criticism.

When you put your work out there, people can comment on it, they can like it or hate it, they can question your motives and your talent. They can judge you.

And let's face it, this is scary. We want people to see what we do favorably and if they love it, we are elated. But if not, if it fails to impress or even worse, if it is trashed, we are devastated. No one wants to be judged in this way. It's dangerous.

Creative people who have been disfavored by critics often make this retort: "What have **you** done that is better? What have **you** created that's so great?"

The artist is saying that it may be easy to be a critic, to dislike something, and a lot more difficult to be the artist and create it in the first place.

My painting teacher, Norman Raeben, had these ten commandments of art, which I wrote about in my first book, *The Creative Path: A View from the Studio on the Making of Art*. One of these commandments was, "Don't be a critic before you are an artist."

He was directing that commandment to us, the artists, not the critics, beseeching us not to trash our own efforts, not to judge them. Why? Because judging them might make it impossible for us to make art in the first place. Can a critic be an artist, after all? It's pretty hard, because they might have that awful expectation of being judged, if not by others, then by themselves.

So, back to the question: Does a critic have to be an artist?

And my answer: Artists might be their own worst critics, but when it comes to criticizing other artists, I suspect we are a lot kinder and more compassionate than a nonartist might be. Why? Because we know how hard it is to express yourself and to do it so well that others approve and even applaud your effort.

Artists who become critics have that extra component of empathy they put into their criticism, and that's a good thing. If a critic disparages the work of an artist, without first acknowledging the effort the artist has made, and the good in the work, I don't think too much of them. I want to tell them to get off the high horse they rode in on. I admit it.

So my final answer: Critics don't have to be artists, but they have to be thoughtful, compassionate people, and recognize the contribution the artist is making. Then the critic's contribution will also have value.

HOW CAN I COMPARE DISPARATE WORKS ON DIFFERENT SUBJECTS, SAY A LANDSCAPE TO A PORTRAIT?

Interesting question. In some respects, it does not matter what the subject is, as similar pictorial factors play regardless of the subject. "Is the work well composed?" is a question that is universal to all subjects. Is the work balanced, organized in an interesting way, can your eyes travel freely throughout the work, or do they get stuck somewhere?

The elements of art that we discussed earlier are always a good reference. Is the light felt? Is the color harsh or tonal? Is the line beautifully drawn? Is the space felt? All of these are present regardless of whether the work is realistic, abstract, or somewhere in between.

As we've mentioned, artists often work on disparate subjects yet do have a decided affinity for certain subjects over others. Part of your discernment may be applied to this question of where the artist excels. Which is more felt: his figurative work or landscape? And always, why? What is it about the figurative piece that makes it more effective?

Asking or wondering "why?" will serve you in good stead as you develop your discernment in art. You are hypothesizing most of the time, because we cannot always be assured of the artist's intention, but just asking and taking that guess means you care, you are engaged, and you are attempting to get the message the artist has sent into the universe via this particular artwork.

The most important questions you ask about art will always be these: How does it speak to me? How does it move me? Why do I love it? What does it mean to me?

HOW CAN I FORM MY OWN OPINIONS, AND NOT BE INFLUENCED BY OTHERS?

This is extremely difficult. We have heard so much from others, and we have so many reasons to consider their opinions as sacrosanct. They are authorities, they have studied longer than we have, they are brilliant, they also are artists, they are teachers, they have written books, they know what they are talking about, and we don't.

But we have something to say. We have been around the block too. We have seen. We have tasted. And in one regard, we have one up on them. We have lived in our own skin for quite a while now, and we kind of know what we like. It's gotten broader since we've studied a bit, but certain things just capture our interest, and that's only growing, not going away.

We know ourselves. We have preferences and that's okay.

So listen to everyone, hear them out, then reflect on your own instincts. Then decide what you think. Just be ready to change your mind when something happens in your life or in your perception to grow another sprout of your brain stem. That's what a free person does.

And finally . . .

IF I HAVE GOOD TASTE, WILL THAT MAKE ME A BETTER PERSON?

Ah, I love this question. I am happy if you develop good taste because that means you have taken the time to learn and be open. But that alone will not make you a better person.

What will make you a better person is to be a better person, to love and to be positive and to share.

I am hoping that I have made a little contribution to making art one of the many joys in your life, and if you would like to take it a step further, turn to the next chapter and my program on how to become a connoisseur of art.

Chapter 13
Becoming a Connoisseur of Art

Sadly, I am approaching the closing pages of this book. I hope it has provided you with some new information and an increased understanding and appreciation of visual art. Perhaps you would like to take this a step or two further, read other points of view, study some of the artists you discovered here and would like to know more about. Carry on, and enjoy. Books on art are readily available.

Maybe this book has awakened an ever more pressing desire—to study art history, to try your hand at art making, or just to become what is referred to as a connoisseur of art. It may be that you are a window shopper and will just start visiting art galleries and museums more frequently or fervently. Or it may mean that you have an interest in acquiring art and becoming a collector.

All of these are exciting and wonderful pursuits, and I encourage them wholeheartedly. Let's break them down and talk about each and what I recommend you do to get started.

TAKING STUDIO ART CLASSES

We all know that empathy and understanding begins with familiarity. Nothing will give you a better appreciation of art than trying your hand at it. Whatever medium you choose, you will very quickly discover that it is a lot harder than it looks. You will learn that each medium has its secrets and commands, and you must accept them and learn to work with them, not resist. You will learn that art is created by indirection—you can't just plop a painting onto a canvas—it has to be constructed piece by piece and this takes practice and making oodles of wrong turns to start to get on track.

Making art is like playing three-dimensional chess. To get to Z, you must master A through Y, and this takes time. You don't know what you don't know until you try, and if you keep at it, you will progress.

Choose a medium you are especially fond of or that appeals to your personality. So many people have a strong decorative sense and are incredibly skilled at design and can put together stunning homes and love crafty activities like scrapbooking. If you are one of these, perhaps take it to the next level and take a course in collage.

If you love to draw, join a life-drawing class. If you like to build things, try woodworking or ceramics. For some reason, ceramics workshops are filled with women; I can't understand why more men do not choose this medium. It demands considerable raw strength and accuracy, and I feel so many men would excel at it, if only they could overcome the gender bias.

If you don't like to get your hands dirty, I don't recommend painting. It is a messy world and to really become proficient, you've got to be all in. It is not a dainty medium by any means. I would suggest fusing glass perhaps—you might get a wee cut from the glass, but it is a clean and fascinating medium.

Considering your main profession is an excellent clue as to what art medium might be best for you. Dentists, for instance, are incredibly adept at modeling and have developed exceptional small motor skills. If they try their hand at sculptural media, especially ones that involve carving, they are likely to go to the head of the class. Being a nurse requires incredible patience and care; perhaps watercolor, a delicate medium, might be a fit. For a more daring person, an athlete perhaps, I'd think about mixed media. In this case, being bold and confidant is an asset.

Whatever you choose, making art yourself will make you more attuned to the art of your fellow students, as well as the professional artists you appreciate in galleries, on the internet, and in museums and other art venues. You will have a much better idea of what it took to arrive at that level of excellence. You will realize that having an idea and an intention does not mean you will be successful in communicating that message. It takes many tries and failures to get there.

Unfortunately, many people do not realize this and think art is created by magic, or by extraordinarily gifted people who can produce this work automatically. It is not so. Most artists, even those that are gifted, toil in their studios and flop a great deal of the time. Remember that for the most part, you only get to see the successes on the walls of the museums. Hidden underneath those successes are the works that did not make it to the light of day. You'd need an X-ray to find them, but they are the keys to the artist's successes. When we learn what not to do, success is on the next page.

BECOMING A CONNOISSEUR OF ART

You know me by now—I love definitions. According to Merriam-Webster, a connoisseur is "someone who understands the details, technique, or principles of an art and is competent to act as a critical judge." A secondary definition specifies "one who enjoys with discrimination and appreciation of subtleties."

This book has been about the keys to understanding and appreciating visual art. I assumed that you were an appreciator even before you read this book, as you were interested enough to read it. But let's consider this: Is it sufficient simply to appreciate art to be considered a connoisseur? Were you already there?

Not according to the dictionary, alas. Even in the second definition, one is called not just to "appreciate" but to "discriminate," detecting various subtleties to do so. Love alone just does not suffice; intelligence is a necessary determinant.

The dictionary tells us we need to "appreciate subtleties" to gain the title we are seeking. That would suggest we need more than general knowledge of names and dates and movements and such. We need to have those eagle eyes recognizing the differences, discrepancies, character, and distinctive approach each of these artists and movements embody. We need to get into the weeds and not only notice these fine points but have the ability to elaborate on them and to articulate them.

Assuming that you already had the love, or at least the interest, before you opened the book, what exactly did you need to become a connoisseur? You needed the information about what subtleties to look for, that's a given. Without the question, there can be no answer.

Understanding the elements of visual art provides the subject area. Once you know the qualities of color, for instance, you are enabled to compare color schemes and judge their effectiveness. Once you understand perspective, you can determine whether the artist applied it appropriately.

And so on . . .

You need the subject, and you also need the language. If you don't know the difference between description and expression, you may have a sense of the distinction, but your ability to articulate it is compromised. You need the words.

So, to summarize, start with the interest, add the information and the language, and you will be on your way. With the basics, the ability to make fine distinctions and the language to explain them, you will almost be ready to lead an entourage through the museum. Being a docent is a great way to practice being a connoisseur of art.

What does a wine connoisseur have that the average wine drinker does not? He or she can probably distinguish the type of grapes used, maybe even the vintage, can surely tell a Pinot from a Merlot, and tell you why Cabernet A is worth $36 and Cabernet B is on the shelves for $8.

And an art connoisseur? An art connoisseur is probably familiar with the elements of art and can opine on the way the light is understood, the iconography of shapes and textures, and may even advance a judgment on the artist's intention in a particular work. He or she will probably recognize the medium employed and have an idea of how that choice effects the message of the work. The connoisseur might instantly recognize a Matisse or Picasso, but so might the ordinary art lover, the difference being that the connoisseur might be able to elaborate on the influence these artists had on their contemporaries and descendants and where they stand in the pantheon of Art with a capital A.

An art connoisseur is just a bit more informed on the general subject, and I would venture to say, that extra knowledge, the care taken to compare and contrast, has the general effect of intensifying the love and respect he has for the art forms and the artists who deliver them. Knowledge is power, but it is also love, and the more of it we have, the more we can truly appreciate wine or art.

What will you gain from doing the work and becoming a connoisseur? Does the wine taste better to a wine connoisseur than to an average wine lover? Not necessarily. It may not taste better but becoming a connoisseur does add another element to the experience.

Knowing about wine is something the connoisseur can share with others to increase their satisfaction. It also is likely to increase the favor and appreciation those people shared have of the connoisseur. They might say, "Oh, if you want to know about wine, ask Jeffrey. He's my go to."

So, you might make some new friends, and it might puff up your ego a bit in the bargain.

It makes us feel good to know things. That's a reward in and of itself. Becoming a connoisseur of art just might make you a more interesting person that other people like to talk to. That would be positive. A new interest will take you inevitably to new places to see art, and there you are likely to meet new people who share your interest. So being a connoisseur makes your world larger.

It might be something you wish to share with your partner or life mate. Having a new shared interest offers you both something new to talk about, to investigate, and to share, so this is another possible bonus to putting in the time and work.

These are all good reasons. But the most important reason to become a connoisseur of art is that art is a way human beings communicate their thoughts, their feelings, their sense of self, and their purpose. Reading and studying these messages from your fellow humans encourages you to investigate your own thoughts, your own feelings, who you are, who you want to be, and ultimately your purpose.

What resonates with you in art gives clues to who you truly are and want to be. Becoming open to many voices makes you a more flexible and open-minded person, and ultimately, is one of the tools you can use to get more in touch with yourself. That's a good thing, and the greatest reason to learn more about art. You already like it, now you will like it even more. And it will enrich your life.

BECOMING A COLLECTOR OF ART

You can become a connoisseur of art without spending a penny. Oh, except for some museum entry fees, but that won't add up to much. Or you can decide that you like art so much that you would not only like to look at it, you would like to have it close to you. You would like to own it and even to contemplate building an art collection.

As an artist, I applaud this decision, especially if you are open to collecting the work of living artists, and most especially, if those living artists are not particularly well known or represented by important gallerists or representatives. I champion getting in on the ground floor, so to speak, and collecting art for one reason and one reason only: because you appreciate it.

Artists will make art whether they can sell it or not. Look at Mr. Vincent van Gogh and countless others who had no financial success in their lifetimes. Art is a calling, and when we have that calling, we are willing to spend the bank to make it possible, whether or not we ever sell a piece of art. But when we do sell it, when someone who is an appreciator, or even better, a connoisseur of art, gives us his or her hard earned money to acquire our art, we are thrilled. You have validated all our hard work and made our piques of doubt vanish. Thank you.

So yes, consider becoming a collector. You can do it on your own or hire someone to help you make choices. There are gallerists and art consultants galore just waiting to work with you. You can even send me a note, and I will point you to absolutely marvelous art that is available around the corner and across the globe.

If I have done anything here to encourage you or to help you become a connoisseur of art or an art collector or both, I have done my job. Thank you for sticking with me to the end. But it is not the end . . . Ha!

I have a big treat for you coming up in the Appendix. I have asked artists I have included here to make a special brand-new work to include in this book. Most of these works have never been exhibited or seen before this book was printed. Isn't that exciting?

Because our Perspectives chapter looked at Mother and Child images, I thought readers would really love to see how this theme is interpreted in contemporary iterations and in different media. Turn the page and have a gaze. You are among the first to lay eyes on this truly exceptional exhibition.

Enjoy!

Appendix

Exhibition of Mother and Child Works by Living Artists

What follows is an art exhibition. Here is the ad for the show:

> **A Fresh Look at an Old Subject: The Mother and Child.**
> Art by living artists on the theme.

What subject is more interesting to the visual artist than the human form? The story of figurative art is long and wide, the subject seemingly inexhaustible. And as viewers, it is a subject that continues to engage us. In addition to the portrait, genre works that show people at work and play, and all variety of classical and romantic pieces, this subject proves to be fertile territory for the visual artist. For religious, sentimental, and familial reasons, as well, Mother and Child is a resonant theme throughout the ages. As in our chapter on "Perspectives," countless ways to present this subject have been and continue to be explored.

These are some of the artistic considerations visual artists make in undertaking this subject:

1. **Medium.** Any medium can be employed in an interpretation of this subject. I have tried to include a few varied mediums in this exhibition to give you a feeling for the breadth of this subject and how each medium can offer a very special means to explore the relationship between two figures. Sculpture is a particularly resonant medium as it can establish the two figures in corporeal relation; look to the sculptures of Henry Moore in particular for excellent examples of related forms.

2. **Composition.** Regardless of medium chosen, artists face the issue of composition. This includes placement on the canvas, relative size

of shapes and forms, intensities, color distribution, aerial and linear perspective, etc. It is in many ways the first order of business in designing a work of art—whether the work will be a vertical, horizontal, or square piece, this orientation will determine to a large extent the character of the work, and also whether it will be a success. A poor orientation will often damn the work just as a proper one will give it momentum. Though the artist will continue to make choices until the work is complete, poor compositional choices are often irremediable.

3. **Intention.** What is driving the work in the first place? Why has the artist chosen the subject and what does she want to say about it? Is this intention best realized in a realistic, semiabstract, or totally abstract format? Does the intention drive the color to be intense, local, muted, tonal? These are the types of concerns the artist contemplates in initiating a work of art and in completing it. Setting the mission, the intention. The why. It is always what viewers are relating to when they come to a judgment of whether the work is a success. Has the work delivered its promise?

4. **Reading for comprehension.** Now let's examine the works and note their characteristics, their moods, and the particular point of view each artist has brought to the task. Each artist has interpreted the theme in a manner that is relevant to them. They have provided clues to those meanings, and I am further elaborating them here.

As you read these works, especially now that we have reviewed so much of what is involved in the process, take note of how you are receiving the message that the artist is settling out in his or her very personal take on the theme. Can you spot the references? The mood? The tone? The perspective?

Each has something to offer. Can you find it and identify it?

JUDITH SCHAECHTER, *MOTHER AND CHILD*

Modern *Pietà*

Schaechter has contributed this work to our exhibition even though it is currently on view at the Hermitage Museum in St. Petersburg. I have made an exception to my search for entirely new works because I find this piece so compelling and believe it is something you should have an opportunity to view.

Stained glass is an old medium, and Schaechter is one of its most modern practitioners—she has reinvented this medium for a contemporary audience. It is one of the more difficult media to master and it requires deft and skill to accomplish at this level. Drawing and painting on paper or canvas is much more direct—stained glass work is sequential and takes planning. Judith's imagery is totally personal and is something we have never seen before, certainly in glass.

As Judith describes it, her *Mother and Child* depicts "a female character bearing the body of her grown son on her shoulders. She is flanked by two red oak trees and the border resembles yellow caution tape.

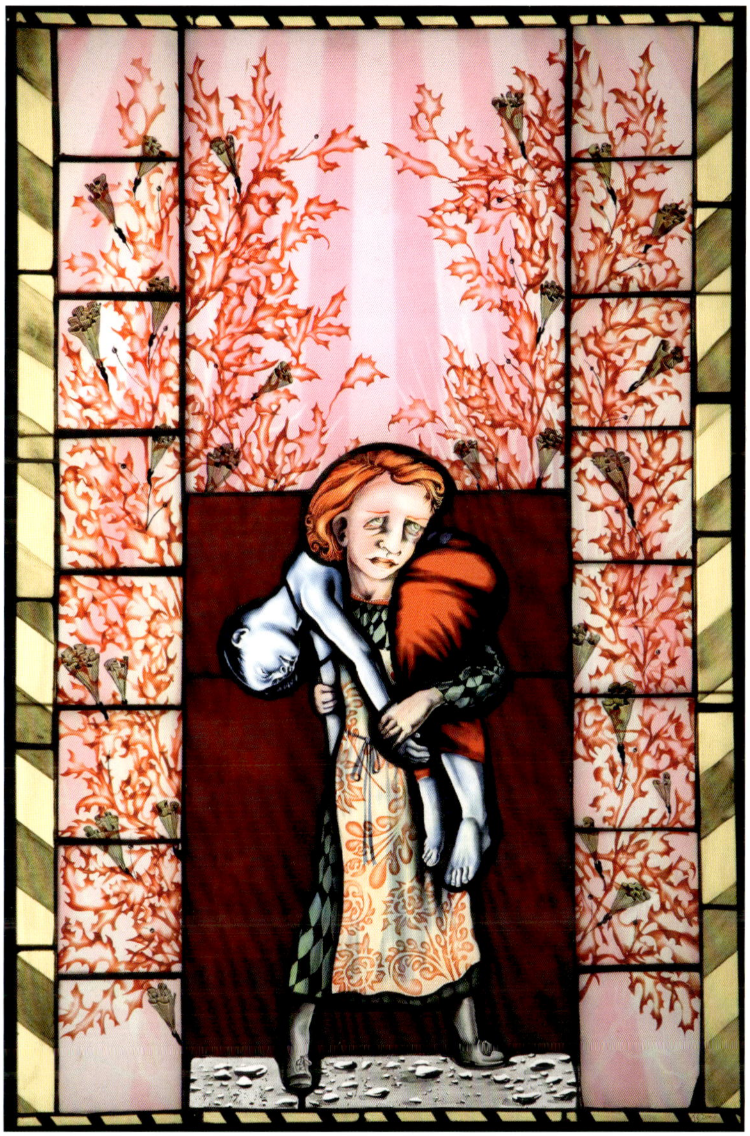

Fig. 133. Judith Schaechter, MOTHER AND CHILD.

Most Mother and Child pieces describe a woman with baby or small child. So I asked Schaechter why she chose to create a work featuring an adult child. Her response: "I wanted to create a contemporary pietà image based on my reading about the American Civil War. Women could not enlist, but many mothers lost their sons. I wanted to express the terrible tragedy of that sacrifice."

Stained glass is a medium that partners with light to express its message. Though Schaechter's intention could have been expressed through painting or other medium, it is so much more powerful here with the light charging through the colored glass to make that tragedy she expresses that much more pungent and piercing. This is a good example of how visual art can move us in a way no words could approximate.

ANN-MARIE BROWN, *COLD CROSSING/MOVING TARGET*

Migration

Ann-Marie Brown elects to enhance her oil paintings with encaustic, a paint made from pigment that is mixed with melted beeswax and resin and affixed by the application of heat. She uses these materials to express two voices in her work. She explains it thus: "The brushwork creates hard point of clarity and the encaustic creates liminal spaces that are finished in the mind of the viewer."

The work she offered for this exhibition is part of a series about migration.

A Canadian artist, Brown's particular focus is on the perils faced by individuals transiting to Canada, as alluded to in the title. As unlike the standard mother and child, this piece is not about the relationship of child to mother, rather their mutuality in facing a difficult situation. To Brown, this depiction is not only description; it is a warning to those who might trifle or think askance about the plight of the migrant.

There is a starkness to this image that suggests this peril, which is very well described in Brown's writing about her intention. Though she acknowledges her renderings have an element of realism—we see recognizable figures—she tells us that she intends for them to "function like Rorschach tests." What does this mean? Is there an ambiguity expressed in her imagery?

The artist clarifies and puts it this way: "The resolved painting contains contradictory elements within its singularity, as we do. In that way, the painting becomes a presence."

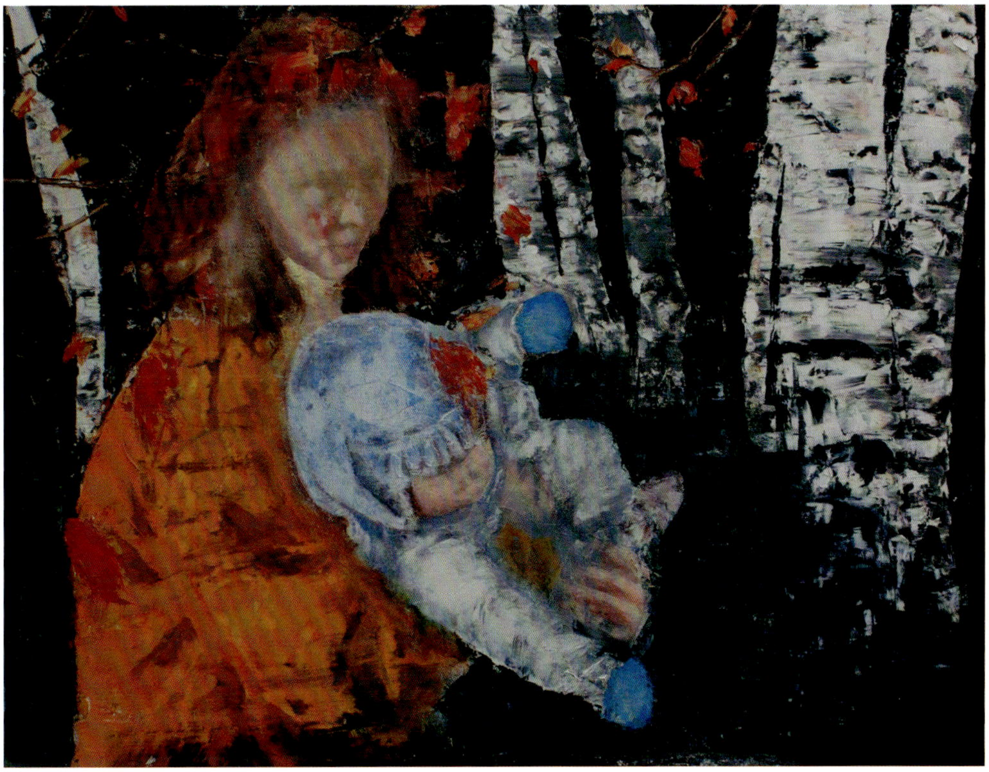

Fig. 134. Ann-Marie Brown, COLD CROSSING/MOVING TARGET.

She is telling us that the work is not descriptive or prescriptive; it is rather a reflection of complex feelings that make their way into paint and wax and onto the canvas for us to ponder.

JIMMY WRIGHT, *BIG MOMMA AT TURKEY CREEK*

Home

Most of the artists who offered me work on this theme of Mother and Child were, not surprisingly, women, so I was very pleased when Jimmy Wright agreed to contribute a work. It comes from his "Down Home" exhibition of decades ago, and I am thrilled to include it here.

Most of Wright's well-known, splendid paintings, especially his floral works, are sophisticated and expertly painted. But here we see another side, a warm, sketchy treatment of a mother and child that is fresh and innocent, very down home indeed.

I love the endearing faces on both Big Momma and her baby, and especially the doll-like treatment of the baby. The down homeness is amplified with the addition of the tree and house in Momma's skirt. I am not sure who the other figure is, maybe an aunt or other relative.

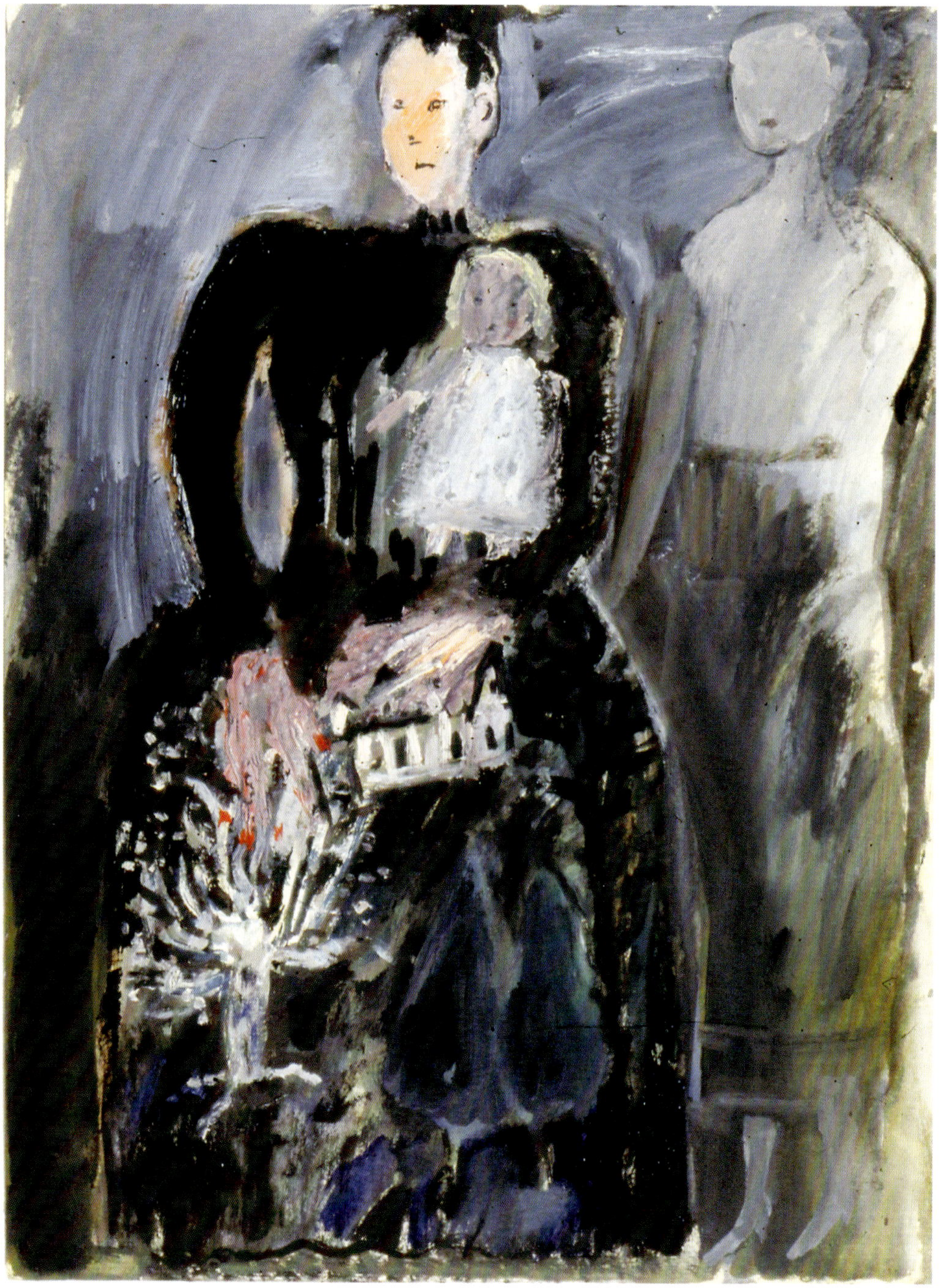

Fig. 135. Jimmy Wright, BIG MOMMA AT TURKEY CREEK.

The thing to remember and celebrate is that artists have many moods and personalities they exhibit through their artistic lives and can and do speak with many voices. One can be ultrasophisticated one day and down home the next. Think of this before you put the stamp on any artist to characterize their work as this or that.

ANNA BOOTHE, *LITTLE HELPER*

A Mother's Love

As a sculptor, Boothe creates meaningful objects that result from psychic investigations. She describes these often multipart works as providing clarity to emotions that may be difficult to articulate in any other fashion. Boothe calls them "icons, pseudo-mirrors, or even prosthetics that aid in self-comprehension."

An example is this work, made in 1994 to celebrate the love she felt for her then three-year-old son. A remarkably engaged and curious child, Boothe included him in her studio practice, teaching him to cut glass at age four and working together creating molds and casting glass.

Boothe described the process of making this work in this way:

> The sculpture itself is a combination of my son's hands first cast in wax, multiples of which were reformed into a broom form and then cast in glass. The "knob" where the base joins the handle is covered in a piece of my husband's baby diaper (saved by his mother!). My overall intention, besides simply eulogizing my toddler, is to portray a generational context and the timeless bond of a mother and child.

Truly appreciating this work takes more than a quick look, during which you may not realize what you are seeing. It requires that you think about the meaning of these little hands. Boothe explains that she often incorporates body parts into her sculptural compositions and that the hands "represent holding on, letting go, and giving as themes that recur in our everyday emotional lives."

I think you will concur that "holding on, letting go and giving" pretty much describe parenthood in a nutshell. The artist has spoken through her art.

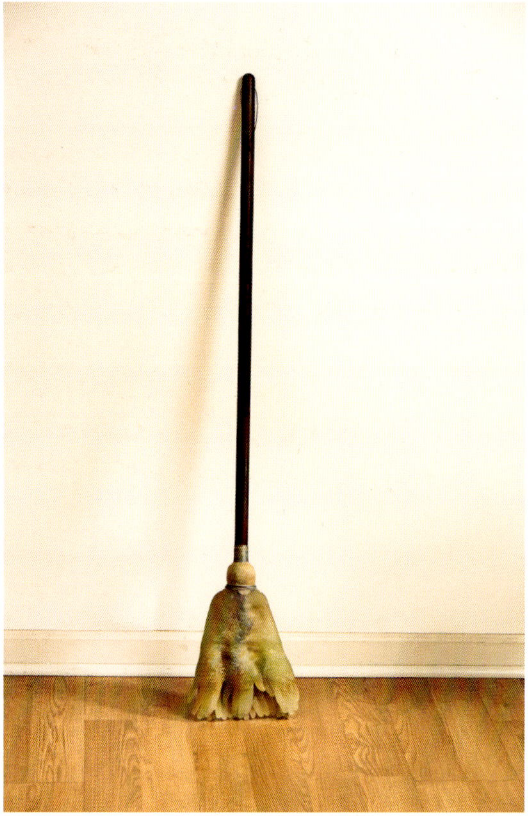

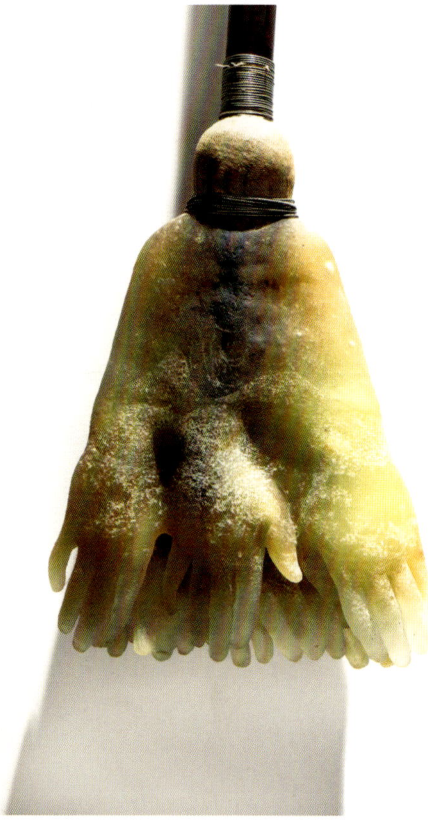

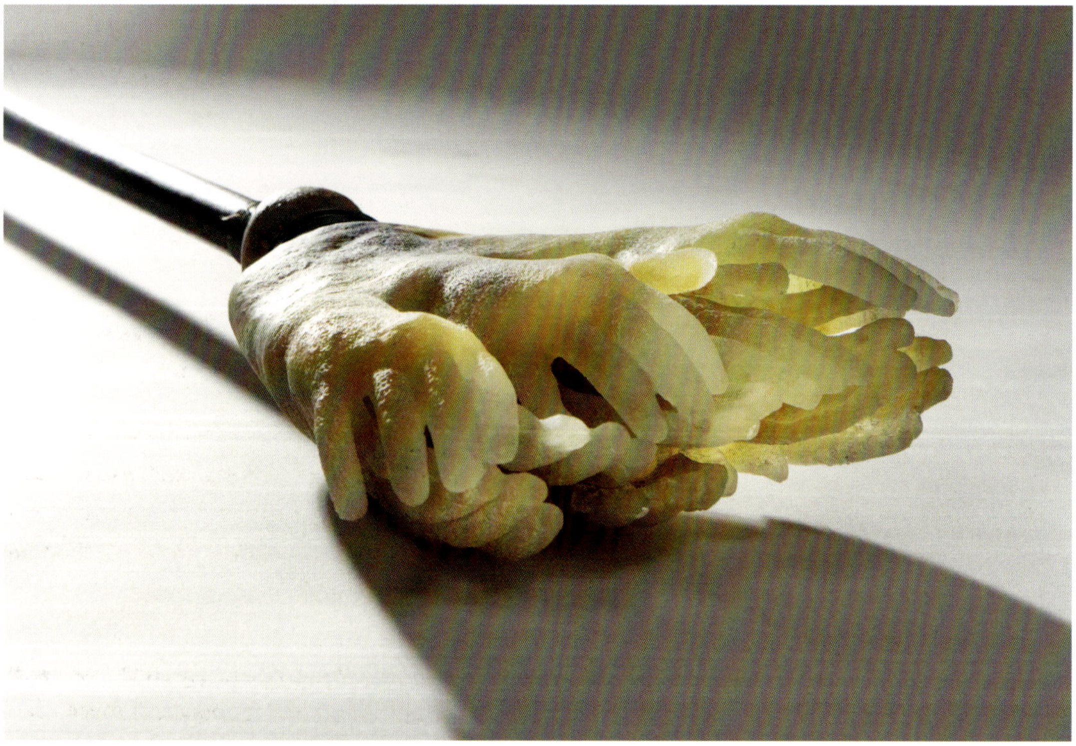

Figs. 136A, 136B, 136C. Anna Boothe, LITTLE HELPER (three views).

LOLA DEL FRESNO, *MOTHER AND CHILD*

Change

We've talked in the book about how ideas are born and how all artists draw from a bank of imagery, some that comes from the history of art, and others from their catalog of memories. We are all constantly using what has come before us and reinventing it in the light of our own existence.

I was thinking of how to discuss Lola del Fresno's *Mother and Child* and the word *transmogrify* popped into my consciousness. I was reacting to the fact that her black-and-white drawing of a mother and child in this work appears quite classical, as if they have sprung from a sixteenth-century work. Have a look. Not only the relative position of the figures suggests such a reference, but also the lack of expression on the mother's face, and the cherubic drawing of the child.

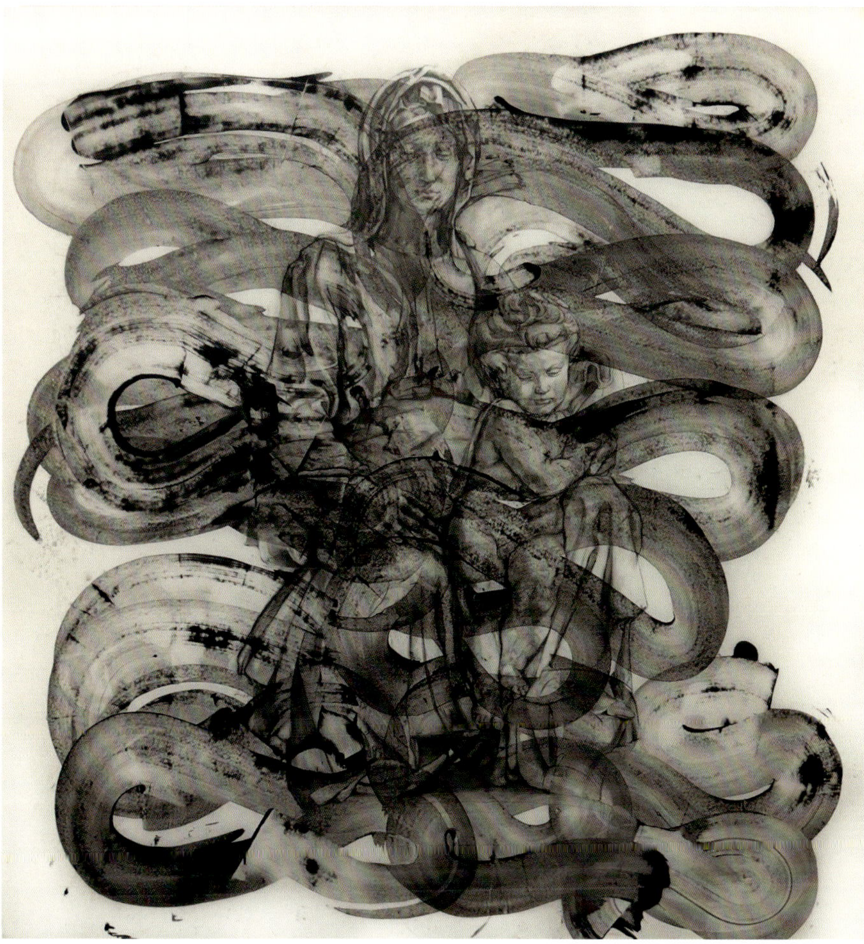

Fig. 137. Lola del Fresno, MOTHER AND CHILD.

But wait. Del Fresno has not called it a day with these classical-like figures. She has almost obliterated them with a swirling overlay. In doing so, she has transformed this image and given it an entirely new take or meaning. Realizing this, I wondered if "transmogrify" is the correct description of what the artist has endeavored to do. So I consulted the thesaurus.

All of the following words mean change: metamorphize, transmute, convert, transmogrify, transfigure. What then are the differences? As Merriam-Webster tells us: transform implies a major change in form; metamorphose suggests an abrupt or startling change induced by or as if by magic; transmute implies transforming into a higher element; convert implies a change fitting something for a new or different use; transmogrify suggests a strange or preposterous metamorphosis; and transfigure implies a change that exalts or glorifies.

Now, trying to choose the most apt word, I am stymied. Why? Because the addition of this overlay onto the classical drawing, the artist has changed its form, created a startling change, transformed it into something else, altered the meaning, all of these.

Is the change startling or strange? Yes.

Does it exalt or glorify?

The last is puzzling. What it does is to challenge us, to make us wonder, to question. I cannot give you the answer to whether it glorifies—that is so subjective. The artist has asked you to come to your own conclusion. I will let you do just that.

VERONICA CAY, *WONDERWOMAN*

Protection

I have the pleasure of including this wonderful hand-built ceramic sculpture by the Australian artist known as Ronnie Cay. It is formed in two pieces and is decorated with colored engobes (white or colored slip applied to pottery) and fired to 1,200 degrees Celsius. The sculpture depicts a female who is protecting a child.

Veronica explains that as both the mother of grown children and the grown child of her own mother, she is steeped in the very challenging and time-consuming mother-and-child dynamic. In this work she delves into what she refers to as "the fiercely protective aspects of motherhood, ready to stand up for her children and fight for their rights."

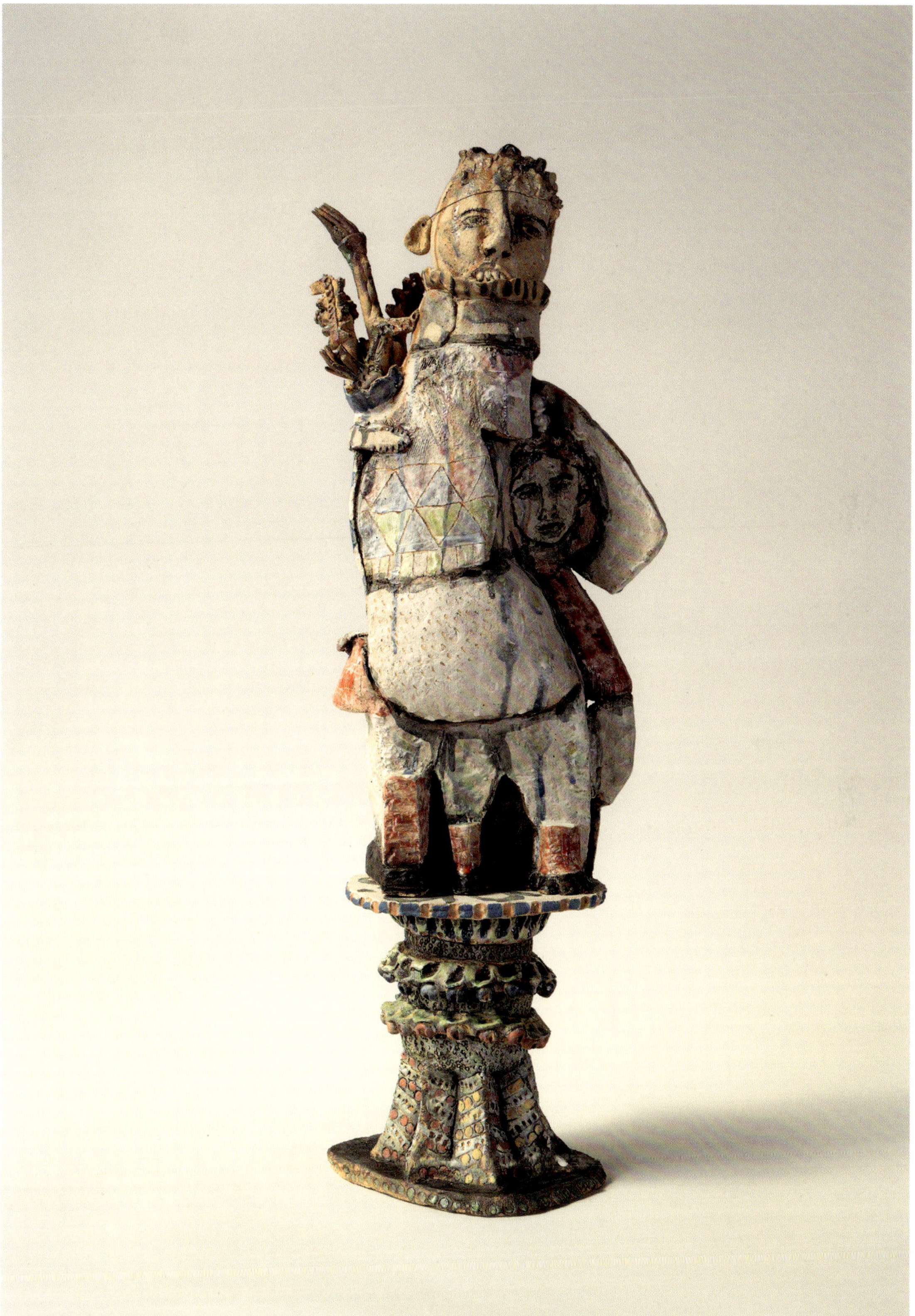

Fig. 138. Veronica Cay, WONDERWOMAN.

She continues her description: "On her back the woman has a set of tools at the ready to perform any task. From the side view they become a vase of flowers setting the scene for an accomplished domestic setting. She stands on a decorative pedestal or her soapbox. She is looking tired and the shine is starting to wear thin."

What a fascinating work this is, and especially so given the medium. The figure of mother stands on a little pedestal or soapbox with the child nesting close to her, under a wing so to speak. Why the pedestal/soapbox? Because she is declaring her plight for all assembled to see and hear. She carries with her all the myriad tools she will need to accomplish her task. She is, as the title confirms, a warrior of love, a wonder woman.

Here we have the power of art to express and explain such a very complicated phenomenon, both the joys and demands of motherhood, and the clash of emotions it engenders. Just have a close look at the mother's face, and read the drama of these conflicting needs and wishes. You might have written a book to explain it, but this little sculpture tells it all in an instant.

SHEILA FEIN, *HEARTBEAT*

Childhood Bliss

Sheila Fein is a devoted mother of four daughters and an artist/illustrator with the unique ability to make her love manifest on paper. She created this wonderful work *Heartbeat* expressly for this book; it was an assignment totally suited to her state of mind and enormous talent.

Instead of a work specifying the relationship between mother and child, Fein elected to concentrate on what she calls "the universal child," which she refers to as "our vulnerability and the mesmerizing mystery of life." She depicts this beautiful child enveloped and ensconced in a world of love, cradled and adored by all this imaginary world of happiness and dreams makes available to this innocent being.

Everything wonderful is possible for this child, unsullied by life's tragedies and confusion.

It is the focus of this creator to present her imagery in the most emotionally positive manner and she does that here, offering the wonder of childhood all of us deserve.

Note that this work was created with colored pencils. This medium is a delicate one and involves stroking the pencil with the hand close to the image. Sheila has clearly put herself tenderly and lovingly into this very tender and loving work of art. I will not be surprised if it brings a tear to your eye.

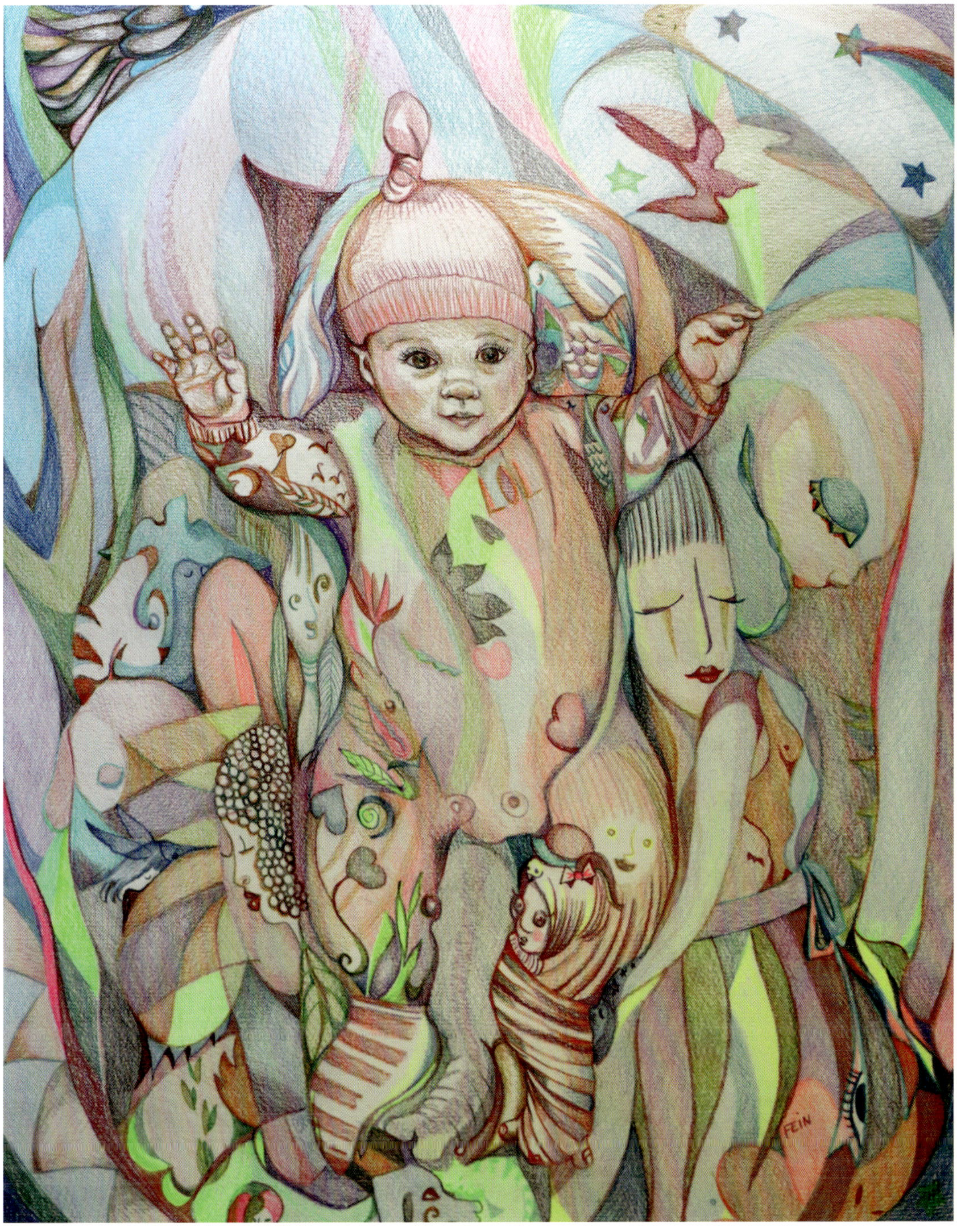

Fig. 139. Sheila Fein, HEARTBEAT.

MICHAEL LEBOWITZ, *MOM AND KIDS*

Journeys

Lots of people take photographs of mothers and children, and they may be charming and adorable, but they don't rise to the level of art. When I first saw this seemingly ordinary photograph by Michael Lebowitz—of anyone's mom and kids, I was struck with how very interesting it was as a composition, and how much there was to see in it if you just open your mind and skip all the names, places, references, and other pictures you have seen.

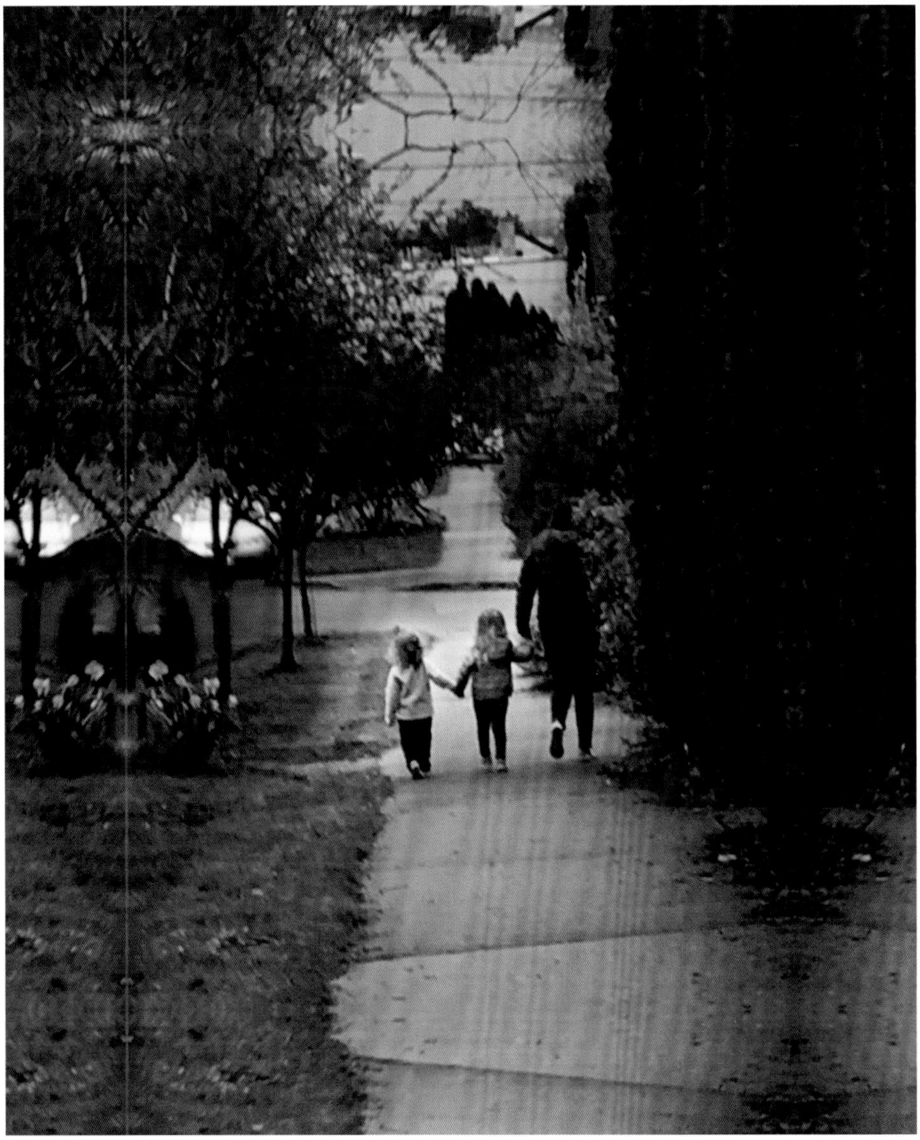

Fig. 140. Michael Lebowitz, MOM AND KIDS.

I love the composition of this photo. At the same time it seems just a captured moment with the three figures on the move, they are also perfectly framed in a cocoon of patterns. Do you see them? The kaleidoscope-like shape on the upper left. And then the mirroring patterns—the weblike structure in the upper center perfectly balanced by the designs in the ground, both the reflection on the left and the sidewalk shape in front of the tree.

It is if the photographer penetrated the scene to reveal these metaphysical shapes in the surroundings, as Mom and kids just merrily walk by. I say it's magic.

The fact that the photograph is in black and white is what makes these designs pop into consciousness. In color, they would disappear. A good argument for eschewing color in this context.

Once again, less is much more.

SIRARPI HEGHINIAN WALZER, *MOTHER AND CHILD*

Visual Poetry

For those not familiar with encaustic, it is a medium that utilizes hot wax to which colored pigments have been added. Sirarpi Heghinian Walzer is a mixed-media artist and encaustic is an important part of her art vocabulary. As different media each offer a unique touch and mood, the combination of media in a work, what we refer to as mixed media, combine to create a dense, enlivened surface.

Just as writers veer toward poetry or prose, so too do visual artists, and Heghinian Walzer lands squarely on the side of poetry. What does that mean for a visual work? I would say that poetry, as opposed to prose, is more likely to evoke, rather than to describe or illustrate a complex idea or emotion. For the viewer, the meaning of the work is sensed, rather than known; it is found rather than told.

We can see this approach brought to bear in this mother and child. The figures are not front and center and surrounded by what might be referred to as a "background." Instead, they are found in the riot of color and light, live in it, and are only a part of the entire picture.

This is an important aspect of modern painting, that the artist does not create all-important isolated figures and the rest of the canvas is the quiet that enunciates

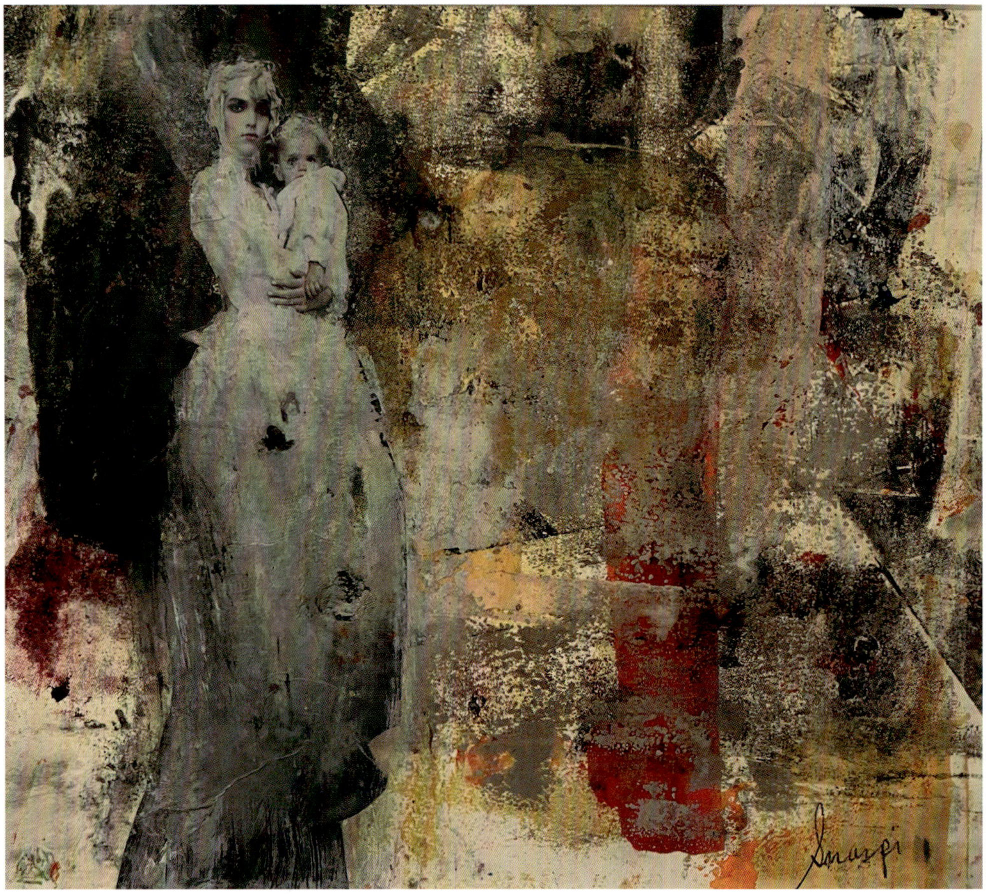

Fig. 141. Sirarpi Heghinian Walzer, MOTHER AND CHILD.

them, but conceives of the entire canvas as significant, just as deserving of painterly treatment as the objects or people represented. It is a more abstract way of thinking about a subject, even if it is a representational one. Heghinian Walzer is a superb exemplar of this methodology, and her *Mother and Child* is a quite riveting work of art.

CAROLYN SCHLAM, *JOY*

Joy

I am not a mother and I have no children. Yet the subject of mother and child is one I have returned to many times over the years. In this iteration, I had no model, no photograph, no outer reference to consider. I tasked myself with portraying the very intimate connection I imagine to only be possible between a mother and her baby.

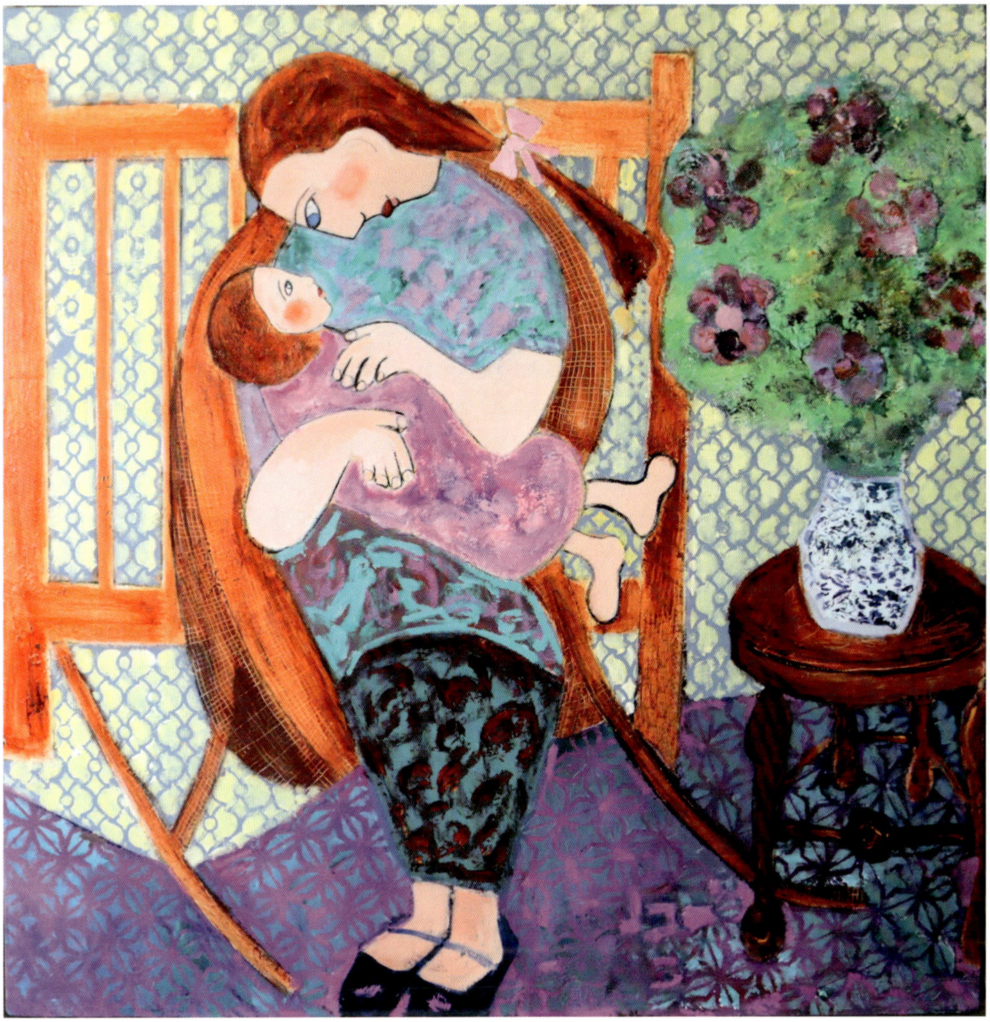

Fig. 142. Carolyn Schlam, JOY.

The mother in this painting looks down upon her child with unquestioned devotion and absolute absorption. She cannot quite believe what she has created. The baby is a reflection of her, part of her, not yet a self.

I do not know about this relationship from personal experience and can only extrapolate as the creator of my art, which is the only baby I will ever have. Like a real mother, I can't quite believe what I have created.

This painting is a reflection of the joy my art has brought me, and I believe it is evident here in the patterning, the composition, the soft colors, the mixtures of notes bouncing off one another. I see the joy as encapsulated in the tender touch of the paint, my effort to make each note as glorious as I am capable of. If I could take my heart and spread it like paint, it would make this painting. I am calling it *Joy*.

Going Forward

I hope you have enjoyed this book and especially being introduced to the living artists whose works grace these pages. If you are interested in learning more about these artists, you will find their contact information in the List of Images. Please do look up their websites and follow their careers. Contact them or their representatives if you are possibly interested in collecting their works.

Endings are difficult. So, let's not call this the end. I hope to continue to share my ideas about art with you as long as I can and you are interested in hearing them. I encourage any reader who has enjoyed this book, or has a question, or would like to share a thought, to get in touch with me through my website at www.carolynschlam.com. I love hearing from you.

Acknowledgments

Many thanks to the kind people who helped me with this book. My publisher, Tad Crawford, who gave me the opportunity to publish this second book in the series; my agent, Susan Schulman, ever faithful and supportive; my editor, Sarah Janssen, offering invaluable and wise assistance, Amanda Pina, William Davies and Clarice de Veyra of Gagosian Galleries and David Barnett of David Barnett Gallery, who endeavored to secure the cooperation of several important artists. Thanks also to the foundations who agreed to waive copyright fees and offered their artists' work for this book.

Most especially my thanks go to Anselm Kiefer, my friend and colleague Jimmy Wright, and all the other living artists who made contributions of their art to this book and complied with all my requests for documents. I would not have been able to write this book without them.

Personally, I want to thank my sister, Rebecca Katechis, and and all my dear friends who listened to endless stories of my efforts on this book, always encouraging me and guiding me forward.

Together, you all brought *More Joy* to the finish line, for which I am eternally grateful.

JOY TO ALL,

Carolyn Schlam

List of Images

Chapter 1: The Vocabulary of Art and Art Criticism

Fig. 1. Edouard Manet (1832–1883), BERTHE MORISOT WITH A BOUQUET OF VIOLETS, 1872, oil on canvas, 21.8" × 15.9", Musée d'Orsay, Paris, France. https://commons.wikimedia.org/wiki/File:Edouard_Manet_-_Berthe_Morisot_With_a_Bouquet_of_Violets_-_Google_Art_Project.jpg. Public domain.

Fig. 2. Edouard Manet (1832–1883), BOATING, 1874, oil on canvas, 38.25" × 51.25", Metropolitan Museum of Art, NY. https://www.metmuseum.org/art/collection/search/436947. Public domain.

Fig. 3. J. M. W. Turner (1775–1851), A MOUNTAIN SCENE, VAL D'AOSTA, c. 1845, oil on canvas, 48.03" × 36.02", National Gallery of Victoria. https://commons.wikimedia.org/wiki/File:J._M._W._Turner_-_A_mountain_scene,_Val_d%27Aosta_-_Google_Art_Project.jpg. Public domain.

Fig. 4. Wassily Kandinsky (1866–1944), HOUSES AT MURNAU, 1909, oil on cardboard, 19.25" × 25", Art Institute of Chicago. https://www.artic.edu/artworks/129849/houses-at-murnau. Open access. Public domain.

Fig. 5. Claude Monet (1840–1926), PALAZZO DARIO, 1908, oil on canvas, 26 1/16" × 32 3/16", Art Institute of Chicago. https://www.artic.edu/artworks/14630/venice-palazzo-dario. Open access. Public domain.

Fig. 6. Edgar Degas (1834–1917), DANSEUSE, c. 1895, drawing, charcoal, 27.1" × 20.8", Museum Folkwang, Essen, Germany. https://commons.wikimedia.org/wiki/File:Edgar_Degas_-_Danseuse,_appuy%C3%A9e_%C3%A0_une_colonne_(1895-98).jpg. Public domain.

Fig. 7. Paul Cezanne (1839–1906), STILL LIFE WITH QUINCE, APPLES AND PEARS, c. 1885, oil on canvas, 11.1" × 12.1", private collection. https://commons.wikimedia.org/wiki/File:Cezanne_-_Still_Life_With_Quince,_Apples,_and_Pears.jpg. Public domain.

Fig. 8. Wooden sculpture in the style of modern Makonde carvings from Tanzania attributed to Munfarid1. https://commons.wikimedia.org/wiki/File:Makonde_sculpture_Elephant.jpg. CREATIVE COMMONS ATTRIBUTION SHARE ALIKE 4.0 INTERNATIONAL LICENSE.

Fig. 9. CYPRIOT SCULPTURE https://commons.wikimedia.org/wiki/File:Sculpture_%22Modern_Aphrodite%22_by_Fort_Paphos,_Cyprus.jpg. CREATIVE COMMONS ATTRIBUTION SHARE ALIKE 4.0 INTERNATIONAL LICENSE.

Fig. 10. Edgar Degas (1834–1917), LE TUB, 1886, Pastel on Paper, 23.6" × 32.6", Musée D'Orsay, Paris. https://commons.wikimedia.org/wiki/File:Edgar_Germain_Hilaire_Degas_031.jpg. Public domain.

Fig. 11. John White Alexander (1856–1915), REPOSE, oil on canvas, 52¼ × 63⅝", Metropolitan Museum of Art, New York. https://www.metmuseum.org/art/collection/search/10065. Public domain.

Chapter 2: Questions and Conundrums

Fig. 12. Henri De Toulouse Lautrec (1865–1901), MOULIN ROUGE, 1891, Lithograph, 74¹³⁄₁₆" × 45⅞", Metropolitan Museum of Art. https://commons.wikimedia.org/wiki/File:Moulin_Rouge-_La_Goulue_MET_DT11780.jpg. Public domain.

Fig. 13. Gustav Klimt (1864–1918), THE KISS, 1907-8, Oil on canvas, 70.8" × 70.8" Upper Belvedere. https://commons.wikimedia.org/wiki/File:The_Kiss_-_Gustav_Klimt_-_Google_Cultural_Institute.jpg. Public domain.

Chapter 3: Beauty

Fig. 14. Jimmy Wright, SUN AND SHADOW, 2001, oil on canvas, 96" × 72", Courtesy of the Artist and Fierman Gallery, New York.

Fig. 15. Albert Bierstadt (1830–1902), AMONG THE SIERRA NEVADA, 1868, oil on canvas, 6' × 10', Smithsonian American Art Museum. https://commons.wikimedia.org/wiki/File:Albert_Bierstadt_-_Among_the_Sierra_Nevada,_California_-_Google_Art_Project.jpg. Public domain.

Fig. 16. J. M. W. Turner, VENICE WITH THE SALUTE, c. 1840, oil on canvas, 20.4' × 10.1 yd, Tate Britain. https://commons.wikimedia.org/wiki/File:Joseph_Mallord_William_Turner_-_Venice_with_the_Salute_-_Google_Art_Project.jpg. Public domain.

Fig. 17. Magdalena Morey, CATCHING THE WAVES, 2022, Acrylic, pastel and gold leaf, 100 × 100 cm, Courtesy of the Artist.

Fig. 18. Pierre Bonnard (1867–1947), MISIA ET VALLOTTON A VILLENEUVE, 1899, Oil on Board, 27⅝" × 20⅛", Private Collection. https://commons.wikimedia.org/wiki/File:Edouard_vuillard_misia_et_vallotton_a_villeneuve.jpg. Public domain.

Fig. 19. Wassily Kandinsky (1866–1944), IMPROVISATION KLAMM, 1914, oil on canvas, 43.4" × 43.4", Lenbachhaus. https://commons.wikimedia.org/wiki/File:Kandinsky_-_Improvisation_Klamm_PA291186.jpg. Public domain.

Fig. 20. Winslow Homer (1836–1910), NOREASTER, 1895, oil on canvas, 34.4" × 50", Metropolitan Museum of Art, New York. https://commons.wikimedia.org/wiki/File:Northeaster_by_Winslow_Homer_1895.jpg. Public domain.

Fig. 21. Mary Cassatt, THE CUP OF TEA, 1880-1, Oil on canvas, 36⅜" × 25¾". https://commons.wikimedia.org/wiki/File:Mary_Cassatt,_1880c_-_The_Cup_of_Tea.jpg. Public domain.

Fig. 22. Marsden Hartley (1877–1943), MOVEMENTS, 1913, Oil on Canvas, 47" × 46⅞", Art Institute of Chicago. https://www.artic.edu/artworks/65916/movements. Public domain.

Fig. 23. Anselm Kiefer (1945–), LILITH AM ROTEN MEER (Lilith at the Red Sea Lilith à la Mer Rouge). Photo courtesy of the Artist, Anselm Kiefer, 1990, Lead, emulsion, fabric and ash on canvas Blei, Emulsion, Stoff und Asche auf Leinwand Plomb, émulsion, tissu et cendre sur toile 280 × 625 cm (110¼" × 246"). Copyright: © Anselm Kiefer Photo: Atelier Anselm Kiefer Collection Nationalgalerie im Hamburger Bahnhof, Museum für Gegenwart. Courtesy of the Artist.

Fig. 24. Edvard Munch (1863–1944), MELANCHOLY, 1892, oil on canvas, 25.1" × 37.7", National Museum of Art, Architecture and Design. https://commons.wikimedia.org/wiki/File:Munch_Melankoli_1892.jpg.

Fig. 25. Paul Klee (1879–1940), GHOST OF A GENIUS, 1922, oil transfer and watercolor on paper, 19.68" × 13.93", Scottish National Gallery. https://upload.wikimedia.org/wikipedia/commons/e/eb/Paul_Klee_-_Gespenst_eines_Genies_%28Ghost_of_a_Genius%29_-_Google_Art_Project.jpg. Public domain.

Figs. 26A, 26B, 26C, 26D. Hieronymus Bosch (1450–1516), THE GARDEN OF EARTHLY DELIGHTS, 1490–1500, oil on panel, 80.9" × 12.6', Museo del Prado. A: https://commons.wikimedia.org/wiki/File:Bosch,_Hieronymus_-_The_Garden_of_Earthly_Delights,_central_panel_-_Detail_lobster_shell.jpg. B: https://commons.wikimedia.org/wiki/File:Bosch,_Hieronymus_-_The_Garden_of_Earthly_Delights,_right_panel_-_Detail_Key.jpg. C: https://commons.wikimedia.org/wiki/File:Bosch,_Hieronymus_-_The_Garden_of_Earthly_Delights,_central_panel_-_Detail_Winged_man_with_fruit_flies_to_heaven_(upper_right).jpg. D: https://commons.wikimedia.org/wiki/File:The_Garden_of_Earthly_Delights_by_Bosch_High_Resolutioncrop.jpg. Public domain.

Fig. 27. Harue Koga (1895–1933), THE SEA, 1929, Oil on canvas, National Museum of Modern Art, Tokyo, Japan. https://commons.wikimedia.org/wiki/File:Sea_-_Koga_Harue_1929.tiff. Public domain.

Fig. 28. Michelangelo Merisi Caravaggio (1571–1610), ST. JOHN THE BAPTIST, oil on canvas, 1602, 50.78" × 37.4", Capitoline Museum. https://commons.wikimedia.org/wiki/File:Caravaggio_(Michelangelo_Merisi)_-_Saint_John_the_Baptist_-_Google_Art_Project.jpg. Public domain.

Fig. 29. Willem de Kooning, WOMAN STANDING-PINK, 1954–1955, oil and charcoal on canvas, 48" × 36", Anderson Collection at Stanford University, Gift of Harry W. and Mary Margaret Anderson, and Mary Patricia Anderson Pence, 2014.1.018. Courtesy of the Willem De Kooning Foundation/Artists Rights Society (ARS), New York.

Chapter 4: Authenticity

Fig. 30. Jean Francois Millet (1814–1875), THE GLEANERS, 1857, oil on canvas, 32.8" × 43.3", Musée D'Orsay, Paris. https://commons.wikimedia.org/wiki/File;Jean-Francois_Millet_-_Gleaners_-_Google_Art_Project.jpg. Public domain.

Fig. 31. Vincent Van Gogh (1853–1890), SHOES, 1888, oil on canvas, 17.9" × 21.7", Metropolitan Museum of Art, New York. https://commons.wikimedia.org/wiki/File:Vincent_Van_Gogh_-_Shoes_2.jpg. Public domain.

Fig. 32. Georges Seurat (1858–1891), THE ARTIST'S MOTHER, 1882-3, Conté crayon on paper, 12⅝" × 9⁷⁄₁₆", Metropolitan Museum of Art, New York. https://www.metmuseum.org/art/collection/search/334652. Public domain.

Fig. 33. Jean-Léon Gérôme (1824–1904), BASHI-BAZOUK, 1868, oil on canvas, 31¾" × 26", Metropolitan Museum of Art, New York. https://www.metmuseum.org/art/collection/search/440723 Public domain.

Fig. 34. Jean-Baptiste Carpeaux, WHY BORN ENSLAVED, 1868, marble, Metropolitan Museum of Art. New York. https://www.metmuseum.org/art/collection/search/824469. Public domain.

Fig. 35. Raphael (1483–1520), SELF PORTRAIT, tempera on panel, 18.7" × 12.9", Galleria Palatina. http://commons.wikimedia.org/wiki/File:Raffaello_Sanzio.jpg. Public domain.

Fig. 36. Alessandro Allori (1535–1607), SELF PORTRAIT, 1555, oil on panel, 23.6" × 18.5", Uffizi Gallery. https://commons.wikimedia.org/wiki/File:Self-portrait_by_Alessandro_Allori.jpg. Public domain.

Fig. 37. Caravaggio (1571–1610), CUPID AS VICTOR, 1601, oil on canvas, 61.6" × 44.6," Gemaldegalerie. https://upload.wikimedia.org/wikipedia/commons/0/0c/Caravaggio_-_Cupid_as_Victor_-_Google_Art_Project.jpg. Public domain.

Fig. 38. Rembrandt (1606–1669), SELF PORTRAIT, 1658, oil on canvas, 52.6" × 40.8", The Frick Collection, New York. https://commons.wikimedia.org/wiki/File:Rembrandt_-_Zelfportret_-_Google_Art_Project.jpg. Public domain.

Fig. 39. Francois Boucher (1703–1770), PORTRAIT OF MADAME DE POMPADOUR, 1756, oil on canvas, 83.4" × 64.5", Alte Pinakothek. https://commons.wikimedia.org/wiki/File:Madame_de_Pompadour.jpg. Public domain.

Fig. 40. John Henry Fuseli (1741–1825), THE NIGHTMARE, 1781, oil on canvas, 40" × 50", Detroit Institute of Art. https://upload.wikimedia.org/wikipedia/commons/5/56/John_Henry_Fuseli_-_The_Nightmare.JPG. Public domain.

Chapter 5: Originality

Fig. 41. Chauvet Caves Horse Panel (detail). Wooden charcoal drawings with fading, flint cropping and scratching with stump. https://commons.wikimedia.org/wiki/File:Panneau_des_chevaux-detail%C2%A9_Patrick_Aventurier_-_Grotte_Chauvet_2_Ard%C3%A8che.jpg. Public domain.

Fig. 42. Petroglyphs of Qobustan (Azerbaijan). https://commons.wikimedia.org/wiki/File:Petroglyphs_of_Qobustan_2.jpg. Public domain.

Fig. 43. Leonardo da Vinci (1452–1519), MONA LISA, c. 1503, oil on panel, 30.3" × 20.8", Louvre Museum, Paris. https://commons.wikimedia.org/wiki/File:Mona_Lisa,_by_Leonardo_da_Vinci,_from_C2RMF_retouched.jpg. Public domain.

Fig. 44. Michelangelo (1475–1564), THE AWAKENING SLAVE, 1519, Marble, 105.1", Galleria del Accademia. https://commons.wikimedia.org/wiki/File:Awakening_slave_by_Michelangelo-Galleria_dell%27Accademia.jpg. Public domain.

Fig. 45. Johannes Vermeer (1632–1675), THE MILKMAID, 1660, Oil on canvas, 17.9" × 16.1", Rijksmuseum. https://commons.wikimedia.org/wiki/File:Johannes_Vermeer_-_Het_melkmeisje_-_Google_Art_Project.jpg. Public domain.

Fig. 46. Francisco Goya (1746–1828), JUDITH AND HOLOFERNES, c. 1819, mixed media, 57.4" × 33", Museum del Prado. https://commons.wikimedia.org/wiki/File:Judith_y_Holofernes_(Goya).jpg. Public domain.

Fig. 47. Gustave Courbet (1819–1877), FRUIT, 1871, OIL ON PANEL, 7" × 14.4", Burrell Collection. https://commons.wikimedia.org/w/index.php?search=gustave+courbet+still+life&title=Special:MediaSearch&go=Go&type=image and https://commons.wikimedia.org/wiki/File:Courbet_Gustave_Fruits_1871.jpg. Public domain.

Fig. 48. Antoni Gaudi, LA SAGRADA FAMILIA, Barcelona, Spain. https://upload.wikimedia.org/wikipedia/commons/2/22/TEMPLE_EXPIATORI_DE_LA_SAGRADA_FAM%C3%8DLIA_24012021_%281%29_18.jpg. Public domain.

Fig. 49. Claude Monet (1840–1926), WOMAN WITH A PARASOL, 1875, oil on canvas, 39.3" × 32.2", National Gallery of Art. https://commons.wikimedia.org/wiki/File:Claude_Monet_-_Woman_with_a_Parasol_-_Madame Monet_and_Her_Son_-_Google_Art_Project.jpg. Public domain.

Fig. 50. Vincent van Gogh (1853–1890), STARRY NIGHT, 1889, oil on canvas, 28.7" × 36.2", Museum of Modern Art. https://commons.wikimedia.org/wiki/File:Van_Gogh_-_Starry_Night_-_Google_Art_Project.jpg. Public domain.

Fig. 51. Paul Gauguin (1848–1903), HAIL MARY, 1891, Oil on Canvas, 44¾" × 34½", Metropolitan Museum of Art, New York. https://www.metmuseum.org/art/collection/search/438821. Public domain.

Fig. 52. Early Cycladic 2, HEAD OF A WOMAN, 2700–2500 BCE, Marble, 9-15,16 Metropolitan Museum of Art. https://www.metmuseum.org/art/collection/search/255176. Public domain.

Fig. 53. Amadeo Modigliani (1884–1920), WOMANS HEAD, 1912, Limestone, 26⅞" × 9½", Metropolitan Museum of Art, New York. https://www.metmuseum.org/art/collection/search/486837. Public domain.

Fig. 54. Henri Rousseau (1844–1910), THE DREAM, 1910, 80.5" × 117.5", Museum of Modern Art. https://commons.wikimedia.org/wiki/File:Henri_Rousseau_-_Le_R%C3%AAve_-_Google_Art_Project.jpg. Public domain.

Fig. 55. Cassius Marcellus Coolidge (1844–1934), POKER GAME, oil on canvas, 41.6" × 50", Private Collection. https://commons.wikimedia.org/wiki/File:Cassius_Marcellus_Coolidge_-_Poker_Game_(1894).png. Public domain.

Chapter 6: Modernity

Fig. 56. Milton Avery, FEMALE ARTIST, 1944, Oil on Canvas. Rights granted by the Milton Avery Trust and Artist Rights Society (ARS).

Fig. 57. Piet Mondrian, CHURCH FACADE 5, 1914, drawing, charcoal on paper, 28¼" × 19⅛", San Francisco Museum of Modern Art. https://commons.wikimedia.org/wiki/File:Mondrian_-_Church_Facade_5,_1940.jpg. Public domain.

Fig. 58. Paul Klee (1879–1940), STRUCTURAL II, 1924, gouache on paper, 10.1" × 8.2", private collection. https://commons.wikimedia.org/wiki/File:Paul_Klee_Structural_II_1924.jpg. Public domain.

Fig. 59. Juan Gris (1887–1927), GLASS AND CARAFE, 1917, oil on panel, 14.5" × 24", Kunstmuseum Winterthur. https://commons.wikimedia.org/wiki/File:Juan_Gris_-_Glas_und_Karaffe.jpeg. Public domain.

Fig. 60. Georges Valmier (1885–1937), LES TULLIPES, 1928, oil on canvas, 36.2" × 25.5", Private collection. https://commons.wikimedia.org/wiki/File:Georges_Valmier_1928,_Les_Tulipes_(The_Tulips),oil_on_canvas,_92_x_65_cm,private_collection.jpg. Public domain.

Fig. 61. Edgar Degas (1834–1917), IMAGINARY LANDSCAPE, Monotype, 1892, 10" × 13⅜", Metropolitan Museum of Art, New York. https://www.metmuseum.org/art/collection/search/359362. Public domain.

Fig. 62. Richard Diebenkorn, OCEAN FROM A WINDOW, 1959, Oil on canvas, 70" × 64" (177.8 × 162.6 cm), Catalogue Raisonne No. 2724, Courtesy of the Richard Diebenkorn Foundation.

Fig. 63. Richard Diebenkorn, STUDIO WINDOW: OCEAN PARK, 1970, Oil on canvas, 84" × 72" (213.4 × 182.9 cm), Catalogue Raisonne No. 4014, Courtesy of the Richard Diebenkorn Foundation.

Fig. 64. Sir Frederic Leighton (1830–1986), FLAMING JUNE, 1895, Oil on canvas, 46.8" × 46.8", Museo de Arte de Ponce. https://commons.wikimedia.org/wiki/File:Frederic_Leighton_-Flaming-June_(1895)_-Museo_de_Arte_de_Ponce.jpg. Public domain.

Fig. 65. Valentin Serov (1865–1911), GIRL WITH PEACHES, 1887, oil on canvas, 35.8" × 33.4". https://commons.wikimedia.org/wiki/File:Valentin_Serov_-_%D0%94%D0%B5%D0%B2%D0%BE%D1%87%D0%BA%D0%B0_%D1%81_%D0%BF%D0%B5%D1%80%D1%81%D0%B8%D0%BA%D0%B0%D0%BC%D0%B8._%D0%9F%D0%BE%D1%80%D1%82%D1%80%D0%B5%D1%82_%D0%92.%D0%A1.%D0%9C%D0%B0%D0%BC%D0%BE%D0%BD%D1%82%D0%BE%D0%B2%D0%BE%D0%B9_-_Google_Art_Project.jpg. Public domain.

Fig. 66. Paul Cezanne (1839–1906), VIEW OF THE DOMAIN ST. JOSEPH, late 1880s, oil on canvas, 25⅝ × 32", Metropolitan Museum of Art, New York. https://www.metmuseum.org/art/collection/search/435885. Public domain.

Fig. 67. Georges Seurat (1858–1891), MODELS, 1886, oil on canvas, 79" × 98.4", Barnes Foundation. https://commons.wikimedia.org/wiki/File:Georges_Seurat_-Models_(Poseuses)_-BF811_-Barnes_Foundation.jpg. Public domain.

Fig. 68. Carolyn Schlam, COFFEE, 2015, Oil on canvas, 48 × 48". Courtesy of the Artist.

Fig. 69. Édouard Vuillard (1868–1940), WOMAN IN A STRIPED DRESS, 1895, 25⅞" × 23⅛", Collection Paul Mellon. https://commons.wikimedia.org/wiki/File:Edouard_Vuillard_-_Woman_in_a_Striped_Dress_-_Google_Art_Project.jpg. Public domain.

Fig. 70. Pierre Bonnard (1867–1947), CONVERSATION IN ARCACHON, 1926–30, oil on canvas, 27.8" × 24.6", Musée des Beaux Arts de la ville de

Paris. https://commons.wikimedia.org/wiki/File:Pierre_Bonnard_-_Conversation _à_Arcachon_-_PPP3181_-_Musée_des_Beaux-Arts_de_la_ville_de_Paris.jpg . Public domain.

Fig. 71. Georges Rouault (1871–1958), SE RÉFUGIE EN TON COEUR, 1922, print, 13.7" × 10.5". https://commons.wikimedia.org/wiki/File:Se_R %C3%A9fugie_En_Ton_Coeur,_Va-Nu-Pieds_De_Malheur_-_Vanderbilt _Fine_Arts_Gallery_-_1969.074.tif. Public domain.

Fig. 72. Käthe Kollwitz (1867–1945), SLEEPING CHILD, 1892, Museo Kathe Kollwitz. https://commons.wikimedia.org/wiki/File:K%C3%A4the_Kollwitz-Enfant _endormi-1892.jpg. Public domain.

Fig. 73. Juan Gris (1887–1927), PORTRAIT OF MME. JOSETTE GRIS, 1916, 55.4" × 38.1", Museo Nacional Centrol de Arte Reina Sofia. https://commons .wikimedia.org/wiki/File:Juan_Gris_-_Portrait_de_Madame_Josette_Gris_-_ Google_Art_Project.jpg. Public domain.

Fig. 74. Kazimir Malevich (1879–1935), BLACK SQUARE, Oil on canvas, 1930, 21" × 21", Hermitage Museum. https://commons.wikimedia.org/wiki /File:Malevich,_Kazimir_Severinovich_-_Black_Square.jpg. Public domain.

Fig. 75. Pieter Brueghel The Elder (1526–1569), THE TOWER OF BABEL, 1563, oil on panel, 44.8" × 61", Kunsthistorisches Museum. https://commons. wikimedia.org/w/index.php?search=brueghel+tower+of+babel&title=Special: MediaSearch&go=Go&type=image. https://commons.wikimedia.org/wiki/File:Pieter _Bruegel_the_Elder_-_The_Tower_of_Babel_(Vienna)_-_Google_Art_Project _-_edited.jpg. Public domain.

Fig. 76. Pieter Brueghel The Elder (1526–1569), THE TOWER OF BABEL, 1568, oil on panel, 23.5" × 29.3", Museum Boijmans Van Bueningen. https: //commons.wikimedia.org/wiki/File:Pieter_Bruegel_the_Elder_-_The_Tower _of_Babel_(Rotterdam)_-_Google_Art_Project_-_edited.jpg. Public domain.

Fig. 77. Monument of the Discoveries, Lisbon, Portugal, Photo by Carolyn Schlam.

Chapter 7: Perspective

Fig. 78. Molded Vessel in the Form of a Mother and Child, 12th–13th century, H. 8 1/16" (20.5 cm) × W. 5 3/8" (13.7 cm), Metropolitan Museum of Art. https: //commons.wikimedia.org/Wiki/File:Molded_Vessel_in_the_Form_of_a _Mother_and_Child_MET_DP262925.jpg. Public domain.

Fig. 79. Leonardo da Vinci (1452–1519), MADONNA LITTI, mid 1490s, tempera on panel, 16.5" × 12.9", Hermitage Museum. https://commons.wikimedia.org/wiki/File:Leonardo_da_Vinci_attributed_-_Madonna_Litta.jpg. Public domain.

Fig. 80. Sandro Botticelli (1445–1510), MADONNA AND CHILD, c. 1470, tempera on panel, 29.3" × 29.4", National Gallery of Art. https://commons.wikimedia.org/wiki/File:Sandro_Botticelli_-_Madonna_and_Child,_c._1470.jpg. Public domain.

Fig. 81. George Romney (1734–1802), MOTHER AND CHILD, Drawing, graphite on paper, 5" × 5.2", Yale Center for British Art. https://commons.wikimedia.org/wiki/File:George_Romney_-_Mother_and_Child_-_Google_Art_Project_(2428623).jpg. Public domain.

Fig. 82. Kitagawa Utamara (Died 1806), MISTRESS AND SLEEPY CHILD, 1798, Woodcut print, 14⅜" × 9⅝", Metropolitan Museum of Art. https://commons.wikimedia.org/wiki/File:%E9%A2%A8%E4%BF%97%E7%BE%8E%E4%BA%BA%E6%99%82%E8%A8%88_%E5%AD%90%E3%83%8E%E5%88%BB_%E5%A6%BE-Midnight-_Mother_and_Sleepy_Child_MET_DP135613.jpg. Public domain.

Fig. 83. Bernard Blommers (1845–1914), MOTHER AND CHILD AT THE SEASIDE, oil on panel, 10.7" × 8.4", Private collection. https://commons.wikimedia.org/wiki/File:Bernardus_Johannes_Blommers_-_Mother_and_child_at_the_seaside.jpg. Public domain.

Fig. 84. Berthe Morisot (1841–1895), MME. GOBILLARD ET SA FILLE, 1875, Watercolor, 6½" × 8⅟18", Private collection. https://commons.wikimedia.org/wiki/File:Berthe_morisot_mme_gobillard_et_sa_fille_paule020016).jpg. Public domain.

Fig. 85. Gustav Klimt (1862–1918), THREE AGES OF WOMAN, 1905, Oil on canvas, 70.8" × 70.8", Galleries Nazionale d'Arte Moderna e Contemporanea. https://commons.wikimedia.org/wiki/File:Klimt_-_Die_drei_Lebensalter der_Frau.jpeg. Public domain.

Fig. 86. Gustav Klimt (1862–1918), Detail, THREE AGES OF WOMAN, 1905, Oil on canvas, 70.8" × 70.8" Galleries Nazionale d'Arte Moderna e Contemporanea. Public domain.

Fig. 87. Harold Gilman (1875–1919), MOTHER AND CHILD, 1918, oil on canvas, 19.9" × 27.4", Auckland Art Gallery. https://commons.wikimedia.org

/wiki/File:Harold_Gilman_-_Mother_and_Child_-_Google_Art_Project.jpg. Public domain.

Fig. 88. Janis Rozentals (1866–1916), MOTHER AND CHILD, 1904, 2.63" × 3.5", Latvian National Museum of Art. https://commons.wikimedia.org/wiki/File:Janis_Rozent%C4%81ls_-_Mother_and_Child_-_Google_Art_Project.jpg. Public domain.

Fig. 89. Mary Cassatt (1844–1926), MATERNAL CARESS, 1890, Drypoint, aquatint and softground etching, printed in color from three plates, plate: 14⅜" × 10⁹⁄₁₆" sheet: 17¼" × 11¹⁵⁄₁₆" (43.8 × 30.3 cm) (36.5 × 26.8 cm), Metropolitan Museum of Art. https://commons.wikimedia.org/wiki/File:Maternal_Caress_MET_DP815284.jpg. Public domain.

Fig. 90. Egon Schiele (1890–1918), MOTHER AND CHILD, 1912, Leopold Museum. https://commons.wikimedia.org/wiki/File:Egon_Schiele,_Mother_and_Child,_1912;_Leopold_Museum,_Vienna.jpg. Public domain.

Fig. 91. Joaquin Sorolla (1863–1923), MOTHER, 1895, oil on canvas, Sorolla Museum. https://commons.wikimedia.org/wiki/File:Joaqu%C3%ADn_Sorolla_y_Bastida_-_Mother_-_Google_Art_Project.jpg. Public domain.

Fig. 92. Santeri Salokivi (1886–1940), MOTHER AND CHILD, 1922, oil on canvas, 24" × 20". https://commons.wikimedia.org/wiki/File:Salokivi_Mother_and_child.jpg. Public domain.

Fig. 93. Edvard Munch (1863–1924), THE DEAD MOTHER AND HER CHILD, 1897–1899, oil on canvas, 41.1" × 70.6", Munch Museum. https://commons.wikimedia.org/wiki/File:Munch,_The_dead_mother_and_the_child.jpg. Public domain.

Fig. 94. Christian Krohg (1852–1925), MOTHER AND CHILD, 1883, oil on canvas, 18.8" × 20.8", National Museum of Art, Architecture and Design. https://commons.wikimedia.org/wiki/File:Christian_Krohg_-_Mother_and_Child_-_Google_Art_Project.jpg. Public domain.

Fig. 95. Bela L. Pratt (1867–1917), YOUNG MOTHER, 1911, WHITE MARBLE, 15½", Worcester Art Museum. https://commons.wikimedia.org/wiki/File:Young_Mother_by_Bela_L._Pratt.jpg. Public domain.

Fig. 96. Henry Moore (1898–1986), MOTHER AND CHILD:HOOD, St. Paul's Cathedral, Travertine marble, 72" high. https://commons.wikimedia.org/wiki/File:Mother_%26_Child,_Henry_Moore,_St_Paul%27s_Cathedral_05.jpg. Public domain.

Fig. 97. Dorothea Lange (1895–1962), MIGRANT MOTHER, 1936, Photograph, 1.9" × 1.5", Library of Congress. https://commons.wikimedia.org/wiki/File:Lange-MigrantMother02.jpg. Public domain.

Fig. 98. Alice Neel (1900–1984), MOTHER AND CHILD HAVANA, 1926, oil on canvas, 26" × 18". https://commons.wikimedia.org/wiki/File:Mother_and_Child,_Havana_by_Alice_Neel,_1926.jpg. Public domain.

Fig. 99. Fritz Stuckenberg (1881–1944), MOTHER AND CHILD, 1920, Oil on canvas, Yale University Art Gallery. https://commons.wikimedia.org/wiki/File:Fritz_Stuckenberg_-_Mother_and_Child_-_1941.696_-_Yale_University_Art_Gallery.jpg. Public domain.

Fig. 100. Milton Avery (1885–1965), MATERNITY, 1950, oil on canvas, 32" × 46", Image courtesy of the David Barnett Gallery, Permission by Milton Avery Foundation Private Collection.

Fig. 101. Carolyn Schlam, MOTHER AND CHILD AND DOLL, paint and cut papers, 30" × 22". www.carolynschlam.com, carolynschlam@aol.com. Courtesy of the Artist.

Chapter 8: Essence

Fig. 102. Photo of Pablo Picasso, 1962. https://commons.wikimedia.org/wiki/File:Pablo_picasso_1.jpg and http://www.magicasruinas.com.ar/revistero/internacional/pintura-pablo-picasso.htm. Public domain.

Fig. 103. Signature of Amadeo Modigliani. https://commons.wikimedia.org/wiki/File:Amedeo_Modigliani_signature.svg.

Fig. 104. Photo of Caroline Remy, "Séverine," by Atelier Nadar, Biblioteque Nationale de France. https://commons.wikimedia.org/wiki/File:S%C3%A9verine_Atelier_Nadar_01.png. Public domain.

Fig. 105. Amélie Beaury-Saurel (1848–1924), PORTRAIT OF SÉVERINE, 1893, Oil, 48.2" × 34.6", Musée Carnavalet, Paris. https://commons.wikimedia.org/wiki/File:Am%C3%A9lie_Beaury-Saurel.jpg. Public domain.

Fig. 106. Auguste Renoir (1841–1919), SÉVERINE, 1885, pastel on paper, 24½" × 20", National Gallery of Art. https://commons.wikimedia.org/wiki/File:Auguste_Renoir,_Caroline_R%C3%A9my_(%22S%C3%A9verine%22),_c._1885,_NGA_46683.jpg. Public domain.

Chapter 9: Living Artists Whose Focus Is on Beauty

Fig. 107. Malcolm Liepke, LADY IN BLACK, oil on canvas, 40" × 60", Represented by Rukaj Gallery, Toronto. https://www.rukajgallery.com/; Pontone Gallery, London. https://pontonegallery.com/; and Arcadia Gallery, New York and Los Angeles, https://arcadiacontemporary.com/.

Fig. 108. Viktor Butko, CLOUDY SUNSET AT DERING HARBOR, oil on linen, 40" × 47", 2021, www.viktorbutko.com, viktorbutkofineart@gmail.com, representative: Grenning Gallery, www.grenninggallery.com. Courtesy of the Artist.

Fig. 109. Chuck Fischer, VILLEFRANCHE-SUR-MER, Aluminum, wood, modeling paste, gesso, acrylic, 36" × 40", 2022. www.chuckfischerstudio.com, chuckfischerstudio@gmail.com. Courtesy of the Artist.

Fig. 110. Veronica Cay, BREATHING DEEPLY INHALING COMFORT, mixed-media collage on polycotton canvas, 140 × 200 cm, Private collection: HOLA (HOUSE OF LOCAL ART BOUTIQUE ACCOMMODATION EUMUNDI QUEENSLAND), Photo: Christine Hall (www.myphotomotion.com.au), instagram @ronniecay.com. Courtesy of the Artist.

Fig. 111. Dan Muller, HOUSES AT NIGHT, mixed media (watercolor, cut and pasted paper, pastel, charcoal) 40" × 52", mullerworksinc@gmail.com, Representative: David Barnett Gallery, https://davidbarnettgallery.com. Courtesy of the Artist.

Fig. 112. Reginald K. Gee, FOOTWORK AT RANDOM, Acrylic on canvas, 48" × 36", Representative: David Barnett Gallery, www.davidbarnettgallery.com. Courtesy of the Gallery.

Fig. 113. Bernice Sokol Kramer, SAID THE TABLE TO THE LAMP, IT'S A PIECE OF CAKE, wood, table, papier mache, acrylic, collage, painted shoes, lampshade, pastel, fabric, 62" × 34" × 24", www.bernicesokolkramer.com. Courtesy of the Artist.

Fig. 114. Phyllis Baker Hammond, BIRD'S NEST, Powder Coated Aluminum, 90" × 60" × 60". Courtesy of the Artist and J. Mackey Gallery Representative:

J. Mackey Gallery East Hampton www.jmackeygallery.com, jm@mackeygallery.com. Quote from Phyllis Hammond from Justine McEnerney's interview with Phyllis Baker Hammond for the 2022 "Taking Flight" solo exhibition at J. Mackey Gallery East Hampton. Photo courtesy of Gary Mamay.

Fig. 115. Carolyn Schlam, WISTFUL, Oil on canvas, 40" × 30", 2020, www.carolynschlam.com, carolynschlam@aol.com, Representative: David Barnett Gallery, www.davidbarnettgallery.com. Courtesy of the Artist.

Chapter 10: Living Artists Whose Focus Is on Truth

Fig. 116. Lola del Fresno, GIRL RUNNING, Graphite, Acrylic on Mylar installed over a photograph, 163" × 77", https://loladelfresco.com, loladelfresno@yahoo.com. Courtesy of the Artist.

Fig. 117. Bob Conge, A REMBRANDT NIGHT, mixed-media monoprint, 41" × 39", https://bobconge.com, bob@plaseebo.net. Courtesy of the Artist.

Fig. 118. Jimmy Wright, NIGHTWATCH: THE ANVIL, graphite on paper, 30" × 22", collection of the artist, http://www.jimmywrightartist.com. Courtesy of the Artist.

Fig. 119. David Provan, WE LIVE WITHIN EACH OTHERS WOUNDS, Corten steel, 39" × 25" × 9", www.davidprovan.com, david@dvidprovan.com. Courtesy of the Artist.

Fig. 120. Michael Lebowitz, I DID NOT GO TO THE WAR, 2010, black-and-white photograph, 35mm DSLR, DPI 300 ht, 300 w. Depth 8, www.longrunpictures.com, michael@longrunpictures.com. Courtesy of the Artist.

Fig. 121. DB Waterman, FOR A BETTER FUTURE, mixed media on canvas, 100 × 70 × 2 cm, www.dbwatermanart.com, dbwaterman@gmail.com, www.dbwatermanart.com. Courtesy of the Artist.

Fig. 122. Carrie Pearce, DOLLY, Oil and found objects on panel, 60" × 24", Private Collection, https://www.carriepeace.com, carrie@carriepearce.com. Courtesy of the Artist.

Chapter 12: Living Artists Whose Focus Is on Emotion

Fig. 123. Ann-Marie Brown, DESI IN HER MOTHER'S DRESS, Oil and encaustic, 30" × 30", Location: unknown (stolen), www.annmariebrownpaintings.com, ambpaintings@hotmail.com. Courtesy of the Artist.

Fig. 124. Anna Boothe, GROWTH, Glass, highway beads, polyester resin, fiberglass, 36" × 11" × 16", www.annaboothe.com, anna@annaboothe.com. Courtesy of the Artist.

Fig. 125. Sheila Fein, BUCKET HEAD, Acrylic on canvas, 24" × 24", www.sheilafein.com, feinfantasypop@gmail.com. Courtesy of the Artist.

Fig. 126. Stephen Maffin, LORE, Acrylic, plaster, burlap, 24" × 24", www.stephenmaffin.com, Representative: Sue Greenwood Fine Art. Courtesy of the Artist.

Fig. 127. Magdalena Morey, FINDING BALANCE, Acrylic, pastel, gold leaf, 100 × 100 cm, Private Collection, www.magdalenamorey.com, info@magdalenamorey.com. Courtesy of the Artist.

Fig. 128. Judith Schaechter, DE-LUXE, Stained glass, engraved, enameled, assembled with copper foil and lead, 28" × 40", www.judithschaechter.com, Representative: Claire Oliver Gallery, www.claireoliver.com. Courtesy of the Artist.

Fig. 129. Phoebe Scott, WITHIN, Ceramic, 53" × 21" × 13", www.phoebescott.com. Courtesy of the Artist.

Fig. 130. Sirarpi Heghinian Walzer, PORTRAIT OF A WOMAN, mixed-media collage, ink, beeswax, 8" × 8", www.swalzer.com, sirarpiwalzer@gmail.com. Courtesy of the Artist.

Fig. 131. Kristin Kwan, THE GOLDEN AFTERNOON, Oil on panel, 24" × 36", Private Collection, www.kristinkwan.com. Courtesy of the Artist.

Fig. 132. Alan Powell, DANCING BY THE RIVER, Oils and etching inks on canvas, 36" × 48", 2019, www.akanpowellstudios.com, Alanpowellstudios@gmail.com. Courtesy of the Artist.

Appendix A

Fig. 133. Judith Schaechter, MOTHER AND CHILD, 2006, Stained Glass, Hermitage Museum, Russia, www.judithschaechter.com. Courtesy of the Artist.

Fig. 134. Ann-Marie Brown, COLD CROSSING/MOVING TARGET, Encaustic and oil on canvas, 30" × 40", www.annmariebrownpaintings.com, ambpaintings@hotmail.com. Courtesy of the Artist.

Fig. 135. Jimmy Wright, BIG MOMMA AT TURKEY CREEK, Oil on paper, 15" × 11", 1987, Courtesy of Fierman Gallery and Courbett vs Dempsex, Chicago, http://www.jimmywrightartist.com.

Fig. 136. Anna Boothe, LITTLE HELPER, 2001, glass, wood, metal, cloth; 48" ht. × 8.5" w × 4" d; www.annaboothe.com, anna@annaboothe.com. Courtesy of the Artist.

Fig. 137. Lola del Fresno, MOTHER AND CHILD, Graphite, Acrylic, Ink on Mylar, 60" × 65", www.loladelfresno.com. Courtesy of the Artist.

Fig. 138. Veronica Cay, WONDERWOMAN, 2023, Ceramic Sculpture, 82 × 30 × 20 cm, Photo by Christine Hall, (www.myphotomotion.com.au), instagram @ronniecay.com. Courtesy of the Artist.

Fig. 139. Sheila Fein, HEARTBEAT, color pencil on museum board, 20" × 25", www.sheilafein.com, feinfanstasypop@gmail.com. Courtesy of the Artist.

Fig. 140. Michael Lebowitz, MOM AND KIDS, 2017, black-and-white, 35mm, iPhone 6, www.longrunpictures.com, michael@longrunpictures.com. Courtesy of the Artist.

Fig.141. Sirarpi Heghinian Walzer, MADONNA AND CHILD, September 2023, mixed-media encaustic collage, 18" × 20", www.swalzer.com, sirarpiwalzer@gmail .com. Courtesy of the Artist.

Fig. 142. Carolyn Schlam, JOY, Oil on Canvas, 48" × 48", 2023, www.carolyn schlam.com, carolynschlam@aol.com. Courtesy of the Artist.

Index

Note: Bold numbers indicate an image on the page.